FLIGHT
FROM THE
REICH

FLIGHT

FROM THE

REICH

Refugee Jews, 1933–1946

Debórah Dwork &
Robert Jan van Pelt

W. W. NORTON & COMPANY

NEW YORK • LONDON

For information about permission to reproduce selections from this book,
write to Permissions, W. W. Norton & Company, Inc.,
500 Fifth Avenue, New York, NY 10110

For information about special discounts for bulk purchases, please contact
W. W. Norton Special Sales at specialsales@wwnorton.com or 800-233-4830

Manufacturing by RR Donnelly, Harrisonburg
Book design by Abbate Design
Production manager: Anna Oler

Library of Congress Cataloging-in-Publication Data

Dwork, Deborah.
Flight from the Reich : refugee Jews, 1933/1946 / Debórah Dwork
& Robert Jan van Pelt. — 1st ed.
p. cm.
Includes bibliographical references and index.
ISBN 978-0-393-06229-8 (hardcover)
1. Refugees, Jewish—Government policy—Europe, Western—History—20th century.
2. Refugees, Jewish—Germany—History—20th century. 3. Refugees, Jewish—Europe,
Western—History—20th century. 4. World War, 1939–1945—Jews—Rescue. 5. Europe,
Western—Emigration and immigration—History—20th century. 6. Germany—
Emigration and immigration—History—20th century. 7. Holocaust survivors.
I. Pelt, R. J. van (Robert Jan), 1955– II. Title.
HV640.5.J4D96 2009
940.53'18—dc22

2008053858

W. W. Norton & Company, Inc.
500 Fifth Avenue, New York, N.Y. 10110
www.wwnorton.com

W. W. Norton & Company Ltd.
Castle House, 75/76 Wells Street, London W1T 3QT

1 2 3 4 5 6 7 8 9 0

*Frontispiece: Twin sisters, sent from Germany to the Netherlands on a
kindertransport, arriving in an orphanage in Naarden on 16–17 November 1938.*

For Miriam Rebecca and Hannah Murray
but for whom this book would have been written much sooner

CONTENTS

INTRODUCTION

ANNE FRANK, POSSIBLY THE MOST FAMOUS AND CERTAINLY THE best loved refugee Jew, is rarely coded as a refugee at all. Not even in the Netherlands, where she and her family sought safety in 1933. A new picture emerged when the Dutch television network aired a program in fall 2004 to elect "The Greatest Dutch Person." Voting from a list of two hundred candidates, the public chose ten, one of whom was Anne. The juxtaposition of her name with the title "greatest Dutch person" shone a bright light on an obvious fact: neither she, her mother, nor her sister ever held Dutch nationality, and her father Otto Frank, the sole survivor of that family of four, was naturalized only on 22 December 1949, sixteen years after he had moved to the Netherlands. Anne was a German-Jewish refugee who officially held German nationality until Berlin stripped all Jews living outside the borders of the Reich of their citizenship. This included German Jews deported to the east and German Jews, like the Franks, who had fled. All became stateless.

The TV show producers proposed that Anne receive posthumous citizenship. Some members of parliament supported this move. Alas, the ministry of justice informed the public, the law did not allow posthumous naturalization. It fell to Micha Wertheim, a popular comedian with an ironic sense of humor, to call the nation's attention to the obvious: refugees need citizenship from host countries while they are alive, not when they are dead. "Anne Frank, and many thousands of Jews like her, undoubtedly would have been only too happy to have got Dutch nationality while they were alive. It is too late now—even for TV." Turning to current affairs, Wertheim pointed out that Rita Verdonk, minister of integration and immigration, had adopted a xenophobic platform, sharply limiting asylum in the Netherlands. "This minister expels people who have lived here for more than ten years already. Without shedding a tear, she claims that Chechnya, Liberia, Somalia, and Afghanistan are safe countries to which people can return without difficulty." And he suggested: "Instead of supplying dead people with passports, the Minister could spend her time better protecting people who are still alive."[1]

If the Dutch no longer recall that Anne was a German-Jewish refugee, it is not surprising that no one else does either. Her history in hiding, followed by deportation and death, elides her family's early response to Nazi persecution. It is most probable that it was precisely the family's status as refugee Jews from Germany that prompted Otto to prepare his family's hiding plans sooner than his Dutch coreligionists who sought to disappear. German Jews held a more vulnerable position than Dutch Jews after the Germans occupied the Netherlands in May 1940. They were ordered to register (28 June) and were specially targeted in violent raids in February and June 1941. When all non-Dutch Jews had to report for "voluntary" emigration on 5 December 1941, Otto Frank (by then stateless, like all German Jews) may well have realized that this was a charade—there was no emigration to anywhere anyone wanted to go. And he was right: the first transports from the Netherlands to death camps in the east were filled with German Jews. In short, his experience as a refugee framed his interpretation of events on the ground.[2]

Few histories of the Holocaust include discussion and analysis of the refugees' experience. At best on the margins, this aspect of Holocaust history typically falls literally beyond the subject bounds. This perspective was illuminated by a query from a fellow historian (in another field) following a presentation on our work. "Sorry," he said, "I know you were invited to speak about Holocaust history. And I am just wondering: what does the history of Jewish refugees have to do with the Holocaust?" Not a foolish question. If the Holocaust is the history of people murdered by the Germans and their allies, the refugees hold a very minor role. Most escaped that fate. Not all, as the fate of the Frank family underscores. But most.

We take a wholly different position. All European Jews who came under the control of Germany and its allies were targeted for death. Some six million were killed. The remaining three million survived camps, endured life in hiding, "passed" as a gentile, fled to safety, or experienced some combination of these. All were victims of the Holocaust. Had Jews not hidden or passed, they too would have been deported. Had they not sought asylum elsewhere, they too would have been caught in the machinery of death.

Fleeing does not write refugees out of the story; it simply takes the story elsewhere. Indeed: it takes it everywhere. The history of refugee Jews during and after the Nazi era is literally, from the Latin *centrifugal*, to flee the center. That center comprised Germany; then Greater Germany, which included Austria, Sudetenland, Bohemia, and Moravia; and finally all of German-ruled Europe. The sites of flight grew ever more distant from the countries adjacent to Germany to all the peopled continents.

The refugees' escape around the world defies traditional plotlines. Unlike other histories that start and end at conventionally established dates, this history has many starting points, even more end dates, and actors scattered across the globe. Realizing that the so-called grand narrative could not encompass the story we sought to tell, we devised a grid to capture pivotal moments and core issues. Focusing on four turning points in a repeat pattern of people, places, papers, and problems allowed us to zero in on individual agency, geographic reach, government and philanthropic organization policy, and the difficulties—quotidian to existential—refugees faced. It allowed us to move from broad vision to narrow opportunities; from petty application of the law to daring defiance of it. It is at once a grand story and a tale of details. If our new narrative form is fractured, so too were the lives of those we study.[3]

The schema we adopted[4] offers the benefit of focusing on crucial themes but also carries the risk of ignoring events that a reader might expect to find. Most significantly, we do not discuss the history of post-war collective and individual indemnification. Every refugee experienced wholesale spoliation, and nearly all were destitute by the time they reached safe shores. Unlike other major refugee groups in the modern era, such as the Russian and Armenian refugees after World War I, survivors of the Holocaust—including those who escaped the Nazi net through flight—won a measure of material restitution. The Luxembourg agreements of September 1952 between the German Federal Republic, the state of Israel, and the Conference on Jewish Material Claims Against Germany (Claims Conference) aimed to support the rehabilitation of survivors through payments in cash or goods of $714 million to Israel, $107 million to the Claims Conference, and hundreds of millions to individuals. The *Wiedergutmachung* (making amends, or compensation) legislation that followed not only helped many to rebuild their lives more quickly than expected. It also created a first, albeit shaky, bridge between the victims and the state that was the legal heir of the German Reich.[5]

The Luxembourg agreements, Wiedergutmachung laws, and subsequent agreements negotiated until the present day are sequelae of the story we tell and thus fall outside its scope. Some key landmarks of refugee history during the Nazi era are missing too, like the story of the *St. Louis*, so well known through Stuart Rosenberg's movie *Voyage of the Damned* or Julian Barnes's *A History of the World in 10½ Chapters*.[6] And while we will not explore the history of Walter Benjamin in the chapters to follow, we take his advice on the writing of history to heart.

A German-Jewish refugee, Benjamin became, posthumously, a towering presence in cultural studies, celebrated as one of the most original thinkers of the twentieth century. His attempt to cross the Pyrenees and his death at the French-Spanish border in 1940 have acquired legendary dimensions.[7] Benjamin lived in Paris from 1933 until May 1940 when he and two-thirds of the population of that city took to the road to escape the German advance. He ended up in Marseille where he was among the first to receive an emergency visa issued by the American government to well known writers and artists. His passport had expired and, as for other German refugees without papers, the League of Nations *Certificat d'Identité des Réfugiés Provenant d'Allemagne* (Identity Certificate for

Refugees Coming from Germany) served as his primary identity document.[8] American visa in hand, Benjamin easily obtained Spanish and Portuguese transit visas, but Vichy refused to grant him an exit visa.

Benjamin decided to cross the French-Spanish border by hiking over the Pyrenees. Despite a heart problem, he insisted upon carrying a heavy briefcase with his latest work. "The manuscript must be saved," he told his guide Lisa Fittko. "It is more important than I am."[9] Arriving at the frontier, Benjamin learned that Spain had just closed its gates and would not honor his transit visa. While this proved a temporary measure, canceled a few days later, no one could know that at the time. He was exhausted and the hour was late, and the Spanish guards permitted him to sleep in the border town of Port Bou; refoulement could wait a day. He died within the next twenty-four hours, perhaps by suicide, perhaps from a stroke.[10] In either case, his demise was marked by ill luck and tragic timing. If Benjamin had arrived at the frontier a day earlier, he would have been let through. And if he had remained in Marseille a day longer, he would have heard the news and waited until the border opened again.[11]

Benjamin was buried in Port Bou. Spanish authorities entered his briefcase in the municipal death register, recording its contents. They did not note a manuscript. It vanished, never to be found.

Benjamin died alone and afraid in a strange town, sharing the fate of many unknown refugees who succumbed during their flight or exile. A monument to him in Port Bou has become a memorial to them all.[12] The site includes a long, dark staircase suspended precariously over the Mediterranean. A cracked glass panel prevents visitors from falling into the sea below. On it is inscribed Benjamin's final advice to historians: *"Schwerer ist es, das Gedächtnis der Namenlosen zu ehren als das der Berühmten. Dem Gedächtnis der Namenlosen ist die historische Konstruktion geweiht."* "It is more arduous to honor the memory of the nameless than that of the renowned. Historical construction is dedicated to the memory of the nameless."[13]

PART ONE

1933

The Schocken department store in Chemnitz, designed by Erich Mendelsohn.

THE END OF
AN ERA

ADOLF HITLER ADDRESSED THE GERMAN NATION IN A RADIO BROAD-
cast on 31 January 1933, the day after his appointment as Reich chancellor. His first words were ominous. Describing the whole period from the
German revolution of 9 November 1918 to his ascent to power on 30 January as an era of destruction, disintegration, and dissolution, Hitler delegit-
imized the very constitution and political institutions he was supposed to
uphold and defend. His administration was a "Government of National
Uprising," and as Reich chancellor he aimed to lead a revolt against the
state, destroy the Weimar Republic, and establish the Third Reich.[1]

No supporter of democracy either in theory or in its practice, Hitler
did not view his assumption to office in terms of a temporary stewardship
to be relinquished in due course. On the contrary. He and his support-
ers considered what they brazenly called the *Machtergreifung* (takeover)
in almost apocalyptic terms. For Hitler and the Nazis, history was the
story of power, and progress in history meant the increase of power. They
swore to use their Machtergreifung to halt the thousand-year deteriora-
tion of racial integrity and heroic unity that had bound the Germans
together in the early middle ages.[2]

According to the Nazis, this disintegration had accelerated in the nineteenth century, and become a free fall in the "catastrophe of the years 1918–1933." Rotten to the core, the Weimar Republic was a *Judenrepublik*— the Jews' Republic. "Jewry—in leadership positions . . . triggered a devastating and total collapse. Jewish parasites mutilated the German face of our culture until it could not be recognized any more," they screamed. "Everything that was important and sacred to German people—courage and loyalty, a sense of responsibility and self-sacrifice, honesty and commitment, God and nation—was made into a joke and drawn through the muck." With their regime, the thousand-year descent had come to an end: "a millennium of constructive history will supersede a millennium of mistakes."[3]

WHERE NAZIS SAW PERDITION and ruin, German Jews experienced progress toward political emancipation and cultural equality. Bismarck's establishment of the German Reich in 1871 had brought full political emancipation, but social discrimination had remained common practice, and Jews were barred from government, the diplomatic and civil services, senior academic positions, and commissions in the armed forces. Participation in the economy was open, however, and Jews made use of this opportunity, achieving prominence in finance and many branches of manufacturing. The professions too were available, and Jews entered the fields of law and medicine. If, as Nietzsche claimed, the great majority of non-Jewish Germans disliked Jews, racial antisemitism—the notion that by virtue of birth alone, every Jew was a threat to civic society and should be barred from full citizenship, socially isolated and, if possible, expelled—held little traction in the political sphere. Those who held such views remained on the fringes, their Jewish Question of marginal importance, and their form of antisemitism socially taboo.[4]

Patriots, monarchists, and very proud of the German culture which they believed to be theirs too, German Jewry formed the most prosperous Jewish community in the world. Few German Jews chose to leave for the new world. From 1899 to 1914 more than 1 million Jews emigrated from the Russian empire, 240,000 Jews from the Austro-Hungarian Empire, and

60,000 Jews from Great Britain for the United States, while only 10,000 German Jews crossed the Atlantic. During the same period, 60,000 Jews from the east settled in the German Reich—which made Germany a country of Jewish *immigration*.[5] They constituted a small percentage of the great transmigration: German Jews watched a tidal wave of Jewish movement from the east to the new world flow away on German ships that left from Bremen and Hamburg. Faced with a constant stream of destitute emigrants, they established the *Hilfsverein der Deutschen Juden* (German Jews' Aid Society) to help organize the exodus from the east and provide support in transit. The founders in 1901 imagined only aid given *by* German Jews *to* other Jews on their way elsewhere.[6]

The Weimar Republic offered Jews significant improvement on Bismarck's Reich. The tension between formal equality and de facto second-class status in many spheres evaporated as Jews ascended to ministerships, joined the diplomatic and civil services, and advanced to professorships in the universities. Jews remained unpopular in the army and navy, but these pillars of the former monarchy held far less significance in post–Versailles treaty Germany. In areas that mattered, Jews made their mark: Salman Schocken modernized the retail economy radically through the establishment of large, beautifully designed department stores to mass-market the best of contemporary design, and the novelist Joseph Roth, architect Erich Mendelsohn, composer Arnold Schönberg, poet Else Lasker-Schüler, playwright Ernst Toller, critic Walter Benjamin, journalist Kurt Tucholsky, theater director Max Reinhardt, and scholar Ernst Cassirer assumed pioneer roles in the experimental, innovative culture of the day. Receiving the Nobel Prize for physics in 1923, Albert Einstein became for all intents and purposes the face of a new and better Germany, one very different from the Germany of Bismarck and the kaiser.

But while Jews now climbed the highest pinnacles, they also faced a new abyss. A brutalization in political rhetoric triggered by World War I and normalized in the maelstrom of postwar social violence melted the social taboo that had prevented a dislike of Jews from degenerating into racial antisemitism. The Jewish Question now became an obsession for many on the right, and rabid antisemites' "solutions" to that Jewish Question became commonplace. They changed the terms of the debate.

Even Christians who denounced Jew-baiting as a disgrace to the German nation conceded that "one has rightly begun to speak of Jews and Germans instead of Jews and Christians."[7]

Still, German Jews did not worry. The Weimar legal system seemed to work, protecting life and property. The well-organized *Centralverein deutscher Staatsbürger jüdischen Glaubens* (Central Association of German Citizens of Jewish Faith) brought civil suits regularly against boycotts of Jewish businesses and professionals, and the courts convicted extreme antisemitic agitators.[8] Few Jews realized that their reliance on the readiness of the authorities to apply the law would be of little help if the Nazis came to power. They simply could not imagine that under a Nazi regime the courts would become a political tool. And many of the four hundred thousand Jews who were German-born and German citizens believed that if there were to be a problem, the almost hundred thousand eastern Jews, most of whom had settled in Germany after World War I and were either citizens of east European countries or stateless, would serve as the target.[9]

A NAZI REGIME APPEARED IMMINENT in 1932, but the Jewish establishment remained sanguine. "The Jewish question, passed off by the Nazis in a thousand ways as the key to world history, plays no decisive role in German politics," the Centralverein newspaper claimed in May that year.[10] The Nazis doubled their representation in the 608-deputy Reichstag, moving from 117 to 230 seats, in elections just two months later. Gaining 38 percent of the votes, they became the largest party. Yet they did not control a majority, even with their nominal ally, the German National People's Party. A political stalemate followed. Some Jews began to consider a worst-case scenario if Hitler were to come to power. "Perhaps the Nazis will beat some poor Jews to death," a banker told the writer Joseph Roth, "but nothing will happen to us." "Jewish pig," Roth replied, and punched him.[11] Few had Roth's insight or moral fiber. Most German Jews trusted their illusions while Hitler repeatedly demanded the chancellorship. And they felt reassured as the political leaders of the German National People's Party and other right-wing parties needed for a majority coalition refused to give it to him. With no other candidates for the chancellery, General Kurt von Schleicher took it on, but he could not build a majority either and he resigned at the end of January 1933. Now it was Hitler's turn.[12]

President von Hindenburg invited Adolf Hitler to assume the chancellorship of a coalition government on 30 January 1933. According to a deal struck earlier, he would be Reich chancellor, and von Hindenburg's lapdog, former Reich Chancellor Franz von Papen, vice chancellor. Von Papen and the other seven gentlemen in the cabinet were confident they could control the oafish chancellor and his two crude cohorts, Interior Minister Wilhelm Frick and Minister Without Portfolio Hermann Göring. In their establishment hubris and cynicism they calculated that they had bought the mass support they had lacked before. And as far as the Jewish Question was concerned, they had nothing to worry about: in their negotiations with Hitler, he had not mentioned that matter at all.

While the elites believed that they could control Hitler and his ministers, most non-Nazis were sure that his government would be another short-lived affair. On average, governments after 1918 had lasted less than nine months and no one had any reason to think this one would be any different. The great majority of German Jews remained optimistic. "The new Reich government will soon notice that it has quite different and more difficult problems to solve than the so-called Jewish problem," the Centralverein newspaper predicted on 2 February.[13] Even Jews engaged on the political left, who clearly saw the threat Nazism posed, believed that nothing much would happen. Years later, Manès Sperber— a psychologist, a communist, and a Jew—reflected with astonishment on his failure to see that danger loomed. "I reasoned that the SA would make raids on Grenadierstrasse and some other streets where poor Jews lived, throw Polish Jews out of their apartments, and bloody some Jewish heads. A *numerus clausus* [quota system] would be introduced at the universities, certainly at the schools of medicine and law, in order to weaken Jewish competition, but otherwise nothing would change."[14]

History proved him and most other German Jews wrong. Within a few months Sperber had left Germany, as had the entrepreneur Schocken, the novelist Roth, the architect Mendelsohn, the composer

Schönberg, the poet Lasker-Schüler, the playwright Toller, the critic Benjamin, the journalist Tucholsky, the theater director Reinhardt, and the scholar Cassirer—and tens of thousands of others. And the Hilfsverein that had been founded by German Jews to help persecuted Jews from Russia leave for countries overseas now turned to help German Jews to find a place . . . anywhere.

THE FIRST
TO FLEE

W<small>E LIVED IN BERLIN FROM 1930 TO 1933,"</small> FRIEDRICH KATZ RECALLED decades later. "During that time, my father wrote for the daily newspaper of the German communist party the *Rote Fahne* and as a correspon dent for the [American] Yiddish newspaper *Morning Freiheit,* and Soviet Yiddish newspapers. My father's specialty was writing satirical articles, especially about Hitler. In 1933 the Nazis took power. After the Reichstag burned, my father went underground and practically did not live at home anymore." But the Nazis had sent someone to spy on his flat. "A few weeks later he came home just to greet my mother and see me and get a few shirts and things. Somebody knocked on the door. It was the police. The policeman began to interview my father." They knew a lot about Leo Katz, communist, Austrian citizen, and prominent literary figure. "My father did not write under his own name. He wrote under a pseudonym because we were Austrian citizens and could have been expelled as unwanted foreigners if it had been known that a foreigner was writing on German political questions in a German political paper, especially a communist paper. But the Nazis had an agent in the communist headquarters who gave them my father's pseudonym, and the police knew about practically every article he had written."

Ironically, this interview may well have saved the Katz family. "My father denied everything. And after an hour, the policeman said, 'Look, Mr Katz, I don't believe one word of what you've said, but I haven't met you. I'm leaving now, and I don't know who will come after me. I hope you understand me.' So my father took the next train to Paris.

"My mother and I stayed for several months before we went to France to join my father," Katz continued. "And I frequently asked my mother, 'Why did we stay?' And she said, 'For two reasons. First, I was working in the Soviet commercial mission, so I thought they would not arrest me. And second, I felt the party might need me to carry out underground work.' Which, since we were Jewish, and looking back on it today, I don't think was the most intelligent decision. But my mother really tried for five or six months to carry out underground work."

Bronia Katz was successful. "She and another member of the party edited an underground paper, distributed it to party members, went from house to house putting it under the doors or throwing it from windows." A risky endeavor, but they did not get caught.

The communist party—its ideology, advancing its aims, and their identity in relation to it—sat at the core of the Katz family. "We lived in a section of Berlin called Wedding, which was the center of the communist party. I think every second person there was a communist. . . . I still remember at night, really huge trucks coming in and arresting these communist workers. At that point the Nazis were not very interested in whether we were Jews or not."[1]

HITLER CAME TO POWER on 30 January 1933, and the legal protection of individual freedoms remained in force throughout February. Few Germans fled the country or remained abroad that month. The famous novelist Thomas Mann, his Jewish wife Katia Mann-Pringsheim, and their adult children Klaus and Erika, who had not hidden their loathing of Hitler and the Nazis, belonged to a very small group of people who voted with their feet during those weeks. Almost all other opponents of the new government believed that it would be politics as usual under what most expected to be a short-lived Hitler government.

The Reichstag fire, set by the Nazis (27 February) and blamed on the communists, suggested that the Mann family had been farsighted. An emergency decree permitted restrictions on civil liberties and on the freedom of the press and of association, and gave the government wide powers to arrest those deemed dangerous to the state. The ensuing dragnets prompted many political dissidents to leave. If the immediate circumstances were dramatic, the means—usually by train or on foot—were quite ordinary. The Nazis did not cancel passports in the first instance, and those who held one relied upon it to cross the border. This included most of the intellectuals and political activists who sought to flee immediately. Their work had taken them abroad before, and they had a passport in hand when danger approached. At first, "I was unable to adapt from living in a constitutional state to living in a state run by a dictator and lawless gangsters," the Jewish author of *Berlin Alexanderplatz*, physician, and well known critic of the regime Alfred Döblin explained. But by the evening after the Reichstag fire, "I had adjusted. My wife agreed. It would just be a brief trip abroad. You'll let the storm pass over you, just three or four months, someone will have dealt with the Nazis by then. . . . I left the house with one small suitcase, alone."[2] Spotting a Nazi waiting at his doorstep, Döblin gave him the slip and made his way to a town near the Swiss border where he spent the night. "A boat trip across Lake [Constance] to Kreuzlingen. Now comes the border crossing by car; everything goes smoothly."[3]

Käthe Frankenthal, also a physician, a Jew, and an elected socialist party representative to the Berlin city council, was on vacation in Switzerland on the night of the Reichstag fire. She returned. Soon realizing there was nothing she could do to improve the situation, she left, like Döblin, by train with only a travel case. Her timing was knife-edge. She departed on 31 March, coincidentally the day before the state-ordered boycott of Jewish-owned businesses. The Nazis were out in force. In Dresden, SA men serving as auxiliary police "stormed the train, went from compartment to compartment, picking out the ones to be arrested." Frankenthal did not know the criteria. Initially apprehended, she was let go the next day, but her passport was confiscated. With little left to lose, she checked herself into the best hotel in town, drank a bottle of good wine, and went to sleep. Luck was with her. Perusing the morning paper on 2 April, she noticed that a new decree forbade anyone to leave the country without permission, but "anyone already traveling was to be let through!" Frankenthal persuaded the officials to return her passport on the basis of this loophole. "I took the next train across the border. . . . Everyone on the train was fleeing."[4]

Some left by car, some by train, and others, like twenty-year-old Helmut Flieg, who had published a poem enraging the Nazis, slipped over "the green border" by walking across the frontier to safety. In the wake of the Reichstag fire, SA men raided his parents' home in Chemnitz, but he had moved to Berlin in 1931. The SA men arrested Helmut's father as a hostage to ensure that he would give himself up, but they had not counted on his mother, who contacted him in Berlin. "Get out. Out of Germany. Immediately."[5] Helmut packed a rucksack and chose Prague as his destination. Fearing that the international train would be heavily patrolled, he lit upon the idea to hike a fifteen-mile trail that ran south from Hirschberg in Silesia to the Spindlerbaude,[6] a well known hiker's lodge in summer and skier's lodge in winter that straddled the German-Czech border: "half-German, half-Czech; when you go to the toilets you in fact cross the border."[7]

Dressed in city clothes, Helmut boarded the local train for Silesia, pondering his decision: shouldn't he return to Chemnitz to obtain his father's release? In one form or another, Helmut's dilemma plagued all refugees. All left family behind and worried that running from danger meant running from their responsibilities. Perhaps encouraged by his mother's command, Helmut did not turn around, alighted in Hirschberg, and began the twenty-eight-hundred-foot ascent up the Riesengebirge to the border. The early spring of the valley turned into late winter on the mountain. Just when he felt too exhausted and in too much pain to continue, he saw lights in the distance. Entering the Spindlerbaude's warm, crowded *Stube* (bar), he noticed that the skiers looked at him askance; his late arrival and his attire drew unwelcome attention. He walked right through to the toilets, thus crossing from German into Czech territory. Exiting through the back door, he found a bus bringing skiers back to Prague. The driver recognized him as a refugee in need of help and offered him a ride to the city. There he took the alias Stefan Heym, which he kept for the rest of his life.[8]

Initially, the German government cared little when political opponents or artists left the country. This changed in the wake of mass anti-Nazi demonstrations in New York in March 1933. Berlin then feared that refugees would agitate against the regime from their country of asylum.[9] Authorities in the host countries harbored the same worries. That year, the British *Daily Herald* newspaper asked the ministry of labor whether its Berlin correspondent, Viktor Schiff, might move "to London for the express purpose of writing up the German situation in their London office." The ministry had no objection but sought concurrence from the foreign office, wondering whether "there may be political objections to allowing this German to use this country as a base from which to carry on what might well develop into a propaganda campaign against the present German government." Foreign office officials considered the matter, referencing other instances in which permission had been given—"the Ukrainian propagandist Korostovetz" and "the Croatian agitator Kosutitch." They noted too that "the members of the political party supported by the *Daily Herald*"—which by 1933 was the world's best-selling daily newspaper and championed a working class agenda—"would not be the only Englishmen" to embrace the principles of asylum and free speech. Furthermore, if permission were denied, and questions asked in parliament, "it would be the Foreign Office who would have to shoulder the responsibility." Common sense prevailed. "On the whole, it would seem that a refusal to admit Herr Schiff . . . might not be easy to defend . . . and it appears doubtful whether his individual efforts could add very much to what is already being written and said here against the present régime in Germany."[10]

THE 1 APRIL STATE-SPONSORED BOYCOTT of all Jewish professionals and all Jewish-owned businesses left no doubt as to who was especially marked for persecution. Hearing that the American Jewish Congress (contrary to the wishes of German Jews) planned a worldwide boycott of German goods, Hitler ordered a one-day pre-emptive strike. The

Nazi leadership called upon the German people to take defensive action against the Jews, "the guilty ones" who "live in our midst and day after day misuse the right to hospitality, which the German *Volk* [people] has granted them."[11] In the party's view, Jews had been reduced to resident foreigners who could be held hostage to ensure the behavior of the outside world toward Germany. This was pure racism at work: people were held responsible not only for their own deeds but for those of the imagined race-community to which they belonged as well. Just as the Germans belonged to a unified race-organism, so did the Jews. Thus, Jews living in Germany were responsible for the actions of Jews abroad.

The boycott was not an economic success. Many Germans found it

A young SA man enforces the 1 April boycott, standing outside a clothing shop in Würzburg owned by a Jew. The sign accompanying the caricature reads: "Shun everything Jewish."

inconvenient or financially foolish. Nevertheless, it proved a psychological success. The twenty-five-year-old, anti-Nazi, gentile lawyer Raimund Pretzel later recalled that "it triggered a flood of arguments and discussions all over Germany, not about anti-Semitism but about the 'Jewish question.'" By threatening the Jews, the Nazis forced a national debate about their right to be part of German society. "Suddenly everyone felt justified, and indeed required, to have an opinion about the Jews, and to state it publicly," Pretzel observed.[12]

Jews experienced the boycott as a rupture that severed their world from the past and from the rest of Germany. Born in 1922 in the small town of Berfelden in southern Germany, Bertha Rosenthal was eleven years old at the time. Perhaps twenty-five Jewish families lived in her town, and no more than ten Jewish children attended her school in a given year. "The synagogue was in very serious disrepair, but the men went to services and most people kept kosher." The Jewish children went to school with their neighbors on Saturdays; "we had to go to school, that was the law, but we didn't have to write." On Saturday, 1 April 1933, Bertha went as usual. "In the morning before classes we would all congregate in the *Turnplatz* [gym field] where we played ball. . . . We were standing there, these four girls, four of us, and no one ever threw the ball to us. That's when we knew. That was it." After school "we went to my house, and there was a Brownshirt walking up and down to make sure nobody would come in. Nobody would have gone in anyway. It was shabbat, and anybody who still dealt with my father [a cattle trader] wouldn't have come on a Saturday." Economically, the boycott had no impact on the Rosenthal family, "but that day of the boycott, April 1, 1933, that was really the watershed. After that, it was as if we weren't there."[13] It took Bertha Rosenthal's family another three years, the bleak prospect of no schooling for her brother and her, and an affidavit from her father's uncle in America to emigrate from Germany.[14]

For Anna Essinger, the director of a progressive boarding school in the Swabian Jura mountains, the boycott served as an immediate catalyst. "We had many friends in the village, but all that happened in Germany on April 1st, 1933, had its repercussions even in that out-of-the-way place." Persuaded that "Germany was no longer a place in which to bring up children in honesty and freedom," Essinger "made up [her] mind then to find a new home for our school." She considered Switzerland and the Netherlands; "in June I came to England for the first time." She had friends to help her and "neither the Board of Education nor the Ministry of Labour raised any objections, and the Home Office gave all necessary permission." Informed of Essinger's plans, the children's parents raised no objections either. Essinger asked Quakers in England to raise the funds to rent suitable premises for the school. Just five months later, in early September, six teachers and the ten oldest pupils left for England in order to prepare for the rest.

Nearly the entire school community, some seventy-five Jewish and "non-Aryan" children and accompanying faculty, left Germany for the village of Otterden in Kent to form the Country Home School, New Herrlingen, renamed Bunce Court in 1936.[15] As the original name implied, Essingen sought to teach children who soon would lose their citizenship an appreciation of German language and culture. If actual teaching was conducted primarily in English, the community spoke German. No one, at this point, imagined that the departure from Germany would prove a permanent rupture. They expected to be reunited with their families and, in due course, to return to their homes.[16]

Essinger had rightly appreciated the boycott as a direct attack. Within weeks, German Jews were politically and socially disenfranchised, stripped of their rights and privileges as citizens. The government passed its first anti-Jewish measure, the Law for the Restoration of the Regular Civil Service, on 7 April. Paragraph 3, the so-called Aryan Paragraph, ordered the immediate retirement of civil servants of "non-Aryan origin." This affected thousands of Jews, as all teachers, professors, physicians employed in state hospitals, as well as government employees counted as "civil servants." A second law passed that day, the Law Concerning the Admission to the Legal Profession, removed Jews from the judiciary. Nor did the Nazis ignore young people. The Law Against the Overcrowding of the German Schools and Universities (25 April) set a 1.5 percent quota on the total number of Jewish students admitted to high schools and universities throughout the country and a maximum of 5 percent for any individual school. The few who managed to surmount these barriers were obliged to carry a yellow-striped student card and were excluded from student associations.

Fired and without prospects for employment, older Jews began to consider life elsewhere. Dismissed from school and barred from educational opportunities, younger Jews looked abroad too. Many left without a firm plan; others prepared with great care. Through his brother-in-law Erich Elias, Otto Frank got a license to establish a privately owned branch office in Amsterdam of the German firm Opekta-Werke, which produced pectin. Otto left for Holland in summer 1933 with fifteen thousand guilders borrowed from Elias, and officially registered his office with the Amsterdam Chamber of Commerce. His wife Edith and daughter Margot joined him in December; Anne arrived in March 1934. Otto Frank thus came to the Netherlands as a German entrepreneur, and the Dutch authorities were happy to issue the Franks a residency permit. Yet the family would not have moved were it not for the

Arriving in Amsterdam on 7 April 1933, a week after the 1 April boycott, German Jews wait outside the central train station.

boycott and its aftermath. For them, Amsterdam was first and foremost a refuge.[17]

WHEN THE NAZIS CAME TO POWER in 1933, Europe faced a refugee problem it had not known how to handle since 1918 and that had been exacerbated by the Depression. Rampant unemployment meant that no one wanted immigrants who would take away jobs or add to the welfare rolls. Nevertheless, thirty-seven thousand to forty-five thousand Jewish Germans and ten thousand gentile Germans who fled that year found safe havens.[18] Threat of arrest and fear of penury shaped the first wave of emigration—primarily men who left seeking safety, and with the hope of securing a place for their families. Urbanites all, they were for the most part renowned politicians, professionals, intellectuals, artists, and businessmen who had international contacts to help them leave. Most imagined a temporary need for asylum until the madness passed.[19] Surrounding countries opened their doors to them even though, due to the strict currency restrictions that applied to all German travelers abroad and the Weimar-legislated Reich flight tax that applied to those wishing to emigrate, they came with few possessions and little money.[20] The French government, cherishing the ideal of asylum, waived its visa restrictions, and thirty thousand German refugees crossed its border.[21] Private charities raised eight million francs (then half a million dollars) to support them. The Netherlands and Czechoslovakia also dropped paperwork and admitted six thousand and five thousand refugees, respectively.[22] Holland's tiny Jewish community established a Committee for Jewish Refugees, raising as much money as in France. In the middle of the Depression, the committee found employment for most and set up an agricultural training program for younger Jewish refugees.[23]

Perhaps one reason for this sympathy was that like the refugees, host nations believed the asylum they offered to be a temporary, emergency measure. Then too, the great book burning held in the center of Berlin on the night of 10 May horrified many abroad.[24] Students dressed in SA uniforms threw twenty-five thousand books by the likes of Karl Marx, Sigmund Freud, Heinrich and Thomas Mann, and Erich Maria

Remarque on a large pyre. Goebbels praised their actions as an appropriate response to the "trash and filth of Jewish gutter literati," although many of the authors were gentile. An article in the *Völkischer Beobachter* hammered home the key message. "The Horst-Wessel song rings out thunderously and the flames are still crackling while stacks upon stacks of the collected Jewish subversive writings are thrown into them. With this demonstration, the continuing fight against the un-German mind has been started."[25]

For once the Nazi newspaper did not exaggerate. In the days that followed, book burnings spread to universities at Heidelberg, Göttingen, Munich, and Münster. Newspapers from as far afield as China and Japan printed accounts of this violence. Not a few journalists remembered the poet Heinrich Heine's prediction a century earlier: "Where one burns books, one soon will burn people."[26]

As books were culled and burned, libraries owned by Jewish individuals and institutions appeared at risk. Fritz Saxl, director of the *Kulturwissenschaftliche Bibliothek Warburg* in Hamburg, worried about the books under his care. The unique legacy of cultural historian Aby Warburg (1866–1929), the library spanned established fields such as science, religion, and philosophy, as well as more controversial areas like folklore, pageants, physiognomy, alchemy, astrology, magic, and witchcraft.[27]

Warburg's brothers Paul and Felix, who lived in the United States, inherited Aby's library which, by the time he died, had become the center of Renaissance studies in Germany and the intellectual home of such famous cultural historians as Erwin Panofsky and Ernst Cassirer. Panofsky, Cassirer, and Saxl—all Jews—were fired from the University of Hamburg in April 1933. Saxl still had his job as director of the library, but he began to imagine relocating the whole institution: books, photo archive, and staff.[28] If there were little future for Jews in Germany, there would not be a future for an institution that, in its study of the continuity of ideas among different peoples, defied Nazi race-based history. Saxl looked at the tea leaves in his cup: public book burnings, purge of library collections, and, happily, the circumstance that the Warburg Library was owned by American citizens whose assets in Germany were not subject to the Reich flight tax.[29] England, with its strong tradition of classical

Die kulturhistorische Bibliothek Warburg

wird von Hamburg nach London verlegt.

Professor Aby Warburg s. A.

Eine einzigartige Einrichtung, die kulturhistorische Bibliothek Warburg in Hamburg, wird in diesen Tagen Deutschland verlassen und nach London übersiedeln. Welche Bedeutung diese Bibliothek besitzt, schildern wir in einem ausführlichen Artikel, der im Hauptblatt der vorliegenden Ausgabe des „Israelitischen Familienblattes" erscheint. Unsere Bilder zeigen die vorbildliche Ausstattung des Bibliotheksgebäudes in Hamburg, den geräumigen Lesesaal (unten), und rechts an der Seite einige Räume des technischen Betriebes. Das obere dieser drei Bilder führt in eines der vorzüglich geordneten Magazine, auf dem mittleren sieht man die Rohrpostanlage und das Förderband zur Beförderung der Bücher aus den Magazinen zum Lesesaal, und unten die dem neuesten Stande der Technik entsprechenden Apparaturen zur Herstellung von Reproduktionen, die aus dem wertvollen Be-

Das bisherige Heim der Bibliothek in Hamburg

stande der Bibliothek häufig von wissenschaftlichen Instanzen aus aller Welt verlangt werden. — Die Bibliothek wird vorläufig für drei Jahre in London untergebracht werden. Ob sie dann wieder nach Deutschland zurückkehren wird, ist bisher noch nicht bestimmt worden.

Blick in den Lesesaal

Article in the Hamburg Jewish newspaper announcing the transfer of the Warburg Library to London.

studies and tolerance of intellectual eccentricity, seemed a natural home for the Warburg collection. The University of London agreed. It would host the library, and if the Warburgs were willing to pay half the moving costs and three years of operating costs, the British textile magnate and philanthropist Samuel Augustine Courtauld pledged the remainder.[30]

It was one thing to offer hospitality to a treasured library and quite another to welcome the authors of books held in that library. Most of the twelve hundred ousted Jewish academics, however renowned in their scholarly fields, were financially dependent upon their lost university positions. The book pyres lit a response abroad on their behalf too. Prominent scientists and scholars in England, France, the Netherlands, Switzerland, and America founded no fewer than fourteen organizations to aid their colleagues.[31]

The plight of world famous scientists like Albert Einstein made great newspaper copy, which also aided the cause of those less well known. As it happened, Einstein and his wife Elsa were in California in January 1933, en route to Princeton where he lectured that winter, as he had done for the past few years. Returning to Europe in mid-March, Einstein landed in Belgium and publicly resigned from his official and honorary positions in Germany. A number of universities in the United States and Europe promptly offered him a post. The American education reformer Abraham Flexner had already organized Einstein's future, however. Flexner had persuaded department store magnate siblings Louis Bamberger and Caroline Bamberger Fuld to endow a new Institute for Advanced Study in Princeton. Chartered in 1930, the institute began operations in 1933 with Einstein as one of its first faculty.[32]

THE NAZI REGIME PERMITTED MOST JEWISH professors, professionals, and civil servants to leave. In contrast with the political "enemies of the state," they typically were not on the government's lists of refugees to be stopped by guards at the border. And indeed: many German-Jewish academics found positions abroad. Of the 1,600 university professors (Jewish and gentile) affected by the 7 April legislation, 800 left Germany by 1937. Age played a large role: 100 percent of the younger scholars and

50 percent of those over age fifty emigrated.[33] The organizations had been remarkably effective: the English Academic Assistance Council, for example, found posts for 178 academics that first year; similarly, the American Emergency Committee assisted 46.[34]

But what of the thousands of doctors, lawyers, architects, accountants, and other professionals and civil service employees? And what of the less well known but equally unemployed writers, journalists, and creative and performance artists? Their problem was to find a country that permitted entry and employment thereafter. The first proved manageable in 1933; the second posed nearly insurmountable obstacles. When Raimund Pretzel, disgusted by the Nazis, told his father that he planned to leave for Paris, the elder Pretzel asked, "And what do you intend to do abroad?" As a refugee he would have no value. Raimund protested that a gutter in exile was better than a life of compromise at home. "Such things are easy to say beforehand," his father replied. "Starvation and destitution are easy to contemplate when you have enough to eat."[35]

Still, the young Pretzel left for Paris but, unable to make a living, he returned to Berlin in 1934. A non-political "Aryan," Pretzel was not on a Nazi watch-list, and he could pick up his life where he had left it. Four years later, his love for Erika Hirsch, a Jewish woman pregnant with his child, forced the issue of emigration. Liable to be convicted for the crime of *Rassenschande* (race defilement), the two left for Great Britain where Hirsch had relatives who sponsored her immigration.[36]

Unlike Pretzel, Jews who left risked much by returning when they hit hard times. As we have seen, the majority of German exiles in 1933 fled to France where the government offered refuge but rarely the opportunity to undertake any job other than agricultural work. They joined "layers upon layers" of emigration, as Rudolf and Ika Olden, who left Germany immediately after the Reichstag fire, put it. "From all countries where there have been national and other revolutions in our time, representatives of their nations found themselves in this most hospitable city" of Paris. "Syrians, Turks, Bulgarians, Hungarians, Russians, Armenians, Italians, Spaniards—and now Germans have moved here too."[37]

"In Paris I feel as if I've been saved," Hermann Kesten, literary director of the Kiepenheuer publishing house, wrote to his colleague Ernst

German Jews in an "asylum" (hostel) established at the corner of Chevalier-de-la-Barre and Lamarck streets in Paris for destitute refugees, 1933.

Toller. And then he went on to ask: "My dear friend, how are we to earn our living now?"[38] The refugees lived on their savings as long as they could. When these were depleted, "they were compelled to find cheap lodgings in Belleville and other very poor quarters in Paris," explained Lawrence Darton in his report on the efforts of a Quaker aid group, the German Emergency Committee (GEC). Käthe Frankenthal, who had persuaded Nazi officials to allow her to continue her journey out of Germany because she fell into the category of those already in transit, had gone to Prague and then to Paris. Her experience mirrored the pattern. "I first moved into a modest hotel. Then into a poor one, and then into a squalid one," she wrote in 1940. "I was familiar with wretched neighborhoods in Germany, but I had only visited them. I don't know if Parisian quarters are worse. But life there was even more terrible than I had imagined the depressing impact of such an environment could be.[39] Hotels "serve as a home for the poor and poorest," the Oldens observed. "Often it is only one step from it to an asylum or the sleeping spots under the Seine bridges. . . . There is nothing beyond the bed, and no space for anything. A round washbasin, often unstable, a chair or two if it is very luxurious, and a small, narrow table. The stairs are steep and angular, the windows dirty, the bathroom a legend from faraway countries."[40]

To earn a living was key. Noting that "'the possibilities of work are very scarce,'" a GEC investigator praised how the refugees nevertheless "'make the best of it. I know an educated woman who goes out as a char [cleaner] in the morning, mends fine linen for a hotel in the afternoon, and manufactures chocolate in the evening, to keep herself and her children.'" Others, the report went on to say, "could find no work and afford no lodging: the subways, benches and doorsteps were their only beds."[41] By autumn 1933 the situation had become so desperate that the French government provided "five barracks in which to house some hundreds of refugees, mostly young men. Conditions in the barracks were at first appalling, there being no heat or light, no tables, chairs or beds, and very poor food. Most of the men were without occupation of any kind."[42]

The British spared themselves such scenes. A specially appointed cabinet committee, composed of high-ranking representatives from the home office, ministry of labor, board of trade, passport control department, foreign office, and colonial office, met on 6 April to consider an urgent proposal from the specially organized Jewish Refugees Committee (JRC), led by Jewish community leaders Otto Schiff, Neville Laski, Leonard Montefiore, and Lionel Cohen. Alarmed by the April boycott and Nazi regime's ferocious edicts to impoverish German Jews, the JRC proposed that all German-Jewish refugees "should be admitted without distinction, and that German Jews already admitted for the purpose of visits or who may be admitted in the future, should be allowed, during the present emergency, to prolong their stay indefinitely."[43] At that time—

and indeed, until 1938—travelers with German, Austrian, and Czech passports were permitted to enter Britain without a visa for a limited period as visitors, businessmen, or students, but they had to satisfy the immigration officer on duty at the border that they had sufficient means of maintenance. In the hope of persuading the government to allow those without financial means to enter the country, as well as to waive restrictions on the duration of stay, the JRC pledged that "all expense, whether in respect of temporary or permanent accommodation or maintenance, will be borne by the Jewish community without ultimate charge to the State."[44]

With no one to speak for the refugees during the cabinet committee deliberations, the officials did not admit of any benefit to be derived by accepting the JRC proposal, even with the guarantee of financing by British Jews. On the contrary. "The Minister of Labour impressed upon the Committee that he was not prepared to take the responsibility of agreeing to any measures involving a perceptible increase in the unemployment figures. There was little question . . . that a number of refugee Jews would, in the course of a few months, either apply for permission to take up employment in this country, or take up employment without that permission." The committee also discounted the idea that the newcomers might bring economically advantageous skills and expertise. Then too, having taken refugees, Britain would come under international pressure to "retain a large number of them permanently," while the colonial office "saw no prospect of Jewish refugees from Germany being able to make their way in appreciable numbers into any of the Colonies." They would not be admitted to Palestine either, where "the governing principle was the economic absorptive capacity of the country" and where "there was very strong Arab feeling against Jewish immigration of any kind." All things considered, the government decided "that there can be no question at the present time of relaxing the restrictions on the entry of aliens." Whitehall even added a new condition: "that the refugee should in every case register himself with the Police immediately on reaching his destination in the United Kingdom."[45] Having made no concessions and having laid on an extra burden, it nevertheless accepted the Jewish community's financial guarantee. All in all, a good day for the government.[46]

This policy shaped practice. "I have a son, who was several years law-yer in Germany and nourished me, his old mother from 74 years," Clara Sutro wrote to "the Noble Minister Lord Chamberlain" on 31 July 1933. "Is it possible, if he makes all Examen in Great Britannia to gain that he becomes there too a lawyer. Because he was not 'arisch' he was thrown out of his Existency. Highest Lord, if you anything to help us, I pray you to give me answer."[47] "I understand," Victor Perowne of the foreign office reflected, "that there is nothing to prevent anyone practising as a barrister in England provided that they carry out the usual procedure of joining one of the Inns of Court and get called to the Bar. . . . It is quite another question of course if Herr Sutro would be let into this country—the H.O. [home office] are the authorities here—and are bound by a Cabinet deci-sion in this respect. The British Jews have undertaken to maintain any Jewish refugees admitted, if necessary."[48] Skirting the issue of admis-sion, the foreign office reply to Mrs Sutro focused on the steps an alien needed to take to become a solicitor in the United Kingdom and sent her to the Law Society for more information about the required exams—to be taken only after her son had become a naturalized British subject.[49]

Mrs Sutro's son was relegated to the netherworld of requirements and permissions because it was not clear to Whitehall that he had any-thing spectacular to offer. By contrast, the British readily accepted the staff of the Warburg Library, who came with their unique collection of sixty thousand books and twenty-five thousand images, and the card cat-alogs, bookshelves, reading tables, binding equipment, and other insti-tutional paraphernalia. Two small freighters steamed out of Hamburg harbor on 12 December 1933 loaded with the library and its staff: Saxl, his wife Gertrud Bing, art historian Edger Wind, librarian Hans Meier, and bookbinder Otto Fein. However relieved they must have been to have secured a safe haven, all of them—like Stefan Heym—left their families behind. For its part, the library, transplanted to new soil, nour-ished the scholarship of such great refugee art historians as Margot and Rudolf Wittkower, Raymond Klibansky, and Ernst Gombrich and pro-vided the materials that prompted a new generation of English academ-ics, including Frances Yates and D. P. (Perkin) Walker, to shape a wholly radical understanding of the Renaissance.[50]

The welcome accorded the Warburg Library reflected British asylum policy: we'll take the best and let the French, Dutch, and Czechs cope with the rest. Just at the time the library set sail for London, Victor Perowne wrote his colleague at the British embassy in Paris: "*For your private information* the Home Office are not at all dissatisfied with the present position as regards the numbers and quality of refugees from Germany over here (which compares very favourably with that of some other countries including France). But we most certainly don't want present numbers increased and it is our policy therefore to do *nothing* to *encourage* further immigration."[51]

The initial surge of public outrage and activism, so evident in the spring, had subsided. Many of the privately funded philanthropic organizations founded to aid the refugees were financially distressed. And no national government took the lead. The fate of German Jews was no one's problem. They could take care of themselves: "The Jews themselves are naturally doing their best to placate the new régime and their inborn cleverness is coming to their assistance," one official in the chancery division of the British embassy in Berlin wrote to his department in London (24 January 1934). "Their intelligence and adaptability have saved them in the past and is helping them again to-day. Like animals they have their protective colouring which changes with the colour of the vegetation in their vicinity."[52] No one need worry about them.

A HOMELAND
IN PALESTINE

Tʜᴇ ɪᴅᴇᴀ ᴡʜɪᴄʜ ɪ ʜᴀᴠᴇ ᴅᴇᴠᴇʟᴏᴘᴇᴅ ɪɴ ᴛʜɪs ᴘᴀᴍᴘʜʟᴇᴛ ɪs ᴀ ᴠᴇʀʏ old one: it is the restoration of the Jewish State." With these words the Viennese-based journalist Theodor Herzl moved the Jewish Question into the international diplomatic arena. "No one can deny the gravity of the situation of the Jews," he asserted, surveying contemporary (1896) conditions in Europe. "Wherever they live in perceptible numbers, they are more or less persecuted. Their equality before the law, granted by statute, has become practically a dead letter." The solution: an idea of seemingly startling simplicity. "Let the sovereignty be granted us over a portion of the globe large enough to satisfy the rightful requirements of a nation; the rest we shall manage for ourselves."[1]

Herzl did not much mind where that spot might be, and in *The Jewish State* he wondered, "Argentine or Palestine?" Each had its attractions. Argentina "is one of the most fertile countries in the world, extends over a vast area, has a sparse population and a mild climate." For its part, "the Argentine Republic would derive considerable profit from the cession of a portion of its territory to us." On the other hand, "Palestine is our ever-memorable historic home. The very name of Palestine would attract our people with a force of marvellous potency." And what would the Otto-man Empire gain? "If His Majesty the Sultan were to give us Palestine, we could in return undertake to regulate the whole finances of Turkey."[2] Evidently, Herzl too had adopted stereotypes of Jews.

Herzl called for a Zionist Congress. It was held in Basel the follow-ing year, with the delegates declaring their resolve "to establish a home for the Jewish people in Palestine secured under public law."[3] For Max Nordau—Hungarian Jew, physician, intellectual, and dedicated Zionist— the homeland could not be established soon enough. He predicted that a rise in antisemitism would create a massive Jewish refugee problem, and at the Fourth Zionist Congress in 1900, he compared the current Roma-nian persecution of its Jewish population and the resulting emigration with the expulsion of the Spanish Jews in 1492. Anticipating the eviction of all 270,000 Romanian Jews,[4] Nordau believed that Austria would fol-low suit and expel its 780,000 Galician Jews, which would inspire Russia to exile its many millions. The only solution for this imminent catastro-phe was to create the homeland Herzl had envisioned.[5]

Herzl's plan called for a slow but steady population transfer, starting with persecuted Jews. Cultivating the land and building the infrastruc-ture, they would create conditions conducive to the success of succeeding waves of immigrants: the poor, to provide a labor pool and consumer demand; the prosperous, to capitalize trade; and finally, the wealthy. Some eighty thousand Jews either heeded Nordau's warning or had come to the same conclusion in the pre–World War I years and settled in Ottoman-ruled Palestine. And as Herzl had imagined, they were primarily from eastern Europe, avid to escape a life without hope and equally eager to bring fruit from the soil.

The Zionist movement got a boost during the Great War. Over-estimating the power of Jews in the United States, the British govern-ment sought to allay the fears of American Jews about the allies—which included both Russia and Romania, the two European countries with the worst records of antisemitism—by promising a Jewish homeland in Palestine. America declared war on Germany in April 1917, before the British government had made any public announcement on the matter, but the foreign office had already started down that path. In any case, a new reason had emerged: revolutionary developments in Russia. The Bolshevik provisional government called for an immediate end of the war. Overestimating too the power of Jews in the Bolshevik movement (and the adherence to Zionism of Jews in it), the foreign office believed that the promise of a Jewish homeland would shore up Russian support for the Allied cause.[6] British Foreign Secretary Lord Balfour issued a declaration on 2 November 1917 affirming that "H.M. Government views with favour the establishment in Palestine of a national home for the Jewish people, and will use their best endeavours to facilitate the achievement of this object."[7]

When the foreign office developed the concept, it was an offer at the expense of the Turks, as Palestine was under Ottoman rule. A month after the declaration, however, British forces entered Jerusalem. The London bureau of the World Zionist Organization (WZO) waxed jubilant. "The Declaration puts in the hands of the Jewish people the key to a new freedom and happiness," WZO—London proclaimed as General Allenby's troops occupied the entire country. "All depends on you, the Jewish people, and on you only. The Declaration is the threshold, from which you can place your foot upon holy ground. After eighteen hundred years of suffering your recompense is offered to you."[8]

At that point no one seems to have been singularly concerned about the Arab majority population in Palestine. On the contrary. The British Zionist Norman Bentwich, who served as a member of the Egyptian Expeditionary Force, saw a mutuality of interest between Jews and Arabs. Writing "during the leisure hours of camp life in the Summer of 1917 while waiting at the portals of Palestine to enter the Promised Land," Bentwich envisioned "a renascent Hebrew people and a renascent Arab people, who will arise after the war, [and] will grow together in unity and share the common pride in the new destiny of the whole Semitic race."[9] If Bentwich hoped the Arabs would embrace the situation he desired, Balfour gave no weight to their wishes at all. "Zionism," he maintained in a memo some eighteen months later, "be it right or wrong, good or bad, is rooted in age-long traditions, in present needs, in future hopes, of far greater import than the desires and prejudices of the 700,000 Arabs who now inhabit that ancient land."[10]

The promise of the Balfour declaration grew when the League of Nations granted Britain mandatory power in Palestine.[11] Mandatory authority was grounded in article 22 of the League covenant, which dealt with "those colonies and territories which as a consequence of the late war have ceased to be under sovereignty of the States that formerly governed them." Believing that these regions were "inhabited by peoples not yet able to stand up for themselves under the strenuous conditions of the modern world," the principal Allied powers decided that "the tutelage of such peoples should be entrusted to advanced nations who by reason of their resources, their experience, or their geographical position can best undertake this responsibility."[12] Palestine was not a colony; it was an independent state-waiting-to-be. A Jewish state, with minority rights for non-Jews, even though the latter constituted a comfortable majority of nine to one. "The Principal Allied Powers have also agreed that the Mandatory should be responsible for putting into effect the declaration originally made on November 2nd, 1917, by the Government of His Britannic Majesty, and adopted by the said Powers, in favor of the establishment in Palestine of a national home for the Jewish people, it being clearly understood that nothing should be done which might prejudice the civil and religious rights of existing non-Jewish communities in Palestine, or the rights and political status enjoyed by Jews in any other country." Recognizing "the historical connection of the Jewish people with Palestine," and accepting the "grounds for reconstituting their national home in that country," the powers charged Britain with the responsibility for "the development of self-governing institutions." To that end "an appropriate Jewish agency shall be recognized," specifically, "the Zionist organization," as the partner "with the Administration of Palestine in such economic, social and other matters as may affect the establishment of a Jewish national home and the interests of the Jewish population in Palestine."[13]

WITH THE ESTABLISHMENT OF "a Jewish national home" in the offing, Palestine emerged as a real option for Jewish refugees. Agonizing over the slaughter of his coreligionists in the Ukraine after the war, Max Nordau proposed the immediate transfer of six hundred thousand Jews to

Palestine. Faced with the certain death of up to a third of the refugees due to Palestine's utter lack of infrastructure, resources, or preparation for such a mass movement, the Zionist leadership rejected his plan. Frustrated, Nordau snapped back: it was better for Jews to die in Palestine, contributing to the creation of a Jewish homeland, than to be murdered by antisemites in Europe. He was overruled, but his proposal and his argument reframed the issue of the importance of Palestine as a place of immediate asylum.[14]

It refocused attention too on the knotty question of how many people Palestine could absorb. Arthur Ruppin, a German Jew who had joined the Zionist movement in 1905 and was sent to Palestine two years later to investigate options for agricultural development and settlement, weighed in on immigration at the Zionist Congress in 1923. Absorption had sat at the core of his concerns for the past fifteen years. He had worked to change the paradigm of settlement from wealthy landowners and poor agricultural workers to the egalitarian kibbutz collectives and moshav cooperatives that became the backbone of the state-in-the-making and a cornerstone of the Zionist vision. In his view, the movement could not afford the risk of admitting too many. As a purely practical matter, "The immigrants cannot attack the soil with their bare hands, or, without equipment, begin to manufacture industrial products." In short, "immigration is a function of the money at our command."[15]

The Mandate government and the Jewish Agency accepted Ruppin's assessment. The number of Jewish immigrants was set in relation to the ability of the economy to absorb them: those who could bring at least £1,000 (or $5,000, or RM15,000), which was sufficient for one farm or to support the immigration of four families, entered without restrictions. (This raised a significant bar; in terms of average earnings, £1,000 equals £128,000 today, or $245,000.) Professionals with £500 and skilled craftsmen needed by the *yishuv* (settlement, i.e., the Jewish community in Palestine) with £250 also were admitted without caveat. And the Jewish Agency supported as many as it could out of the £200,000 it had available for this purpose, calculating the absorption cost at £50 per person.[16] The yishuv grew at a measured pace, tripling from some 60,000 to 170,000 in the first decade of British rule.

The British decided how many Jews could enter; the Jewish Agency determined who they might be. Left-wing Zionist groups, committed to a solid socioeconomic base of farmers and manual laborers, dominated the yishuv. They sought strong, young immigrants who had lived as pioneers (*haluzim*) and had received vocational training and ideological education in agricultural schools before leaving for Palestine. These Jews were to discard their European identity and start anew as Hebrews in the Jewish homeland. In the words of the Zionist leader and future prime minister of Israel David Ben Gurion (born David Green in Plonsk, Poland), this meant "taking masses of uprooted, impoverished, sterile Jewish masses, living parasitically off the body of an alien economic body and dependent on others—and introducing them to productive and creative life, implanting them on the land, integrating them into primary production in agriculture, in industry and handicraft—and making them economically independent and self sufficient."[17]

Palestine fired the imagination of Polish Jews who lived in a rabidly nationalist and fiercely antisemitic country. Desperately poor, with no prospects in sight, young Polish Jews embraced the political solution Zionism offered and flocked to its proliferating youth movements.[18] Traveling in Europe in 1935 to assess Jewish communal conditions, Oscar Janowsky, an American scholar of and participant in Jewish affairs, remarked upon the central role of Palestine in the collective hope of Polish Jews. Janowsky happened to see the same propaganda movie, *Toward a New Life*, in Geneva (which he visited rather than a German city, in order to avoid the Nazi regime) and Warsaw. In Geneva, he said, the audience had "'contributed' to make the new life possible," but "they did not share in it." In Warsaw, by contrast, "the audience hummed the tunes; it anticipated the action; it thrilled to the hopes and joys and labors of the pioneers." Bidding a son farewell, "a Jew from Krakow who had seen better days" explained, "'In Palestine, my boy may find joy and hope and work.'"[19]

The contrast Janowsky observed in 1935 certainly pertained to German and Polish Jews in 1933. When Hitler came to power, only twenty thousand German Jews (4 percent) belonged to Zionist organizations. Most of them had no interest in emigrating to the cultural desolation of

Palestine.[20] As a result, German Jews comprised only 1 percent of the yishuv population.

For German Jews desperate to escape the Nazi regime, such considerations lost significance. Anticipating pressure to admit large numbers of refugees, the British government set up a cabinet committee. "The number of Jewish refugees who could be allowed to enter is strictly conditioned by what the country can absorb," the committee reported on 7 April 1933. "There is no reason to suppose that room could be found in Palestine in the near future for any appreciable number of German Jewish refugees."[21] The sole concessions the British government allowed were administrative. After the 1 April boycott, the high commissioner issued 1,000 certificates as an "advance" on the quota for the next half year; 618 of these went to German Jews. Extra certificates were issued for German Jews with financial resources, as per the existing formulary.[22] The Depression had increased the value of these sums in terms of average earnings since 1922; by 1933, £1,000 equaled £180,000 today, or $347,000.

The Zionist leadership agreed with the British authority's rationale and its measures. Then too, it was those who had shown little interest in the project of Palestine before—the German Jews—who needed asylum now. They had few friends among the Zionist leaders who wrestled with the conflict between their established long-range vision and abandoning those plans in light of the crisis in Germany. As the labor leader Berl Katznelson declared, it was impossible to resettle all German Jews in Palestine, and therefore the leadership "will have to choose on the basis of the cruel criterion of Zionism."[23] Addressing the Eighteenth Zionist Congress in Prague (August 1933), Arthur Ruppin, whose demographic expertise hampered his political imagination, calculated that Palestine could absorb only one hundred thousand German Jews in the next ten years: "In order that the immigration not flood the existing settlement in Palestine like lava, it must be proportionate to a certain percentage of that settlement." Ruppin dreaded "disorganized flight." Even "the condition of Jewish youth," which he acknowledged as "desperate," did not move him from his insistence on "escape" through "organized emigration."[24]

Financial resources were key to "organized emigration." The Zionists therefore parleyed with the Nazis. And the Nazis, for their part, were willing to negotiate. Whatever their attitude toward German Jews, the Nazis' worldview accorded Zionists a peculiar place. "The fundamental idea of the Zionists to organize the Jews as a nation among nations in their own land is sound and justified, as long as it is not connected with any plan for world domination," the prominent Nazi ideologue Johann von Leers declared in August 1933.[25]

Nazis and Zionists agreed that Jews had no place in the diaspora: Nazis believed that Jews had harmed western civilization; Zionists that two thousand years of European antisemitism was more than enough. Both saw Palestine as the solution. The *ha'avara* (transfer) agreement they hammered out allowed German Jews the sum required by Britain for unrestricted entry into Palestine. It also permitted transfer of capital in the form of German products or commodities. German Jews sold their possessions in Germany, depositing the marks gained in a German bank. A trust company then spent the money on German cars, building materials, dyes, pharmaceuticals, and the like, which were shipped to Palestine and sold for Palestinian pounds by another trust company and given to the settlers. Thus German Reichsmarks deposited in Germany were changed into Palestine pounds without straining the foreign currency reserves of the Reichsbank.[26]

German Zionists loathed making a deal with the Nazis that implicitly agreed to the liquidation of the German-Jewish community, but they saw they had no choice. The Jewish Agency regretted that the agreement broke the international boycott led by Jews against Germany and moved Jews who were not ideal settlers to Palestine, but understood the financial value of the deal for its long-term goals.[27] Chaim Weizmann, a Russian-born, naturalized British subject who served as president of the World Zionist Organization from 1920 until 1931 and president of the Jewish Agency from 1921 until 1930, expressed the sentiments of many of his colleagues in a letter he wrote on 19 October 1933 to the American Zionist leader Louis Lipsky. "I think everyone would prefer to do without it, but unfortunately it is a Hobson's choice: we have to get as much of the property of Jewish emigrants out of Germany as we can, and since the export of money is out of the question, goods are all we *can* export."[28]

The number of Jews who wished—and had the financial resources—
to benefit was limited: between August 1933 and early 1937 only 12,000
German Jews used the ha'avara agreement to transfer a proportion of
their assets to Palestine. Even so, this influx of money stimulated such
economic growth that it allowed another 20,000 young German Jews
without resources to immigrate to Palestine during that period. In 1933
Palestine served as the destination for 19 percent of German-Jewish refugees; that figure rose to 37 percent in 1934 and more or less held steady
at 36 percent in 1935 and 34 percent in 1936.[29] The ha'avara agreement
also opened up places in Palestine for the besieged Polish Jews. Thus during the first years of Nazi rule the number of Jews in the yishuv doubled
from 200,000 to 400,000 (or close to 30 percent of the territory's population of 1.3 million), and what had been disconnected enclaves in 1930
grew together. Palestine appeared to be on its way to Jewish statehood.[30]

PERMISSION TO EMIGRATE WAS ONE THING; earning a living once arrived
was another. *Palästina Aufbau Gesellschaft* (the Palestine Development
Society) rushed a second edition of its *Das Palästina Informationsbuch*
(*The Palestine Information Book*) into print in response to an explosion
of interest in immigration to the Jewish homeland. "Palestine is a small
country, and the country's needs are therefore limited; and the possibilities of export are also quite limited," the authors warned. "Most professions are glutted, but every month hundreds and thousands of Jews
arrive here, people from all corners of the world, with and without capital, with some plans and also—sadly without plans." Doctors, lawyers,
engineers, pharmacists, and teachers were not needed. Palestine, like the
rest of the world, enjoyed a surfeit of "intellectual workers." Immigrants
needed to think creatively: "physicians who have a lot of capital and who
can build up a private clinic, or chemists who are willing to begin to
manufacture specialized products," would do well, as would industrialists who made products currently imported. Furthermore, the authors
declared, "We want to shout to all Jews who voluntarily or are forced to
find a new profession in a new home: Go as farmers to Palestine!" And
while "there are no opportunities for civil servants," jobs abounded for

manual workers, "especially for young, strong people who have learned a trade well."[31]

"About artists we do not need to speak," the authors cautioned. "They have great difficulty earning a living anywhere, and only very few very great masters who are famous everywhere have an easier time of it—as is the case in Palestine, too." The most renowned German-Jewish author to immigrate to Palestine in 1933 was the writer (and Zionist) Arnold Zweig. From his letters it would appear that his challenge was adaptation, not earning a living. A friend of Sigmund Freud, Zweig carried on a voluminous and illuminating correspondence with the famous psychoanalyst. Writing to Freud in January 1934, Zweig explained how minor difficulties mounted major obstacles to adjustment. "You will find, dear Father Freud, that I am expatiating too much upon central heating, but these questions of practical life, where the apparatus of civilisation functions only creakingly, are the main problems in this country. We are not yet prepared to give up our standard of living and this country is not yet prepared to satisfy it. And since the Palestinian Jews are rightly proud of what does exist and since we are rightly irritated about what does not, there is much friction on the quiet, especially among the women, much vexation about the immense expense of effort these trifles demand." A year later, Zweig admitted, "I have established quite calmly that I do not belong here. After twenty years of Zionism that is naturally hard to believe." The nationalism, especially where it concerned Hebrew, depressed him. "I am a German writer and a German European and this fact has certain consequences." Freud counseled him to stay; at least Palestine was safe.[32] And Zweig took his advice.

In hindsight, it is easy to be baffled by Zweig's lack of insight and to overlook Freud's prescience. We know that Freud correctly saw that safety was the sole issue and that Zweig's complaints were trivial. At the time, however, no one could even imagine what lay ahead. German Jews who sought refuge in 1933 knew only that they had to flee the Nazi state, and Palestine offered safety.

Unlike their east European counterparts, German Jews had not prepared for life in the new land. Most lacked the skills required for the kinds of work available, and they had neither ideological training in

Zionism nor personal interest in Jewish history, culture, and language. If in central and western Europe and the United States, German Jews had considered themselves and their culture superior to the *Ostjuden* (eastern European Jews) and their ways, they found an inverted social hierarchy in Palestine.[33] "The wheel has turned," the Zionist leader and founder of the women's Hadassah organization Henrietta Szold observed. "In Palestine today there is helpfulness in full measure, yet no lack of unkind criticism of the refugees as Jews of inferior rank. Palestinian Mayflower Jewry is East European!" Born in Baltimore and a key figure in the American Zionist movement, Szold went to Palestine in 1920 at age fifty-nine. When Hitler came to power she was seventy-two, with plans to retire in America "to be coddled by my sisters." Now she had a new job to do, and she remained.[34]

The settlement of German Jews loomed large for Szold. As she confided to her diary in June 1933, "I hope we shan't bungle the business of absorption and adjustments." She worried too whether the refugees would manage. "The three hundred or four hundred men whom we have pushed into the *kibbutzim*, the workers' groups who are employed in the agricultural villages—while gradually in their 'leisure' time developing their own plots of ground—are fitting themselves into the conditions as they exist, but not too easily," she wrote in September. "It is their will that is making them successful, not their natural inclination."[35]

They had little choice. People who feel that they can hang on or hold out do not flee. German Jews who left during the first year of the Nazi reign knew they could do neither. And thus, for example, a renowned pediatrician from Berlin, Theodor Berger, and his wife were found in "a tiny shop—a mere cubby-hole" in Jerusalem. They sold cold cuts and salads and declared themselves satisfied. "We have two rooms in back of the store. They are not so light but they are enough."[36] The urgent situation shaped expectations and, in the short term, making do sufficed. But, as Arnold Zweig experienced, that sense of relief did not guarantee long-term adaptation. Indeed: Zweig abandoned Zionism for communism and left Palestine for East Germany in 1948.

In Szold's view, the most important factor was age. "Those who have passed the forty-year milestone are bound to suffer," she observed. "They long for the fleshpots of their German Egypt. They would return—they

Standing in a Kibbutz Ein Harod field, this girl was a member of the first youth aliyah group from Germany. PHOTOGRAPHER: ZOLTAN KLUGER, 1934.

say to themselves—in a jiffy if the Hitler regime were ended. And many of them believe it will end soon."[37]

BY THE TIME SHE WROTE that diary entry, Szold had embarked upon the greatest initiative of her very accomplished life: an effort to settle teenagers from Nazi Germany in Palestine. Palestine had served as a safe haven for a small group of orphans (thirty-seven boys and fourteen girls) after the Kishinev pogrom (1903), and for a few thousand after the massacres in the Ukraine in the wake of World War I. Perhaps the Jewish national home could provide an escape for Jewish youngsters, with or without parents, now.

This idea did not occur to the Zionist leadership either in Palestine or in Europe. They focused on immigrants of majority age who had the skills and capital to develop the economy and infrastructure. The youth aliyah movement, as the project to send teenagers to Palestine came to be called, developed in response to a request for help by impoverished, unemployed boys in Berlin. Nathan Höxter was sixteen, a member of a Zionist-socialist organization, and a choirboy in the Heidereutergasse synagogue. He knew Rabbi Moritz Freier and his wife Recha, a teacher and ardent Zionist. Höxter and his friends called upon Recha Freier early in 1932. "There they stood, thin, excited, gloomy, despair on their pale faces," she recalled nearly thirty years later. "They told me they had been sacked from their jobs for no other reason than that they were Jews. They were looking for a way out. Could I help them to get to Western Germany? They had heard that there were chances of finding employment in the coal-mines. Perhaps I had other advice for them?"[38]

Hitler had not yet come to power, and antisemitism was perceived as less important than the Depression. Freier followed up with the director of the Jewish labor exchange in Berlin, who was also a member of the Zionist movement. He believed that "'this state of affairs is undoubtedly due to the general unemployment in the country.'" When the economy improved, "'the Jewish boys will get work again.'" Freier might have been satisfied with his reply but for her chance sighting of the boys at a communist meeting spot near the Schoenhausertor in north Berlin. She understood: "If Zionism found no answer to their problem, then they would have to get it from other sources."[39]

As it happened, Freier herself found an answer in Zionism. "The boys should go to Palestine, to the workers' settlements, where they would receive a training for the land of Palestine." Once conceived, it was—to her—an amazingly obvious idea. "Should Jewish youth, ready for work and life, go to ruin somewhere or other, when their people needed them for its own work of rebuilding?"[40] Others saw problems where she saw possibilities. The Zionist Organization in Germany was doubtful.[41] The German Federation of WIZO (Women's International Zionist Organization) "laughed."[42] Nor did Henrietta Szold see its merit at this point.[43] Without endorsement, there was no hope for admission certificates. There the matter stood until the director of the Ben Shemen children's village visited Berlin in summer 1932 and offered places for twelve youths. The group had hoped to go to work on a kibbutz, not join an educational institution. Still, it was a start, and off they went at the end of 1932.[44]

The exodus of German Jews in early 1933 changed the situation on the ground. When Freier arrived in Palestine in May to garner support, she found key people willing to listen. Her plan depended upon the willingness of kibbutzim and moshavim to accept the youngsters, and the executive of the *Histadruth* (Workers' Federation) called delegates from these agricultural collectives to a meeting in Tel Aviv. There, to Freier's delight, "the basic principles of the system were laid down." The representatives determined the age and gender constitution of the groups to be settled on kibbutzim and moshavim, the type of training these fifteen- and sixteen-year-olds would receive, and the per person cost.[45] The way was now clear for the *Vaad Leumi* (Jewish National Council in Palestine) to sponsor the youth aliyah movement and to request immigration certificates for these young people.

While Freier brought her mission to Palestine, Chaim Arlosoroff, the head of the political department of the Jewish Agency, visited Berlin. Russian-born and German-educated, Arlosoroff had grown up in the German Zionist movement and had been a member of *Blau-Weiss* and *Ha-Poel Hazair*. As he was a leading figure in Palestine, his voice carried weight. At the forefront of his agenda loomed *"the question of children."* He advocated for the migration of thousands of haluzim, young people typically over age eighteen who had trained in Europe for life in Palestine, as well as thousands of school-aged youngsters to be trained and educated in the national homeland.[46]

Palestine beckoned. The number of haluzim increased from five hundred to fifteen thousand in a single year. Training centers sprang up across

Germany.[47] And the promise of youth aliyah appealed to parents eager to get their children out of harm's way and to youngsters eager for opportunity.

If Freier had the vision, Szold had the skills, competencies, and connections to establish the infrastructure in Palestine. Then head of the Vaad Leumi social welfare department, Szold began the painstaking task of persuading the Jewish Agency to support a request to the British to grant immigration certificates to five hundred young people under age eighteen. These were to be additional permits beyond those for new immigrants allowed in on the basis of absorption capacity. It fell to her too to contract about work, housing, and education with each kibbutz and moshav willing to take the young recruits and to settle the sum required by the agricultural collectives for these obligations. They agreed upon a maintenance fee of four pounds per month per person and, most important, a two-year apprenticeship and adjustment period.[48] However enthusiastic the young people were, they would need practical, ideological, and academic training. Few knew how to work the land, understood the principles of collective life, or spoke Hebrew. At the close of the two-year period, the young people would choose whether to remain together as a group or strike out individually.

In the meantime, Freier began to register youths wishing to go to Palestine. While they waited for immigration certificates, they set up a preparatory camp on the grounds of the Schocken family estate near Berlin. This became a regular part of the emigration process. The aim was to forge the girls and boys into a collective with a group identity and a sense of mutual responsibility. The preparatory camp also served another function, allowing the teachers and leaders to determine the fitness of each member for the challenges to come. Each place was precious, and those who were not suited for the program would not be allotted a permit.[49]

The Palestine administration granted the first 350 certificates in November 1933, and the Jewish Agency allotted the first batch to Berlin. Arie Appel belonged to that group. "On 12 February [1934] the first youth group left Germany, and large crowds came to the railway station to see them off," he recalled nearly half a century later. "When they landed at the port of Haifa on 19 February, Mrs Henrietta Szold and a number of people from [Kibbutz] Ein Harod were there to receive them." Writing

Youth aliyah refugees dance at Kibbutz Ein Harod in March 1936.
PHOTOGRAPHER: ZOLTAN KLUGER.

in the third person, he described the situation as he remembered it and also as he had learned it from the others. "Strong and often contradictory feelings ran through the minds and hearts of these young newcomers. Those with a deeply religious background felt that they were going-back to the Holy Land, while the secular-minded saw it as the beginning of a future nation as well as the starting point of their own personal achievement. Others, of course, were attracted by an adventure into the unknown, but for all of them, whether they realized it or not, this was the beginning of a totally new life. Climate, landscape, food, living on a *kibbutz*, farm work, language—everything was different and hard to get used to." Still, in Appel's memory, "there was no shortage of confidence and determination to overcome these difficulties."[50]

As it transpired, Arie had recorded his impressions a year into his stay at Ein Harod. Marveling at the transition he had lived, he observed, "Today all this may seem natural to us, but it is a miracle that a whole generation managed to sever all links with the past and assume an entirely new physical and spiritual foundation." He accepted the Zionist ideology as his own. "There can be no transition more remarkable and inspiring than our own, that of a largely assimilated Jewry regaining its freedom and pride, of merchants becoming workers, of a foreign language giving way to Hebrew, of becoming acclimatized to a farming life instead of the city, of the creation, in fact, of a radically new society." And he had gained a new appreciation of work: "only a whole day of hard work can give you the right to bear full responsibility and make you really understand the meaning of work."

Yet he wondered what sort of Jew he was. He came from an assimilated family, and his "first impetus towards Judaism flowed from the Zionist Movement. This being so, what will my way be in this country, and towards what kind of Judaism should I aspire?" Nor had he mastered Hebrew, perhaps because the youngsters spoke German among themselves. For Arie—unlike Arnold Zweig (in his forties)—this was a difficulty to master, not a reason to withdraw. Concluding his assessment of the first year at Ein Harod, he observed, "It is a way of life of a generation in search of new horizons."[51]

The vision of "a generation in search of new horizons" took root across the ideological and religious spectrum of the Jewish community and prompted support from Jews on both sides of the Atlantic. As Norman Bentwich, who by then was director of the League of Nations High Commission for Refugees (under High Commissioner James McDonald), observed, "Palestine offered a healing from the deadly miasma of anti-Semitism and from the sick feeling of helplessness. It was brought home to all, non-Zionists as well as Zionists, that boys and girls could grow there to freedom and service." It was, he said, "a combination of idealism and practical necessity [that] launched Youth Aliyah as a popular movement."[52]

Jewish organizations, no matter the stripe, appealed to Szold for help. Writing from Jerusalem to his brother in Baltimore, one of Szold's nephews described his surprise to see a letter from Jabotinsky's Zionist Revisionist movement to his aunt. "I asked Aunt Henrietta why Revisionists wrote to her at all. It turned out that although the Revisionists have withdrawn from the Zionist organization they nevertheless want her to take an interest in Revisionist Youth Aliyah." And she did. She was equally open

German-Jewish boys sent on youth aliyah to Kibbutz Rodges read the Torah.
PHOTOGRAPHER: ZOLTAN KLUGER, 1935.

to requests from the Orthodox, even if she could not satisfy their needs. As her nephew continued, the Orthodox organization Agudat Israel (also not a member of the Zionist movement) "want a German Youth Aliyah too, but they want a guarantee that boys and girls will be kept strictly separate, a thing the Zionists find it practically impossible to do."[53]

Youth aliyah served the children of refugees as well as youngsters still in Germany, and opened a branch in Paris for that purpose. The political philosopher Hannah Arendt, who had left Germany in 1933, was appointed director of the Paris office. Writing in 1935, she observed that adolescent children of refugees suffered from neglect because "their parents, overburdened with worries, have no time to take care of them." The adults thought about neither the past nor the future "and, focusing their concern only on the immediate present, forget the situation of their children."[54] Reaching out to refugees with children, Arendt was met with suspicion. And when they came to her office, the emotional strains of their refugee life hindered constructive action. Listening to his father "recounting their odyssey, the son is silent and unsociable. He is ashamed of their many misfortunes; he is annoyed by them; he behaves as if none concerned him, as if it were someone else's story and he were in the room by accident; he doesn't want to be identified with misfortune!" But, she learned, he claimed to be "an 'old Zionist.'" The boy returned by himself the next day, and they spoke more openly. "He shouldn't be ashamed of his misfortune!" Arendt enjoined him. "He shouldn't give it personal significance, for it isn't a personal misfortune; it is the misfortune of his entire people. Nothing is changed or improved by silence or hypocrisy. Yes, he will go to Palestine, not as a remedy to his own troubles, but as a member of an entire, large group, not because he is indigent, but because he is needed over there; he will build the country for himself and others, and for those who will come there after him. He will not be alone over there. And already here, he no longer has the right to feel alone, for he is showing a sense of solidarity with all those who share the same fate."[55]

Word of mouth recruitment by the youngsters "is the best propaganda," she found. Yet they—like older refugees—were loath to renege on their familial responsibilities. "A young man of fourteen walks in. He wants to 'get information.' Where are his parents? 'I would rather not worry them unnecessarily,' he says, 'before really making up my mind.' He sees Palestine as 'the only solution to the Jewish question,' but wonders if he has the right to leave his father, for he handles all his French correspondence." Encouraged by Arendt, who works out his placement, "he informs his parents, and two weeks later he is in the camp, where he begins to solve the Jewish question in a practical way by learning agriculture."[56]

BY THE END OF 1935 the situation in Palestine appeared positively prosperous. "I am glad to be able to say," Ruppin reported to the Zionist Congress of September 1935, "that the German immigration, which broke in upon us with the volume and unexpectedness of an avalanche, has been 'absorbed.'"[57] He was especially pleased by the immigration of German-Jewish youth. "As a phenomenon this is one of the most inspiring things in Jewish life," he enthused to the Council of the Jewish Agency a few days later. "Every child, who has been snatched from the inferno of hatred which Germany has become for the Jews, has been saved and restored to life."[58]

Zionists had cause for joy: immigration to Palestine stood at an all-time high, and the yishuv enjoyed a booming economy while the rest of the world suffered the Depression. The Arab population, by contrast, saw these developments with increasing alarm. The Arab Palestinian leadership had rejected the legitimacy of the Mandate in 1922, and they had refused to develop an "Arab Agency" to organize the Arab community in Palestine and provide a platform for its interests, as the Jewish Agency did for the yishuv. Without access to the administrative structures of the Mandate, the Arabs had no effective political mechanism to participate in or deal with the rapid transformation of the society in which they lived, and in which their economic and demographic share worsened apace.[59] The yishuv had doubled in size since 1933; by the end of 1935 Jews accounted for 28 percent of the population. Demographic projections suggested that if the 1935 level of immigration (66,472 people) carried forward, Jews would gain a majority share of the population by 1947. Worse: the new immigrants had fostered an expanding economy, which set a higher absorptive capacity, and thus increased immigration.[60]

The Arab revolt of 1936 targeted the British and their Mandate, not the Jews and their settlements. The Arabs calculated that if the British surrendered the Mandate and withdrew, or at least prohibited immigration of Jews, the yishuv would cease to function as the dynamic core of a future Jewish state. Without the support of British imperialism, the Jews in Palestine would be forced to abandon the Zionist agenda and accept their time-honored position of a docile minority, as in other Arab lands.[61]

The British crushed the Arab revolt ruthlessly. With more than one thousand dead, violence in the streets, and no solution in sight, Jews in Germany stopped in their tracks. Perhaps the United States would be safer? Reporting in May 1936, John Erhardt, American consul general in Hamburg, alerted the secretary of state "that the pressure of German Jewish immigration to the United States . . . may shortly become more acute." He noted that "the recent disturbances in Palestine . . . may force the curtailment of immigration there." And he observed "a growing conviction among the Hamburg Jews, which, I am certain, reflects the attitude of their co-religionists elsewhere in the Reich, that emigration to the Holy Land would be, for them, taking the serious chance that after settling there, they might well, within a few years, have to undergo the same uprooting which they are now experiencing here." Many German Jews "now believe it would be hazardous to plan to settle there and consider the United States, with its annual quota of 25,000, as the sole remaining haven."[62] Erhardt had assessed prevailing sentiment correctly. Writing in *Der Morgen*, a leading German-Jewish intellectual monthly magazine, the economist Arthur Prinz, who worked for the Hilfsverein der Deutschen Juden (German Jews' Aid Society), worried about the possible consequences of the turbulence in Palestine. "In this deteriorating Jewish-Arab relationship," he warned, "the Jewish minority communities in the Arab world can easily become hostages." Consider emigration overseas, he urged his coreligionists; stop focusing on Palestine.[63]

The British government in London worried about the Arab uprising too and appointed a royal commission to travel to Palestine to "ascertain the underlying causes of the disturbances . . . and to ascertain whether . . . either the Arabs or the Jews have any legitimate grievances."[64] Chaired by William Wellesley Peel, former secretary of state for India, the commission submitted its report in July 1937. The Mandate had ceased to work, it found. The sole solution lay in partition: "While neither race can justly rule all Palestine, we see no reason why, if it were practicable, each race should not rule part of it. . . . Partition seems to offer at least a chance of ultimate peace. We can see none in any other plan."[65] It envisioned a massive population transfer, primarily of Arabs, as there were few Jews in the territory allocated (on paper) to Arabs. "If Partition is to be effective in promoting a final settlement," the commission asserted, "it must mean more than drawing a frontier and establishing two States. Sooner or later there should be a transfer of land and, as far as possible, an exchange of population."[66]

The House of Commons referred the Peel commission findings to the Permanent Mandates Commission of the League of Nations which, in the end, supported its recommendation for partition.[67] The German foreign office was dismayed. It had never imagined that the Jews would be so successful in Palestine, and it dropped their former advocacy of the Zionist cause with alacrity. "The formation of a Jewish state . . . is not in Germany's interest," the foreign office wrote its embassy in London and consulate general in Palestine. It "would not absorb world Jewry but would create an additional position of power under international law for international Jewry, somewhat like the Vatican State for political Catholicism or Moscow for the Comintern."[68] Within weeks of the Peel report, Referat Deutschland, the department responsible for liaising between the foreign office and the other state and party offices, had determined that getting rid of the Jews by sending them to Palestine was less urgent than preventing the establishment of a Jewish state. "The Jewish question as a domestic problem would be replaced by the considerably more dangerous one of an opposition of world Jewry to the Third Reich based on recognition by international law."[69]

While the Referat Deutschland organized the state and party machinery to oppose the proposal, the Zionists, meeting that same month (August) in Zurich, split on the specifics of partition. The Zionist Congress roared with varying plans, compromises, and declarations of intransigence. "It is our belief that Eretz Israel in its totality belongs to us," the religious Zionist rabbi Meir Bar-Ilan thundered. If relinquish-

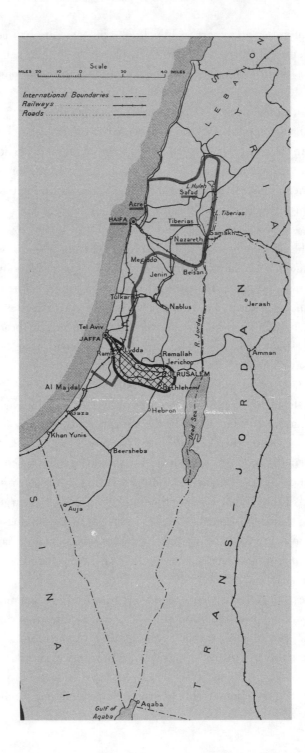

ing historic land claims was painful, abandoning the dream of control over Jerusalem, which the British were to continue to control, was not to be borne. "A Jewish State without Jerusalem would be a decapitated body," the labor leader Berl Katznelson maintained. Chaim Weizmann pleaded with the delegates to accept a small but sovereign Jewish state that, while it could not accept older people—"they are dust, economic and moral dust in a cruel world!"—would provide refuge for as many as two million young Jews. Invoking the prophets Isaiah and Jeremiah, who spoke only about safeguarding people not land ownership, he pled his case for a state to save one-third of the six million European Jews he believed at risk. "Two millions, and perhaps less—*Sche'erit Hapleta*—only a remnant shall survive. We have to accept it."[70] In the end, the Twentieth Zionist Congress narrowly passed a motion to consider partition. But the moment had passed.[71]

Nahum Goldmann was one of many delegates devastated by the debate and its outcome. Reflecting upon it some forty years later, his judgment had only sharpened in light of the history that followed. The Zionists' failure to grasp this slim but quite real opportunity to found a state in 1937 flowed from an "inability to compromise, determination to hold on to every inch of Palestine as something historically sacred, the obstinacy and fanaticism of a persecuted people that for two thousand years had set beliefs and ideals above reality and practical necessity, an unwillingness to recognize that a people not content with waiting, hoping, and having faith must reckon with realities, even if it means sacrificing some cherished historic ideas as a means toward shaping its own destiny." And he conjectured: "If the Zionist movement had accepted the proposal then, spontaneously and without delay, it is quite conceivable that it might have been implemented. We would then have had two years' time before war broke out and a country to which hundreds of thousands, possibly millions, of European Jews might have escaped."[72]

We will never know. It remains one of the heartbreaking "what ifs" of the miserable history of refugee Jews from Nazi Europe.

Peel Commission proposal for partition. Taken from Palestine Royal Commission, Report (1937).

PASSPORTS IN
A CLOSED WORLD

Hannah Arendt, german-jewish political philosopher, fled from the Reich to France and from there to the United States. By war's end she had experienced life on the run, internment in a camp, and the precarious existence of a refugee. Much of her postwar writing pondered the political framework of the catastrophe both abetted and endured by millions. She saw World War I as pivotal. "The days before and after the First World War are separated not like the end of the old and the beginning of the new period, but like the day before and the day after an explosion," she observed in her seminal work, *The Origins of Totalitarianism* (1951). Among the events Arendt identified as sequelae of the Great War, she included "bloodier and more cruel" civil wars "than all their predecessors; . . . followed by migrations of groups who, unlike their happier predecessors in the religious wars, were welcomed nowhere and could be assimilated nowhere. Once they had left their homeland they remained homeless, once they had left their state they became stateless; once they had been deprived of their human rights they were rightless, the scum of the earth."[1]

Like Arendt, the Austrian-Jewish author Stefan Zweig was prompted by his life as a refugee to search for the key moment of social rupture, and he too marked the outbreak of World War I. Stateless, after Nazi Germany annexed Austria, Zweig learned the hard lesson he had heard from a Russian refugee a decade earlier: "Formerly man had only a body and soul. Now he needs a passport as well, for without it he will not be treated like a human being." How different had been the world before the outbreak of the Great War, when "people went where they wished and stayed as long as they pleased. There were no permits, no visas. . . . One embarked and alighted without questioning or being questioned, one did not have to fill out a single one of the many papers which are required today." After the war, by contrast, "the world was on the defensive against strangers," Zweig remembered.

> The humiliations which once had been devised with criminals alone in mind now were imposed upon the traveler, before and during every journey. There had to be photographs from right to left, in profile and full face, one's hair had to be cropped sufficiently to make the ears visible; fingerprints were taken, at first only the thumb but later all ten fingers; furthermore certificates of health, of vaccination, police certificates of good standing, had to be shown; letters of recommendation were required, invitations to visit a country had to be procured; they asked for addresses of relatives, for moral and financial guarantees, questionnaires, and forms in triplicate and quadruplicate needed to be filled out, and if only one sheet of paper was missing one was lost. . . . Human beings were made to feel that they were objects and not subjects, that nothing was their right but everything merely a favour by official grace.[2]

Nostalgia did not shape Arendt and Zweig's view. As legal texts of the day and Werner Bertelsmann, a German scholar of passports, explained (1914), "most modern states have, with but a few exceptions, abolished their passport laws or at least neutralized them through non-enforcement." Foreigners "are no longer viewed by states with suspicion and mistrust but rather, in recognition of the tremendous value that can be derived from trade and exchange, welcomed with open arms and, for this reason, hindrances are removed from their paths to the greatest extent possible."[3] In Europe, only Russia, Turkey, Romania, and Bulgaria—states that had maintained the eighteenth-century habit of issuing internal passports for policing their own citizens—remained notorious exceptions to the general rule.[4]

The relative insignificance of papers, permits, and passports before 1914 and their tyranny after that date mark a social and political sea change. Startling as this new course appeared to people like Zweig, the bureaucrats who developed the systems drew upon precedents of long standing. The term "passport" came from the fifteenth century and derives from the French words *passer*, to pass, and *porte*, a gate. Needing permission to enter a fortified city, travelers presented a paper, such as a letter of introduction by a person of rank, to establish their identity and function. The gatekeeper endorsed the paper by writing *visé* (seen) or "passport."[5]

Initially an informal procedure, the first passport regulation was issued by Louis XI of France in 1464 when he established a system of royal couriers. They carried official passports that allowed them to travel without hindrance and, at the same time, enabled the royal bureaucracy to track their movements: in every town they entered their passports were stamped and the details recorded in a ledger that was forwarded to a central register.[6] Soon envoys received passports, and before the end of the century these were used to monitor the movements of mercenary soldiers and prevent desertion. Passports issued by church authorities became important identity documents for pilgrims, giving them free passage and admission to hostels. Conversely, people without passports came under suspicion as vagabonds, paupers, Roma and Sinti, Jews, or other transients that cities sought to keep outside their walls.[7]

With the rise of mercantilism in the seventeenth century, passports emerged as a key tool to control the population and thus the economy, and they served to establish administrative order. Louis XIV decreed that people leaving his realm needed a passport that authorized them to do so. Significantly, none was required to enter the kingdom.[8]

Enlightenment philosophers objected to passports as contrary to

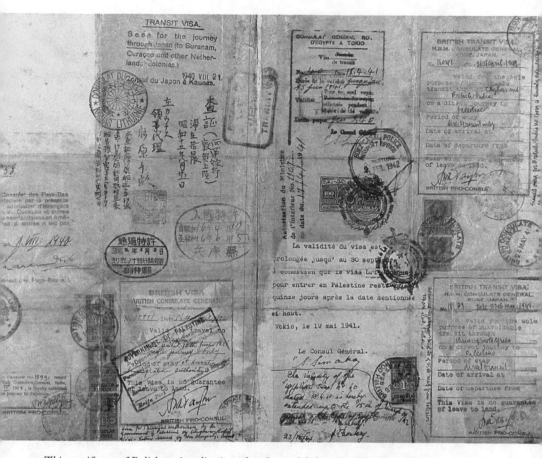

This certificate of Polish nationality issued to Samuel Solz, a Jewish refugee from Bialystok, by the Polish consul in Vilna shows the visa stamps Solz obtained as he fled to Kovno, where he got a transit visa from the Japanese consul Chiune Sugihara, through Japan, China, India, and Aden to reach Palestine.

liberty and natural law, and they were abolished in the first days of the French Revolution.[9] But faced with Louis XVI's escape attempt, royalist uprisings in the Vendée, and military interventions by Prussia and Austria, the revolutionaries quickly restored the passport system. They aimed to prevent anti-republican movements, suppress vagrancy and banditry, avert infiltration by foreign agents, and control the departure of citizens.

For the first time, passports became a state document issued to every-one, and it was assumed that foreigners who wished to enter the country would also produce such a paper. Yet while the use of passports grew, no internationally recognized and accepted passport system developed to regulate the admission of foreigners, and no standard obtained as to what such a document should be and what rights and obligations it carried.[10]

The liberalization of national economies and the advent of mass travel by train and steamship in the latter half of the nineteenth century led to the elimination of passport obligations. As laws requiring passports could not be enforced, they were canceled or, as in the case of France, lay dormant.[11] Still, passport or no passport, countries needed no excuse to bar unwanted foreigners. Those who belonged to groups most often refused admission, such as traveling musicians, itinerant peddlers, and Russian and Austro-Hungarian Roma and Sinti, tried to obtain passports to facilitate movement between countries and to obtain consular help if in trouble (an expectation of protection that was rarely honored).[12] For others, however, passports established identity and nationality and thus the right to diplomatic and consular protection abroad and the right to return to the country that had issued the document.[13] This latter proved singularly important, as states were loath to admit an alien who had no place to which to return.

After borders closed in 1914, passport laws were reactivated. New wartime passport and visa requirements soon became standard through-out Europe. The documents themselves, previously an uncomplicated single sheet, now required a photograph and a full physical description.[14] Intended to be temporary, these passport and visa requirements were not abolished when hostilities ended. On the contrary. In many instances the rules were sharpened—to the chagrin of German legal scholar Ernst Isay, who called for the rapid abolition of "this heritage of medieval diplo-macy which gives both States and individuals only inconvenience and not a single advantage."[15] Government officials disagreed. Economic crisis, massive unemployment as a result of troop demobilization, fear of revolu-tion, displaced populations, and an influenza pandemic that killed three times as many people, civilians and combatants combined, as had died during four years of war (40 million as compared with 15.2) strengthened the xenophobia born in 1914. States feared beggars, vagabonds, refugees, deserters, spies, political agitators, and those who tried to profit from contemporary currency problems.[16]

Many supported the maintenance of tight control over the movement of strangers for a very different reason: the practical benefits that accompanied citizenship. The postwar economic crisis left many veterans unemployed, and states imposed elaborate systems to prohibit or restrict "permissions to work" on foreigners so as to regulate and protect the native labor market. In most places, the right to employment became a corollary of citizenship. And with the rise of the welfare state and the introduction of education, unemployment, health, and old-age benefits for citizens, the gap widened between national and foreigner. If outsiders could merge easily into a new society before 1914, it became very difficult after 1918. To make matters worse, the United States and the British dominions, sites of mass immigration at the turn of the century, slashed the total number allowed to enter and delimited the countries from whence they came.[17]

NINE TO TEN MILLION PEOPLE sought asylum in 1920s and '30s Europe. Few had valid passports. In the reconfiguration of Europe, minority groups—or those who feared becoming one because of the shifting boundaries—fled to countries where they were "nationally" attached. These millions of refugees belonged somewhere and were relatively well absorbed into their "national homes."[18]

A different type of refugee, however, those who fled genocide (Armenians) or revolution (Russians), posed an intractable problem. The slaughter of Armenians by Turks under cover of World War I sent more than two hundred thousand Armenians surging into Syria and France. And the Russian Revolution led some seven hundred thousand people to flee to Germany, Poland, France, Romania, and elsewhere. These refugees carried the ominous burden of statelessness, which deprived them of the rights, privileges, and protections accorded to citizens.[19] As a contemporary legal text explained, stateless people "enjoy no protection whatever, and, if they are aggrieved by a State, they have no way of redress, since there is no State which would be competent to take their case in hand. As far as the Law of Nations is concerned, apart from morality, there is no restriction whatever to cause a State to abstain from maltreating to any extent such stateless individuals."[20]

This previously minor problem ballooned in the 1920s. Millions of citizens of the former Austro-Hungarian Empire found themselves stateless due to the new citizenship rules of the successor states. In the newly configured Europe, ethnic Hungarians, for instance, now lived in Czechoslovakia. But stateless people such as they had their homes and livelihood. They could not travel. Yet for the most part, they could remain quietly where they were and hope for naturalization in due course.

Not so Russians and Armenians. The Russian government unrolled the largest denationalization in history with its decree on 15 December 1921 stripping citizenship from nationals who had lived outside Russia for five years and had not got new passports from the Soviet Union, those who had left the country after 7 November 1917 without permission, and those "who have voluntarily served in armies fighting against the Soviet authority, or who have in any way participated in counter-revolutionary organizations."[21] Some 863,000 Russians thus suddenly found themselves stateless refugees.[22] Turkey proved just as ruthless. First, the government confiscated all the property in Turkey of Armenians living abroad (1923). It then passed a law (23 May 1927) that stripped nationality from "Ottoman subjects who during the War of Independence took no part in the National Movement, kept out of Turkey and did not return from July 24, 1923."[23] A subsequent law stipulated that "those who are deprived of their Turkish citizenship shall be expelled if they are in Turkey. The return to Turkey of all persons deprived of their Turkish citizenship is prohibited. Their property is subject to liquidation by the Government."[24] These decrees affected as many as 200,000[25] to 900,000[26] Armenians.

The Soviet Union and Turkey denationalized citizens they saw as impediments to their revolutionary vision. Belgium, France, and Italy adopted similar decrees to denationalize anyone the government perceived as a threat to public order or state interests.[27] The League of Nations stepped into this legal vacuum. Accepting responsibility to provide for Russian stateless refugees, the Council asked the famous and enormously respected Norwegian explorer Fridtjof Nansen to serve as "High Commissioner on behalf of the League" to deal with this problem.

An international celebrity for his North Pole adventures in the 1890s,[28] the charismatic Nansen had served the League before. At the request of then Secretary-General Eric Drummond, he and his energetic and efficient colleague Philip Baker had organized the repatriation of 250,000 Central Powers[29] (as the countries that fought against the allies were called) soldiers still in Siberian prisoner-of-war camps in 1920 and 200,000 Russian prisoners of war in Germany. With that task behind him in spring 1921, Nansen accepted the League's mission. Working with Baker, he sought to develop a means to provide political and legal protection to Russian refugees, as well as to coordinate the efforts of the numerous organizations that offered relief services.[30]

Baker lit upon the idea of an identity document that derived prestige from Nansen's name. The 1922 treaty called the document a *Certificat d'Identité*, but Baker used the term "Nansen passport," and the name stuck. Issued by individual countries on behalf of the high commissioner's office, the Nansen passport was recognized as a valid international identity document by twenty-four nations by the end of 1922 and fifty a few years later. Valid for one year, the Nansen passport did not grant the privilege of residence citizens enjoyed or the right to seek employment.[31] But it looked like a passport, was called a passport, was associated with the most noble name of its day, and it worked.[32] As one of Nansen's aides put it, "what the identity certificate lacked in substance it . . . gain[ed] in moral prestige."[33] Nansen's Nobel Peace Prize in December 1922 sealed that moral authority and raised the platform for international acceptance of the passports that bore his name, including the establishment of quasi-consular offices in many countries to help Nansen passport holders. Issued first to Russian refugees, the Nansen passport was extended to Armenians in 1923 and Assyrian, Assyro-Chaldean, and Kurdish refugees in 1926.[34]

Buoyed by this success, Nansen convened an inter-governmental conference in Geneva (1926) to press governments to include the right for Nansen passport holders to return to the country that had issued the document, should the holder travel abroad. Twenty-three nations agreed. They also agreed to allow their consuls to issue visas to Nansen passport holders, just as they would if these persons held a national passport.

Many saw an answer in sight for stateless people. The League of Nations' Organization for Communications and Transit held a passport conference that same year. The German delegation proposed a generic passport for stateless persons, people whose nationality was unclear, and nationals whose government refused to renew their passports.[35] This last issue arose from fascist Italy and affected political opponents abroad. When their passports expired, they faced two choices: remain where they were without valid papers, or return to Italy to be sent into internal exile, imprisoned, or killed.[36] The Italian delegate understood that the generic passport had Italian exiles in view and, supported by the Polish delegate who argued for an absolute distinction between nationals and stateless, defeated the proposal.[37] This victory for fascist Italy soon faded, however, as Mussolini found it preferable to keep a close watch over his opponents, which the passport renewal process facilitated.[38]

The compromise document that emerged was a bland and neutral *Carte d'Identité et de Voyage* (Identity and Travel Document).[39] It never grew in stature, while the Nansen passport steadily accrued additional rights: limited diplomatic protection; legal assistance; eased labor restrictions; limitations on expulsion. By the time Nansen died in 1930, refugees with passports in his name enjoyed many of the same benefits as nationals.[40] "It is a fantastic commentary on the inhumanity of our times," the American journalist and activist Dorothy Thompson observed in 1938, "that for thousands and thousands of people a piece of paper with a stamp on it is the difference between life and death, and that scores of people have blown their brains out because they could not get it. But there is no doubt that by and large, the Nansen certificate is the greatest thing that has happened for the individual. It returned to him his lost identity."[41]

THE NANSEN PASSPORT REACHED its zenith just when a new problem overwhelmed its scope. In October 1933 an inter-governmental conference sponsored by the League's Nansen International Office for Refugees (IOR) adopted a Refugee Convention that extended even greater rights to Nansen passport holders than they had held to date.[42] A significant achievement from the vantage point of the 1920s, the convention paled in the face of what officials feared would be a new refugee flood from Germany. Within days of the Nazis' April boycott, a cabinet committee in London discussed whether "steps should be taken forthwith to have the question of Jewish refugees from Germany considered by the International Office for Refugees of the League of Nations."[43] The catch here, Orme Sargent of the foreign office explained, was that the IOR "deals with White Russian and certain other stateless persons who cannot obtain national passports. The German Jews now leaving Germany are German nationals, and possess German national passports. Though they are leaving Germany owing to persecution, they are not technically refugees." Political considerations obtained too, as Sargent's chief, Foreign Secretary John Simon, pointed out. "A suggestion by His Majesty's Government that the League should consider measures of assistance for German nationals leaving Germany would be regarded in that country as an act of unwarranted interference, if not hostility."[44]

The farther removed from responsibility for friendly relations with Germany, the stronger the language seeking a solution for refugees from the Nazi regime. If the foreign office had its worries, other agencies had theirs. Thus Arthur Henderson, head of the World Disarmament Conference, urged Simon in no uncertain terms to take up the matter with the League. German refugees deserved a Nansen passport, just as Russians and Armenians had. "I have no doubt in my own mind that the giving of such protection to these unhappy people would be right in principle and would be simply applying to a new situation the decisions made ten years ago in respect of Russian and other refugees who found themselves in an identical position," he wrote. "The experience of the great advantages reaped by the Russians from this protection has shown how important this form of help might be to the German Jews and political refugees today."[45] Henderson understood that the Soviet Union had not been a member of the League when Nansen had been asked to deal with Russian refugees, while Germany was now an important member. To stymie Reich objections, he suggested that the Nansen passport extend its protection to "all stateless persons." The British League of Nations Union agreed; it proposed widening the definition of "stateless" to those "whose nationality is doubtful and to persons having a nationality who are unable to obtain a national passport or have a valid reason for not applying for such a passport."[46]

Possession of a valid passport was of vital concern to refugees. Fleeing Germany in March 1933, Walter Benjamin knew that his passport would expire in August. "One can obviously not count on its being renewed under the present circumstances," he wrote (20 March) his friend Gershom Scholem in Jerusalem.[47] He had heard rumors that consular officials asked German nationals to hand over their passports for safekeeping. "I am going to pretend that mine has been lost. But of course I don't believe that I will get another one," he confided two months later.[48] He had gone to Ibiza and feared getting stuck there, unable to carry on to Paris. Assuring Benjamin that he worried unnecessarily, Scholem noted that he did not understand "why an expired passport would be an obstacle to crossing the French border at a time when hundreds of people from Germany are constantly doing it without any passport—and without being deported."[49] Fortunately for Benjamin, he did not have to resort to that course. "The steps I took in the matter of my passport have been rewarded with success," he reported at the end of July.[50] Claiming that his passport had been stolen, he had obtained a new one, valid for five years, from the German consul in Palma.

A moment of luck: Benjamin got a new passport just before German refugees ceased to qualify for consular services and the newly passed (14 July) Repeal of Naturalizations and the Adjudication of German Citizenship Law, which allowed the government to withdraw citizenship, took effect. A decree two weeks later clarified that eastern European Jews in Germany formed the main target, but German refugees were at risk to become stateless as well.[51] This appeared ominously like the Russian denationalization law of 1921, and as the regime used the act to strip high-profile opponents of Nazism like Albert Einstein and Arnold Zweig of their citizenship, no one abroad knew where it would stop.

Stateless refugees from Germany (primarily eastern European Jews who had come to Germany in 1918 and had never been naturalized) had fled with the 1927 Carte d'Identité et de Voyage which afforded few rights. When its validity expired after six months, the holder had to return to Germany or get German consular officials to renew them.[52] Both impossible. With the July legislation, German nationals abroad faced the same problem when their passports came due. The Nazis had learned much from fascist Italy, but while Rome had abandoned the idea, Berlin pursued it. Consuls got their orders: no passport renewals, no other consular services, and no diplomatic protection.

STILL, NO GOVERNMENT STOOD WILLING to refer the matter to the Nansen office. As pressure grew from many quarters to establish a new office responsible for refugees from Germany, London and Paris sought invisibility. The creation of such an agency, foreign office official Victor Perowne wrote in a note to his colleagues, "would lead to a vast increase in the numbers of refugees and might encourage the German Government cynically to get rid of all undesirables at the expense of other countries." Furthermore, he added, "such a body could scarcely fail to make recommendations which it would be inconvenient for H.M. Government to implement and embarrassing for them to reject."[53] Perowne advised the British delegation at the League Assembly meeting in Geneva later that month "to lie as low as possible."[54] Paris urged the same strategy. Nansen had done much good "in a global economic situation that was quite different"; it then concerned "refugees of whom many were ready to become farmers or factory workers—much easier to place than the bank clerks and commercial employees, the intellectuals and semi-intellectuals."[55] The French had long shaped their refugee policy according to the country's labor needs, and they had no wish to change course at the direction of the League.[56]

Fearing that the opportunity to bring the refugee problem to the League would slip away, the prominent Anglo-Zionist Norman Bentwich turned to David Cohen, lay leader of the Jewish community in the Netherlands.[57] Cohen was deeply involved in the reception of German-Jewish refugees in Amsterdam, and he had access to the Dutch foreign minister, Andries de Graeff.[58] It took little for Bentwich to persuade de

Graeff, who believed the Netherlands had shouldered more than its share of the refugee burden. A new high commissioner would do nicely.

Berlin wanted none of it. The German foreign office considered a legal limbo policy for the refugees, drafting language to say that refugees from Germany were free to return to the Reich at any time. But Hitler had no patience for such diplomatic niceties: under no circumstances should any German representative suggest that Germany stood willing to take back the refugees, he ordered. The German ambassador to The Hague sought to prevent de Graeff from raising the matter at all, but the Dutch proved determined. To a point. De Graeff took up the refugee problem in the League Assembly in September, but he stepped away from discussion of Germany's racist policies, which affected the Jews, nor did he mention the Reich's violation of the rights of neighboring states that had taken in the people Germany had thrown out. "Nothing is further from our thoughts than a desire to interfere in internal affairs coming under Germany's sovereignty," de Graeff hastened to explain. "We have no wish to examine the reasons why these people have left their country, but we are faced with the undeniable fact that thousands of German subjects have crossed the frontiers of neighboring countries and are refusing to return to their homes, for reasons which we are not called upon to judge. For us, therefore, it is a purely technical problem, and its solution must be found by common agreement."[59] De Graeff simply accepted Germany's aggression toward Jews and toward its neighbors as a fact of political life. The surrender to Hitler had already begun.

De Graeff suggested a new and parallel organization under the direction of a League commissioner. Its success, he insisted, depended upon its bonds with the League and the mantle of authority and prestige the international body bestowed upon it.[60] Negotiations emasculated his proposal. Some delegates insisted that the high commissioner should try to find "work for the refugees in all countries which are able to offer it" (and who had work to offer during the Depression?); Britain's William Ormsby-Gore demanded the exclusion of Palestine from the high commissioner's reach;[61] and the German delegate Karl Ritter opposed the bland formulation that governments could be asked merely to assist the high commissioner "to the best of their abilities."[62]

The Assembly accepted a severely compromised solution and, with Germany abstaining, created the International High Commission for Refugees (Jewish and Other) Coming from Germany, which received no money from the League and was not responsible to the League Council.[63] With no hero in sight, no one like Nansen to fire public imagination, the League, always eager to enlist American cooperation, offered the position of high commissioner to James McDonald, formerly a professor at Indiana University and then chairman of the Foreign Policy Association. A devout Christian with a huge social network, McDonald was a Germanophile with good contacts with liberal Jews.[64] Like Nansen, McDonald was to coordinate activity between the states confronted with the refugee crisis. And like Nansen, he was not to undertake any direct relief work. But unlike Nansen, McDonald was explicitly forbidden to deal with the refugee problem in a political manner: he was prohibited from intervening directly with the German government because of its hostility toward the League of Nations.[65]

Robert Viscount Cecil of Chelwood (left) chairs a meeting in London on 9 May 1934 of the League of Nations high commission for refugees from Germany. High Commissioner James McDonald is at his side.

As part of the compromise to avoid a German veto, McDonald reported to a separate Governing Body chaired by the British statesman Robert Viscount Cecil of Chelwood, principal draftsman of the League of Nations Covenant in 1919 and a pillar of the League thereafter. This arrangement undermined McDonald's authority; he could neither speak nor act with the authority of the League. Treated like a cast-off child of the League and starved for resources, McDonald's high commission consisted of two small rooms and a staff of six people located in Lausanne, physically and symbolically removed from the Geneva headquarters.[66]

As pragmatic as he was idealistic, Norman Bentwich volunteered to serve as director of the tiny high commission, helping McDonald negotiate Europe's bureaucracies. The need for a new identity document loomed large. They aimed to cut through the bind in which German refugees were caught: legally nationals but in fact stateless.[67] Two years of intensive effort knocking on chancery doors in every capital of Europe yielded the creation of the *Certificat d'Identité des Réfugiés Provenant d'Allemagne* (Identity Certificate for Refugees Coming from Germany). Accepted by Belgium, Denmark, France, Ireland, the Netherlands, Norway, Spain, and Switzerland, this certificate was for a refugee "who does not possess any nationality other than German nationality, and in respect of whom it is established that in law or in fact he or she does not enjoy the protection of the Government of the Reich."[68] It accorded the crucial right of return to the country of issue and the opportunity to apply for visas from other countries. Unlike the Carte d'Identité et de Voyage, it provided protection against expulsion. Most particularly, even if "reasons of national security or public order" justified eviction, "the Governments undertake that refugees shall not be sent back across the frontier of the Reich."[69] A flawed remedy, the certificate never carried the power and prestige of the Nansen passport, and it was not supported by a network of quasi-consular services that offered Nansen refugees a measure of diplomatic protection and much practical help. But for German refugees whose passports had expired it was better than no paper at all.

GERMANS LIKE IKA AND RUDOLF OLDEN hoped against hope that McDonald would prove a powerful force in refugee affairs. A well-known journalist and anti-Nazi, Rudolf escaped to Prague the day after the Reichstag fire and moved on to Paris where he was joined by his wife, a psychoanalyst. Reflecting in 1934 upon their first year of life as refugees, they took comfort from the creation of a high commissioner. "To give refugees a great leader, social worker, spokesman, and negotiator; to give them a guardian of high rank and official position—that was a riveting idea. Just imagine what a lost soul a refugee is in this world of confusion and chaos. A human being abroad who fears his own consul, rather than being able to seek help from him. And a poor man to boot."

The Oldens envisioned what a strong and authoritative representative for refugees might do. "When harassed by the Alien Police or anyone else, [a refugee] can say: 'Sir, I will lodge a complaint with my High Commissioner!' And immediately the unfair official will snap to attention, and become sympathetic and kind." As they well knew, refugees risked unceremonious expulsion back to Germany, which meant, perhaps, "extradition to concentration camps and steel whips." In their view, only the high commissioner could protest and prevent such actions. Yet they realized "that these are just daydreams which have not yet come true. Perhaps they never will."

The high commissioner functioned within straitened circumstances in 1934. "The task of helping German refugees is greater than anything Nansen faced and more difficult to bring to resolution," the Oldens acknowledged. "The worsening Depression has raised boundaries between countries and between minds." McDonald's choices narrowed to "diplomacy and polite conversation with government representatives, or a resounding call to arms and a protest directed at all nations." As they believed that "he will not achieve anything following the first way, we hope that he will choose the second road with inner conviction and passionate aplomb. We wish him relentlessness, intransigence, an unbending sense of what is just and the genius of a great agitator. Then he will be of use to the refugees and, beyond them, to the world. Otherwise he will be an embarrassment to all."[70]

McDonald soon agreed. By fall 1935 he realized that he would not be remembered as a second Nansen, his diplomacy had yielded little, and the passage of the Nuremberg Laws in September defied the principles of his mandate. Try as he might to protect refugees from Germany, the Nazi regime insolently created ever more. The heart of the matter lay in Berlin, not Paris, London, or The Hague. In a last effort to effect change, McDonald wrote a letter of resignation, on 27 December 1935, that he released to newspapers and journals around the globe. Designed to shake the conscience of the world, he called for "friendly but firm intercession" with Germany: "The problem must be tackled at its source if disaster is to be avoided."[71]

McDonald's dramatic resignation and bold plea for direct intervention captured attention in many quarters. But the moment passed, the papers thrown away. And the sole attempt by a responsible official to change the paradigm from dealing with German refugees to dealing with the German regime became yesterday's news.

MINORITY RIGHTS
AND JEWS AS
A MINORITY

THE JEWISH REFUGEE PROBLEM AROSE FROM TWO KEY FACTORS: antisemitism and the status of Jews as a minority. Antisemitic policies could be fought only through protest, which promised little success. The status of the Jews as a minority, by contrast, might provide grounds for possible intervention, as minority rights—a legal concomitant of the nation state—were firmly embedded in international law.[1]

When Allied leaders had convened in Paris in 1919 to shape the map of Europe, they had heeded Woodrow Wilson's call for national self-determination and accepted nationality as the guiding principle to establish state borders. Wilson, the president of a country comprised overwhelmingly of immigrants from around the globe, should have known better. It was a blindingly stupid idea. If new states like Finland, Estonia, Latvia, Lithuania, Poland, and Czechoslovakia that emerged out of the collapse of the German, Russian, and Austro-Hungarian empires were to serve as the national homes of previously marginalized peoples, no boundaries could be drawn along strictly national lines. All the states that were supposed to reflect a perfect unity of nation and territory included minorities. And these minorities now found themselves in a much more awkward position than in the multination empires. The basic assumption that structured the new nation states gave rise to implacable hostility against them. They did not belong.[2]

Of all the minority groups, the Jews were among the most vulnerable. Unlike, for example, the Magyars in Romania or the Germans or Lithuanians in Poland, they could not take comfort in the knowledge that their group formed a majority elsewhere. Jews were in the minority everywhere—often a tiny minority—and so they did not waste energy seeking improvement of their lot by claiming independence or clamoring for a change in boundary that would allow them to join their majority nation. With no such nation in sight, Jews focused on their future as a minority. How, Jews in the old and new world asked, could they best protect themselves and their coreligionists?[3]

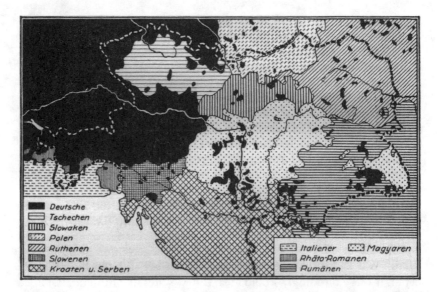

Map showing the ethnic patchwork of the former Austro-Hungarian Empire. The dotted line delineates the borders of the empire. Taken from Richard Henning, Geopolitik *(1931).*

In the United States, the American Jewish Congress sought to persuade the American delegation in Paris to demand that all new states guarantee minority rights in perpetuity, including "equal civil, political, religious and national rights without distinction of race or faith."[4] Organized into congresses and assemblies, Jews in central and eastern Europe formulated similar political demands and sent delegations to attend the peace conference. Astonishingly, they achieved unity. Representing more than ten million European Jews, the delegations merged into the Committee of Jewish Delegations (CJD) and developed a proposal for minority protections. For them, Jews were but one of many minority groups, and all such populations were entitled to basic human rights and to protect themselves against cultural assimilation. Measures included, for example, the right to become a citizen of the country in which they dwelled, "to establish, manage, and control their schools and religious, educational, charitable, and social institutions," to observe their Sabbath, and to work on Sunday. Equally important, "any person may declare his withdrawal from such a national minority."[5]

The allies established a special Committee on New States and for the Protection of Minorities, which used the CJD document as a model for its first undertaking, the Polish Minorities Treaty. Newly re-created Poland had got large tracts of former German territory and, with it, a significant German population. The German delegation demanded minority rights guarantees for them, pledging in return that "Germany on her part is resolved to treat minorities of alien origin according to the same principle."[6] The Polish prime minister, Ignace Jan Paderewski, fought the treaty fiercely. Germans in Poland would enjoy minority protection, while Poles in Germany would not, he objected. The imposition of minority rights was external interference in internal Polish affairs. Furthermore, he warned, Jews accustomed to their new privileges in Poland will migrate elsewhere and demand the same rights.[7] The allies addressed one complaint, assuring Paderewski that Germany would need to accept a minority treaty when it applied for admission to the League of Nations.[8] And with that, the prime minister had to be satisfied. Poland signed, and the Committee on New States and for the Protection of Minorities scored its first success. The Czechoslovak, Romanian, Greek, and Yugoslav del-

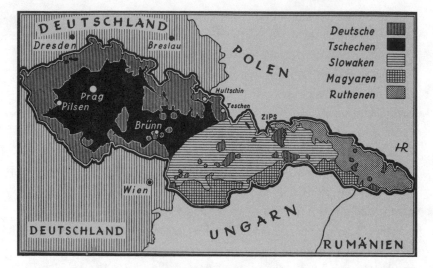

Map showing the ethnic patchwork of interwar Czechoslovakia. At the center are the core Czech (50 percent) and Slovak (15 percent) peoples, and at the borders the German (23 percent), Hungarian (5.5 percent) and Ruthenian (3.5 percent) minorities. The Jewish minority is not represented on this map. Taken from Walther Pahl, Das politische Antlitz der Erde *(1938).*

egations quickly accepted minorities treaties too.[9] These achievements fostered new ambitions. Minorities treaties had been intended to protect people who, due to land redistribution, passed from the sovereignty of a country in which they had been part of the majority population to another, where they were in the minority.[10] Now the committee wrote treaties to be signed by states that, far from gaining land after the war, lost it to others. Austria, Hungary, and Bulgaria[11] signed without much protest; Turkey held out longest. Albania, Finland, and the Baltic countries accepted minorities treaties when they applied for admission to the League in 1922. By the time Germany was admitted in 1926, no one bothered to impose a minorities treaty. For many reasons, the League was eager for Germany to join and, as there had been no complaints against the new member to bring the issue to the fore, the opportunity just slipped away.

The Committee of Jewish Delegations was as pleased as the Committee on New States. Its document had served as a model in the formulation of minorities treaties, and it envisioned a constructive role ahead. Declaring itself a permanent body, the CJD emphasized its mandate to fight for the rights of Jews.[12] It had ample scope to do so: throughout the 1920s, Jews in the new or enlarged states that had signed treaties were under continuous attack, and the CJD saw those very treaties as their primary line of defense.

Jewish groups on the ground in each country refused to turn to the League of Nations to defend their rights, however. They fought against discrimination at the municipal, state, and parliamentary level. But they feared that taking their case to Geneva would exacerbate the situation at home. "Long experience has taught them that winning a case against their government was often a Pyrrhic victory at best," the American Jewish Committee noted.[13] A key problem for the Jewish groups was that Jews had no state of their own to champion their cause at the League. Petitions by German minority groups, for example, were submitted and supported by Germany's delegates. Who would serve this function for petitions submitted by Jews? The CJD had no official standing, and the Jewish Agency was recognized as the official representative of the Jewish inhabitants in Palestine alone. Then too, Jews in central Europe who had cause for grievance did not identify as a minority group. They embraced the assimilationist project wholeheartedly, demanding full civil rights as citizens equal to all other citizens, not as members of a minority protected by a League of Nations treaty.[14]

Seeking a means to be more effective, the CJD joined forces with other organizations. Their aim was to form a World Jewish Congress, and a conference, held in Geneva (14–17 August 1932), was a preliminary step. For Nahum Goldmann, a German Jew who, as the publisher of the *Encyclopedia Judaica*, had a lively network of contacts and saw the situation of the Jews in global terms, the World Jewish Congress was to "provide the Jewish people with an address."[15] His coreligionists disagreed. Significantly, if perhaps predictably, the major German-Jewish organization, the Centralverein deutscher Staatsbürger jüdischen Glaubens, refused to participate.[16]

If mainstream central European Jews were appalled by the prospect of differentiating themselves from the majority population, Zionists embraced it. Emil Margulies, head of the Jewish Nationalist Party in Czechoslovakia and a Zionist, argued that the future of Jews in Europe lay in their status as a recognized minority. Attempts by Jewish organizations in Germany, France, or Poland to defend the rights of Jews because they were Germans, Frenchmen, or Poles were doomed, he declared. Speaking at the World Jewish Conference, Margulies insisted that Jews claim civil rights on the grounds that "one is part of the Jewish community, . . . that one is different." In short, he declared, "We claim equal rights for the Jewish ethnic community. And for the individual as a member of this community." He held no illusions. "The world of assimilation has collapsed, and we ought not act as if we were blind to it."[17]

IF FOR JEWS THE MINORITY ISSUE was a matter of identity, for the Nazis it was a question of safeguarded status. In January 1933 large German populations lived throughout central and eastern Europe, protected by minorities treaties. The German foreign office worried that measures against Jews in the Reich would worsen the position of ethnic Germans elsewhere. These trepidations spiked with the very visible and widely reported 1 April boycott. Foreign Minister Konstantin von Neurath pondered the problem. Anti-Jewish actions, he wrote to Interior Minister Wilhelm Frick a few weeks later, would have "a strong effect on our general policy on minorities, which in the first place aims to maintain those German groups abroad that are important to the Reich." Germany would lose its moral right to defend those ethnic populations and would encounter significant legal problems in Upper Silesia, the sole region for which Germany had signed a minorities treaty. "The new [Nazi] laws create a conflict with international obligations that the Reich has accepted," he observed. Frick brushed aside such concerns. Anti-Jewish measures were central to Nazi policy and took precedence over foreign office protocols. In any case, he soothed von Neurath, German anti-Jewish measures would serve as a model the Poles would copy and "would not justify an abolition of the Geneva Convention in general, so we do not need to worry that our German compatriots in Poland will be endangered."[18]

Not knowing what to think or what to do, the foreign office turned to Max Hildebert Boehm, a leading scholar and activist for German minorities in Europe. Working with specialists in the foreign office, Boehm wrote an article on "Minorities, the Jewish Question, and the New Germany," which was sent to all German embassies and consulates. The core principle of the minority movement, he argued, is "the protection of organically grown, self-conscious minorities that are proud of their special ethnic character against absorption into the majority populations." The Jewish policy of the Nazi regime "does not seek assimilation, but dissimilation, not absorption, but exclusion." Thus discriminatory measures against Jews did not contravene the minority principle or Germany's international obligations. German Jews did not consider themselves a minority that needed to defend against assimilation into the majority population. And as they did not seek a separate identity, they could not claim "the rights of an ethnic group."[19] If minorities as defined in a League treaty sought to be protected from pressure by the majority population to assimilate, German Jews sought a degree of assimilation that the majority population resisted and resented. Boehm's formulation pleased the foreign office.[20]

Von Neurath had been right to worry about Germany's liability in Upper Silesia. When the League of Nations partitioned that ethnically mixed district between Poland and Germany in 1922, it had imposed a fifteen-year convention on both governments that, among other matters, protected minorities' rights.[21] Leo Motzkin, chairman of the CJD, and Emil Margulies saw the 1922 German-Polish convention as an opening to combat the Nazi anti-Jewish measures of April and May 1933 since they applied to German Upper Silesia as well and clearly contravened the agreement Germany had signed.

Still, Motzkin and Margulies held little hope for success. The League's poor record was no secret. "For years the petitions of mal-treated populations had vanished without trace and without reply in the League filing cabinets and wastepaper baskets," the journalist Max Beer explained in *The League on Trial*, "while the memoranda of ruling Governments were dealt with care and distributed with respect."[22] Yet as the dimmest prospect was still a prospect, and as there was no better tool at hand, the CJD submitted a petition in Geneva on behalf of Franz Bernheim, a thirty-four-year-old shop clerk.[23]

Born in Salzburg, Bernheim had obtained citizenship in Württemberg and thus German nationality. He had moved to Upper Silesia in the early 1930s and had found employment. Fired on 30 April solely because he was Jewish, Bernheim went to Prague where he signed his petition for redress on 12 May. As head of the Jewish National Party in Czechoslovakia, Margulies submitted the petition accompanied by one hundred letters of support from Jewish organizations to the League.

Bernheim had asked the Council to "treat this petition as urgent,"[24] and it did. Friedrich von Keller, the German permanent representative to the League, contacted the foreign office, informing it that this could be the start of a general attack on Germany's anti-Jewish policy and counseling against a battle on this case. Von Neurath agreed. Charged with damage control, von Keller was to try to disqualify the petition on a series of grounds and, failing that, should treat the case as a purely local problem.[25]

The Bernheim petition came before the Council on 26 May. Von Keller hastened to stifle discussion with an official declaration of limited responsibility, claiming that "this can only be due to mistakes on the part of subordinate organs acting under a mistaken interpretation of the laws."[26] Von Keller did not address the question of redress or restitution. The Council adjourned to consider the matter for a few days.

Von Keller sought to take advantage of this hiatus. He tried to kill the petition by persuading Sean Lester, the Irish delegate who served as rapporteur for the Council, that Bernheim had no standing: he had no long-term ties to Upper Silesia, he had no right to submit a petition on general questions, and was he really a "minority" as the term was used in the 1922 convention? But Lester would not yield. Worse for Germany, in his report on the matter, Lester noted that "persons who, because they belong to the minority, have lost their employment or found themselves unable to practise their trade or profession in consequence of the application of these laws, will be reinstated in their normal position without delay."[27] This was more than von Keller could accept, and he rejected the conclusion on behalf of his government, even though doing so prompted more discussion rather than less.

As it happened, the World Court in The Hague had just handed down a landmark decision in a territorial dispute between Denmark and Norway over eastern Greenland that had bearing on the issue. During a visit to Denmark in 1919, the Norwegian minister of foreign affairs had made an off-the-cuff statement relinquishing claims to eastern Greenland. The Norwegian government disavowed the statement and supported the occupation of the uninhabited territory by a Norwegian whaler in 1931. The Danes brought the case before the World Court, and the remarks by the Norwegian foreign minister in 1919 proved crucial. The court found his oral declaration officially binding.[28]

The French delegate Joseph Paul-Boncour probably had not yet learned of the World Court decision when he reminded the Council that when Germany pressed the allies to protect German people beyond its borders with minorities treaties, "she had at the same time insisted very strongly—and her attitude was deserving of appreciation—that she would herself, in her own territory, ensure respect for the rights of minorities." Edward Raczynski, the Polish delegate, referred too to the declaration on 29 May 1919 by the German delegation at the peace conference. He inferred from this oral declaration that "the Members of the Council had . . . at least the moral right to make a pressing appeal to the German Government to ensure equal treatment for all Jews in Germany."[29] In short: declarations were not simply air, and minority rights pertained to Jews throughout Germany, not solely Upper Silesia. In his response, von Keller ignored all references to Germany's pledges in 1919, reminding everyone that the discussion at the Council table should be limited to the situation in Upper Silesia and could in no way exceed the Council's competence.[30] No one argued the point or staked out a larger claim.

While the Council came to its final decision, German Jews grew anxious about the effect of the Bernheim case. It called into question how they saw themselves and how the regime saw them. "The great majority of German Jews remains firmly rooted in the soil of its German homeland, despite everything," one of the leaders of the Centralverein, Alfred Wiener, wrote in the association's newspaper. Acknowledging that "according to the laws and regulations directed against us, only 'Aryans' now belong to the German people," he asked: "What are we, then?

According to the law, we are non-Germans without equal rights; to ourselves we are Germans with full rights." But, he assured his readers, "we
reject the idea that we are a folk or national minority, perhaps like the
Germans in Poland or the Poles in Germany, because we cannot deceive
our innermost core. We wish to be subject to the new government as Germans with equal rights, and not to some other entity whether it is called
the League of Nations or something else." Speaking directly to the Bernheim petition, Wiener concluded, "As far as we are concerned, that settles
the Geneva case, which at present preoccupies Jews everywhere."[31]

The Council reached its decision on 6 June. Franz Bernheim "must
be regarded legally as belonging to a minority," it ruled. None of the
objections von Keller had raised was valid. The petitioner had suffered
illegal discrimination, and Germany was obliged to abide by the internationally binding document it had signed.[32]

Berlin backed down. Anti-Jewish laws were not to be applied in
Upper Silesia, the government proclaimed. And it publicized its acqui-
escence widely, to ensure that all the world knew how eagerly Nazi Germany fulfilled its legal obligations.[33] A great public relations coup.

Many felt they had won. The Jews of German Upper Silesia gained
a few years of calm. The International Federation of League of Nations
Societies, the organization that supported the League in each country and
pursued an internationalist, democratic agenda, welcomed the League's
attention to the situation of Jews in Germany and passed a resolution
at its annual congress in June calling for the restoration of equal rights
throughout the country, and not in Upper Silesia alone.[34] Not even the
German delegate voted against it; the best he could do for the regime was
to abstain.[35] The second Jewish World Conference, meeting in Geneva in
August, examined the League's conclusions closely. Pleased that he had
managed to bring "the Jewish Question into the League of Nations,"
Emil Margulies noted that while German Jews may not see themselves
as a national minority, they experienced the fate of such groups.[36] Perhaps because he was a German Jew, Nahum Goldmann spoke passionately about the need to combat the disenfranchisement of German Jews
in Berlin as well as in Geneva: "If we 20th century Jews permit and
accept it when a great European country disenfranchises and declasses its

Jewish population, then the basis for the equal rights of all Jews around the world is destroyed; it means that the Jewish people have surrendered their rights everywhere."[37]

One way to fight was through the Minorities Congress, established in 1925 as a meeting ground for representatives of all minority groups in Europe.[38] Whenever minorities had suffered assault, the congress had taken a position. Yet it had not taken up Nazi legislation against the Jews. The Jewish World Conference resolved to boycott the Minorities Congress to be held in September if Nazi persecution were not on the agenda. CJD chairman Leo Motzkin put the Jews' position plainly to the chair of the Minorities Congress. It fell to the congress, including the representatives of the German minorities, to defend the rights of Jews, as it had the rights of others. A resolution was needed to condemn "the disenfranchisement of Jews . . . as a violation of the laws of humanity and the minority movement."[39] The chair did nothing. The Jewish delegates boycotted. And the German minorities delegates attacked: "We believe that the exclusion from a nation of people who are different in character or race is justified." They had "fought assimilation fiercely" (while the Jews had not), and they did not "condemn the right of a people to dissimilate a national group."[40] In no uncertain terms, the German minorities gave the Nazis their permission to continue to assault the Jews.

THE NAZIS NEEDED NO ENCOURAGEMENT. They just wanted to move their agenda forward with as little trouble or interference as possible, and they did not know how far the League would go to confront the fledgling National Socialist state. The German cabinet met on 12 September to discuss the meeting of the Assembly in Geneva later that month. "Attacks against the Reich government on account of the handling of the Jewish Question in Germany are expected," von Neurath told his colleagues. He advised a fierce offense as the best defense. The German delegation should take the initiative, choose the battleground and the terms of engagement, emphasize that "the quarrel with the German Jews is the Reich's own affair," and present a bold new definition of minorities. To ensure the best possible representation, he asked Hitler to permit "Reich

Minister of Enlightenment and Propaganda [Josef Goebbels] join the delegation."[41] Hitler agreed: Goebbels was to save the day in Geneva.

Goebbels agreed too. And he was confident he would prevail. "Yesterday," he wrote in his diary on 25 September, "my arrival in Geneva is a great sensation. Today, Monday. With Neurath to the League of Nations. Depressing. An assembly of dead people. . . . How far superior we Germans are to all this. All of it lacks dignity and style."[42] Maybe so. But he got a chilly reception. Trouble loured. Senior civil servants met with Hitler to discuss the situation in Geneva. The Dutch government, they heard, was to bring up the matter of the refugees. They had become a burden on the neighboring states, and this was an act of aggression. Attempts to stop the Dutch action had proved unsuccessful, but Hitler would not hear of any softening of the Nazi position.[43]

Goebbels chose his time and his venue. A master of his craft, he was silent in the meeting rooms, saving his punch for a two-hour speech before three hundred journalists in the Carlton Palace Hotel. After all, he was not there to work within the League of Nations; he had come to Geneva to present the National Socialist case.

"The nation and the government in Germany are one thing," he told the journalists. "The will of the people is the will of the government and vice versa." Given such identity of purpose, other freedoms could be surrendered. How could they be "compared to a work of reconstruction through which millions of men were reinstated in the process of production and by which a whole nation is moving away from a feeling of despair over the hopelessness of the situation towards a new faith?" The policies and the practices of the Nazi regime were for the best, he asserted. The Jews, who were not Aryans and therefore not Germans, had too much power and influence. "It must be remembered that the Jews in Germany were exercising . . . a decisive influence on all intellectual life, that they were absolute and unlimited masters of the press, of literature, of the theatre and the cinema." What country would have acted differently? "By settling the Jewish problem legally, the German government adopted the most humane and loyal method."[44]

Perhaps Goebbels persuaded the journalists, but he did not move League members. Senator Henri Bérenger was among the many who remained cold to Nazi arguments. Approaching Goebbels, Bérenger asked him what he had against the Jews. "His answer was: 'They are not Aryans.' . . . He did not mention a single substantial objection. He could not claim that the Jews had bad morals or that they acted in a treasonous manner—in a word, nothing *that would justify even in the smallest way the persecution of the Jews*."[45] Goebbels noted this encounter in his diary too: "Conversation with Bérenger. . . . Make good impression. He is a smart old man. . . . Everything unfolds with the best manners."[46]

One after another, delegates to the Assembly challenged Germany's policies and practices. The Swedish delegate Richard Johann Sandler reminded his colleagues of the "unquestioned human values, the conservation of which the League, in the interest of peace and humanity, cannot neglect." Andries de Graeff, the Dutch delegate, noted that "thousands of German subjects have crossed the frontiers of neighboring countries." He could have pointed out, as we have seen, that according to established international law, this should be interpreted as a move by Germany against bordering nations but, cowardly on this matter, he emphasized instead how heavily the refugees weighed on the public purse. Still, he had raised the issue, as others did too.[47] But Goebbels heard none of it. He had left.

Following the plan developed in the foreign office, von Keller took the initiative on the minorities question in a major speech on 3 October to the League's Sixth Committee, which dealt with political questions. Von Keller presented Boehm's definition of a minority group, carefully crafted to exclude the Jews. "First and foremost, the Jews in Germany are neither a linguistic nor a national minority. They do not look upon themselves and have never expressed any desire to be treated as a minority." As Jews did not constitute a minority, he continued, the Jewish Question was not a minority question. "It is a problem *sui generis*, for which, accordingly, a special settlement will have to be found."[48]

As von Keller had raised the Jewish Question, Henri Bérenger took the opportunity to discuss the Bernheim petition and the questions it raised about "the laws of the Reich." Greek legal scholar Antoine Frangulis, who served as delegate for Haiti, then argued that all citizens—whether a member of a majority or a minority—"should be equal before the law and enjoy the same civil and political rights, without distinction of race, language or religion." The British representative, William Ormsby-Gore, stood with his French and Haitian colleagues, rejecting the German notion of "the racial homogeneity of political units and States." The British empire, he pointed out, was peopled by "every race, every colour, every creed!" Even "in our own little island of Great Britain we have a population of the most mixed stock." No one on the committee even nodded in agreement with von Keller, and Edvard Benes, the Czech delegate, told him bluntly that his theory of ethnic nationality made no sense.[49]

Von Keller grew angry, especially with Bérenger for raising the Bernheim case. "I must make a vigorous protest against this roundabout attempt to open a discussion here on German law."[50] Unperturbed, Bérenger responded: "Was it not the German delegation which inaugurated the present discussion?" Proposing that he had done them a "greater honour" by discussing their ideas rather than passing over them in silence, he concluded by introducing a draft resolution. The first paragraph reaffirmed that states not bound by the minorities treaties must nevertheless observe in their treatment of their own minorities "at least as high a standard of justice and toleration as is required by any of the treaties and by the regular action of the Council." Bérenger's second paragraph was more important and had real teeth. It stated that the Assembly "consider that there is no justification for any interpretation of the Minorities Treaties [to] exclude certain categories of citizens from the benefit of the provisions which, in those treaties, refer to all nationals 'without distinction of race, language or religion.'"[51] All except von Keller voted aye.

Bérenger's draft resolution was incorporated in the Sixth Committee's final proposal to the Assembly. When it was put to a vote on 11 October, von Keller opposed the second point. As all resolutions before the Assembly had to be ratified by unanimous agreement, this was an effective veto. The League stepped away from confrontation, taking the decision to separate the robust second paragraph from paragraph one with its reference to the time-honored 1922 recommendation. Unmooring Bérenger's paragraph two from the rest of the resolution served Germany well. Its delegation voted for the defanged version and against the stand-alone ballot on paragraph two.[52]

A pivotal moment lost. In autumn 1933 the League had power but chose not to use it. Too many of the key states had a version of minorities problems of their own. Britain and France, both colonial powers, well knew that while they could speak about equal rights at home, no such rights obtained among the native peoples of their empires. Perhaps Ormsby-Gore wondered how Mahatma Gandhi would use paragraph two. In any case, Berlin got the message. The League posed no threat. The German delegation would walk out later that month. The immediate issue was disarmament. But the minorities question had opened the exit door.

THE WITHDRAWAL OF GERMANY from the League on 21 October did not bring negotiations between Geneva and Berlin about the Nazis' antisemitic policies and practices to an end. Wherever the League had a legal interest, as in the Saar, the CJD pressed for political action. Under sovereignty of the League after World War I, the Saar population was to decide its national identity in a plebiscite set for January 1935.[53] No one doubted that it would choose union with Germany. In 1932 the Nazi party had got only 6 percent of the vote in Saarland, but rapid nazification directed by Berlin had changed facts on the ground by mid-1933. Local party members surreptitiously imposed a boycott of stores owned by Jews and of Jewish lawyers and physicians. The situation grew increasingly dire each month. Fearing reprisals against their coreligionists in Germany, the tiny Saar Jewish community moved clandestinely, forming an unnamed resistance committee, using code when speaking on the telephone, and posting appeals to foreign organizations from mailboxes in France. Perhaps to avoid calling attention to themselves, or perhaps because they underestimated the peril they faced, few Saar Jews exercised their right as inhabitants of the region to French citizenship.[54]

Responding to the community's distress, the CJD submitted a petition to the League requesting the imposition of minority protections in the Saar after the plebiscite to come in 1935.[55] The League appointed a committee of three, chaired by the Italian delegate Pompeo Aloisi, to prepare a convention with Germany on the matter. More than one prompt was needed, and on 1 September the CJD filed a second petition. Reaffirming its earlier request, the CJD emphasized the worsening conditions and reiterated its call for permanent minority protections. But facing vanishing prospects for success, the CJD also developed a compromise proposal for a one-year grace period for Saar inhabitants to leave the territory with all their property tax-free, thus shielding refugees from the Reich flight tax.[56]

The committee of three met in Rome, to accommodate Aloisi. CJD president Nahum Goldmann went to Rome too. According to the German embassy in Paris, he "was urged to make this journey by the well-known Senator Bérenger, with whom he has had a long conversation."[57] It was a good suggestion: in 1934 Mussolini still had the political will to wrest a concession out of Germany. To everyone's surprise, Mussolini granted Goldmann an audience.

ACCOMPANIED BY THE CHIEF RABBI OF ITALY, Angelo Sacerdote, Goldmann called upon the duce on 16 November. Mussolini stood as he greeted them. With no invitation to sit, Goldmann remained on his feet as he presented Mussolini with a report on the deteriorating situation of the Jews in many European countries. Finally, Mussolini offered them a chair, Goldmann recalled in his memoirs.

> "'After you,' I said.
> 'I prefer to stand,' he announced in oratorical tones.
> 'Do you know Nietzsche,' I asked.
> 'Do I know Nietzsche? He's my favorite philosopher.'
> 'Then you probably remember, Your Excellency, that Nietzsche says there are two kinds of thinkers, sitting thinkers and walking thinkers. You, Your Excellency, are a standing thinker.'
> The Duce was about to smile but the imperial role he was playing prevented him, and he suppressed the beginning of a smile.
> 'I'm not a thinker,' he exclaimed. 'I'm a man of action.'
> 'But I hope you think carefully before you act.' "

Now at ease, Goldmann turned to the Saar Jews. "Whatever happened, [the League] must get a clause included in the Saar agreement obliging Germany to allow any Jews from the Saar who wished to emigrate to do so, taking with them all of their assets in French currency."

Mussolini, however, had little faith in the League. "'You want the League of Nations to do this? You want the League of Nations to act? Are you naïve enough to believe that the League of Nations can take any decisive action?'" he thundered. "'What are you saying, Sir?' he shouted. 'That the League of Nations ought to act? The League never acts! It's a debating society, a senate of old windbags who talk and talk and talk. Jews are intelligent people. You are certainly an intelligent man. And you expect this academy of windbags to do something? The League of Nations can only talk. It can't act.'"

He was right. Still, Goldmann persevered. The League was all he had.

"'But you're a member of the League, Your Excellency. You could act.' . . . I reminded him of Italy's particular responsibility, since Baron Aloisi was chairman of the three-power commission on the Saar, and to this he replied: 'I'll force Germany to let the Saar Jews leave and take their money with them.' He picked up the large scratch pad and a pencil, tore off a sheet and scribbled, 'Saar. Jews. Emigration.'

"'That takes care of that,' he said. 'You can rely on me.' And he kept his word."[58]

AND INDEED, HE DID INSTRUCT BARON ALOISI to take care of it. The Rome agreement permitted inhabitants of the Saar to liquidate their assets and export all their goods and money without paying any taxes. And it protected all inhabitants of the region from discrimination on account of their language, race, or religion for a period of one year after the plebiscite.

This served the Jews well when 91 percent of their neighbors in the Saar voted to join Germany. "One Year Stay of Execution for the Jews of the Saar," ran the title of an article in an Austrian newspaper by Lothar Rothschild, the rabbi of the largest community in the territory. "Anyone who can, will leave," he predicted. "The young almost without exception will go to Palestine, and we are busy obtaining a number of refugee certificates for the young Saar Jews."[59] Older people would emigrate to France or Luxembourg. By June 1935 the community had shrunk from 4,638 (in January 1933) to 3,117. And by the time the year ran out that figure had dropped to 2,000. According to the census of 17 May 1939, only 558 Jews, 243 "half-Jews," and 191 "quarter-Jews" remained. Thus, Saarland had the smallest percentage of Jews of any German region, and it had seen the greatest reduction of its Jewish population since 1933.[60]

PRESSED BY THE CJD to protect Jews through the application of minorities rights treaties, the League of Nations had enjoyed limited success in Upper Silesia in 1933, soon after the Nazis came to power. Within a few months the Reich had asserted its power: the German delegation had blocked Bérenger's proposal in the League's Sixth (Political) Committee. By 1934 it fell to Mussolini to address the problem; the League could but "manage" it, providing the cover for Jews to leave quietly, with their assets (if they found buyers) in French francs, within a year. The League's good-bye gift to them was a Nansen passport to protect them wherever they might land.[61]

PART TWO

1938–1939

Sculpture of the Reich eagle holding the swastika at the Nazi party rally grounds in Nuremberg. Taken from Gerdy Troost, Das bauen im neuen Reich *(1938).*

THE SCREWS
TIGHTEN

THE NAZIS MOVED FORWARD FEROCIOUSLY TO CONSOLIDATE THEIR regime. They aimed to construct a Führer state, in which laws, policies, and practices flowed from the will of the Führer and in which legal protections became mere scraps of paper. Not even party activists were protected if they were seen as an obstruction to this goal. Thus, during what came to be called the Night of the Long Knives (30 June 1934) the SS, acting on Hitler's orders, murdered the leaders of the SA, the party's paramilitary arm. The army saw the SA as competition, and Hitler needed the support of the military. The Night of the Long Knives also consolidated Hitler's power in the party; no one dared challenge him now.

President Hindenburg's death some five weeks later gave Hitler the opportunity to complete his ascent to power. A new law combined the offices of Reich president, chancellor, and Führer of the National Socialist movement. Embodying all three, Hitler was empowered to lead the German nation. The day Hindenburg died, 2 August 1934, every officer and soldier in the German army took an oath of allegiance not to "nation and fatherland," as had been the custom, but to their new commander-in-chief Hitler personally.

As Hitler's grip on the government tightened, German society became increasingly Nazified and individual liberties fell one after the other. Most important, the government accrued the right to execute anyone if "necessary for the self-defense of the State." Legal protections evaporated as the Gestapo, operating beyond the control of the courts, developed a whole system of prosecution and incarceration through commitment to a concentration camp. All Germans understood that they were at risk. Few stood prepared to challenge these developments. Some applauded. Most, including the great majority of Germany's five hundred thousand Jews, presumed the violence would pass and awaited an equilibration.

The situation of Jews in Germany had stabilized after the 1 April boycott and the first waves of legislated economic discrimination. As the state appeared to pursue a more pragmatic policy, the exodus of 1933 slowed. Then too, the doors that had opened to Jewish refugees in March 1933 began to close a year later. The Depression, fear of a refugee flood, and apprehension that the asylum seekers would stay longer than initially anticipated prompted France and the Netherlands (the countries that had taken the greatest number) to tighten immigration procedures. In 1933, fifty thousand Jews had left Germany; in 1934 the number dropped to twenty-three thousand.

Planned emigration overtook panicked flight. Jews looked to sell their property and ship their possessions, and they looked too for an asylum that offered them the prospect of earning a living. Palestine became a major destination: rather than running from horror, Jews left with honor to build up the Jewish Home. And the ha'avara agreement allowed them to do so with a good portion of their assets.[1] In 1934, 37 percent of German Jews went to Palestine, 37 percent to European countries, and 26 percent to countries overseas. The number of Jewish refugees fell again in 1935, to twenty-one thousand. The percentage destined for Palestine remained about the same, while European countries received fewer (28 percent), and those leaving for overseas increased (36 percent).[2] Emigrants sold their assets at a figure far below their real value. The proceeds were subjected to the Reich flight tax, which creamed off a quarter. Initially, the tax applied to persons with assets of two hundred thousand Reichsmarks and up, but from 1934 it applied to those with fifty thousand.[3] The remaining sums went into blocked accounts, which could be sold only to foreign importers of German goods and at 40 percent (1934) to 20 percent (1936) of the official value. The regime and those in business with Germany profited handsomely with the Jews' departure.[4]

As the figures suggest, most Jews believed that if they accommodated sufficiently, they might remain in their native land. The terms appeared to be straightforward: they would be tolerated if they were invisible. "Jewry can rest assured that we will leave them alone as long as they retire quietly and modestly behind their four walls, as long as they are not provocative, and do not affront the German people with the claim to be treated as equals," Minister of Propaganda Josef Goebbels announced.[5]

The message to vanish rang clear. "Jews not welcome," "No profit for Jews here," "No Jews served," "Jews and dogs not admitted," "The Jews are our misfortune," read signs all over Germany. And people, organizations, and institutions showed individual initiative to ensure that Jews would be invisible: shopkeepers refused to sell to them, libraries and museums closed to them, nor could they gain admission to theaters or other places of public entertainment. Joachim Prinz, a rabbi in Berlin, observed the dissolution of social life. German Jews found themselves locked in a new ghetto—not one with physical walls, but "the isolation that neighbourlessness means, a fate crueller than any other, and perhaps the fiercest that can be suffered in the social life of man."[6]

Reaching ever more deeply into the private sphere, the regime's anti-semitic policies took a sexual turn in summer 1935. In addition to random acts of violence against individual Jews—harassment, beatings, vandalization of property—Jews and gentiles in relationships became the foci for Nazi fury. Responding to open talk about a ban on marriages between gentiles and Jews (or perhaps acting on their own recognizance), officials at some registry offices refused to perform such marriages, and SA men paraded outside these couples' homes. Arrests for "race defilement" increased, and partners forced through the streets with placards around their necks. Uneasy about these independent expressions of hostility, though eager to benefit from such popular energy, Hitler forbade (8 August) all "individual actions." The regime needed to take control, and the Nuremberg Laws were its means to do so.

The Reichstag assembled for the annual Nazi party rally in Nuremberg on 10 September, and the leadership marked the occasion with stun-
ning legislative action. The Law for the Protection of German Blood and
German Honor prohibited marriages and sexual relations between Jews
and "citizens of German or kindred blood." The Reich Citizenship Law
restricted citizenship only to subjects "of German or kindred blood." As
to who was a Jew, it did not take Nazi lawyers long to introduce a formulary. Anyone with three Jewish grandparents was a Jew. Those with
two Jewish grandparents were "half-Jews," and those with one Jewish
grandparent "quarter-Jews."

The Nuremberg Laws shocked the leaders of the Centralverein
deutscher Staatsbürger jüdischen Glaubens—now forced to rename
itself *Jüdischer Centralverein* (Central Jewish Association) as Jews had
ceased to be *Staatsbürger*, German citizens. So committed to Jewish life in
Germany that they had taken a principled anti-Zionist stance, the Centralverein now shifted ground completely. The laws spelled the end. The
association turned to immigration, supporting two now equally important streams—Palestine and overseas—in a targeted effort to get one
hundred thousand younger Jews out of the country over the next five
years.[7]

Many were eager to go. By late 1935 economic considerations had
become a major stimulus for emigration. As more and more Jews saw no
future in Germany, and Palestine could not receive everyone, many set
their sights on emigration to countries overseas. If in 1933 refugees wished
to stay near Germany to be able to return easily when the regime toppled,
by autumn 1935 few thought the Nazis would be booted out so soon.
Then too, the worst of the Depression had passed and prospects abroad
opened. In 1933, 8 percent had moved overseas; in 1935 the percentage
equaled that of Jews immigrating to Palestine (36 percent); in 1936 the
figure reached 43 percent;[8] and in 1937 overseas countries absorbed 60
percent of the Jews leaving Germany, while Palestine dropped to 15 percent, and Europe, 25 percent.[9]

Jews assessed their prospects everywhere. South Africa, the first
of the British dominions to recover from the Depression, glimmered
brightly. Some 3,350 German Jews landed in 1936, and others wished

to follow. Local Nazi anti-Jewish agitation soon closed that door, however, and in 1937 immigration to South Africa dropped to 900.[10] Looking
to South American countries, German Jews recognized that the governments did not welcome refugees, religious intolerance prevailed, and
the local economies were insufficiently industrialized to accommodate
middle class settlers easily. Still, tens of thousands immigrated to that
continent in the mid–1930s thanks to the great efforts of local South
American Jewish communities.[11]

Liquidation of the Jewish community through emigration had
become a de facto goal of the German government by fall 1936. In an
interministerial discussion (29 September 1936) on Jewish policy, senior
civil servants pressed the removal of all Jews from Germany as the best,
and perhaps the only, solution to the Jewish Question. "The fundamental principle of all measures is to foster the emigration of the Jews,"
State Secretary Wilhelm Stuckart of the interior ministry reminded his
colleagues. "All measures relating to politics concerning Jews must be
focused on that goal." State Secretary Hans Posse of the economics ministry agreed. "Jews should be permitted a certain degree of business activity in Germany until emigration became possible."[12]

The words "a certain degree of business activity" meant less every
month. In a so-called "Aryanization" process, Jewish entrepreneurs,
shopkeepers, and artisans came under increasing pressure in 1937 to sell
their enterprises. Government agencies refused to deal with businesses
owned by Jews, Nazi party members informally but effectively boycotted them, and by the end of that year remaining firms suffered from
severe reductions in foreign currency and material allocations. Increasing impoverishment, unemployment, and loss of professional capacity
affected all sectors of the Jewish community.

With that domestic "problem" on its way to resolution, Hitler turned
to scoring a foreign policy success. The time had come to keep his promise of *Ein Reich, Ein Volk, Ein Führer* (One Empire, One People, One
Leader): to bring all the Germanic peoples "home" to the Reich by creating a Greater Germany. The first territory to be claimed for that empire
was Austria.[13]

Austrian Nazis had attempted an *Anschluss* (merger) through a coup d'état in 1934. Their effort failed, mostly because Mussolini would have none of it.[14] He rightly feared Hitler as a neighbor. But Mussolini became increasingly dependent on Hitler, and Austria lost his support. Making the best of a bad situation, Austria's chancellor Kurt von Schuschnigg negotiated a pact with Hitler in July 1936 that recognized Austria's independence but legalized the Austrian Nazi party, permitted Nazi rallies, and admitted two thinly disguised Nazis into the Austrian government. Undermined by local Nazi activities, Austria descended into chaos; civil order collapsed in 1938 and the government's resolve to defend the republic melted away. Faced with the choice of hostile invasion or Nazi government, Schuschnigg resigned. The new chancellor, Arthur Seyss-Inquart, invited his German brothers to cross the border. The German army marched triumphantly into Vienna on 13 March 1938. Popular euphoria for Hitler, National Socialism, and unification with Germany was matched by hatred for and violence against the Jews, surpassing any such open display in Germany to that date.[15] Now Austrian Jews joined their German coreligionists in the search for asylum elsewhere.

OFFICIALS AND
THEIR SOLUTIONS

CHURCH BELLS PEALED AND PEOPLE CHEERED AS THE FÜHRER'S motorcade entered Vienna on 14 March 1938. Most of Austria's 191,000 Jews lived in the capital city, where they accounted for 10 percent of the population; after Warsaw and Budapest, the Jews of Vienna constituted the third-largest Jewish community in Europe. But numbers did not matter. Enthusiasm for Hitler, Anschluss, and Nazism ignited a frenzy of popularly supported brutality. SA men and other Nazis pulled Jewish men and women off the streets, forcing them to clean barrack latrines or scrub the pavement with their bare hands and, sometimes, just for "fun" with their own undergarments or toothbrushes.[1] Gentile Viennese enjoyed the show.

The violence and concomitant social isolation energized Jews' efforts to emigrate, especially to the United States.[2] America had long glowed in its reputation as a refuge for the oppressed, and in the wake of the Anschluss a key opinion maker of the day, the formidable journalist Dorothy Thompson, reminded the reading public of America's responsibility. "If the present strong currents of migration continue to push anarchically upon those states still open to immigrants; if it is now further to be horribly augmented; if it is not consciously directed; if assistance is not furnished to immigrants so that they are sure not to become a burden upon their hosts, and instead can be turned into definite economic assets—then there is a catastrophe ahead for more than the immigrants and the would-be immigrants," she warned. "Until now the problem has been largely regarded as one of international charity. It must now be regarded as a problem of international politics."[3]

Thompson urged the American government to initiate negotiations with Germany to create an agreement similar to the ha'avara scheme, in which Berlin would make available Jews' frozen funds to help them start anew overseas. She believed that the Nazi government had a vested interest to cooperate, as "a great number of people starving in the midst of any community is neither economically nor politically attractive."[4] It was up to the United States to act, "if only as a testimony to the vitality of our faith in the democratic principles which we profess to live by. On those principles our institutions are founded, and with them are integrated the fundamental concepts of our civilization. Therefore, the attempt must be made not out of pity for the exiles, actual and potential, but as a reaffirmation of our own beliefs, lest they become hollow dogmas to which, eventually, not even lip service will be given anywhere."[5]

Perhaps Thompson's call for action pricked President Franklin Delano Roosevelt's conscience. Perhaps it presented him with what he saw as a political opportunity. Shortly after reading an early draft of Thompson's article, he announced (25 March 1938) his intention to call an international conference on the refugee crisis at the French resort town of Evian-les-Bains in July and subsequently issued invitations to twenty-nine countries. To allay fears that the United States would demand great concessions, the invited nations were told that "no country would be expected to receive a greater number of emigrants than is permitted by its existing legislation."[6] All new programs would be financed by private agencies, not public monies. The purpose of the meeting that in the end included representatives from thirty-two countries was to facilitate the emigration of "political refugees" (not Jews) from Germany and Austria.

Eager as the British were for American engagement with Europe, they remained perturbed about the use of violence against a minority population as blackmail. "The effect of the constitution of an inter-governmental committee for the purpose of opening the door more widely to emigration of Jews and others from Germany is certain to encourage the German government to force persons, whom it does not want, to leave the country," Roger Makins of the British foreign office commented. "Other European countries with surplus populations, and particularly Poland and Roumania, may well intensify the persecution of Jews and others whom they do not want in the hope of getting rid of them through the good offices of the Committee. Unless great caution is exercised, the constitution of the Committee may therefore intensify the pressure on the Jews in Europe, and make the refugee problem even worse than it is at present."[7] Perhaps, an interdepartmental meeting con-

Myron Taylor, chair of the American delegation, addresses the conference at Evian in July 1938. James McDonald, high commissioner for refugees, sits to the left of Taylor, and Georges Coulon, Henri Bérenger's secretary, to the left of McDonald. Robert Pell, assistant to Myron Tayor at the time and to George Rublee later, sits to the far right, facing forward.

cluded a few days later, the American embassy should be advised that the very existence of Roosevelt's initiative might well result in greater persecution.[8] If the Americans were told, they were not deterred.

Henri Bérenger, head of the French delegation, served as host to the conference, welcoming two hundred representatives, observers, and journalists in Evian on the French side of Lake Geneva on 6 July 1938.[9] William Shirer, reporter for the *New York Times*, took the measure of the proceedings within twenty-four hours. "I doubt if much will be done," he wrote in his diary. "The British, the French, and the Americans seem too anxious not to do anything to offend Hitler. It is an absurd situation: They want to appease the man who was responsible for their problem."[10] Shirer was correct. Only the delegate from Colombia, M. J. M. Yepes, raised the question of "principle: Can a State, without upsetting the basis of our civilization, and, indeed, of all civilization, arbitrarily withdraw nationality from a whole class of its citizens, thereby making them Stateless Persons whom no country is compelled to receive on its territory?" Yepes both accused and cautioned. "The whole tragedy lies in the fact that this preliminary question was not settled in time." And he concluded, "The worst thing is that the bad example of the Old World may be copied in other continents, and the world will then become uninhabitable."[11]

The Dominican Republic alone offered a practical proposal: large-scale agricultural colonies worked by German and Austrian refugees and supported by the DR government.[12] Racism made strange bedfellows in 1938. Holding European blood "superior," General Rafael Trujillo, dictator of the Dominican Republic, had ordered the massacre and violent expulsion of Haitian workers the previous year (1937).[13] The Evian conference provided him with an occasion to improve his blood-stained image, to obtain a share of the millions of dollars undoubtedly to be made available for refugee settlement and, best of all, to increase the "white" population by offering asylum to European Jews.[14]

JEWISH OBSERVERS WERE DEEPLY DISAPPOINTED by the results. Norman Bentwich, who attended the conference as a representative of the Council of German Jews, noted that "it was remarked that Evian spelled backwards gave 'naïve.' The democracies had little conscience but less faith. Their governments were still unwilling to try to solve the problem and fell back on palliatives. The more difficult the task, the smaller their will to deal with it radically."[15]

The chair of the American delegation, by contrast, returned pleased. Myron C. Taylor reported to Secretary of State Cordell Hull that the meeting had accomplished its purpose by spawning the Inter-Governmental Committee (IGC), which would convene in London on 3 August.[16] If the refugee problem were to be solved rationally, Taylor told Hull, Germany would have to become involved, and Taylor took hope that it would do so. If not, he feared the status of the "undesirables in its population, that is undesirable from its point of view," would be "little better than serfs."[17]

The aim of the IGC was to move from disorderly exodus to orderly immigration. No one spoke of urgency or rescue or even of Germans or Jews. Vague generalities and highflown rhetoric ricocheted around the Locarno Room in the foreign office building. Chairing the meeting, Taylor talked about "challenges to civilization" and compared the movement of peoples to the movement of goods. "Just as forces have operated in some instances to restrain and in other instances to stimulate artificially the flow of goods, similar forces have acted in some instances to bar and in other instances to force artificially the flow of peoples." It followed that now that statesmen "are labouring to re-establish the orderly course of world trade and commerce, similarly the time has come when governments, recognizing that disorderly movements of peoples in great numbers makes for general unrest, must strive to re-establish the orderly course of migration."

Bérenger, representing France, did not mention Germans or Jews either, but he sounded a slightly more somber—and practical—note, reminding those assembled of increased suicide figures and that the "brusque displacement of these human masses menaces not only Europe." Furthermore, he saw the situation within the context of minority rights that, as those assembled did not need to be told, were protected by the League of Nations.[18] Once mentioned, however, the principle of minority rights and protections faded away. Two issues emerged and held sway: land and money. For the next year the course of refugee policy lurched back and forth, as government officials, diplomats, and Jewish community leaders focused on identifying places to send refugees and instituting a mechanism to pay for their relocation.

Jewish philanthropists had initiated large-scale agricultural projects in the late nineteenth century considering far-away land and its capabilities to support settlers. Such non-Zionist ventures were an immediate response to mass violence against Jews in eastern Europe. Antisemites latched on to such prospects with alacrity in the 1930s and introduced their own sites, with no thought of practical problems. The quest for agricultural colonies to solve the refugee problem was discussed by so wide a spectrum of people that schemes hatched out of thin air by no one at all sometimes hit the headlines. The Portuguese government intended to settle over five million Jews in its west African colony, a *Daily Herald* front-page article reported, although that government knew nothing about any such plan.[19]

The island of Madagascar in the Indian Ocean had caught the fancy of European antisemites when France imposed a protectorate there in 1885. A French antisemite, Paul de LaGarde, immediately saw its potential as a destination for French Jews. Decades later a British antisemite, Henry Hamilton Beamish—who linked up with the Nazis in the early 1920s—elaborated upon this idea in the *Völkischer Beobachter* (1926), claiming that the island could accommodate fifty million people or more. Madagascar became a staple of antisemitic speculation. The *Stürmer* (1933) envisioned a closed ghetto, with "fast and vigilant patrol boats circl[ing] the island continuously."[20] Germany had no corner on the Madagascar project. Poland sought it as a destination for its own unwanted Jews. Initially deaf to the Poles' persistent requests, France agreed in 1937 to allow a Polish commission to explore the possibilities for Jewish settlement on the island, and the investigators arrived in June. Their two-month survey revealed that Madagascar could not support mass immigration, and Polish newspapers reported it fit for twenty-five to thirty thousand Jewish families. French and Polish negotiators continued to discuss the matter through 1938, and the Germans watched these developments closely. While the Evian conference met, Alfred Rosenberg, then head of the Nazi party's Foreign Policy Office, published his solution to the German-Jewish refugee problem in the *Völkischer Beobachter*: Madagascar.[21]

COLONIZATION OR RELOCATION, mass movement or individual move, called for money. Max Warburg, a prominent Hamburg banker and president of the Hilfsverein in 1936 (and one of Aby Warburg's younger brothers), proposed the establishment of an "Advance and Transfer Corporation." Wealthy German Jews would pledge their assets to the corporation and receive loans from banks outside Germany against these funds. One estimate held that this system would enable one hundred thousand men aged seventeen to thirty-five to emigrate, establish themselves, and help their families leave within four years. But talks broke down when Berlin would not give its assurance that it "will at all times protect such assets against interference of any kind whatsoever."[22]

Questions continued to circulate. Under what financial conditions would the Nazi regime allow Jews to emigrate? And what about impoverished Jews? The creation of *Allgemeine Treuhandstelle für die jüdische Auswanderung G.m.b.H.* (Altreu) in May 1937 appeared to answer these questions. Jews with thirty thousand Reichsmarks for two people and fifty thousand Reichsmarks for families of three or more were permitted to hand over their capital to the Germany treasury, which gave them back a small amount in foreign currency for emigration purposes. Keeping most of the balance, the treasury created the Altreu fund with some of its ill-gotten gains. These sums were disbursed to poor Jews who needed to prove financial independence to consular officials in order to get entry visas, and just over a thousand people left under this plan.[23] The Jews were a "race-community." They could take care of each other, with no loss to the German race-community.

The Altreu ran out of funds within the year, but the racist principles in which it was grounded lived on in the Vienna-based Gildemeester action.[24] A Dutch resident of Austria, Frank van Gheel Gildemeester was a racketeer with some philanthropic notions, connections with the Quaker aid society, and ties to the Nazis after the Anschluss. He sought to help wealthy baptized Jews primarily, but not exclusively. In

order to emigrate, these "non-Aryans" gave their assets in trust to Bank
Krentschker & Co. A 10 percent "special contribution" was paid to the
Gildemeester fund to cover the travel costs of poor Jews. The bank did
well, pocketing 3 to 3.5 percent in fees. At best the Jews retained some
30 percent of their capital. But that 10 percent from eighty-eight families allowed thirty thousand Jews to flee.[25] The Gildemeester action fell
under Eichmann's Central Office for Jewish Emigration in December
1938 and ceased to operate a year later. All "legal" emigration was now
controlled entirely by Eichmann's office, which held fast to the principle
that the wealth of rich Jews must be used to pay for poor Jews also.

Eichmann's boss Reinhard Heydrich flaunted his subordinate's
operation at a meeting chaired by Hermann Göring after the infa-
mous November pogrom (the so-called *Kristallnacht* of 9–10 November
1938).[26] Charged with the Jewish Question, Göring focused on expelling
Jews from the economy. Heydrich raised the stakes, turning to "the main
problem, namely to kick the Jew out of Germany." Eichmann's operation
had worked wonders: from April through October, "we have eliminated
50,000 Jews from Austria while from the Reich only 19,000 were eliminated during the same period of time." Stung, Göring suggested that the
Jews were moved "illegally" from Austria through other countries until
they "landed finally on an old barge in the Danube. There they lived,
and wherever they tried to go ashore, they were barred." Heydrich continued, unfazed. "At least 45,000 Jews were made to leave the country by
legal means." "How was that possible?" queried Göring. "We extracted
a certain amount of money from the rich Jews who wanted to emigrate,"
Heydrich explained. "By paying this amount, and an additional sum in
foreign currency, they [the *Kultusgemeinde* (Jewish community)] made it
possible for a number of poor Jews to leave. The problem was not to make
the rich Jew leave but to get rid of the Jewish mob."[27]

Once introduced as fact on the ground, everyone—host government
officials, philanthropic agencies, the Jews—seems to have accepted the
Nazis' view of the Jews as a race-community that had to pay for the
forced emigration of all its members. The November pogrom brought
home the urgency of the situation to receiver governments, and the IGC
sought renewed negotiations. With his government's tacit approval, Hjal-

mar Schacht presented a proposal in London in December 1938. If Warburg had focused on the individual, Schacht saw a collective. All Jews'
assets in Germany would be pooled in a trust to guarantee an international loan. Able-bodied Jews, rich and poor, would get a loan, leaving
some two hundred thousand elderly Jews to be tolerated until they died.
The trust would use German exports to service the loan.[28]

Schacht's plan supported the Germany economy, as it boosted German exports using property confiscated from Jews. The IGC found the
terms too advantageous to the Reich. Schacht proved willing to negotiate.
The Reich foreign office was not: Jews' assets did not belong to the Jews.
"According to our National Socialist understanding, the Jew, a being of
alien race who moved to Germany without possessions, obtained his property by removing it from the German national wealth through a particular way a Jew has of doing business." The regime was under no "obligation
to give Jews an opportunity to transfer their wealth": it wasn't theirs.[29]
Still, Schacht and IGC director George Rublee pressed on, with Rublee
making all sorts of concessions that flattered the Nazi worldview. Rublee
agreed, for instance, that the "German government cannot forthwith give
categorical assurances regarding the principle of 'freedom of molestation'
so long as he [Rublee] cannot promise Jewish elements outside Germany
will likewise cease their criticisms and attack on the Third Reich"—as if
the "German government" and "Jewish elements outside Germany" were
parties with equal power and equal opportunity to attack or protect.[30]

WHILE RUBLEE AND SCHACHT PARLAYED, IGC member government officials searched the map for a place to put refugee Jews. Someone lit upon
the Soviet Union's Jewish autonomous province of Birobidzhan, located
on the Soviet-China border.[31] Established in 1928, it counted twenty thousand Jewish settlers in 1938. But the Soviet constitution did not grant
refugee status to individuals persecuted on the basis of "race."[32] British
Chargé d'Affaires in Moscow Gordon Vereker cautioned against pressing the issue. In the Soviet xenophobic and spy-obsessed political culture,
Jewish refugees would likely "fall victims to the 'purge' at no distant date."
Indeed, he noted soberly, "an infinitely larger number of Jews have in all

probability been executed in the Soviet Union during the last two years than in Germany under the National Socialist régime, while an equal if not larger number have been placed in concentration camps."[33]

The *Times* held a rosier view, claiming that Birobidzhan offered support for at least one hundred thousand refugees. Recognizing that the matter would be of interest to parliament, Lord Winterton, chairman of the IGC, took up the issue, although he was persuaded that the immigration of German-Jewish refugees would "place them in a position of even greater personal peril and economic distress than they are in Germany." Still, he "mooted the matter" to the Soviet ambassador, Ivan Maisky. Perhaps the Soviet Union might look sympathetically on communists in concentration camps who would be difficult to place elsewhere. "I confess that I felt slightly disingenuous in making this point . . . but it seemed to me that they should be given the chance at any rate of a short period of freedom, with the possibility of escaping 'liquidation', as a better alternative to lifelong imprisonment and misery in a German concentration camp."[34] Maisky offered little to Winterton other than his opinion that "the Jewish community in various countries could find sufficient money to settle the whole of the German Jews." Give up pressing the Reich to allow Jews to emigrate with their assets, he advised, but "bring all pressure to bear on the Jewish community outside Germany."[35]

NEITHER WINTERTON NOR NEARLY ANYONE ELSE on the IGC needed persuasion on this point. Hjalmar Schacht had been fired in January, and the IGC was in heavy negotiations with Helmuth Wohlthat, a high-ranking official in Göring's Four Year Plan Office and a personal confidant of his boss. These negotiations suited all concerned: Göring wanted glory for getting rid of Jews; Rublee and his assistant Robert Thompson Pell needed something to show for their efforts; Wohlthat knew a good deal when he saw one. A man of considerable ability and energy, a serious art collector and bibliophile, he had enjoyed an enviable career in the Nazi regime since 1934 when Schacht had made him responsible for foreign currency matters, but he had never joined the party. Then too, he felt at ease with Americans, having earned an M.A. degree at Columbia

University in political science and having married a German woman then living in Philadelphia. Taking over where Schacht had left off, Wohlthat saw an opening to rake in foreign currency for Germany, please Göring, and solve a pesky problem in his preferred fashion: reasonably.[36]

As the German government still refused to recognize the IGC, Wohlthat met with Pell and Rublee and, later, with representatives of the Reichsbank, foreign office, and economics, food, labor, and interior ministries. At crucial moments he consulted Göring who, once, checked with Hitler.[37] Through this elaborate ritual, Wohlthat and Rublee came to an understanding. The Wohlthat-Rublee plan addressed the organization and finance of emigration and the status of those left behind. Protection of Jews was couched in vague language; depredation of the Jewish community to pay for its own forcible removal was crystal clear.[38]

Through Wohlthat's efforts, senior German government officials agreed to coordinate emigration with countries of immigration and to stop further persecution of Jews.[39] Henri Bérenger remained doubtful. According to a report from the German ambassador in London, Herbert von Dirksen, to the foreign office in Berlin regarding the IGC response to the plan, Bérenger "refused to participate in the London conference 'because the German proposals are not in accord with the dignity of France.'"[40] Unperturbed, Wohlthat moved forward his colleagues in Berlin on myriad matters from the specifics of the trust fund, to who would be helped with the funds raised under the agreement, to noting that "antisemitic propaganda abroad should be stopped temporarily by a Berlin department in the countries to which Jews were to emigrate, in order not to endanger Jewish emigration."[41]

German civil servants were making fine progress when their army invaded Bohemia and Moravia in March 1939. The prospects for "peace for our time" sought by British Prime Minister Neville Chamberlain dimmed; Hitler's move proved that his ambition went beyond his long-sworn goal to unite all Germans in one Reich. In the midst of increased speculation about war, Pell traveled to Berlin via Paris, where he got an earful from Bérenger.

.   .   .

"I LEFT FOR PARIS ON APRIL 3RD," Pell began a memo to his colleagues. As many on the IGC well knew—and Pell was about to learn—Bérenger had long scorned the Nazis for their racism and lack of logic. He held equal contempt for politicians who refused to confront them on these grounds. Pell had set an appointment with the senator through his secretary Georges Coulon but learned upon arrival that no meeting was scheduled. Pell reached Coulon, who asked whether Pell could see him instead. The American demurred and tried to reach Bérenger through another channel. There too he met a dead end. Phoning the next day, Coulon offered Pell an appointment with Bérenger at six-fifteen that evening, precisely when Pell's train was scheduled to leave for Berlin— which Coulon knew. Pell promptly accepted, however, and rearranged his Berlin travel and appointments. On the way to Bérenger, Coulon suggested "that I should indicate to Senator Bérenger that the German conversations were carried on merely for the purpose of putting Germany in an awkward position." Pell was surprised; he had no intention of lying about his aims.

"In any event I was not given an opportunity to say anything to Senator Berenger because when he arrived home to keep the appointment— at 7.0 p.m.—he burst into the room almost shouting 'I have had enough of this whole business; I have had enough.'"

An astute observer, Bérenger did not hesitate to detail the history of international action on behalf of the refugees as he perceived it. "In March of last year President Roosevelt gave the world to believe that he was about to do great things for the Jews," he fumed. "Naturally the world assumed that he was going to throw wide open the American quotas or give Alaska to the Jews or at least do something concrete. But what happened? First France was bullied into calling a conference at Evian. Then after some months, Mr. Taylor came floating along on a cloud. From where? Why, from Italy, of all places! And what did Mr. Taylor do? He came dripping honeyed words and distributing culinary largesse. And everyone assumed that he was about to place his great industrial experience at the service of the Jews; that he was about to emerge as a second Herbert Hoover [who had distinguished himself running relief operations after World War I]. And then what happened? He sailed off on his cloud, probably back to Italy.

"And then what happened?" Bérenger continued. "Why, a gaunt prophet came out of America accompanied by a pale romantic acolyte [Pell himself]. They went around for months crying 'Woe! Woe! Woe!' until, all of a sudden they found their dear friend, Hermann Goering. Ah, then the world took on another hue. Everything was beautiful. It was dear Hermann Goering this and dear Hermann Goering that."

By this point Pell may have felt he needed a scorecard. But Bérenger was not done. "And then what happened? Pooff! The prophet and his acolyte disappeared in smoke, no-one knows why, no-one knows whither!"

The diatribe had not yet come to an end. "And then what happened? Mr. Taylor came sailing back on his cloud again, after having hobnobbed with the Lord knows whom in Italy—Mussolini and Hermann Goering, who knows? And what did he come back for? Why, to exploit a private corporation, a nice trap prepared by the Germans to catch stupid little fish. But France was not a stupid little fish. The French Jews were not stupid little fish. Robert de Rothschild was not a stupid little fish. Mr. Taylor could have his trap. He could put his head in it. Anyway, Mr. Taylor having sailed in on his cloud sailed off again! A very charming man!

"And what was left? Nothing was left except the League Commission [for Refugees], which had been there before President Roosevelt's initiative and which would be there after President Roosevelt's initiative was no longer remembered—and Mr. Pell—and who is Mr. Pell? Why, Mr. Pell is a 'fonctionnaire', and what is Mr. Pell's 'fonction'? Apparently to go to Berlin every week or so and salute Hitler's or is it Goering's behind. Well, if the American Government wished Mr. Pell to engage in this function, naturally it could do so. But France had its honour to consider." France, he told Pell, "washed its hands of the whole affair." France "would have nothing to do with the German negotiation." It would remain on the IGC solely as a presence, not an active body. "Evian was a year ago," he reminded Pell pointedly. "It might surprise [Pell] to learn that a great deal had happened since."

Finally, Pell managed to interject the reason for his visit. Would Bérenger object if he handed the memorandum to Wohlthat at their meeting the next day? An explosion followed. "Memorandum—Ah, yes, the memorandum! Which you did not even have the good grace to

translate into French. After all, there is a French language, which is the
diplomatic language. France is a member of the Committee. The French
Vice-Chairman should at least expect to have communications addressed
to him in his own language!" Previously, "he had decided when Mr.
Rublee had written to him in English that he would not reply. He would
not reply to any communication addressed to him in English." Admitting
that the foreign office had translated it for him, he allowed that it was
"innocuous." Pell had got what he had come for, and Bérenger had said
what he wished Pell to hear. The senator rose and declared the conversation concluded.[42]

BÉRENGER HAD REALIZED A KEY POINT: while the IGC fluttered to
accommodate the Germans, no one had asked German Jews if they
would participate in the trust scheme or had solicited the views of Jewish
philanthropic leaders elsewhere. "Robert de Rothschild is violently hostile" to the plan, Pell reported. "He is convinced that it involves a great
danger not only to the Jews inside Germany who will lose their fortunes
with the blessings of the Intergovernmental Committee, but to Jews outside who will be dunned in the guise of negotiation for the transfer of the
money set aside in trust. . . . He has conferred with his cousins in London
and finds they are of the same opinion."[43] The de Rothschild family had
given enormous sums and expended great effort on behalf of refugees.
But they—not Wohlthat or Rublee or the Nazi regime or the IGC—had
taken that decision. The plan, as they and other Jewish leaders saw, was
little more than legalized blackmail.[44]

Journalist Dorothy Thompson agreed. This proposal was extortion
to obtain ransom money from Jews around the world and had nothing
in common with the agreement she had envisaged. "If you begin paying ransom money to kidnappers you are subsidizing kidnapping," she
warned her readers. "If this pretty idea works for Germany, so that the
rest of the world finances her export trade in order to save people from
being willfully starved and killed, why should not other governments
who think they have a minority problem adopt the same technique?"[45]
Emphasizing that this kind of agreement would serve to increase the

refugee problem, she urged that this insight should "take precedence over even humane considerations, for unless it is borne in mind, no humanitarianism will be able to cope with it. If governments get the idea that they can expropriate their citizens and turn them loose on the kindness of the rest of the world, the business will never end. A precedent will have been created; a formula will have been found."[46]

Despite increasing doubts, negotiations continued, with Wohlthat making a return visit to London in June. The regime was prepared to create the trust; in its view it was now up to the IGC to provide settlement opportunities and to establish the international foundation to guarantee mass emigration costs. Confusing Nazi ideology for fact, Wohlthat assumed that a "group of bankers or financiers," Jews of course, "were prepared to finance the whole of the scheme of emigration." Sir Herbert

George Rublee, who had recently resigned his position as director of the Inter-Governmental Committee, surrounded by reporters upon arrival in New York on 23 February 1939 aboard the SS Queen Mary.

Emerson (who had succeeded George Rublee in February as director of the IGC) managed to disabuse him of that notion, while assuring him that "the Jewish community had contributed most generously" and that "they would carry on so far as they reasonably could in the way in which they had done in the past." Summarizing their negotiations, Emerson noted the need to establish the external foundation, but the key issue was mass emigration sites. "The Germans will not believe that those concerned mean business unless a start is made with settlement."[47]

BACKED BY A PLEDGE OF SUPPORT from the American financier Bernard Baruch, the U.S. state department sent the intrepid journalist Linton Wells to investigate the possibility of settling Jews in Angola.[48] "Portuguese rule in Angola stinks to high heaven," he reported. "There you will find one of the rankest systems of conscienceless exploitation existing in the world today, directed by a leechlike bureaucracy insatiable in its desire to suck every drop of the colony's life blood—and no transfusions contemplated." The land was rich and could support at least a million Jewish refugees, "PROVIDED, first absolute sovereignty is acquired from its present maladministrators and exploiters." He estimated that one hundred million dollars would buy out the Portuguese.[49] Not even Baruch could meet that price tag.

The British contemplated equally outlandish schemes, including Socatra, an arid, hot island off the coast of Somalia beset by monsoon winds.[50] Prompted by the November pogrom and the subsequent IGC negotiations, the colonial office looked for more serious proposals and asked all the territories under its administration, except Palestine and TransJordan, how many German and Austrian Jews had settled in each domain. The grand total came to two thousand.[51] Hearing that the outgoing governor of Northern Rhodesia had suggested that there might be opportunities for Jewish refugees in the Mwinilunga district, British Secretary of State for the Colonies Malcolm MacDonald pressed the new governor, Sir John Maybin, to develop a proposal. When the Rublee-Wohlthat negotiations appeared likely to yield results, a commission was sent to Northern Rhodesia to investigate large-scale settlement.

The colony had allowed fewer than a hundred refugees to immigrate, and Maybin remained dubious about many more. The only role open to them was as subsistence farmers, which would create a "poor white problem," marked by malnutrition and debilitating disease, and thus damage the position of the white man. Racism of another form barred their entry here.[52]

In addition to each country's investigations and inquiries, the Americans and British formed a joint committee to explore the possibility of British Guiana. Traveling to the colony in February 1939, the commission concluded that hinterland territory suited large-scale settlement.[53] The climate was manageable, the soil fertile, and the local people welcomed European immigrants. Populated by black people who held government jobs and supplied the police force; East Indians, who had been brought as indentured laborers on the sugar plantation and remained poor; small groups of Portuguese, Chinese, and Britons; and nine thousand natives, British Guiana was not "'owned'" by any one group. Black people in particular welcomed immigration of Jews, expecting that they would develop the economy.[54] Starting with a grand vision, the commission reduced its ambition to a trial group of three to five thousand, and then to two village communities with a total of five hundred people.

Whitehall hoped that an announcement of British financial support for the Guiana option the day after it closed Palestine to immigrants would diminish anger about the latter. "By so doing we should to some extent meet the very hostile Jewish criticism which the publication of our Statement of Policy in Palestine would certainly provoke."[55] A clumsy strategy at best. Its timing fooled no one, and a sense of betrayal abounded. In any case, just a few settlers arrived before the project fell flat.

THE DOMINICANS DELIVERED what neither Washington nor Whitehall accomplished. While the latter pressed others, the Dominicans offered their own land—for a price and with a racist agenda. Pursuing Trujillo's proposal at Evian, the American Joint Distribution Committee and its subsidiary, the American Joint Agricultural Corporation (Agro-Joint), created the Dominican Republic Settlement Association, Inc. (DORSA)

which, with Robert Pell's help, negotiated with the Dominican government. Trujillo guaranteed the settlers freedom of religion, granted them
expedited migration procedures, and offered them tax and customs
exemptions. It fell to DORSA to select the immigrants and cover relocation and settlement costs. The first contingent of 50 refugees arrived in
Sosúa in March 1940, but the enterprise did not grow beyond the first
phase of 500 settlers. The war launched by Germany in 1939 had closed
transit routes and turned officials' attention to other matters. An analysis of the project undertaken by the Brookings Institution concluded
that there was little likelihood of success.[56] Published in 1942, the survey
served little purpose, and the 472 refugees who had reached Sosúa made
the best of their situation.

Marie Syrkin, journalist and Labor Zionist, traveled to Sosúa in January 1941. Her description of the immigrant selection process, training,
and the importance of timing with regard to the war spoke for many
such initiatives at the time. "Settlers for Sosúa are chosen in countries of
Europe from which it is possible to secure emigration," she explained.
"The range of choice has been shrinking as the war develops. For
instance, 250 prospective settlers were chosen in Amsterdam. Only 37 of
the 250 were actually able to arrive." The criteria were equally practical:
"Healthy young people, of sturdy physique, and preferably with some
agricultural training are chosen." When Syrkin visited, she found that
"the settlers looked young and husky; the average age is about 26. The
broad-shouldered, bronzed chaps that I saw bore no visible signs of the
experiences that they had been through in Europe."[57]

The success of the project depended on many factors, including
farm experience. Some of the settlers had got practical experience in
the agricultural training camps run by the Jewish community throughout
Greater Germany,[58] but DORSA did not rely on this alone. New arrivals spent three to six months in a reception camp to learn "gardening,

*Previously interned in Italy, this group of Jewish refugees from Germany, Austria,
and Czechoslovakia sail to the Sosúa settlement in the Dominican Republic via
New York on the SS* Cherokee, *19 October 1940.*

dairying, cattle-raising etc. While in this camp, all expenses are paid by Dorsa, and the settlers get 10¢ per day as pocket money." When ready to proceed independently, settlers got a bungalow, ten acres of land, and an initial supply of tools and livestock.[59]

Arriving in Sosúa in the middle of January, Syrkin was struck "like everyone else at the loveliness of the place." This did not negate "the real difficulties of pioneer colonization." These abounded. Still, the settlers made a go of it on the fields and they soon organized group social activities. She joined "a dramatic reading given in the entertainment barrack on a Saturday evening. . . . The audience of over a hundred young people listened intently to declamations of Goethe, Heine, and other German classics. There was also a humorous part to the program. I heard a number of grim jokes about Hitler, and less grim ones about the immigrants' status—a kind of specific brand of 'refugee' humor."[60]

The settlers established a village that in time boasted its own waterworks, sanitation system, clinic, pharmacy, school, library, synagogue, theater, newspaper, shops, and bank. Their physical isolation prompted them to process perishable agricultural products; a longer shelf life allowed them to ship their wares to market. Thus cheese and sausage industries were born. Productos Sosúa, the common name of these now very large factories, which were owned until recently by descendants of the first settlers, remains a leading brand in the Dominican Republic. And some of the early immigrants stayed too. Luis Hess, one of the first Jews to arrive in Sosúa, was ninety-four in 2002. The school he had founded, Colegio Luis Hess, counted a student body of over six hundred.

After the war some of the settlers left for the United States, others remained, and still others, like Joe Benjamin, arrived. Benjamin's parents had escaped to Shanghai where Joe was born; in 1947 the family made their way to Sosúa. In his view, Sosúa "'was an ideal place to grow up. We went to school for half a day, from 8 to 12, and rode our bikes and played until dark. Everybody watched out for each other. Everybody knew everybody. If you didn't go to the beach one Saturday, friends came over to make sure you were okay.'" Like Hess, Benjamin married a Dominican woman. Their daughter Erika went to the United States to attend college, remaining tied to her community by happy childhood memories. "It is a wonderful place to live and feel safe."[61] A Jewish enclave in a Catholic country, European and Latino, Sosúa endures as the sole constructive achievement of all those settlement schemes.

It is little enough. But it is possible that even worse flowed from the officials' willing engagement with resettlement as a "solution" to the "Jewish problem." Hitler and his colleagues probably needed no encouragement on this matter, but possibly they may have been emboldened by international acceptance of the idea that with population transfer an unwanted people could be made to disappear. And

Jewish refugees from Germany and Austria in a Sosúa settlement dining hall, 1940–1. PHOTOGRAPHER: DR KURT SCHNITZER.

A one-family bungalow under construction at the Sosúa settlement in the Dominican Republic, 1940–1. PHOTOGRAPHER: DR KURT SCHNITZER

if the Inter-Governmental Committee could undertake such action, surely the Reich could do so too. In the years that followed, Berlin cast its eye on successive dumping grounds: Madagascar, the Nisko reservation near Lublin, arctic Russia. Each promised a territorial "solution" to the "Jewish problem." All failed. Murder proved easier.

· PLACES ·

A LIFE

ANYWHERE

Robert rosner's family was so poor in 1938 they could not afford a radio. "My father, my mother, and I—I don't know where my [older] sisters [Erna and Paula] were that night—went to a café" to hear Austria's chancellor Kurt von Schuschnigg's farewell address on a public loudspeaker. Faced with the choice of hostile invasion by Germany or craven acceptance of a Nazi government for Austria, Schuschnigg had chosen to resign. "My father said immediately, 'We'll have to leave.'"

Perhaps, Robert Rosner surmised half a century later, his father was one of the "very few Austrian Jews who decided on that very day that they were going to leave" because he had come to Vienna from Radauti in Bukovina at the start of World War I, and his roots were not so deeply embedded in the capital city. "Probably Vienna was just one station in his life." Whatever the reason, his reaction was: "We'll have to leave; we won't be able to stay here; how can we get away with no money?"

While prescient, they were impoverished. The family remained in Vienna, where civility vanished and antisemitic cruelty became mass sport. By the close of Robert's academic year in June, "We were all talking about emigration and how we can get out. My father found a cousin who lived in the United States on a chicken farm somewhere in New Jersey. He wrote to that cousin. And we went through telephone directories of New York looking for Rosners and wrote letters to all of them also." At the same time, the family sought immigration papers from the consulate in Vienna. "My parents couldn't get on the quota because they were born in what was by then called Romania." His eldest sister Erna, in her final year of medical studies at the University of Vienna, "got married in September or October of '38. My brother-in-law Hans was Vienna-born, so he fell under the German quota, and there was plenty of room in the German quota."

Robert had joined Hashomer Hatzair, a socialist Zionist organization, in order to be together with other young people, but also with "the idea that perhaps I could go on hachshara [training farm]. I could go to Palestine. I had to do something. The Kultusgemeinde started a retraining scheme for kids. First, I wanted to learn to be an electrician, but I wasn't accepted. Then I got in as a chemist. I was always interested in chemistry. In Vienna, I started chemistry, learning to make shoe cream [polish]; that's about it."

Robert's mother had two sisters and a brother, and the family's social life revolved around these relationships, especially among the sisters. One by one, family members managed to emigrate, and their relatives in Vienna hoped that they would help from abroad. Robert's maternal aunt, his uncle, and their son moved into the Rosner family flat; their older children "somehow managed to emigrate." Another maternal aunt moved to Peru through her husband's family, and "the idea [was] that they would help us get into Peru." Meanwhile, Robert continued with his Zionist and chemist pursuits.

Emigration activities—their own, and those of the entire Jewish community—shaped Robert's life in unexpected ways. Jews stood on line at embassies, consulates, shipping companies, and government offices, desperate for papers: exit visas, transit visas, receipts for tax payments, clearance forms, ship tickets, train tickets. These formalities led to an unanticipated way for young people to make money. "We kids did this work of queuing up. One had to start at eight in the morning, and one had to queue up until eleven or twelve, so an adult would say, 'Would you queue for me?' Sometimes they had to get a form, and then I could get it. But when it came to doing serious business, they had to be there."

Robert's sister Paula took on the task of obtaining the family's tax clearance form, which they needed to obtain an exit visa. "My father went bankrupt in '28, so he hadn't paid all the taxes. Paula queued up and, as we had moved from the eighth district, where we'd lived in '28, to the second district, his name was not known to the officials in the second district." Choosing not to check with the office across town, "somehow, the man who was there said, 'Oh hell. Nothing is normal. Let's give the all clear that there are no tax debts.'"

With the form he gave Paula, they were able to obtain an exit visa. But where could they go? Which country would let them in? "We tried the Palestine Office; we tried with family in Palestine. We were thinking, if the situation changed, if we could get to Romania. One uncle of mine tried to leave immediately for Romania, but he didn't succeed. He got sent back. One of my cousins went to Italy and one to Australia. And everyone said, 'We'll try to help you.'"

The Rosners—one of the few fortunate families—ultimately made their way to Britain. His sister Erna and her husband Hans got an affidavit from the cousin the family had found who lived on a chicken farm in America. While they waited for their quota number to be called, Hans's professor in Vienna arranged a scholarship for him in Manchester. The British had relaxed their entry policies after the November pogrom for those with secure prospects to go elsewhere, and Erna and Hans fit that description.

Setting to work straight away after they arrived in December 1938 to make arrangements for the rest of the family, "they found a professor there, Professor Littler, who took me as child. They also managed to find somebody who took Paula as a maid. Paula left somewhere around February, and I left on a children's transport in April."

And what of their parents? "We were still waiting for my parents. Will they be able to come?" They too needed an entry visa. Hans and Erna rented rooms in a house owned by a working class woman. "She was so much impressed with what Hans and Erna were studying that she decided to guarantee for my parents with her life savings of one hundred fifty pounds." With all the paperwork in order, Erna, Hans, Paula, and Robert grew increasingly anxious for the older Rosners to emigrate. "We saw that the war was coming. One day we managed to phone Vienna, which was expensive and *very* difficult at that time. We managed to get my father on the phone, and he said that he's waiting to get his furniture (which was really *their* life savings) across. Hans said, 'Don't wait! Come.'" They took his advice.[1]

VIENNESE JEWS EXPERIENCED IN THE SPAN of six weeks what German Jews had endured in the course of five years. By the close of 1938 they had reached the same conclusion: there was no future for Jews in Greater Germany. Adults faced few ways to make a living, and young people, with schools closed to them and no jobs ahead, had no prospects. In nearly all homes, emigration offered the sole solution. "For the first time I couldn't do things I had done before," the then-fifteen-year-old Marianne Braun recalled. "So we spent more time in each other's houses, talking about what our parents were doing, which was preparing for emigration. So the children talked about all this too."[2]

How to get out? Men in a position to do so tried business connections. Irene Hasenberg's father was a banker in Berlin and he "was offered a job with American Express. He had two choices, either to go to Amsterdam or to Curaçao." Never imagining what would transpire later, Mr Hasenberg chose Amsterdam in 1937. "Curaçao seemed very distant and a very strange place to go to, and it would have been very far from the rest of the family."[3] Marianne Braun ended up in the same city a year later. Her father was one of three principals in a wholesale paper export firm. The director of the company, one Herr Greiner, organized to set up the business in Amsterdam.[4]

Most Jews had no such possibilities, and those who did understood how uncertain they were. As civil society disintegrated, kinship networks emerged as key escape routes. Many pursued the same strategies as the Rosner family: to contact relatives who had settled abroad years before and to depend upon those who now emigrated. The Rosners were particularly successful and lucky. Then too, Erna and Hans were professional people at just the right age to be energetic and resourceful. Robert's aunt who went to Peru was not able to help family left behind in Vienna. Still, she tried, and they hoped. Such mutual expectations abounded.

As they looked for a host country, the Jews of Greater Germany acquired skills and competencies to support their applications for immigration. A common joke circulated in the Jewish community: "What language are you learning?" "The wrong one." Advised by informational bulletins about prospects in various countries as well as by letters from émigrés published in the Hilfsverein journal, young and middle-aged people took classes in all manner of skilled labor. Lore Saalheimer was graduated at age sixteen from a Jewish secondary school in her hometown of Fürth in March 1938. "One talked about emigration all

Jews hoping to emigrate study Spanish in a course offered by the Berlin Jewish community in 1935. PHOTOGRAPHER: ABRAHAM PISAREK.

the time and what one was going to study for emigration," she recol-
lected. "I ended up in a school for laboratory assistants in Berlin." Sending young people from smaller to larger cities to gain such training had
become so common that it provided some newly impoverished Jews in
those cities with an unexpected source of income. "I stayed in the posh-
est part of Berlin, Grunewald, with a widowed lady with a daughter a
year younger than I, who took in seven young girls like me who were all
doing something in Berlin. There were various places like the one I was
sent to. [The landlady] made a living out of [boarding] young girls who
were training for something that would help them in their emigration."[5]

The press to emigrate prompted other opportunities too. Unemployed Jews with skills taught others seeking a marketable competency.
Hilda Zadikow-Löhsing, a highly successful applied artist whose skills
would later save her life in Theresienstadt concentration camp, turned to
teaching when the Germans occupied Bohemia and Moravia in March
1939 and thus supported five members of her family. As her daughter
Mariánka explained, "She was teaching groups of women who came
from office jobs to become arts and crafts experts, to make handmade
and hand-painted lampshades, to paint pictures, to draw from nature, to
do things so that they could make a living in another way, should they
not learn English or French fast enough. If they should be able to emigrate, they could make their living in the art world." The classes were
held in the Zadikow home. "There were groups of five Jewish women
coming three times a day. . . . My mother did this from the time the Nazis
marched in—'39—until we were deported to Terezín."[6]

Either these middle-aged, middle class Jewish women office workers were paying no attention to the emigration information offered by
the Hilfsverein, or the Jewish self-help organization's emphasis on agricultural skills was so far beyond their ken that they could not turn their
energy and attention to such work. Young people, by contrast, heard
the message, in part because of their age but also because many had
embraced the back-to-the-land ideology of the Jewish youth movement.
Like its German counterpart, the early-twentieth-century Jewish youth
movement believed that the remedy for urban tensions and the social
upheaval of modernization lay in a return to nature.

Manual labor was central to the youth movement vision of an anti-bourgeois, -materialist, -cosmopolitan, -capitalist society.[7] Originally, the Jewish youth movement in Germany held that this way of life was the answer to antisemitism: a genuine relationship with German soil would lead to full emancipation and acculturation. Focusing on character development, the central purpose of this non-Zionist youth movement was to educate and develop each individual to "enable him, in full consciousness, to fulfill his national and social purpose."[8] The Zionist youth movement, of marginal importance in the German-speaking lands prior to 1933, held different goals. "Palestine needs workers prepared for any job, capable of taking over any position likely to meet the requirements of collective living," a Habonim (stripe of Labor Zionism) spokesman explained.[9] Young Jews had to be educated to meet the practical needs of the Jewish state. If the former emphasized internal work and the latter external work, both recognized that the context in which they operated shifted

Jewish boys learn woodworking skills in a workshop run in the Grosse Hamburgerstrasse and Auguststrasse schools in Berlin, 1936.
PHOTOGRAPHER: ABRAHAM PISAREK.

radically when the Nazis came to power. Manual labor offered a ticket out of Greater Germany for young people.

While the youth aliyah movement trained young people primarily in Palestine, the Jewish communities of Greater Germany prepared young-sters locally for emigration to the national homeland. "When the Nazis came, of course, definitely I wanted to emigrate and my parents wanted me to go," Otto Suschny recalled. Born in 1924, he was not yet fourteen at the time of the Anschluss. "My parents tried to get me to England, onto one of the child transports. (I would have liked to go to England.) Then I joined the Netzach [another branch of Labor Zionism] youth group in order to be able to go to Israel. I remember there was a place called the *Krugerheim*, it was a Jewish-owned building, where we met." The Nazis approved of these efforts. "At that time, the Nazis didn't really interfere with Jewish emigration, including Zionistic activity. There was even, to a certain extent, cooperation, because at that time the German policy was still to encourage Jews to leave the country and leave behind all their money. That was what they were interested in." Joining Netzach meant preparing for life in Palestine. "First of all, lectures in the Krugerheim."[10] The smaller group to which Otto was assigned met regularly to become acquainted and to discuss matters.

He pursued other emigration possibilities too. "I attended lectures in Spanish for a while because there was a chance of going to a South American country. Then, the Kultusgemeinde started arranging so-called *Umschulungskursen* [retraining courses] for Jews who had intel-lectual lives before to learn some trade which they could use somewhere, Latin America, or wherever they could go." Otto's mother's family had a soap-manufacturing business, "and the Kultusgemeinde asked my uncle to run a number of training courses for Jewish people wanting to emi-grate to learn that." Otto "assisted as an apprentice in the running of these courses for two or three subsequent courses; I did this for two or three months."[11]

The Palestine-bound track gathered speed. Ideologically and intel-lectually prepared by the meetings at the Krugerheim, Otto and his group went to the *Vorbereitungslager* (preparation camp) Ottertal "to test us to see if we fit in." Located in the Semmering, a summer resort area outside

Vienna, Ottertal served as an agricultural and ideological training camp. This month-long experience was followed by a stint of more intensive farm work at the Moosbrunn camp. Georg Überall (who later Hebraized his name to Ehud Avriel), "on behalf of the Jewish Agency, had arranged for us to go to that camp." Supervised by a Hungarian fascist, an Arrow Cross member, Moosbrunn housed a few hundred young people waiting to emigrate. "It was really meant to get us out of town, to be somewhere we could do work which was liked by the government. On the other hand, it was meant by the Jewish Agency to prepare us for going to Israel." In Otto's memory, these training experiences followed one on the other in the spring and summer of 1939. "I remember weeding, turning the soil with a shovel, and picking potatoes. I remember the farmers giving us a meal of potatoes with lard. They were rather friendly to us; they rather liked us. They really saw to it that we ate." Above all, it was a social experience. "I remember the room I slept in, the discussions we had, and that there definitely were girls there. At that age, one remembers whether girls are nearby." Called back to Vienna to attend to the last paperwork, Otto's group stayed "together as long as we were physically there." Some youngsters were sent to another country as an interim station to Palestine. "But everyone who was in Vienna participated" in the group activities: "lectures, Hebrew lessons, and we were singing Hebrew songs, we were taught Jewish history, we had Oneg Shabbat." Comprised of some thirty-five fifteen- to seventeen-year-old boys and girls—"about two to one, boys to girls"—the corps "soon developed a sense of belonging together. This was encouraged, of course, because we were told that when you go to Israel, this will be your family. And it was like that."[12]

THE JEWISH COMMUNAL ORGANIZATIONS of Greater Germany dedicated energy and resources to schemes to help children and young adults. Concerned as they were about the entire community, they were especially anxious about the fate of the young. "The transplantation of the young generation as soon as possible is our greatest priority," Käthe Rosenheim, a German-Jewish social worker, explained in 1936. In Germany itself, some 83 percent of Jews under the age of twenty-four managed to escape by 1939.[13] The Austrian-Jewish community in 1938, and the Czech community a year later, quickly adopted their coreligionists' aims and achieved similar results.

The figures bespeak success; they do not reveal the toil, foreboding, and persistent fear of failure Jewish communal workers experienced as they sought to respond responsibly to the catastrophe they faced. The Hilfsverein solicited information about the labor needs of host countries overseas and published their findings with letters from newly settled immigrants. "Almost all the letters and other information we have received describe over and over again that every immigrant *who is skilled in a manual trade*, or who at least possesses some technical knowledge may count on obtaining a position sufficient to make a living in a relatively short time," the editors wrote in the Argentina section in a 1936 issue of *Jüdische Auswanderung* (*Jewish Emigration*).[14] Among the many trades needed: construction and industrial workers, electricians, blacksmiths, turners, carpenters, upholsterers, weavers, leather cutters, car mechanics, hairdressers, bakers, cooks. A letter from an immigrant confirmed this analysis. "It is certainly easier to make a living in manual trades of every sort. For example, a person with whom I shared my cabin on board, and who was not yet seventeen when he arrived, and who had only six months' training as an electrician, immediately obtained (admittedly with the help of his cousin) a job that earned 30 pesos, which has since been increased to 60 pesos. . . . I can therefore say that while jobs are not lying in the streets in Buenos Aires, it is possible to survive and advance with skills."[15] An immigrant to Brazil sounded the same note. Money was not required for success. Skills, competencies, and physical health were key. "Strong skilled workers in any field are needed. They get jobs immediately, even when they don't know the language, and they earn a lot. This means they can live, buy some things, and have an occasional glass of beer." His advice: "Anyone who is not a skilled worker must retrain."[16]

That prescription for survival resonated with the youth movement anti-bourgeois stance, the Zionist ideology of the new Jew who worked in all the jobs that had long been closed to him in traditional Christian Europe (guild-protected trades and farming), and the antisemitic twist on that historical development: blaming the victim, antisemites argued that Jews were not a normal people with a normal occupation distribution.

With facts on the ground and ideology aligned, the Jewish community, often in conjunction with the Zionist youth movement, hastened to offer retraining courses in such areas as wood and metalwork and as electricians. Reporting in 1939 on the progress of vocational retraining in Germany between 1933 and 1938, Rudolf Stahl (who had headed this effort in Frankfurt) noted that there were too few Jewish craftsmen in Germany to train the thousands who needed this education. "The only way to meet the situation was to set up training workshops, in which a class, usually consisting of twenty pupils, could work with one master." Despite their deficiencies as "real trade workshops"—forbidden to sell their products to the public; more of a school than a workshop; delimited responsibility of the apprentice—these institutions flourished. Berlin hosted six by 1937; another ten were in other large cities. Each served between one and two hundred men and boys at a time.[17]

As these trades were considered male occupations, traditionally female job training opportunities were needed for girls. They learned to cook, wash, and clean in Jewish public service institutions: old-age homes, orphanages, hospitals, and soup kitchens. In addition, girls were offered "special courses in sewing, dressmaking, simple needlework, and tailoring." By 1937 there were thirteen such training sites in Berlin and seventeen in other cities.[18] One M. Mitzman, an officer of the Central British Fund who traveled to Berlin, Breslau, and Vienna in 1939, reported back to London on initiatives on the ground to train youngsters for emigration. "In Vienna [they] have organized an excellent curriculum for their children. They have opened workshops all over Vienna where boys and girls receive instruction in all forms of handicrafts." He noted too that "in another part of Vienna there are gardens and allotments where the children and adults learn agricultural work."[19]

Jews eager to emigrate filled the classes to overflowing. As we have seen, Robert Rosner got a place in a practical chemistry program and learned to make shoe polish.[20] Otto Suschny served as an apprentice when the Kultusgemeinde asked his maternal uncle to run a soap-making course. Lore Gang learned chemical laboratory skills in a "commercial laboratory in Jewish ownership."[21] And while Hilda Zadikow taught women applied arts, her daughter Mariánka took a number of courses organized by the Kultusgemeinde in Prague. Mariánka learned to be a nursemaid for newborns and their mothers. A second course "in early development and educating young children" was followed by a third in medical laboratory techniques. "I was crying when that course finished. I wanted to stay. I loved that laboratory work." Finally, Mariánka also took a culinary class.[22]

Agricultural training and ancillary trades to support farm settlements promised the greatest possibility for transferable skills. Zionist organizations pressed forward with these initiatives in the hope of building the Jewish state. The non-Zionist Jewish Colonization Society (ICA), building upon earlier initiatives, saw the establishment of farming communities across the globe as a way to assist Jewish emigration. Founded in 1891, the ICA funded ventures in South America, North America, Cyprus, Turkey, and Palestine, as well as Russia and Romania. When the Nazis came to power, these ICA settlements offered hope. According

German-Jewish boys learning to use agricultural tools on a hachshara in Germany, 1935.

to the *Jüdische Auswanderung*, by 1937 some forty thousand Jews lived in ICA colonization areas in Argentina; about half of them were colonists. Jews from Greater Germany sought to join their coreligionists. "In January, 1936 the ICA settled a first group of 19 Jewish families from Germany in its colony Avigdor (Entre Rios) in Argentina." Plans for a further 150 families were in progress.[23]

Ardently as many Jews wished to obtain a place at a training farm, Nazi regulations delimited the number of positions available. All agricultural programs—whether run by the Kultusgemeinde, Zionist youth movements, or non-Zionist movements—required special approvals from the *Reichsnährstand* (Agriculture Bureau) and the Gestapo, and administrators had to submit detailed reports on their farm activities, students, and emigration figures. The police did not hesitate to dissolve an enterprise on the slightest pretext.[24]

Philanthropic organizations and individuals therefore founded agricultural programs outside Germany, in Belgium, Denmark, Italy, Yugoslavia, Sweden, and the Netherlands. By 1937 one-seventh of all German-Jewish trainees were in such programs. Although German students in these countries were not officially emigrants, ongoing expenses were paid by the host Jewish community, as well as by the students themselves and the Council for German Jewry. Training was to last six months, but experience proved otherwise. Agricultural education took a full year or two; learning handicraft skills called for two to three.[25]

The *Werkdorp* in the Wieringermeer, one of the best-known training farms at the time, stood in a polder reclaimed from the Zuiderzee in 1930. The Werkdorp thus developed on new land that the Dutch government leased rent-free to the *Stichting Joodsche Arbeid* (Jewish Work Foundation) for ten years. Originally intended to train refugees who had come to the Netherlands in 1933 so that they would have the skills to immigrate elsewhere, the Werkdorp population grew to include some of the students from Germany who could not be placed on farms in the Reich.[26]

Hans Lubinsky, a pediatrician and pedagogue who served as the first director, held high hopes for the Werkdorp. Insisting upon the importance of personal attitude, he believed that "the willingness to become part of a new social class, to say 'yes' wholeheartedly to a new vocation in all its dimensions" was "fundamental to the success of the process."[27] The Werkdorp was not aligned to the Zionist movement; no age limits or religious or political affiliation obtained. Lubinsky held community building and the agricultural enterprise dear and worried that a great percentage of the urbanized Jewish intellectuals who trained would not manage as manual laborers. He had little reason for concern. As of October 1936, only 15 of the 317 admitted had abandoned the program.[28]

The commitment these figures reflect was elaborated in a series of essays by young hachshara Jews published the following year. White collar workers, and the children of white collar fathers, the writers stressed the radical shifts in values and life style they had adopted. To succeed in retraining, they'd had to accept manual labor as a permanent vocation, not a temporary means of emigration. This carried a paradox. To embrace the values of manual labor as a way to earn a living negated the principles of their former bourgeois life, but if they held on to those bourgeois values, they would find their new occupations demeaning. Worse: they found themselves far less competent at their new jobs than they had been in their former professions. "This feeling, to be substandard in one's work, makes it twice as difficult to surrender one's old values," one of the essayists explained.[29]

However inadequate they felt, necessity trumped nostalgia. Manual trade skills and agricultural training aided emigrants' chances to obtain a visa and served when they arrived. Some 40 percent of German-Jewish refugees residing in South Africa in 1937, for example, earned their living as workers.[30]

At the Werkdorp, as elsewhere, girls were offered fewer options to learn wage-earning skills than boys. Conventional gender roles applied at home and abroad. If it was the man's role to make money, women were key to successful emigration, just as they traditionally had been held crucial to a harmonious home. As an article on "The Housewife and Emigration" emphasized, the woman "not only has her own problems to deal with, she has those of the rest of the family." Deploring that the "many problems, concerns, and cares that precede emigration" prevent women from preparing properly for "the enormous difficulties they will face," the

editors identified tasks and responsibilities to which housewives needed
to attend before departure, in transit, and once arrived. Women, they
urged, "must dedicate time" to learn the host country language. They
needed "to become acquainted with the local currency and weights, and
the way daily life is carried on." Reminding their readers that the climate
would be different, the editors suggested "simple, useful clothing, sturdy
shoes, resilient garments for hot and cold weather, leather jackets." Prepare to live without running water, sewage systems, or electricity. Take
tools: "hammers, drills, saws, pliers, screwdrivers, many different types
of nails." Knowing how to cook and clean would prove so crucial that
"anyone who does not know how should take a course before departure." Learn to cook with local ingredients, the editors advised. Take pre-
cautions, like always boiling water. Finally, women needed to attend to
the family's health and hygiene. Make sure everyone's teeth and feet are
checked and treated before departure, as problems will "limit the ability to work and to adjust." Take extra pairs of eyeglasses. Housecleaning
will prove a special challenge, they warned, but is essential to maintain
health. "The kitchen sink and the toilet must be continuously disinfected,
and garbage quickly removed."[31] Notwithstanding this daunting prospect, young and middle-aged Jewish women fled, although their emigration rate lagged behind that of their male counterparts. In 1933 women
accounted for 52.3 percent of the German-Jewish population; by 1939
their proportion of the by then much reduced community had increased
to 57.5, most of whom were elderly.[32]

THE NOVEMBER POGROM SWELLED the number of Jews seeking asylum. Desperation gripped the community. For a long while, many had
believed that the Jews would be outcasts but still tolerated. This myth
vanished overnight; literally turned to ash. The physical demolition of
Jews' property, from the destruction of nearly every synagogue to the
attacks on businesses owned by Jews, on 9 November left no place for
Jewish religious or economic life. The imprisonment of thirty thousand
Jewish men swept out of their homes the next day (10 November) into
concentration camps left no place for Jews at all. The sole escape lay in

emigration, and all hope for release from concentration camps lay in an exit visa.

Businesses throughout the district where Robert Rosner's family lived had been shattered the night of 9 November. "But we didn't realize what was happening generally. And life goes on, you know. My father, in the morning, went on a business meeting. My father was walking in the midst of the textile district; this is quite close to where the Gestapo was. A car came up and arrested him and his friend. But they hadn't come to arrest him, but to arrest the people in that building full of Jewish offices. When they collected the people from the building, there wasn't enough room for him in the vehicle, so they told my father and his friend to get out, somebody else would collect them. My father went straight home. His friend, who was 'Jewish-looking,' went into the Vienna woods."[33]

The Rosners' apartment building was no more secure than the offices in the textile district. "They came during the day. We heard the SS com-

Jewish men force-marched through the street of Regensburg, Germany, on 10 November 1938. The banner reads: "Departure of the Jews." They were sent to Dachau.

ing and arresting people. But we lived on the fourth floor completely in the back [in a rear courtyard, where the poorest people had apartments]. There were many arrests in the lower floors. Perhaps they filled their arrest quota before they arrived on the fourth floor. No one in our part of the building was arrested." In Robert's memory, "from this point on only one question remained: How to get out; where to go?"[34]

Lore Saalheimer's parents phoned her at the boardinghouse where she was staying while doing her laboratory training course in Berlin. They said, "'Come home.'" The family had moved to Nuremberg in 1935, and she returned on an express train the next day. "I knew enough, I wasn't that stupid that I didn't know something bad had happened. I don't think I realized how bad things were until I got home. My parents were on the platform. My mother was in a sweater and skirt, no makeup, no jewelry, no anything. My father looked awful."[35]

Their home stood in shambles. "An atmosphere of complete gloom and no ornaments, no anything anywhere; the house was in mourning. . . . My parents had had a huge sideboard full of the best china, and [the Nazis] had taken an ax and smashed it, smashed the china. They had had a glass display cabinet with a lot of pretty things in it, and also glasses and so on. [The Nazis] had just taken it and thrown it over. I mean every little tiny last bit of it was broken."[36]

Lore's father had not been arrested. That was the sole good news. As for the rest, life became extremely difficult terribly quickly. "I remember my father not being allowed to go to his [toy] factory," Lore recounted. "I remember food being a problem. I remember money being a problem. The other thing I remember is waiting for letters from England. We were waiting for letters from my uncles, from anybody at all from England. There were no letters." Lore had three paternal uncles and an aunt. One of the brothers had emigrated to London years before. Her father's two other brothers followed him, emigrating illegally in 1936. "They went on holiday. Somebody got their money out for them, and they just didn't go back." Their sister joined her three brothers in London a bit later. Only Lore's father and his family remained in Germany, and they waited anxiously for help from their relatives. "It transpired that they thought we might get in trouble if they wrote to us. We felt terribly cut off."[37]

Safety now meant departure papers. Few thought about retraining in the aftermath of the November pogrom. In fact, as Robert Rosner observed, "The Nazis plundered and closed the workshops organized by the Kultusgemeinde during the Kristallnacht, so the whole project came to a close."[38] If the retraining courses reflected a tenuous sense of a constructive future, an image of a new life in a new land with a new job skill, that vision held no more. And if the apprenticeships and courses and language classes had fostered a sense of expectation about the future and some degree of control over it, all of that evaporated. Emergency overwhelmed planning, however tentative it had been. The November pogrom marked, as Lore observed, "a quantum step. This was the real thing."[39]

With no sense of control, no map or plan, no one knew how best to proceed, and everyone was tense. Stress increased daily and fear spurred many arguments. But her parents agreed unequivocally on one matter: "There was no question that my parents wanted me out, me in particular, me out as quickly as possible, out of Germany as quickly as possible."[40]

By the middle of December, Lore's uncle had obtained a student permit for her, which led to a visa to study in England. He then helped her parents leave. Family ties had worked in their favor.

FOR THOSE WITH NO CONTACTS ABROAD and no prospect for an immigration visa anywhere, one destination glimmered—almost an afterthought, located at the end of the earth: Shanghai. One of five Chinese cities opened to foreign residents and trade as a result of the Opium War (1840–3), Shanghai allowed Europeans and Americans to establish extraterritorial "concession areas" or settlements, each governed by its own consul.[41] Efficiently run and lightly taxed, the concessions became an economic engine attracting nearly all the foreign investment in China. By the 1930s the so-called International Settlement measured 5,583 acres and the French Concession 2,525 acres, with a combined population of 1.5 million people, of whom 60,000 were foreigners who enjoyed extraterritorial status. These two areas were embedded in a great metropolis under full Chinese jurisdiction of another 1.5 million people, which made Shanghai the fifth-largest city in the world.

According to the nineteenth-century agreements, Chinese officials had no right to refuse a visa for Shanghai to Americans and Europeans so long as they paid a set fee. In the twentieth century the city known as "the Paris of the Orient" thus became "the Home of the Homeless" and "the Haven of Undesirables."[42] More than twenty-five thousand Russians found refuge there after the defeat of the White forces.[43] Some got jobs as policemen, watchmen, or doormen or pulled rickshaws, but most fell into destitution and survived because their wives earned meager sums as barmaids, "dancing hostesses," masseuses, or prostitutes. Other westerners did not look kindly on the Russians; their poverty weakened the status of Europeans in the city. But attempts to expel the refugees failed.

The Japanese occupation of Manchuria brought horrendous destruction to Shanghai, as anti-Japanese riots by the Chinese prompted the Japanese to attack. Still, the International Settlement remained intact and open for business. When Japan occupied most of northeast China in 1937, including greater Shanghai, they too respected the extraterritorial integrity of the International Settlement and the French Concession. But the economy plummeted, and the situation in the two concessions deteriorated further with the arrival of one million Chinese refugees. Isolated in an area under harsh occupation, Shanghai began to unravel. Thousands of foreigners left for their home countries, and well-to-do Chinese moved to Hong Kong.

Timing is everything, and just at this moment Jews in Greater Germany grew desperate. The allure of Shanghai, a destination for those who had nowhere else to go, bloomed ever greater. "Every day, the Consular offices are stormed by people who ask: 'Can I get a visa to go to . . . ?' 'No.' 'Can I get a passport? . . . I can pay what it costs?' 'No.' 'Is the quota still open?' 'No, No, No, No, No, No.' One cannot travel, then?" a contemporary account reported. "Everywhere the same answer is given: No . . . nein . . . non . . . impossible . . . lo siento mucho . . . I am sorry. . . . All these negative answers prevail in every country in the world . . . except in the city of Shanghai." And the author went on to explain, "Here there is no one to say NO. No one exercises any right to refuse you a visa, if you are prepared to pay the Chinese Consul his fee of three dollars. . . . No necessary papers, no references. If you have a passport . . . that's all right. If you have no passport . . . don't let that worry you . . . you can still get into Shanghai."[44]

The Jewish leadership in Germany did not support immigration to Shanghai, even after the November pogrom. Writing in early 1939, Dr Julius Seligsohn, a member of the *Reichsvereinigung* (Reich Association of Jews in Germany) executive, readily acknowledged the gravity of the Jews' situation in Germany. "A great part of the Jewish population which has not yet emigrated is in danger of being arrested and sent to the concentration camp if the emigration does not take place soon."[45] Yet he did not see Shanghai as an option because "there is no way for them to earn a living." Furthermore, he argued, "it is more honorable for a Jew to die as a martyr in central Europe than to perish in Shanghai. The first is Kiddush Hashem [martyrdom], the second is simply a misled Jewish emigration policy."[46]

As wrongheaded as it seems now, Seligsohn and his colleagues envisaged doom for Jews in Shanghai, a city in the middle of a country at war. They believed that the structure of their community was strong enough to hold out and carry on with planned dispersal. Orderly emigration would allow the Jewish leadership to maintain contact with the newly established exile communities and, after the horror had passed, organize repatriation. They considered Jews who fled to Shanghai lost. That thought pleased the Gestapo. As all berths on regular Shanghai-bound ships were booked for at least a year, Eichmann detailed the Hanseatic Travel Office to charter Greek and Yugoslav tramp steamers to send Jews to China. His scheme for additional transit opportunities offered by the Gestapo at a price failed because the shipping companies demanded foreign currency, which the regime did not want to expend. Plan B, to lay on German ships for the purpose, failed too, as the Reichsbank would not purchase fuel for this purpose.[47]

Frank Foley, the British passport officer in Berlin, well knew that many Jews had no prospect of visas. Desperate applicants denied British visas had raised the idea of Shanghai with him and, as he reported to London in January 1939, he and his colleagues had warned Jews not to go there. "They refuse to listen to us and say that Shanghai under any conditions is infinitely better than a Concentration Camp in Germany. One

A Chinese youth stands outside an office shared by several Jewish doctors (note consulting hours) who found refuge in Shanghai.

can perhaps understand their point of view." Foley added that the German government supported immigration to Shanghai because it believed Jews would perish there. "One has to remember that the declared wish of the N.S.D.A.P. [Nazi party] is that Jews should 'verrecken' [croak]. If they have to 'verrecken', it is of minor importance to the party where the process takes place," he observed. Still, he felt it "humane on our part not to interfere officially to prevent the Jews from choosing their own grave-yards." Foley framed their choice in stark terms. "They would rather die as free men in Shanghai than as slaves in Dachau. The people who sail for Shanghai have usually been warned to leave Germany within a few weeks or enter or return to a Concentration Camp. They know the horrors of a Concentration Camp, but remain hopeful about Shanghai in spite of warnings."[48]

Panic-stricken German and Austrian Jews continued to buy tickets issued by Nord Deutsche Lloyd, Lloyd Trieste, and Nippon Yusen Kai-sya, knowing that upon arrival they would have to fend for themselves in an utterly strange metropolis that promised nothing but the most desti-tute and temporary refuge from persecution—a squalid waiting room for better times. Abandoning the idea that learning a trade would help them earn a living and giving up on acquiring the local language, Jews clutched at hope and set sail. By the outbreak of war, seventeen thousand Jews had arrived in the city, without a future, but safe from the Germans.[49]

VISA STAMPS
OFFER HOPE

Sascha and Ludwig Marcuse fled to France after the Reichstag fire. A writer, philosopher, theater critic, and a Jew, Ludwig was too well known for his liberal views to remain in Germany. Indeed, the Nazis considered husband and wife to be such dangerous opponents of the regime that they were stripped of citizenship in 1937. This mattered little to the Marcuses, who felt at home in France until the Munich agreement (29 September 1938), which Chamberlain believed offered "peace for our time" but in fact simply delivered Czechoslovakia into Hitler's hands without a shot. The atmosphere curdled. Previously banned anti-semitic magazines appeared for sale on the boulevards of Paris, and a new spirit of political conformity seized the Riviera. Stability and peace mattered, not Hitler's concentration camps, Franco's fascist rule in Spain, or Mussolini's racial laws. France no longer seemed hospitable to the Marcuses, and nowhere in Europe looked better.

Fortunately for the Marcuses, Ludwig had been offered an affidavit of support from the Institute for Social Research at Columbia University. "My first reaction then, in spring 1938, had been *nein, jamais,* never (I did not yet know that third word at the time). But out of courtesy to the

American consul, I drove to Marseille, my case entered the bureaucratic machine . . . and I forgot all about it." By the end of that year the United States emerged as a promising option. Imbued with European prejudices about America, Ludwig did not look to the new world to offer culture and contentment. "I simply wanted to get as far away from Europe as possible. After Munich, I was convinced that a German thousand-year Europe was not a slogan, but (for our lifetime) a very precise prediction." He promptly began to go "every day to the American consulate in Paris; all my wishes vanished in comparison to one single object: a visa." Assigned a quota number valid for the month of February 1939, the Marcuses believed all was in order. But they were called back to the office on 15 February: their marriage certificate, issued in Frankfurt, was missing. "'When can we have another visa?'" Ludwig asked. "'There is no date,'" the American consular official replied. "'And you must return your quota number.'" Utterly downcast, they felt they had "lost the race with Hitler."[1]

With no hope, and solely to pursue the goal of gathering all their documents, Ludwig "wrote to the Frankfurt Registry Office. In less than a week I had what I needed. Shocked to the core, the American consul sat down." Amazed by the German civil service which, he observed, "'works like a precision machine,'" indeed *was* "'the Thousand Year Reich,'" he also felt great regret. "'Too late! I have already given your quota number to the American consulate in Berlin.'"[2]

Ludwig accepted defeat. Sascha would not. The consul "thought about it: our number had probably arrived in Berlin on Friday. No one worked on Saturday and Sunday. Not on Monday either, because the consulate had been closed for Washington's Birthday. Now it was Tuesday afternoon." While the case formally was closed and no further action was required of him at that point, the official extended himself. "'If you want, I'll call Berlin during my afternoon break.'" No one could accuse him of taking work time from his active caseload. The cost of the phone call fell to the Marcuses. Ludwig declined. Sascha said yes. "Berlin answered: 'We were about to give the number to someone else.'"[3] With the number reassigned to them and all their papers in order, they received a visa to enter the United States.

For Sascha and Ludwig Marcuse, this paper—an American visa

Antisemitic cartoon showing Jews as unwanted by the United States, published in
Kladderadatsch, *a German magazine, in 1933.*

—served as their ticket to life. Proof of official approval to enter
another country, visas developed in the early nineteenth century and
originally took the form of a small written note by an official in whatever document served as the traveler's passport. The term "visa," from
the Latin *videre* (to see), implied that the official had inspected or
viséed the passport.[4] In the twentieth century the handwritten note
gave way to stamps imprinted by a consular official onto one of the
twenty-eight empty visa pages of the by then standardized thirty-
two-page passport.

The Marcuses were lucky: American immigration laws and policies barred the door to most Jews. Refugees held no status in the American system. As Assistant Secretary of State Wilbur J. Carr put it in April 1933, there was no legal basis "to provide special treatment for the class of aliens known as refugees."[5] The ever-worsening situation in Europe failed to move the Americans. "The free admission of aliens into the United States on the basis of their allegations that they were suffering from racial, religious or political persecutions in their own countries would be almost sure to lead to delicate and hazardous diplomatic situations which would not be in the public interest,"[6] Undersecretary of State and flaming antisemite Sumner Welles declared in 1939. His position exacerbated extant conditions. In the wake of the stock market crash (1929), the state department had ordered consular officials to enforce a provision in the law that denied entry to those at risk "to become a public charge."[7] With unemployment rampant in the United States throughout the 1930s, no one who depended upon finding a job on arrival was allowed entry. Another provision in the law prohibited everyone—except artists, ministers, professors, nurses, and domestic servants—to negotiate a job in advance.[8] And German law forced Jews to leave their assets behind.

Caught in this maze of contradictions, refugees fell in the ordinary immigration system, and responsibility for their maintenance shifted to family and friends in America who were called upon to provide an affidavit (from the Latin *affidare*, to trust), a sworn assurance of financial means to care for the would-be immigrant. As the state department intended, this proved a major obstacle for Jews desperate to leave Greater Germany. Martin Gumpert, a dermatologist who specialized in venereal diseases and pioneered social rehabilitation programs for patients, was forced to abandon his medical work in 1933. A writer as well, Gumpert turned his hand to biographies of scientific researchers and physicians. Two years later the regime prohibited him from earning a living in this way too. Gumpert looked for a way out. From the American consulate he learned he needed an affidavit. "I had never heard the word 'affidavit' before," he explained in a memoir (1941) to educate Americans about refugees' dilemmas. "It is one of those terms without which one seems to be able to get along very well, until one day they give us to understand that our life depends on them. The affidavit—this word with its magic, Biblical sound—is the key to the American paradise."

Gumpert quickly learned what was at stake. "Without such a document a Consul will not even look at you. It is most effective when given by a close relative." He had no such relative. But he had friends in London. "I helped myself out of this unpleasant situation by going to London, which was then still possible, and obtaining from friends some money that would be placed at my disposal after my landing in New York. Thus I possessed something that did not yet belong to me, and so I evaded the [American and German] legal pitfalls."[9]

As the situation worsened, many consuls grew skeptical of the assurances promised by the persons offering support. Affidavits carried a moral obligation but were not legally binding. "Misled by sympathy, a few people whose financial situation does not warrant their taking on added responsibility, have sent affidavits of support," noted an article (1939) on refugees and American immigration law. "This is cruel kindness. When an American consul finds, for instance, that a school teacher who, judging from her bank statement, has been able to save little of her salary, had made affidavits of support for ten of the visa applicants on his waiting lists, he is less likely to attach weight to this class of documents."[10] As Gumpert observed, consuls therefore valued relatives over friends and asked about the precise kinship tie. The closer the better.

Not all consuls followed the state department line or accepted its prejudices. If the affidavit system was used solely to support family members, the American consul general in Hamburg John Erhardt observed (1936), only five thousand German Jews would qualify every year, while the quota allowed twenty-five thousand immigrants from Germany. And the system contradicted American values. It favored those with "well-to-do American relatives willing to make out affidavits of support" but did not consider "their potential suitability to adapt themselves to the American scene."[11]

Responsible for determining whether an applicant would become a public charge, consuls wielded a great deal of autonomous power. The consul general in Zurich routinely rejected affidavits submitted to him by Austrian-Jewish refugees who had been admitted into Switzerland for a short sojourn and sought to move on to America. Almost none passed muster with him. Alarmed by this abuse of power, gentile refugee workers took the affidavits to the consul general in Vienna, who accepted them. Unfortunately, this did not help the applicants; they could not return to Austria to be processed.[12]

Perhaps because they witnessed the abuse of Jews, the consulate staff in Vienna tried to do its best. Far too often this was far too little, but the civility with which employees behaved differed so markedly from the actions in the street that refugees commented upon it. Remembering the consulate buildings, the Austrian-Jewish journalist and essayist Anton Kuh mused that Jews found more than their "dreams and desires" within those doors. "When we look back we find that our predilection for these Consulate buildings sprang from a more intimate personal motive. Here, we felt, we were not different from other people. It was not the pitying looks of the officials nor their gentle manners and voices which bespoke their understanding and solidarity that pleased us so much, but rather the way we were made to feel that our dignity and equality with all other men had been regained. It may sound paradoxical but it was not the welcome accorded us as potential Americans but the fact that we were treated as *fully privileged Europeans* that raised our morale."[13]

No matter how humane the consul, an affidavit from close kin remained key, and Jews in Europe sifted through old letters and scrutinized telephone directories in search of family in America. As we have seen, it was in just this way that Robert Rosner's family found a cousin in New Jersey; he supplied the affidavit that served as the first step toward the rescue of the entire family. Bernhard Mansbach's affidavit came from someone with the same family name, but no family connection. A thirty-seven-year-old salesman in Worms, Bernhard Mansbach lost his job when his firm was "Aryanized." He wrote to a certain Manfred Schiff, an acquaintance who had left earlier and settled in Baltimore. Schiff was not in a position to provide an affidavit, but he offered to approach his wealthy cousin George Mansbach, who ran the Baltimore branch of the family retail clothing business. Charitable and childless, he had already sponsored five German-Jewish refugees. George was certain that the two Mansbach families were not kin, but he agreed to provide affidavits for both Bernhard and his brother Leo.

In the affidavit he signed (11 October 1938), George declared that he earned fifteen thousand dollars a year as vice president of Mansbach Brothers, and his bank account balance averaged well over five thousand dollars. "I am the friend of Bernhard Mansbach, born December 29, 1899, at Worms," he wrote. "I am familiar with the background, education, character and ability of Bernhard Mansbach. For this reason and because of my sympathy for him under present conditions in Europe, I am anxious to help him as much as possible."

The consular officials in Stuttgart were not persuaded, objecting that at sixty-seven George was too old to guarantee financial support. "I wish to state that I am in perfect good health, attend to my business affairs every day," George replied. "Attached is a photograph of myself which shows that I am far from being old and decrepit but am still sturdy and [in] best of good health." Still, to bolster the case George asked his nephew Harry Mansbach, a lawyer from Norfolk, to provide a second affidavit.

As the process crawled forward, events moved on the ground. Arrested in the November pogrom, Bernhard was sent to Buchenwald. Fortunately, he was already on the visa track, and thus his family could obtain a form letter issued by the consulate to everyone whose release from concentration camp depended on a guarantee that they would leave the country. The documents in support of emigration had been examined and found sufficient, the letter affirmed. As soon as the quota number became available, a visa would be issued. This paper freed Bernhard from Buchenwald. It also enabled him to travel in May 1939 to England, where he joined his brother Leo and his parents, who had left earlier. Like Robert Rosner's sister Erna and her husband Hans, Bernhard Mansbach was allowed into Britain because he could provide credible proof of intent to move on. And he did. Granted visa number 9089 by the American consulate in England (September 1939), Bernhard traveled to New York with a ticket George bought for him on the Dutch liner *Volendam*.[14]

.   .   .

BRITAIN, UNLIKE THE UNITED STATES, never envisioned itself as a country of immigration. Not before 1933, not in 1933, and not in 1938–9. America sought to keep Jews out as immigrants; Britain stopped them at the door as refugees. The question Whitehall faced was how to effect this. As London, Berlin, and Vienna had abolished their mutual visa requirements in 1927, German and Austrian Jews did not have this step to negotiate to enter Britain in 1933. Alarmed, London discussed the need to reintroduce a visa in order to control the influx of refugees, but the decision was taken to rely instead upon a muscular prohibition of leave to land at the ports and borders.

Germany's denationalization law of 1938 triggered fears of incoming hordes, and Britain slapped a visa obligation on everyone with a German or Austrian passport.[15] The British Jewish community and refugee organizations agreed with this policy. Endorsing the decision, Otto Schiff, chairman of the German Jewish Aid Committee, observed that it allowed British officials and representatives of his organization to select those to be admitted locally. "The experience of the last five years had shown that it was very difficult to get rid of a refugee when this course seemed desirable once he had entered and spent a few months in this country," Schiff declared at a meeting with Home Secretary Sir Samuel Hoare and members of the Jewish Board of Deputies. "The imposition of the visa was especially necessary in the case of Austrians who were largely of the shop-keeper and small trader class and would therefore prove very much more difficult to emigrate than the average German who had come to the United Kingdom."[16] Raising the ante, Hoare pointed out that "it would be necessary for the Home Office to discriminate very carefully as to the type of refugee who could be admitted to this country. If a flood of the wrong type of immigrants were allowed in there might be serious danger of anti-Semitic feeling being aroused in this country. The last thing we wanted here," he concluded, "was the creation of a Jewish problem."[17]

There the matter stood. The new visa regulations went into effect in May 1938, and the sieve was meant to strain fine. Whitehall warned consuls and passport officers that many people would seek a temporary visa but, after arrival, apply to remain indefinitely and expulsion would prove nearly impossible. Therefore, everyone was to be treated like a potential emigrant, including those who had traveled to Great Britain regularly in the past and who "may in present conditions be anxious to establish himself in the United Kingdom." Jewish businessmen and commercial travelers fell into this category. "Such persons, especially those who appear to be of Jewish or partly Jewish origin, or have non-Aryan affiliations, should be discreetly questioned as to their family circumstances, and how their business or employment has been affected by recent events; and if it is suspected that emigration is intended the applicant should be invited to say so frankly."[18] With such a frank statement the chance for a visa vanished.

Consular authorities were empowered to deny visas to many groups of people: "small shop-keepers, retail traders, artisans, and persons likely to seek employment. Agents and middlemen, whose livelihood depends on commission and therefore on trade activity. Minor musicians and commercial artists of all kinds. The rank and file of professional men— lawyers, doctors and dentists." They could grant visas to "those of *international* repute." Applications by merely "leading" scientists and artists and wealthy industrialists were to be referred to London.[19]

Refugee policy, in short, was a means of enriching Britain's intellectual, cultural, and business capital. Thus Sigmund Freud received a warm welcome.[20] Ernest Jones, a psychoanalyst and great admirer, flew to Vienna to help after the SA looted Freud's apartment. Returning to London, he chatted with Hoare, who belonged to the same ice-skating club as he. Jones soon obtained permission for Freud, his family, and a few associates to move to Britain. Still, it took Anna Freud some weeks to organize papers, see to payment of the Reich flight tax of RM31,329 by Freud's disciple Marie Bonaparte (as his accounts were frozen), and pack the family's furniture and her father's books and collection of antiquities. The Gestapo ordered Freud to sign a document stating that the authorities had treated him "with all the respect and consideration due to my scientific reputation." Obtaining permission to include an addendum before he signed, Freud wrote: "I can heartily recommend the Gestapo to anyone." Shortly after their arrival in London, Freud rejoiced in a letter to his brother Alexander in Switzerland, "We have been inundated with flowers and could easily have suffered serious indigestion from fruit and sweets."[21]

Few ranked so high on the ladder of fame as Freud, and those who fell one rung below fared poorly; no one rushed to their aid. Dr Lothar Fürth owned and ran one of the most important obstetric and gynecological clinics in Vienna. Housed in an imposing six-story structure built by the prominent Swiss architect Hans Wilhelm Auer, the Sanatorium Fürth attested to the reputation and success of the Fürth family.[22] But his was merely local renown, and that counted for little in spring 1938. Fürth wrote a letter to his acquaintance Martin Sherwood in England on 28 March, a fortnight after the Anschluss. "I am coming to you now with a great, great favour I have to beg for: could you possibly do something for me? I am no Airan & so probably my work here will be at an end very soon I know of the great difficulties to get a license in England but I am in a state to accept any proposal even a not medical one if I could come to your country & earn a modest living for me & my wife, who would work too if necessary. Perhaps I could help you in your work?" Fürth understood that he would arrive with nothing, and he wanted Sherwood to know in advance that he would be penniless. "I can only leave here letting *every thing* behind me so that migrating would be landing without money even to buy food or a room."[23]

Sherwood wrote (5 April) to the German Jewish Aid Committee, which in turn tried to get in touch with Dr Fürth through its Vienna representatives. The committee reported back that the agent "made the terrible discovery that he & his wife had meanwhile committed suicide."[24] Hauled out of the clinic by a mob, they had been forced to clean the pavement in front of the building with toothbrushes. They killed themselves the next day.[25] Lothar Fürth was one of thirty-two hundred Jewish medical practitioners in 1938 Vienna and one of the fifteen who committed suicide between March and May. Would he have been one of the fifty physicians from all of Greater Germany the British Medical Association permitted into Britain?[26]

If Britain admitted only fifty Jews with permission to practice medicine, Whitehall opened the door to fourteen thousand Jewish women willing to work as domestic servants.[27] British middle class women had scrambled to find servants since World War I, and they pressed the government to ease the labor market in this arena. At its annual meeting in October 1937, the two-million-member National Council of Women of Great Britain adopted a resolution claiming that the "difficulty of obtaining domestic help tends to restrict families to an extent dangerous to the State" and called on the minister of labor "to grant permits freely to approved young women of other nationalities, who desire to come to this country to enter domestic service."[28]

This amounted to a mandate. And Jews in Greater Germany offered a new pool of potential domestics to fill in for the gentile German and Austrian women who no longer needed work now that rearmament generated full employment at home. Whitehall relaxed some of its regulations (fall 1938), allowing married couples to obtain domestic permits and lowering the age limit for women from eighteen to sixteen. With the whole operation under the administrative umbrella of the Central Office of Refugees, a streamlined system developed to send refugees to Britain as domestic servants.

Typically, an advertisement by the hopeful emigrants appeared in a British paper. "Austrian émigré couple, English speaking, wife excellent cook, husband chauffeur all branches, help house, garden. Go anywhere England, Colonies. JOSEF SCHLESINGER, Haupostlagernd, Stettin," read one ad in the *New Statesman and Nation*. Single people, nearly all women, placed notices as well. "Viennese lady (25), Jewish, good family, fond of children, excellent domestic work and sewing, seeks position in household or with children. IRENA KOFLER, Vienna II, Vereinsgasse 24/15."[29] Interested employers contacted the ministry of labor and the coordinating committee. These agencies verified the offer of employment and that the potential employees were indeed Jews seeking asylum. Finding all in order, they submitted a file to the home office, which sent a visa authorization to the consulate. It was left to local passport control officers to make the final decision.[30]

Sometimes those judgments baffled the officers working on the ground. Writing to the director of passport control Maurice Jeffes, the passport officer in Paris observed, "I have always considered that healthy young females with home experience may be accepted, but there are other cases where I feel sure that the word 'suitable' is a euphemism. For instance, I recently had an ex-actress who, while physically able to do domestic work, did not seem the kind of person who would settle down to it easily."[31] Should he issue a visa?

Some Jews eager to emigrate found the interview with the passport control officer a bit of a challenge too. Thea Scholl and her sister had offers of domestic servant positions, their tax papers settled, and valid passports. With all these papers in hand, she stood "for a night in the Wallnerstrasse" to enter the British consulate. "I was 22 at that time, and had never done any housework," she recalled years later. "Our mother never wanted us to do anything." To her surprise, "I had to show my hands at the consulate, probably to prove that they were not manicured and that I was able to work. . . . Then I had to clean a bathroom, to show that I was able to do so. My sister had to cook." The consulate had instituted an "exam to show that we knew how to do domestic work." Thea's family flat had no bathroom, and so "I was not used to cleaning tiles. But the tub, thank God, that I managed well." She passed. "I thus received absolution. I got my visa from the Jewish community in Vienna, and I left on 24 December 1938." Relief and grief mingled. "The farewell was very sad. We stood there at the station, my parents in tears."[32]

Jeffes inspected George Berry's visa operation in Vienna. "I was very favourably impressed with the admirable way the business of this office is now being conducted," he reported to the home office. "Berry, the Passport Control Officer, had managed to eliminate the queue nuisance." Jeffes was, however, "appalled to see the bad type of refugees" who had been approved by the committee and the ministry of labour. Several women "were so filthily dirty both in their person and their clothing that they were utterly unfit to go inside a decent British home."[33] Antisemitic tripe, perhaps: the dirty Jew. More likely, Jeffes expressed the thoughtless disdain of the privileged. He did not stop to consider the restricted shopping hours and sharply limited access to goods like soap and detergent under which these Jewish women labored.

Clean or dirty, Jewish women rightly saw domestic service in "a decent British home" as their salvation. Within days of the German-imposed protectorate of Bohemia and Moravia (March 1939), Anna Roth-Steinova, then thirty-four, wrote to an English colleague, Doris Campbell. The two women belonged to the Girl Guides movement and

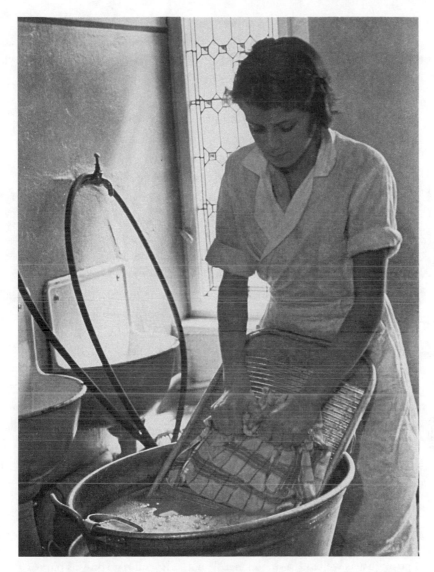

Hoping to emigrate, Jewish girls and young women learn to do housework in a course run by the Berlin Jewish community in 1936.

PHOTOGRAPHER: ABRAHAM PISAREK.

had met at an international jamboree in 1930. "After the recent changes
in the last days you most probably have thought of your friend in Prague,"
Anna wrote to Doris on 17 March 1939. "The purpose of my letter today
is to ask you if you could find a post for me in England as a cook so that
I could get permit for coming there and work there." She had done her
homework. "I have just looked into the form where all the conditions
are under which people can enter England. I shall copy it for your information and enclose it with this letter." Single when Doris had met her
in 1930, Anna was married and had a six-year-old daughter, Milena, in
1939. "I think for me as married woman, two comes into consideration.
For the married couple, she as cook and domestic worker, he as gardener,
chauffeur, and other work in the same family." At that point, Anna's plan
was to organize employment for her husband and herself. "We should
then see what could be done with our little daughter."[34]

Through Doris or another source, Anna got an offer for a post and
her work permit application was accepted. Doris evidently agreed to
furnish a guarantee for Milena, and by 23 June Anna hoped that her
daughter would be included in a transport of children scheduled to leave
Prague for London on 15 July. Perhaps because of the time it took to
organize Milena's departure, Anna's job offer fell through. In the meantime, however, Doris's servants had left and she needed domestic help.
The prospect now opened for all three to live together in Doris's house
with Anna and her husband Emil working as cook and gardener. With
this in view, Anna and Emil sent Milena ahead.

For a time it seemed that their dream would materialize. "Now
imagine, have you heard THAT I HAVE GOT MY PERMIT?" Anna
crowed to Doris on 12 August. One problem resolved, but Emil's permit
was still pending. Anna worried whether he could get "a Domestic Work
Permit just as well as I, a single one." If not, if he could go only as part of a
couple, "then it would be more advisable for us to wait both together here
for this Permit, because, there would then be no more chance for Emil
to get him over." Learning that Doris applied for a double permit, Anna
and Emil waited to join Milena. "I think I shall be able to leave something ROUND ABOUT THE 20TH SEPTEMBER," Anna wrote. "I
don't think it will be quicker, but I do hope will not take longer."[35]

War intervened. "9th September 1939 . . . I feel awfully sorry that I could not leave in time. It means that I shall live in great sorrows and unquietness, when she [Milena] is there and I am here."[36] Milena never saw her parents again. Instead of a couple to serve them, Doris and her husband Arthur received a foster child. If Anna's energy and agency had not yielded the result she intended, surely her pursuit of a domestic service permit had saved her daughter.

Thousands of Jewish women in the major cities of Greater Germany sought to avail themselves of the opportunity offered by domestic service in spring 1939. In Berlin, the Hilfsverein took control over the selection of prospective maids in an attempt to avoid duplication of effort and perhaps too to maintain their relationship with the local passport control officer, Frank Foley. They quite rightly counted Foley as a friend to such prominent members of the Hilfsverein as department store owner Wilfred Israel and Zionist activist Hubert Pollack,[37] as well as to ordinary Jews with whom he had no personal relationship. As one contemporary observer recalled, Foley "felt a genuine compassion for the throngs that day-in and day-out besieged his office with their applications, requests and enquiries." Nor did he ever forget that he dealt with human beings. "The winter of 1938 was a harsh one, and elderly men and women waited from six in the morning, queuing up in the snow and biting wind. Captain Foley saw to it that a uniformed commissionaire trundled a tea-urn on a trolley along the line of frozen misery."[38]

The Hilfsverein did not know that Foley was a British secret service agent. Nor did they know that although it was in his interest to protect his cover as a passport control officer by following regulations closely, he did not; through clandestine means he saved thousands. The Hilfsverein's initiative to regulate the selection of women for domestic service appears to have aimed at ensuring that the women who applied for permits were sufficiently qualified for Foley to approve. Motivated by a wish to avoid awkwardness, streamline the system, and also to enable the women to do their jobs well, the Jewish community established domestic service training schools. Women seeking a visa through employment as a maid now had to pass an exam. Perhaps this dissuaded many; only two hundred women left Germany to take up domestic service each week in early spring 1939 although four hundred such permits were issued.[39]

Even so, employers found much to fault in their new maids, and many refugee women found domestic service more daunting than they had expected. The Domestic Bureau of the Central Office for Refugees issued a pamphlet to help everyone adjust. It explained to employers that "English Homes are Different from German Ones!" and that "English Food is Different." Perhaps most important, it reminded the employers, "For most of the Maids this is a New Career." Addressing the political circumstances, the authors observed, "England is a Foreign Country for these Maids, and they may be home-sick, even though their homeland has become for them intolerable." As for the refugee servants, they needed to remember that "they are received into English households through friendliness and good will and it behoves them to be a credit to their people and to their religion, as the public are apt to judge all from one."[40]

Jewish refugees took work as domestic servants because that offered just about the sole route into Britain. Other avenues opened after the November pogrom, thanks in no small measure to Philip Baker, who had worked with Nansen and in 1938 served as a member of parliament for Derby. In a powerful speech to the House of Commons that situated the Jews in the context of the refugee problem as whole, Baker mustered the imagination, empathy, and confidence of his colleagues. He detailed the Nazis' antisemitic program of the past five years and described the violence of the pogrom less than a fortnight earlier. "Where is this going to end?" he asked. And, he added, "What is it going to mean to us before it is ended?"[41] Home Secretary Samuel Hoare rose to speak in response. Hoare too had worked with Nansen, "dealing with the Russian refugees in Constantinople and in the Balkans." His view of Britain's refugee policy now, after the November pogrom, clearly was informed by his memory of "this tragic experience, these thousands of men and women stranded on the streets of Constantinople without a means of livelihood, upon the verge of starvation, in a no-man's land which did not wish to receive them."[42]

Britain would do more than it had. To mollify potential critics, Hoare hastened to explain that the new policy aimed at easing the way for "trans-migrants" furnishing proof that they would not become a burden on the state. "While the absorptive powers of this country might be limited as far as permanent residents are concerned, we certainly could take in larger numbers of refugees for a temporary period, provided they were eventually to be settled in some other part of the world."[43] Adducing credible proof of further emigration within the next two years, thousands of German, Austrian, and Czech Jews who had obtained an American quota number valid for immigration in 1940 or 1941 could move to Britain immediately. Thus, as we have seen, Bernhard Mansbach entered the country, as did Erna Rosner and her husband Hans. Other groups were eligible for entry as well. Children under the age of eighteen qualified for a temporary stay, as did people between sixteen and thirty-five who were to attend a vocational training program to prepare them for emigration overseas. Perhaps this provision opened the door to Lore Saalheimer, who came to Britain on a student visa after the November pogrom. Persons over sixty with guaranteed support qualified for permanent residence. Finally, London unofficially relaxed the rules to help imprisoned Jewish men who needed visas urgently to be released from concentration camps. Anxious about their fate, the Council for British Jewry negotiated a deal with Whitehall in January 1939; the council established a refugee camp to house the men, while Whitehall agreed to recognize them above and beyond the officially identified categories of refugees.[44]

BRITAIN WAS A MAJOR POWER, separated from Germany by land and water. Weighing national priorities against international relations, London introduced a visa requirement (1938) on everyone with a German or Austrian passport, no matter the risk of antagonizing Berlin. Switzerland, by contrast, was a small nation right on the other side of the border from the Reich. Economic and social bonds between the two countries militated against visa obligations. Reluctant to provoke its aggressive neighbor or to disrupt those ties, Switzerland also worried about *Überfremdung* (overrun by foreigners). According to the census of 1910, 14.7 percent of the Swiss population were foreigners, compared to 3.1 percent in Belgium, 2.7 in France, 2.1 in Austria, and 1.7 in Germany. Unless drastic measures were taken, the cabinet warned the federal assembly in 1924, half of the inhabitants of Switzerland would be foreigners by 1990. A special police department, the *Fremdenpolizei* (Aliens' Police) was established to keep Switzerland for the Swiss, and by 1930 it had reduced the total number of foreigners to 8.7 percent. Strict policing during the 1920s and '30s ensured that refugees of all stripes got only a short respite in their "onward migration" to a country of permanent asylum.[45] But by 1938 Bern feared that these measures might not suffice. Perhaps imposing a visa on German and Austrian passport holders—which Berlin would interpret as a diplomatic slap—provided the sole solution to Überfremdung.

The Überfremdung discourse initially pertained to all foreigners. Influenced by Nazism, however, antisemitic rhetoric linked the perceived problems of Überfremdung and *Überjudung* (too many Jews).[46] Heinrich Rothmund, head of the Fremdenpolizei and chief of the police department in the ministry of justice and police, explained the connection in a lecture he delivered in Zurich in April 1937. "The Jewish Question," he declared, was a pure "Überfremdung problem." Deploring the antisemitism rampant in Germany, Rothmund affirmed national acceptance of the small, long-established, and well assimilated Swiss-Jewish community. They belonged. Foreign Jews did not. "Working for our country's best interest, the Aliens' Police will carry on its strict practices, even when this gives rise, as has happened, to the accusation of anti-Semitism."[47] Rothmund had served as the Swiss delegate on the Governing Board that oversaw McDonald's work as high commissioner and, later, as the Swiss delegate in Evian. He helped shape as well as enforce Swiss refugee policy. And his sentiment reflected that of most of his countrymen.

The Swiss policy of serving as a transit station worked well until 1938. All but one hundred of the nearly six thousand Jews who had arrived since 1933 had moved on.[48] With the Anschluss, however, trains filled with Jewish refugees crossed the border. In less than three weeks some four thousand Jews poured into Switzerland.[49] Alarmed, the federal council (the Swiss cabinet) met to discuss the refugee situation (28 March). The Swiss foreign ministry soon instructed its envoy in Berlin, Paul Dinichert, to discuss this matter with Gustav Rödiger at the German foreign office. In the course of their negotiations, Dinichert devised his own solution, which he suggested to his superiors first. "The simplest solution, of course, would be to limit the visa obligation to non-Aryan German nationals," he proposed. "This goes against our principles of course, but could be justified in that it is also in the interest of Swiss Jews to resist a further influx of foreign Jews."[50]

Before the matter was resolved, government attention veered from visas, which controlled legal entry, to the clandestine influx of refugees over the green border. Reporting to the federal council (19 August 1938), Rothmund announced that over a thousand people had slipped into Switzerland in July and at certain points more than two hundred refugees crossed the border every night, often accompanied to the frontier by SS men. The local Jewish communities, which took care of the refugees, were at a breaking point. Departure for other countries was impossible. The federal council ordered the reinforcement of border patrols and the return of all illegal immigrants to Germany.[51]

Neither Rothmund nor the members of the federal council dealt with refugees face-to-face, and they had no sympathy for them or their plight. Notwithstanding the direct contact that ensued from their job, few policemen guarding the Swiss border evinced compassion or pity, either. St. Gallen police chief Paul Grüninger stood in contrast to his colleagues, and spoke his mind at a meeting chaired by Rothmund of federal and cantonal authorities. "Expelling? How, when fifty come together? From a humanitarian point of view this is just impossible. Heartbreaking scenes! And in any case, there are many who call themselves political refugees. We must admit many."[52] He could have saved his breath. Rothmund dispatched military units to help seal the border. Appalled, Grüninger turned to "illegal" rescue efforts, issuing false documents to all who managed to make their way across the border in his region.

Now that the green border problem had been solved, Rothmund returned to the visa issue. Diplomatic fallout was not his problem, and he pressed the federal council to impose a visa obligation on all German passport holders. The council followed his advice (30 August), and Rothmund met with German envoy Otto Köcher in Bern a few days later. Köcher suggested another solution. If the German government marked the passports of German and Austrian Jews identifying them as Jews, would the Swiss forgo a general visa obligation? In his report of the conversation, Rothmund wrote that although "technically" possible, this procedure was politically delicate. And he repeated, underlining the crucial word, "I could only tell him that this solution was *technically* possible."[53] Rothmund believed that he had convinced Köcher that there was no alternative to a visa for all German nationals. Köcher saw the matter differently: Rothmund's willingness to discuss the option of marking Jews' passports opened the door to a different set of negotiations, and the envoy needed no encouragement to pursue the idea. He cabled Berlin immediately after the meeting. "Dr. Rothmund states adoption of visa only for Jews technically feasible, if border officials can see at first glance that bearer of pass Jew."[54]

Berlin greeted this news with relief, and Rödiger met with the Swiss chargé d'affaires in Berlin, Franz Kappeler. The German government was eager to help the Swiss deal with the situation, Rödiger assured Kappeler. They stood ready to mark the passports of Jews and to accept a visa requirement for passports thus marked. Perhaps a stamp in the top left corner of the first page: a large letter *J* surrounded by a circle two centimeters wide? Kappeler agreed that this would do nicely. Nor did he blink when Rödiger mentioned that as a matter of course, the German government would have to insist on reciprocity—as customary in international relations.[55]

Kappeler argued that "the number of Swiss Jews who wish to travel to Germany in the present circumstances must be small" and therefore inconvenienced or offended few, but Rothmund was furious. "*Unacceptable* in my opinion for Swiss Jews," he barked down the phone to the chargé in Berlin and followed up in a memo to the federal justice and police department.[56] Indeed, even if the Germans were to drop the demand for reciprocity, the Swiss should be wary of accepting their proposal to mark the passports of German Jews. First, German authorities could not be trusted. Furthermore, the moment they had solved the problem of how to expel Jews, the Nazis would turn against the church, causing another stream of refugees. And finally, the government should consider Switzerland's reputation abroad. "It is very clear Germany's actions until now, and especially with its last proposal, attempts to push us toward anti-Semitism, or at least attempts to make us appear so in the view of other countries," Rothmund warned.[57]

The Germans wooed Rothmund. German Minister Plenipotentiary Köcher called on him in Bern. His government wished to avoid the visa obligation at all costs, he explained; it feared it would inspire other countries to follow suit. Rothmund remained adamant. Köcher returned the next day accompanied by Dr Hans Josef Maria Globke, a high-ranking bureaucrat in the ministry of the interior who had helped draft the Nuremberg Laws. He too tried to soothe the Swiss chief of police.[58] Seeing the energy the Germans invested, the Swiss government worried about a diplomatic crisis. Hoping to co-opt Rothmund by making him responsible for negotiating an agreement, the federal council sent him to Berlin. Its strategy proved successful. He capitulated. His assent, he clarified, "pertains only to the technical side of the control." The larger political and moral issues fell to the federal council, and it had to decide whether to endorse the proposal.[59] The Swiss government saw no difficulties. And the German government promptly declared all passports held by Jews invalid. Jews had to turn in their passports for revalidation "with a symbol designated by the Reich Minister of the Interior, which will mark the holder as a Jew."[60] The service was provided "free of charge."[61]

Still, the St. Gallen police chief Paul Grüninger continued to provide false papers to refugees who stole into Switzerland, and he somehow managed to send Swiss entry permits to Jewish inmates in Dachau, which released them and got them out of the country. He routinely submitted false reports to his superior Valentin Keel about the numbers of refugees refused, expelled, received, and housed, admitting to perhaps 10 percent of the actual number of Jews he had let in. Keel knew Grüninger was lying, Rothmund assumed he was. Rothmund leaned on Keel, and Keel, who had condoned Grüninger's actions with a "don't ask, don't tell" policy, now suspended the police chief's authority with regard to refugees and commissioned a secret inquiry into his activities. Grüninger was refused access to his office in April and fired in May 1939. Put on trial in 1940, he was convicted for falsifying documents, fined, and stripped of his job, benefits, and pension. The judges noted that he had not sought personal profit; his actions arose from the "objectively illegal, but subjective humanly understandable and forgivable" wish to give shelter to people in need.[62] If the judges showed sympathy, Grüninger's neighbors did not. Shunned, he led a life on the margins of St. Gallen society, surviving on odd jobs until shortly before he died in 1972.

And what of Jews who fell into others' hands? Border guard Fehr intercepted five refugees from Vienna near Basel on 19 December 1938: an assistant fitter Leo and his wife Irma Preis, both aged twenty-two; a shop assistant named Otto Klein; a tailor's apprentice Walter Kornfein; and a roofer Jakob Kurz, all three aged eighteen. Accompanied by three policemen, the five refugees were brought to the local customs office "and at 5:00 handed over to the German frontier officials." No hope of return. "The note 'Turned back' was entered in their passports. When Mrs Preis found out that she had to return to Germany, she collapsed unconscious and had to be carried to the border."[63]

From the Yad Vashem database of Holocaust victims we learn the fate of all five. Leo and Irma ended up in Brno, whence they were deported in November 1941 to Minsk ghetto where they died. Otto Klein and Walter Kornfein ended up in Yugoslavia, where they were murdered in 1941. Jakob Kurz fled to Lvov in eastern Poland. He was murdered in 1941, shortly after the German army entered the city.

THE RUPTURE
OF DEPARTURE

Wʜᴇɴ ᴛʜᴇ ɢᴇʀᴍᴀɴs ᴡᴀʟᴋᴇᴅ ɪɴᴛᴏ ᴀᴜsᴛʀɪᴀ ɪɴ ᴍᴀʀᴄʜ 1938, thirteen-year-old Gerda Geiringer and her eleven-year-old sister Ilse lived in a private children's home in Vienna. Their parents had divorced in 1926; after seven years of custody battles, a judge had sent the young-sters to live in a children's home. Owned and run by a Jewish direc-tor, the nondenominational institution was shut down shortly after the Anschluss, and the Jewish children—including Gerda and Ilse—went to an orphanage run by the Kultusgemeinde. Herr Geiringer, from a well-to-do family, remained in the city. Frau Geiringer, who had had a lot of trouble making ends meet and who had accumulated a substantial tax debt, realized that she had better leave the country. "She thought that she would have great difficulties leaving the country with all these debts hanging over her, so that was the reason she went over the green border to Switzerland. She went alone with the intention of coming back to call for us in the home she would make for us there."[1]

Leaving in 1938 before Rothmund reinforced the Swiss border patrols, Frau Geiringer made it to Zurich and established herself. "She wasn't allowed to work, but she spoke Italian and German, and she could type, so she did black [off the books] labor." In July she sent word to Gerda that the two children should attend a certain cousin's wedding and that she would smuggle herself back into the country, pick them up at the wedding party and take them back with her by the same illegal route. "The wedding day arrived, and I and all the other children from the orphanage returned to the home from school. The way things worked there was that we all had to line up in front of the dining room, and as we went into the dining room they looked at our fingers, were they clean, and 'Have you washed your ears and your face and the front and back of your hands, and off you go to lunch.' I was on that line and they looked at my ears to see if they were clean—and they found lice. That was the routine every day, and the day before I didn't have lice, but *that* day I had lice. . . . So [my sister went to the wedding and] I was left behind. A little louse changed my life." Her mother and sister crossed the border successfully and made it safely to Zurich. Gerda and her father remained in Vienna.[2]

Gerda's father "had taken up work in the Kultusgemeinde, making all sorts of plans for groups to go to Uruguay, Paraguay, to Australia, to everywhere." He looked too for exit routes for himself and for Gerda. "He was to go with a group to Australia which actually should have left Vienna on the fifth of September 1939 and never left. He sent me on a children's transport to England, which he had access to, being on the staff."[3]

With the permission of the British, Dutch, and Swedish governments, aid organizations in Greater Germany organized kindertransports, special trains laid on to send endangered children west to safety. The children on board these trains left their parents and other family members at the railway stations of Prague, Vienna, Frankfurt, Berlin, Leipzig, the free city of Danzig, and the Polish city of Zbonszyn. Descriptions abound of chaos, and tears, and the unending pain of the parents.

In Gerda's memory, community staff filled spots on the train on a first come, first served basis. As her father worked in the Kultusgemeinde, he acted quickly to sign her up; wealth did not enter into it. This may be correct. Robert Rosner (as we have seen), also from Vienna, the same age as Gerda Geiringer, got on a transport in April 1939, and his

German-Jewish kindertransport children on a bus in the Netherlands, c. 1938.

family had no connections and was so poor that his mother waited for her husband to come home with his earnings every day so that she could go out to shop for their evening meal.

Gerda remembered the preparations for the trip. "From the moment I knew I was going on that transport, I made myself clothes. I made three or four dresses for myself. I can draw them still. My father went with me to get material in Judengasse; he had friends there."[4] Robert's preparations were of a different sort. "I remember I went to Wiener-wald, because I wanted to say farewell to those places which were of importance to me. It had always been part of our family life, because my mother went with us on Sundays to the Vienna woods. So I remember I went to Wienerwald."[5]

The kindertransports from Austria chugged into Germany, through Cologne, over the border into the Netherlands, up to the Hook of Holland, across the North Sea, to dock at Harwich. Gerda crossed into Holland late at night. "It was dark. There had been rumors in the train that we had already passed the Dutch border. 'No, we're still in Germany . . . no . . . no . . .' The train came to various stops, pulled up and started again, pulled up, started again. Our spirits went lower and lower and lower. Suddenly the light came on and there were hundreds of people at the platform, everyone with a package in his hand and they handed all those packages in. There were ham and cheese and chocolate sandwiches. Something to drink too. But those chocolate sandwiches with white bread and butter and chocolate—it was a funny taste, a surprising taste, but we liked it."[6]

Children going on to England went by boat to Harwich. Some, like Robert, were sent from there to London. Others, like Gerda, went to Dovercourt Bay, a holiday camp taken over to accommodate arriving youngsters.

NEWSPAPER REPORTS DESCRIBING THE VIOLENCE of the November pogrom prompted public sympathy and government action in Britain. The Munich Gestapo ordered all Jews to leave the city in forty-eight hours and "to let the police know by 6 p.m. today at what time they would hand over the keys of their dwellings and garages,"[7] the *Times* reported on 11 November. "Misery, terror, and despair," an article following developments in that city observed a few days later. Nearly all the Jewish men had been arrested, and the women were unable to buy food. "This morning Jewish women were heard imploring to be served with milk, not for themselves but for their children."[8] Conditions in Vienna were no better, readers learned. "The position of Austria's Jews is becoming daily more precarious," an article of 14 November reported. "Although the more violent demonstrations have ceased the Nazis have prohibited non-Jewish stores, restaurants and cafés from selling to Jews. As no Jewish shops have been allowed to reopen the effect has been to reduce many Jews to a position dangerously near starvation."[9]

The plight of children struck an especially resonant chord. Stories circulated about attacks against Jewish orphanages and children roaming the countryside on the verge of starvation. These accounts were all too true. Yitzhak Herz, director of the Dinslaken orphanage, recorded the Nazi assault on that particular children's home. Satisfied with their frenzy of looting and trashing the orphanage, SA and SS men ordered the children and staff to march through the town. "The news of the *Judenparade* or *Judenzug* . . . spread like wild-fire through the streets of the town. Three to four rows deep, the Germans filled the pavements of both sides of the street, waiting for the procession," Herz reported in his daily notes. "The small children of the orphanage were forced into a wagon with a long shaft, which was pulled by four teenage boys from the orphanage." The older boys were pushed into a horse stable and terrorized into doing exercises in the middle of the night by a drunk SA man. Children and staff were soon sent back to the now destroyed premises. "Our food reserves had reached a dangerously low level . . . the Nazi Party had prohibited storekeepers from selling us food or doing us any favors . . . the 'junk' we still had (some pots, bags of food, cushions, brooms, etc.) was to be carried by the children. Thus burdened with the remaining belongings of the orphanage we were forced to march through Dinslaken's main street, and this—as was to be expected—during the peak shopping hours."[10]

The Anglo-Jewish community marshaled its resources to mount an effort to rescue children. Helen Bentwich, member of the education committee of the London County Council (and wife of Norman Bentwich, and niece of Sir Herbert Samuel, the first high commissioner of Palestine), and Dennis Cohen, chair of the emigration department of the Jewish Refugees Committee, presented a plan to the Council for German Jewry in a matter of days. They had one aim: to rescue as many youngsters as possible. They envisioned an initial group of five thousand children brought to England two to five hundred at a time and housed in holiday camps that stood empty at that season. So intent were they on rescue that they did not stop to consider details. Whether these camps were winterized, for example, simply did not occur to them. The Council adopted the Bentwich-Cohn plan and, at an emergency session on 14 November, appointed a delegation headed by Lord Samuel to take the matter to the prime minister.[11]

The cabinet committee on foreign policy also met on 14 November. The November pogrom was a great embarrassment for Chamberlain who, on his return from Germany only six weeks earlier, had declared that he had achieved "peace for our time" and had assured the House of Commons that the surrender of the Sudeten to Hitler cleared the way "to make further progress along the road to sanity."[12] On the very eve of the pogrom he had spoken to great approval at the Lord Mayor's Banquet about the Munich agreement.[13] The violence across Germany shone a most unwelcome spotlight on the prime minister's error in judgment, and the cabinet committee sought a path out of the government's political predicament. Home Secretary Hoare worried that if they were not seen to act, "the House of Commons and the country might get out of hand." Chamberlain agreed. The government needed to respond to the "very general and strong desire that something effective should be done to alleviate the terrible fate of the Jews in Germany. Some such action, taken in collaboration with America, would ease the public conscience."[14] But no one adduced a viable proposal, and no one even mentioned Palestine, an obvious option for refuge.

Thus, when Lord Samuel's delegation presented the Bentwich-Cohn plan to Chamberlain the next day, the prime minister listened. The proposal called for the admission of children and young people under age seventeen who would leave Britain after education or training had been completed. Jewish organizations guaranteed that no public funds would be required. In short: a politically advantageous plan from every point of view.

Pressure continued to build. The *Times* carried an appeal (16 November) by the Council for German Jewry to "save all whom it is possible to rescue, especially the young."[15] An editorial entitled "German Jews' Future" depicted the British consulate in Berlin. "A visit to the passport control office here this morning showed that families were often represented by their womenfolk, many of them in tears, while the men of the family waited in a concentration camp until some evidence of likelihood of emigration could be shown to the Secret Police." Most were not eligible for a visa, "since the great number appeared to be 'stateless' through the loss of their German citizenship." Education and apprenticeships had come to an end, "since the training camps in various parts of the Reich in which young Jews were taught farming and prepared in other ways for a new life abroad, were all wrecked during the recent 'demonstrations' and their inmates in many cases severely beaten. State schools of all kinds have now been closed to Jewish children by order of the Minister of Education."[16] All Jews would be expelled from their houses, the *Times* reported two days later.[17] In a letter to the editor in the same issue, Henry McMahon, president of the YMCA, declared that his organization agreed to train Jewish boys between fourteen and eighteen in its farm centers and that Britain needed such workers. "At no time has there ever been any difficulty in finding suitable employment on a farm in this country. There is an admitted shortage of agricultural farm-help of this type in many parts of England largely due to the fact that 42,000 agricultural workers left the land last year."[18]

When Philip Baker brought the refugee question to the floor of the House of Commons, Hoare was fully prepared to support action. It was in the course of this discussion that the government laid the groundwork to open Britain's doors to transmigrants, and it was on that same occasion that Hoare introduced the idea of child transports. And just as he drew upon precedent—his work with Nansen—to set the context for generous action on behalf of adult refugees, so too did he reference the example of Britain's hospitality toward Belgian children during World War I to frame discussion about the Bentwich-Cohn proposal. "We gave homes here to many thousands of Belgian children," he reminded the House, and "we played an invaluable part in maintaining the life of the Belgian nation. So also with these Jewish and non-Aryan children, I believe that we could find homes in this country for a very large number without any harm to our own population." An opportunity to do good had opened. "Here is a chance of taking the young generation of a great people, here is a chance of mitigating to some extent the terrible sufferings of their parents and their friends."[19]

If the action came at a price for Britain, it was far dearer for the parents involved. Speaking of their pain and of the emotional sacrifice they would make, Hoare moved the discussion to another level. "I could not help thinking what a terrible dilemma it was to the Jewish parents in Germany to have to choose between sending their children to a foreign country, into the unknown, and continuing to live in the terrible conditions to which they are now reduced in Germany," the home secretary reflected. Yet he had learned that "Jewish parents were almost unanimously in favour of facing this parting with their children and taking the risks of their children going to a foreign country, rather than keeping them with them to face the unknown dangers with which they are faced in Germany."[20]

There was little to say in opposition to the proposal. A foolish backbencher tried to raise the question of the taxpayers' burden, as the children would attend state schools, and got silenced with the sharp retort "that this disgraceful suggestion should cease to be repeated in the interest of the good name of the house."[21] The sole outstanding policy issue concerned the number of children. Again, Philip Baker had set the agenda. Asking in the House of Commons if the government was willing to admit ten thousand children to Palestine, he got nowhere. But the figure he introduced circulated through Whitehall.[22] Remarkably, by the end of the kindertransports a total of ten thousand children had come to Britain.

The Dutch government too proved willing to help. Soon after the November pogrom, the Dutch consul general in Berlin and senior Gestapo official Werner Best met to discuss, among other issues, "the children problem." The Reich raised no objections: a passport and exit visa would be issued to all youngsters the Dutch government was willing to admit.[23] The Hague, for its part, allowed philanthropic agencies to support refugee children in Holland with private funds, on the principle that they would be educated or trained "for emigration to definitely selected lands."[24] Transmigration shaped policy and practice. Minister of the Interior Hendrik van Boeyen wished to settle children in families; ministry of justice official Coenraad Tenkink preferred to place them in children's colonies. "I fear difficulties when we begin to house children in families," Tenkink cautioned. "The chances of emigration will diminish as a result." Therefore, only those children whose plans to move on came to naught would be taken into families.[25] The government had accepted some fifteen hundred children, van Boeyen informed the cabinet. A few hundred would go to foster families, two hundred were destined for a youth aliyah training camp, and the rest

German-Jewish kindertransport children on the steps of the Ons Boschhuis
children's home in Driebergen, the Netherlands, in May 1939.

would be housed with adult refugees in a central camp.[26] Thousands
more traveled through Holland on their way to England.

WITH POLICY IN PLACE and a transit route established, Jewish communities under Nazi rule and the Movement for the Care of Children from
Germany acted quickly to fill the transports. "The most difficult task had
then to be faced," the first annual report of the movement acknowledged.
"It was known that there were 60,000 children in Austria and Germany,
all anxious to seek safety and refuge in this country. How was it possible

to choose from these the limited number that safely could be gathered in?" Letters poured in from Greater Germany "begging for help, enclosing photographs and particulars . . . yet, how were we to know which children to choose since we could not take all? We obviously could not adopt the principle of 'first write, first come.'"[27] The organization sought a more equitable approach, relying upon the judgment of the Reichsvertretung in Berlin, the Kultusgemeinde in Vienna and, as there was no centralized Jewish body in Bohemia and Moravia, a small committee of English representatives in Prague.

The welfare department of the Kultusgemeinde had created a register of children looking to emigrate after the Anschluss. Within weeks they had recorded more than ten thousand names.[28] The November pogrom set the process in motion in Berlin. Thus, when word came of the opportunity to immigrate to the Netherlands and England, the Kultusgemeinde and the Reichsvertretung had lists of children eager to leave. Community officials in the first instance chose healthy, physically fit youngsters at greatest risk: "danger of internment, death of parents, absence of any means of livelihood." They composed lists and sent them to the movement offices in London, where the names were sent on to the records department, which issued home office permits. A simple card with particulars and a photograph, these permits stood in place of a passport. Stamped by the passport control office, the papers were flown to Berlin, Vienna, and Prague where the Jewish authorities submitted them to Reich officials for permission to emigrate. Stamped again, the cards were given to the leaders of the transports to show upon arrival in England.[29]

The youth aliyah movement, with its goal of immigration to Palestine, also had lists of young people seeking to leave. When the first call for children came to Vienna, the Kultusgemeinde turned to the Zionist organization and its registers. Fritz Deutsch worked in the Palestine Office at the time, although he was no Zionist. Encouraged by his father, Fritz had joined the Boy Scouts when he was twelve. "As I stayed ten years, I got quick promotions and I ended up a group scoutmaster" by age twenty. Fritz's leadership skills and experience with young people stood him in good stead after the Anschluss. Banned from university, he needed something to do, and the youth aliyah movement needed him.

Many of its leaders had immigrated to Palestine, creating a vacuum just when hordes of parents crowded into the offices to register their children in the hope of a speedy departure. Fritz helped to organize preparatory classes for the children and collated eight partial card indexes into a master register of Palestine-bound children.[30]

"Whilst I was working on these records, an urgent message arrived from the *Israelitische Kultusgemeinde*." A first transport of three hundred children was to be organized, and the youth aliyah movement had been allocated a hundred spots. Fritz employed his scout alarm system. "We got eight of our patrol leaders. They came with their bicycles," he recalled. "We got the lists from the Palestine Office of parents who could possibly at very short notice get their children ready to leave. Half an hour or so, we got all eight scouts with their bicycles, and they were given lists. We were working frantically, [sorting names] according to districts, to get as many people as possible as quickly as possible, to get the forms and so on." Their efforts met with success. "Within a few hours, we had hundreds of people queuing up to get the application forms. Then we had to work nonstop: they [the youngsters] had to be photographed, they had to be medically examined and application forms had to be filled in, and all that was done."[31]

Fritz did not compose the lists. "My job was to go through the papers, to interview parents with the children, make the necessary notes and give them papers." He found it "a strange, moving and exhausting experience. Anxious parents were begging and pleading, often crying, trying to make sure that their child would be on the list." Fritz turned to the paperwork after dealing with the people. "I was then typing the list all night. Together with Mrs Grünwald, a very efficient typist. They wanted eight copies. We had two typewriters, and this lady was using one and I was typing the other. I never typed so well in all my life! We typed the lists of the people that were ready with all their documentation." Inevitably, not all children were chosen according to the established criteria. "People misused their positions sometimes. Let's call it favoritism."[32]

Children sent under this system were "unguaranteed cases," as no one in particular had guaranteed to maintain them until the age of eighteen or to send them to school. The movement served as guarantor.

Gerda Geiringer emigrated in this way. Robert Rosner and Milena Roth, by contrast, came under "guaranteed" status: Professor Littler and Doris Campbell vouched to care for Robert and Milena, respectively. Neither the Kultusgemeinde nor the Prague committee selected these children. They had found guarantors through personal channels.

Touched by newspaper reports and movement appeals, guarantors sprang up across Britain. "Offers of hospitality poured in from all areas and classes. Within a fortnight, 500 suitable homes were found," the organization reported. Press coverage of the first transports opened still more doors. "They came from all kinds of homes; from well-known figures of everyday life and from artisans; from the wealthiest homes and from the unemployed." The leadership set up a department to investigate these families and instituted a decentralized system of local guardian committees to "intensify the search for homes, look after the children when they had settled down, and help the Movement." These too proved popular: twenty-six functioned by mid-December, and another forty-one were in process of formation.[33] Guardian committees faced numerous challenges. As Yvonne Kapp and Margaret Mynatt, who worked in Bloomsbury House (refugee aid headquarters), put it, "Their function demanded the combined talents and skills of a mother, hostess, an accountant, a labour manager, a language teacher, a psychologist, a solicitor, a Public Assistance administrator, an education officer, a trained nurse and philosopher. It required further fluency in German, the patience of a saint and the tact of the devil himself."[34]

The warm response by individuals all over the country shaped the guarantee system. Anyone—British citizen or foreigner—who deposited the required cash sum of fifty pounds could sponsor a particular child.[35] Phyllis Shepherd, wife of the vicar of Holme St. Cuthbert in Cumberland, wrote to the movement office in Bloomsbury House. "Thank you for your letter of 15th May," Mrs McClelland of the hospitality department replied. "I have now received particulars of a girl from Germany and I am wondering if she would suit you. The girl's name is Susanne Neuwalder and she was born in Vienna on 17th January 1935. She has no religion, so I hope you will not consider the fact that she has not been baptized too great a difficulty. Her father was a physician and we are told that Susanne is a lively and charming little girl. I enclose her photograph and a guarantee form." With thousands of children to place, the hospitality department pressed for an answer. "Will you kindly let us know your decision as soon as possible as we are most anxious to place this child?"[36]

Susanne Neuwalder; her brother Herbert (a year older than she); their father Herbert, a physician and a Jew; and their mother Maria, an artist, born Roman Catholic, lived in an area called Neuwaldegg at the end of a tram line on the outskirts of Vienna. Recalling her emigration, Susanne did not know how her brother and she came to be registered, but she believed it was through the American Friends Service Committee.

Phyllis Shepherd liked Susanne's photo and description. "Many thanks for your kind letter of 23rd May enclosing the guarantee for Susanne Neuwalder," Mrs McClelland wrote. We are most grateful for your kindness in accepting this girl."[37] Dr Neuwalder too wrote to Mrs Shepherd. Although dated 14 June, his letter reveals that he did not yet know the Shepherds had agreed to serve as guarantors. "Many thanks for your interest in an emigrant child in general and in my little daughter Susi in particular," he began. Assuring Phyllis Shepherd that neither he nor his wife was religious, he gave unqualified permission for Susi to be baptized and educated in the Christian faith. He then turned to more important matters:

> Susi is generally a quiet child playing with her toys for hours, but sometimes rather lively. She is a moderate eater and chattering out what she thinks, causing slight shocks of her severe relatives. She likes to play with other children and is accustomed to many a thump of her brother. Susi goes to bed at 8 p.m. and does not sleep during the day. Till now she slept with her mother, but also alone she falls asleep without further ceremony.

> She does not know an English word, but she is especially voluble and very dexterous in general too. Of peculiarities I may mention that she still sucks her thumb, what we left her up to now, though her sucking is not without influence on the position of her teeth in the lower jaw. She is used to much air, light, and freedom of motion.[38]

Heartily as Dr Neuwalder hoped the Shepherds would accept Susi ("we should be very glad"), he grieved bitterly. "When my father waved good-bye to us, he was laughing and smiling, my mother told me [after the war]: he was doing this to try to keep up our spirits."[39]

The children's departure fell heavily on parents, however desperate they were to secure the youngsters' safety. Julie Stock's husband Leo was arrested in the November pogrom and incarcerated in Buchenwald, and her children Ernst, then fourteen, and Lotte, ten, yearned to leave Germany. "The phrase 'child emigration' became a catchword from one day to the next—and what mother does not want the best for her child?" Julie wrote in her diary. An astute woman, she contacted the director of a Jewish orphanage "the moment I heard about sending away the children." She assumed, correctly, that the Jewish community would evacuate orphanages first, and she moved quickly to include her children in that group. Ernst moved quickly too. His best friend's family had settled in France in July 1936, and Ernst wrote to him now. "The Schweber family generously invited both children to come," Julie recorded.

Ernst and Lotte got places on the kindertransport. "I said good-bye to the children on 7 December in the morning, having decided only shortly before, and without having consulted Father, who remained in B[uchenwald]. They wanted only one thing—to escape the situation here—but neither of my children had any idea what would happen in the future."[40]

Leo Stock returned from Buchenwald three days later. Julie had got him released on the strength of a British visa she had obtained for him. It was not an entirely happy homecoming. "His eyes searched in vain for the children. What could he do? He faced a fait accompli. He wished to travel to England via France soon, to visit them."[41]

The Stock family history spoke for many, as a confidential report by a Quaker monitor of human rights, William R. Hughes, made clear. "I was greatly impressed by the speed and efficiency with which the work of the children's emigration to England was tackled on the German side, in spite of the general absence of the normal machinery," he wrote on 16 December 1938 to the Society of Friends Germany Emergency Committee upon his return from a fact-finding mission. "The mothers leapt

*Refugee girl arriving in Harwich on 14 December 1938 with the third
kindertransport from Germany.*

unanimously at the chance and without exception put their children's
names down. (The fathers could generally not be consulted)." They, like
Leo Stock, had been picked up and sent to concentration camps. German
Jews lived throughout the country, and "the children's forms were assembled at the local centre, where the most urgent cases were underlined and

the whole lot then sent to the central Berlin office." The criteria held constant: "firstly, those in which the children had no home, or no parents, or no means; and secondly, as a group, the big boys, who were held to be in special danger of arrest or ill-treatment."[42]

"I became involved with the Kindertransports after the Kristallnacht," Norbert Wollheim remembered years later. Working for the Jewish community in Berlin, he found his task physically and emotionally demanding. "Some parents became impatient and frantic to get their children out and many times we were accused of favouritism. Time and again we had to tell parents that the permits for their children had not yet arrived from London and we could only include those children for whom we had permits." Difficult as this was, "what was even more difficult was to tell parents at the railway station to say good bye to their children in the waiting room, as the police would not allow them on the platform in order not to have heart-rending scenes in public." But not even the Nazis could control everything. "There were terrible scenes; many children were crying; in some cases there was an eerie silence; always there was tension."[43]

Hertha Nathorff was one of the parents at the Schlesischen Bahnhof; her fourteen-year-old son Heinz had a place on a kindertransport to England. A physician married to a physician, Hertha counted Albert Einstein and Carl Lämmle, the founder of Universal Pictures in Hollywood, among her relatives. Increasing social isolation forced her to consider emigration, and she traveled to Switzerland in August 1934 to discuss the matter with her first cousin Carl. "'If you insist, you can have an affidavit,'" she reported him saying in her diary. For her part, Hertha "only heard 'No' in all" he said.[44] By the summer of 1938 the situation had deteriorated so markedly that she determined to try again. "*Now* he must realize that I have ample reason," she fumed to her diary on 5 August.[45] And of course, worse soon came: her husband Erich was arrested in the November pogrom.

Lämmle sent them a telegram on 17 November, inviting them to California, but Hertha had no success at the consulate. Like thousands of other Jews, she followed multiple leads: "A visum for Chile for RM3,000 to be obtained through an Austrian Nazi"; a possibility of legal passage to Cuba. Most important: "A patient of my husband, who is here from

England to attend a conference, sends his secretary to ask me if he can help me. 'Save my child!' "[46]

Unexpectedly, Hertha got a quota number for the United States on 8 December and, with that, she managed Erich's release from concentration camp a week later. Luck—such as it was at that time—was with the Nathorff family. A week later the parents got a permit to travel to England and remain for six months while awaiting immigration to America. "At last, a glimmer of hope!"[47] And the English patient came through for Heinz. For Hertha, getting him out as soon as possible overwhelmed all other considerations. 1 March 1939: "Tomorrow my boy will travel with a kindertransport to England. For a last time I went with him through the city at dusk, through the familiar streets to the Tiergarten, to the playground, which was his daily routine, to the zoo and back to the Kaiserallee to his old school." She told him "that we will follow soon, and he will help me then, and I laugh, and my heart could rip open from sadness. . . . Tomorrow I will give my child away, my last, my deepest happiness; this too they have taken from me."[48]

Hertha brought Heinz to the Schlesischen Bahnhof at six in the morning the following day. The hour alone guaranteed few witnesses. But in any case, the Gestapo-imposed procedure aimed to avoid perturbation of gentile Germans by scenes of human distress. "Parents are forbidden to accompany [the children] to the platform. I kiss my boy and whisper to him: 'Look out of the window at Zoo station.'" She had a plan. "I throw myself in my car, and speed to Zoo, buy a platform ticket, run up, and I am there before the train." It was a good idea. "The platform is relatively empty, and no one forbids me to approach the train. And my boy looks out of the window and sees his mother one more time." She ached for him to feel calm. "'Look, son, how beautiful the spring sun rises over the planetarium and how beautiful the Gedächtniskirche looks from up here.' . . . [H]e bends out from the window, another kiss, and the train kidnaps him from me."[49] A telegram arrived from London the next day: " 'Arrived safely.' How happy I am. My child is secure. Now I can begin to dissolve our home, the house in which we do not feel at home anymore."[50]

Hertha and Erich had papers in hand for England en route to America. Other parents had nothing but desperation. "630 Children Quit Vienna: One Jewish Mother Dies on Seeing Child Depart for Holland," a *New York Times* headline announced on 11 December 1938. Departing from the suburban Hutteldorf station, 530 youngsters were destined for England and 100 for the Netherlands. "Mothers and relatives were not permitted to enter the station. They held what may have been their last meeting with the children at near-by hotels." According to the Associated Press reporter, "the emotional strain of parting was too much for some of them. One mother died of a heart attack after kissing her 5-year-old child good-bye. The child was not told. Seven mothers fainted as the children marched to the train."[51]

The Society of Friends in Vienna addressed the awful dilemma the parents faced in the fall of 1939. "One can easily understand how hard it is for the parents to part with their children." To send them abroad, to a foreign country, to people they did not know, would have been madness, a dereliction of duty in any other circumstance. "Therefore it is comprehensible that there are many parents who could not make up their minds and in the last moment withdrew their application, often shortly before the departure of the child."[52] The parents faced a situation they had never encountered before and for which they had slim precedents at best to guide them. A decision to go forward was an act of great courage. And perhaps, in that pre-war period, an act of great faith: they believed they would be reunited in a matter of months. Few were so fortunate.

And the children? According to the *New York Times* article of 11 December, the ten-coach train was filled with "630 happy Jewish children aged 2½ to 16." And indeed: many former kindertransport children remember a feeling of excitement about the journey and great relief on leaving Germany. But older youngsters, the fifteen- and sixteen-year-olds, worried about getting their parents out: how to manage? Whom to ask? And young ones like Susanne Neuwalder did not know what to make of it at all. She was four when she and her brother emigrated, yet more than half a century later she recalled their departure clearly, including what they had brought with them. "I remember exactly what we had: we each had a bag, and we each had a little pillow with little handles to use on the journey." Susi wanted to carry the two pillows and have her brother carry the bags. "I do remember really thousands of kids milling around the station and I remember getting on the train and I remember waving good-bye." She remembered one more thing: "And always the overwhelming feeling that I had on that train and for the next several years was confusion. I was always confused."[53]

GUARANTORS MET THEIR CHARGES in Liverpool Street station, if the transport came via Harwich, or Charing Cross station, if via Folkestone. "I remember arriving at the train station in London, on a platform with all these other kids," Susanne recalled. "I remember my new mother, mother number one, referred to as Auntie Phyl, coming to pick me up." And then she lost her brother. Another vicar and his wife had guaranteed for him. The two foster mothers "waited until he turned around to look at something, or I did. And they whipped him away, or whipped me away. I don't know which way it went, but they separated us. For the nine years we lived in England, we actually saw each other only one day, a very memorable day in my life when I was ten and he was eleven."[54] They lived thirty miles distant from one another. Perhaps war rationing and transport difficulties influenced the decision to keep them apart. Possibly the notion that the children would adjust more easily unencumbered by former family ties. And maybe the foster parents simply did not think at all.

For the first few months, while refugee aid workers focused on "unguaranteed urgent cases," children went directly to the summer holiday camps the Bentwich-Cohn plan had identified. Conveniently located near Harwich, Dovercourt Bay opened first and housed the greatest number of youngsters. Anna Essinger, founder and director of Bunce Court School, was asked to run it. Arriving with some of her staff and a number of older students to help her, Essinger established order quickly.[55] C. F. Roundell, chief general health inspector, and Miss Montagnon, woman inspector, found much to praise on their visit shortly after the camp opened, including the modern kitchen, and the way "Messrs. Marks and Spencer have fitted out these children with clothing where required from 'top to toe', including gum boots." They were particularly impressed that "children, including the bigger girls, were all working or occupied in organised groups and there was a general impression of good management under very difficult circumstances." This was due to "Miss Essinger, who is head of the camp" and "a teacher with great experience."[56]

"None of us will ever forget those heartbreaking days and weeks there," Essinger wrote some years later. "Thousands of children were saved, but these were necessarily hurried arrangements, and perhaps it was only natural that serious mistakes could not be avoided."[57] Among these, according to Veronica Gillespie, her co-worker at Dovercourt Bay, ranked "the 'cattle-market' as [Anna] called the system by which representatives of local committees looked along the row of children at meal times and picked out those they fancied. Plain adolescent girls or pimply boys were never picked, which did nothing for their morale. It was really cruel."[58]

Gerda Geiringer recalled that cattle market vividly—only she had another name for it. "It was done like this: people who wanted to take children in their homes were sent along to the camp. They were then put into an office, and a number of children were asked to please come and be shown, something like a slave market, and we called it that as a joke but not quite as a joke. The people were nice. They saw the point, and they came because they were nice. But it did seem like a slave market to us. You know, 'How do you like this one? She's got blue eyes, she's twelve years old, you can still mold her.'" Gerda was taken by Ethyl Hayden, who had thought to foster two little children but accepted two older girls instead. "She had her car, and she said, 'Well, get packed.'"[59]

For Kitty Pistol, it was more like a dog show. Kitty and her best friend Ilse Maurer got spots on the kindertransport of 10 December that left from Hutteldorf station on the outskirts of Vienna. "One day there was a call, there was a Mrs Jacobs there from Manchester. She was looking for ten girls to the age of fourteen. So Ilse and I just ran. Left everything. I said, 'Let's go to the dog show. Maybe they'll take us!' We called it the dog show because they looked at us like an exhibition of dogs. . . . So we ran there. And she did take us."[60]

When they got to Manchester, Mrs Jacobs explained that the girls were destined for Southport where they would stay with local Jewish families until a house was outfitted for them. Opened in February 1939,

*Kindertransport children from Germany stand outside the bungalows at
Dovercourt Bay holiday camp in December 1938.*

the Southport hostel provided a home for Kitty, Ilse, and other girls until
March 1940. A collective journal from the time recorded the girls' activities and experiences. They served apprenticeships, trained for domestic
work, and took jobs in local shops and enterprises. And they worked to
find guarantors or employers for their relatives at home. A few managed.
"On the 12th of February the hostel was opened," one girl wrote. "We
settled down very quickly and felt soon very comfortable." Like the other
girls, she lived on two levels. "I was worrying about my younger sister
who was still in Vienna. I was longing to see her again and to have her
with me." A guarantor emerged. "Mrs Livingstone was so good to take
my sister over. We feel very grateful and are very happy to be together in
our nice Home."[61]

Declaration of war brought the girls' efforts to an end. "Then the war came as a big blow to all of us," Gina Bauer wrote. And she went on: "My sister had arranged everything for my parents to come over to England. We expected them to arrive on the 6th of September and on the 3rd the war broke out. It was a great shock for my sister and me."[62] Half a century later Kitty remembered being there the moment Gina heard the news and realized its significance. "She threw herself on the floor, and she was screaming and shouting. She just had a nervous breakdown, the poor thing. She never saw them again." Kitty never saw her mother again, either. "If the war would have started two weeks later, my mother would have made it." A family in Liverpool had offered her a job as a cook. Returning to Vienna in 1946, Kitty found her mother's packed trunk addressed to Liverpool, hidden with a non-Jewish friend for better times. She did not find her mother.[63]

PART THREE

1942

Deportation of Jews from Brussels, 1944.

· 1939–1942 ·

TOWARD GENOCIDE

On 30 JANUARY 1939, THE SIXTH ANNIVERSARY OF HIS ASCENT TO power, Hitler addressed the newly expanded Greater German Reichstag. "Nothing," he screamed, would "sway Germany from its reckoning with Jewry." And, he observed, no one seemed intent on doing so. "It is truly a shaming display when we see today the entire democratic world filled with tears of pity at the plight of the poor, tortured Jewish people, while remaining hardhearted and obstinate in view of what is therefore its obvious duty: to help."[1] Mocking the democratic states that talked so much and did so little, Hitler highlighted the fact that no one stood ready to take the Jews. "Should the rest of the world be outraged and protest hypocritically against Germany's barbarous expulsion of such an extraordinary, culturally valuable, irreplaceable element, then we can only be astonished at the consequences such a stance would imply. Should not the outside world be most grateful to us for setting free these glorious bearers of culture and placing them at its disposal? In accordance with its own statements, how is the outside world to justify its refusal to grant refuge in its various countries to these most valuable members of the human race? . . . How will the states so infatuated with these 'great guys' explain why they are suddenly taking refuge with all sorts of pretenses just in order to deny asylum to these people?"[2]

If Jews were welcome nowhere, Hitler reasoned there was no place on earth for them. And that might be their fate. He had been a prophet before, he said. "Once again I will be a prophet: should the international Jewry of finance succeed, both within and without Europe, in plunging mankind into yet another world war, then the result will not be a Bolshevization of the earth and the victory of Jewry, but the annihilation of the Jewish race in Europe."[3]

Eight months later Hitler—not "international Jewry"—invaded Poland (1 September) and plunged Europe into war. Great Britain and France had guaranteed Poland's security and Australia, New Zealand, and Canada joined forces with them. But after declaring war on Germany, the allies did nothing, and the Polish army was defeated. Backed by a secret agreement (the Molotov-Ribbentrop pact) with Germany, the Soviet Union invaded Poland from the east on 17 September. The Germans and Soviets ratified their agreement (28 September) to split the country; the new border ran along the Bug river. The Soviets annexed their occupation zone, while the Germans divided theirs into two, annexing the western part. Intent upon subjugating the Polish people, special SS units, *Einsatzgruppen*, terrorized and killed prominent leaders in all sectors of Polish society.[4]

The Einsatzgruppen murdered thousands of Jews as well. With the conquest of western and central Poland, Germany acquired control over two million Jews. It was as if the policy of emigration had come to naught. For six years the German government had been able to get rid of hundreds of thousands of unwanted Jews through emigration, and now they gained millions through conquest.

How was Germany to get rid of them? The regime did not yet contemplate annihilation of all Jews. Taking one piece at a time, Berlin opted to expel Jews from territory annexed to the Reich into what was left of Poland, now called the Government General. Appointed in October to oversee the "ethnic cleansing" of the annexed territories, Heinrich Himmler ordered the deportation of hundreds of thousands of Poles and Jews into the Government General. His subordinate Adolf Eichmann planned to send the Jews to a reservation to be located between the Vistula and the Bug.[5]

Eichmann had gained a reputation in post-Anschluss Vienna, where he headed the Central Office for Jewish Emigration and oversaw the emigration of 150,000 Austrian Jews in one year. After German occupation of the Czech lands, he was moved to Prague, where he did less well because by then Czech Jews found it nearly impossible to get visas. Fearing failure, Eichmann looked for another solution. In late September he found a new "home" for Czech Jewry: the region around the town of Nisko in Poland's Lublin district. Eichmann explained his plan to his superior Reinhard Heydrich, who told Himmler, who in turn told Hitler.

Deportations to Lublin began within weeks, and many died from starvation and disease. The Germans shrugged at the high mortality, even though journalists in Britain and America wrote about it in major papers. The German plan to create "a Jewish State" in the Lublin area was a "remarkable example of political cynicism," the *Times* of London contended. "To thrust 3,000,000 Jews, relatively few of whom are agriculturists, into the Lublin region and to force them to settle there would doom them to famine. That, perhaps, is the intention."[6] The American writer Oswald Garrison Villard agreed: "This mass-migration by force has been begun now, in the dead of winter, and in a manner that cannot be interpreted as anything else than a determination to create, not a Jewish state, but a most horrible concentration camp, which can certainly become nothing else than a habitation of death."[7] None of this criticism daunted the Germans. They were daunted, however, by practical difficulties, the sheer mechanics of moving so many people. By the spring of 1940 Eichmann's project had collapsed. A total of ninety-five thousand Jews had been moved to Nisko.

The outbreak of war had enabled Eichmann to institute a new and more deadly plan to remove Jews from German territory. And the Nazi regime's "solution" to the Jewish Problem had become ever more violent, from individual emigration to pressure on the community as a whole to emigrate to a "territorial" solution: a reservation. The war had also shut the door for the Jews of Greater Germany to Allied countries. British consulates in Germany closed on 3 September, and thus no new visas could be issued to German nationals. Furthermore, "all visas granted or authorized before the outbreak of hostilities should be regarded as void."[8]

Only the door to Palestine remained ajar for a few months. People who had received a certificate from the Jewish Agency before the war and had also obtained a visa for Palestine at a British consulate were permitted to proceed to Trieste and from there to Haifa. Some 2,800 German, Austrian, and Czech Jews who had got certificates, but not a visa, before the British consulates closed became a more contentious diplomatic problem, but they too ultimately were allowed to emigrate. Stacks of unused Palestine immigration certificates in the safes of the now shuttered British consulates, some blank, others with the name of the applicant, posed the greatest dilemma. These certificates included 345 minors registered with youth aliyah.[9] Moshe Shertok, head of the political department of the Jewish Agency, met with British Colonial Secretary Malcolm MacDonald on 23 October to discuss the certificates. "We attach the greatest importance to every opportunity, however limited, of saving such young people from Germany," Shertok urged. MacDonald told him not to worry: the youngsters were safely at home with their parents. Challenging MacDonald's smug response, Shertok replied: "Some of their parents have in the meantime emigrated, being assured that their children, too, would soon leave Germany. The fathers of many others, being of Polish origin, have recently been interned in Buchenwald, and thus a large number of the children have no homes to go back to." But MacDonald would not budge.[10]

British intransigence and antisemitic violence had already persuaded many haluzim to forgo certificates; some 1,650 illegal immigrants from Poland had reached Greece and sailed to Palestine between July 1934 and October 1938. The November pogrom and Britain's White Paper (May 1939) limiting Jewish immigration to 75,000 in the next five years increased the allure of illegal entry, known as *aliyah bet* or class B immigration.[11]

"What we need is neither a selective aliyah nor a broad-based aliyah, but a mass aliyah of hundreds of thousands. . . . We must wage a battle not *for* aliyah, but *through* aliyah,"[12] Ben Gurion stated flatly in November 1938. Nine months later, more than thirty ships had brought over six thousand illegal immigrants to Palestine's shores. In Zionist labor leader Berl Katznelson's view, the illegal immigration of refugees to Palestine heralded a new era in Zionist history. "We may ask why it is that history did not choose free, wealthy and well-behaved Jews to be the bearers of its mission, but preferred instead the Jewish refugees, the most wretched of all humankind, cast adrift on the seas. But this is a fact we cannot change. This is what history determined, and it is left to us to accept its choice and to follow the refugee."[13]

ILLEGAL IMMIGRATION INTO PALESTINE was the least of Britain's problems in 1940. German forces occupied Denmark and Norway in April that year and went on to capture the Netherlands, Belgium, and Luxembourg in May. By that time the *Wehrmacht* (German army) had reached deep into France. The French prime minister Paul Reynaud resigned on 16 June, and the eighty-four-year-old Henri Philippe Pétain succeeded him and sought an armistice. Agreeing to harsh terms—among them, German occupation of the industrial north and west including Paris— Pétain nevertheless was to be the recognized head of the French state. Headquartered in the resort town of Vichy, Pétain's government was to control an unoccupied "free zone" that covered the agricultural southern third of the country.

The fall of France confirmed German dominance on the continent, and Italy, Hungary, Romania, and Bulgaria lined up with the Reich. Officially, Yugoslavia was neutral, but Yugoslavs were not: Serbs were anglophile; the Croats admired Germany; many Montenegrins looked to Italy for support; and Macedonians to Bulgaria. In early 1941, Germany pressured Yugoslavia to become an ally. Italy had invaded Greece in October 1940 and was stuck. Mussolini needed Hitler's help, and Hitler wanted to launch his Greek operations from Yugoslavia. Choosing between the Axis or an invasion, the Yugoslav government joined the Tripartite Pact. Pro-British Serbian nationalists revolted and took control of the country on 27 March 1941. Hitler exploded at this intolerable affront and ordered an attack. The Yugoslav army capitulated on April 17, and Yugoslavia was no more. The Germans carved it up and served pieces to Italy, Hungary, and Bulgaria. The German army invaded Greece the same day as Yugoslavia and quickly defeated the Greek forces. By the beginning of June all of continental Europe except the remaining neutral countries Sweden, Switzerland, Spain, and Portugal, and the half-allied Soviet Union, was under direct or indirect German control. It was not enough for Hitler. On Sunday, 22 June 1941, the Wehrmacht surprised the Soviets with an all-out offensive, an ideological crusade to destroy the Judeo-Bolshevik conspiracy to rule the world.

THE WEHRMACHT'S SUCCESS BROUGHT GERMANY land it wanted and Jews it didn't. More than three million Jews—including one hundred thousand German and Austrian refugees who had found refuge in various European countries between 1933 and 1939[14]—were now in areas under direct German rule, and this problem could not be solved through emigration. A "territorial final solution" was needed, Heydrich told a German foreign office official.[15] Drawing from older ideas to settle Jews in Madagascar and Eichmann's plan to send Jews to a reservation near Lublin, Heydrich envisioned the wholesale deportation of European Jewry to the African island of Madagascar. The Germans simply assumed that Madagascar would be ceded to them, and the transport could be worked out.[16]

The Madagascar plan showed that the Nazis had learned to think big about the Jewish Problem. In 1933, they shrieked about Germany's mission to get rid of all Jews in the Reich. In the late thirties their scope widened to Greater Germany. Now that they ruled so much of Europe, it was their job to free the whole continent from the "scourge" of the Jews: ship them to Madagascar. But the plan came to naught. France did not cede the island, and the war did not end. Göring's *Luftwaffe* failed to subjugate England; there was no negotiated peace, and that was the end of that.

AWAITING THE DEPORTATION OF POLISH JEWRY to Madagascar, the Germans isolated the Jewish population in occupied Poland by establishing closed ghettos nominally ruled by Jewish Councils but practically under direct control of German administrators. Insufficiently supplied with food, medicine, and other resources, these overcrowded ghettos became deathtraps. Starvation led to contagious disease. In Warsaw, 18 percent of the Jewish population died in the three years that separated the fall of that city in September 1939 and the deportations to death camps in August 1942. In total eight hundred thousand Jews died in the ghettos erected in eastern Europe.

No ghettos were established in western Europe. But the Germans and their allies like the Vichy French government soon initiated a process of political disenfranchisement, social isolation, and economic expropriation that repeated the pattern developed in Germany in the 1930s. In Holland and Belgium initiative rested wholly with the German occupiers; in France, the Vichy government instituted its own measures, imprisoning German-Jewish refugees in internment camps or setting them to slave labor in the Sahara; stripping naturalized Jews of their citizenship; excluding French Jews from the civil service and specified professions; robbing many of their businesses and property. Compared to Vichy France, fascist Italy proved much less enthusiastic in persecuting its Jewish population. Certainly, antisemitic legislation was passed but, in general, it was applied without much enthusiasm.

The fascist regimes in southeast Europe were not so benign. Romanian dictator Marshal Ion Antonescu announced his desire to expel the whole Jewish community of three hundred thousand, and Romanian troops massacred hundreds. Wave upon wave of antisemitic legislation expelled Jews from schools, universities, and the professions, removed them from commerce, and expropriated properties and businesses. Fascist Iron Guardsmen butchered hundreds of Jews and destroyed synagogues. Hungary too passed antisemitic legislation, forbidding all manner of economic activity and banning marriage between gentiles and Jews.

NONE OF THIS WAS OF MUCH CONSEQUENCE to anyone but the Jews. The citizens of occupied countries were too concerned with their own suffering to notice that their Jewish neighbors had it even worse. And many people profited from the Jews' losses, gaining jobs, property, possessions, power, and prestige.

The great majority of the three million Jews who found themselves under direct German rule and the many millions who suffered from the antisemitic legislation of Hitler's allies looked for ways out. Neutral countries like the United States and Argentina in principle still accepted Jewish immigrants from Europe, but few Jews had any assets left, and both exit visas and transport were extremely difficult to secure. Some thirty-seven thousand Jews nevertheless managed to emigrate from Europe to the United States, and ten thousand to other countries overseas in 1940. At least another ten thousand reached Palestine, more than half by aliyah bet and detained by the authorities as illegals. The ever-tightening strictures reduced the number of Jewish emigrants from Europe to thirty-five thousand in 1941, with twenty-four thousand to America and forty-five hundred to Palestine, of whom eight hundred were detained.[17] These figures bear witness to the refugees' desperate efforts. They do little to relieve the stark picture of millions facing lethal persecution.

European Jewry reached a historical nadir by summer 1941. The greatest restrictions in the middle ages paled by comparison. Political, social, cultural, economic, biological, religious, and moral genocide ruled; within a generation European Jewry would have died. But while hundreds of thousands of Jews had been murdered, the Germans had not yet instituted the policy and practice of systematic murder.

The German invasion of the Soviet Union in June 1941 inaugurated the Holocaust. The first mass murders of Jews were not by Germans, however, but by their Romanian allies. Massacring Romanian Jews in the border districts with the Soviet Union, the Romanian army continued to slaughter Jews in Romanian territory formerly occupied by the Soviets in 1940 but quickly recovered in June 1941. The Romanians then turned on Jews in Soviet territories granted to Romania. The Romanians set new standards for cruelty; the Germans, by contrast, were to show the blessings of Teutonic rationale and efficiency. Einsatzgruppen followed the advancing Wehrmacht to identify, concentrate, and execute communist leaders and Jews. Initially targeting male Jews, the killing squads began murdering all Jews they encountered—men, women, and children—in August. The German army joined forces. And more than

1.3 million people were shot and machine-gunned in their streamlined operation to annihilate Russian Jewry.[18]

Once the German leadership had decided that murder was the solution to the Jewish Problem in Russia, it soon became the "Final Solution" to the Jewish Problem in all of Europe. The Nazi leadership forbade emigration in autumn 1941. Annihilation had taken its place.

Hitler passed a death sentence on all Jews soon after America entered the war on the allies' side. In a speech to his *Gauleiters* (administrative district leaders) on 12 December, he announced "a clean sweep" to solve the Jewish Question. Recording this event in his diary, Josef Goebbels noted that in Hitler's speech of 30 January 1939, "he had warned the Jews that if they again unleashed a world war, they would be destroyed. That has proved no empty threat." Paraphrasing Hitler, Goebbels continued: "The world war has arrived, and the destruction of Jewry must follow."[19]

PASSEURS: GUIDES
TO FREEDOM

THE NOOSE TIGHTENED ABOUT JEWS IN THE NETHERLANDS IN 1942, and they knew it. During the first half of the year, the Germans forced Jews throughout the country to relocate to Amsterdam. Permitted to lodge only in traditional Jewish quarters or to live with Jewish families, they found themselves in a ghetto without walls. With the star decree in May, they were marked and trapped.[1]

Jenny Gans-Premsela and her husband Mozes (Max) Heimans Gans had discussed immigration to South America a year earlier. "Legal" (with purchased passports) emigration seemed possible at that time, and they were young and healthy. But they did not go. Perhaps family ties rooted them to Amsterdam; Jenny's parents did not wish to leave. Perhaps their well established family jewelry and silver business provided a sense of stability, if not security.

Forced to wear the star, Jenny and Max, like many other Jews in western Europe, scrutinized the map. Beleaguered Britain, separated by the North Sea and the Germans' high-speed patrol boats, appeared impossible to reach. That left Spain and Switzerland, both long shots, but Switzerland by far the more imaginable. Many western European Jews knew someone who had traveled to Switzerland or had done so themselves; few had any contact with Spain. Many spoke German or French; few Spanish. And Switzerland had a long history of neutrality and a tradition of asylum. Spain, by contrast, had just endured a civil war. Jews in the Netherlands, Belgium, and France knew that hundreds of thousands of refugees had fled Spain and doubted the prudence of traffic the other way. Most important, Franco's fascist regime held the country in its grip, and it owed much to Nazi Germany. A future for refugee Jews in fascist Spain appeared a murky prospect indeed.

Dutch Jews had vanishingly few opportunities to disappear. Flat, wide open, and populated throughout, the Netherlands offered little in the way of natural hiding places. If thousands of desperate Dutch Jews sought to hide in the homes of more or less willing gentile countrymen, others looked to flee to Switzerland. The route from the Netherlands traversed Belgium and France: three borders to exit and enter. The challenges were too numerous to list. Who would help? How to find such persons? How much would it cost? Jews who embarked on this clandestine journey were not trained in covert missions. They did not know where to go or to whom to turn. And their experience since occupation had dashed their prewar expectations of trustworthiness. Still, deciding they had little to lose, some Jews took their chances. A few—Jenny and Max among them—had strong business connections in Switzerland and assumed if they reached the border, their contacts would offer hospitality.

Rumors of wholesale deportation of Dutch Jews to the east flew by the end of June 1942, and they were well founded. The Germans informed (16 June) the Jewish Council that they planned to send "police-controlled labor contingents" of men and women aged sixteen to forty to the Reich. Meeting the next day, the Council considered resignation but chose instead to cooperate with the Germans in order, they believed, to save as many people as they could. Max visited (28 June) Dr David Mozes Sluys, a member of the Council and a good friend of the Gans family. Initially, Sluys reassured him but, accompanying the younger man to the door, he asked: "Do you have an opportunity to get out?" When Max allowed that he might, Sluys responded, "'Let's shake hands, as we will not see each other again in this lifetime.'"[2]

For the Ganses, as for others, the first step toward "illegal"—according to the Nazis—emigration consisted of nothing more tangible than a suggestion. In Jenny's memory, someone mentioned the name of a man who lived on a street called Parallelweg in Bergen op Zoom, close to the Belgian border. This person, it was whispered, helped people on their way to Switzerland. For a fee.

Jenny and Max expected that they could manage the sum, as did their friends Abraham (Bram) Horodisch and Alice Horodisch-Garman, stateless Jewish refugees from Germany. Planning to meet in Bergen op Zoom on 2 July, the couples traveled separately. Jenny and Max unfastened their stars and, with borrowed identity cards, only a briefcase for Max, and a purse for Jenny, they walked to the station.

An unanticipated problem beset them: they were no longer used to acting "normally," not, as Jenny put it, "to look anxiously over our shoulders."[3] Detraining in Bergen op Zoom and joining their friends, they realized that Parallelweg was not, as they had assumed, a village street, but a major roadway. A telephone directory listed a name connected to a moving company, and they guessed that the business had acquired a new line: people. "He was a rough character, who . . . immediately understood our intentions," Jenny recalled. "We would discuss Switzerland later. First we had to pay and then he would arrange for someone to take us to Belgium." Unfortunately, he asked for more than they had. "We had to call home for the rest of the sum. There was no other choice." He promised that by the following morning "he would find someone to accompany us—a passeur."[4]

He was true to his word. They took a streetcar in the direction of Belgium and a passeur met them at the end of the line. He led them through a forest over the border to Heide, near Antwerp. Leaving them, he explained that a Belgian passeur would contact them. So far so good. Yet however closely stories of clandestine crossings resemble adventure tales, they ultimately rest on tragedy: the tragedy of forced departure, betrayal, rejection. The two couples got to Antwerp where, as they did not have Belgian identity papers, they rented rooms from a café owner who calculated risk against profit and charged them three times the posted rate. The Belgian passeur brought them identity papers and trouble in the form of a man they feared was an informer. Suspecting a trap, the two couples sought shelter with a Jewish butcher they knew. Mr Beem and his wife felt safer in Antwerp than the Ganses and Horodisches had in Amsterdam and they saw no reason to leave. They were wrong. They were deported and murdered within a year. At that moment, however, they hid the young couples in a friend's attic while two German trucks pulled up to the café.

Clandestine rescue depended upon luck, fortuitous circumstance, and links. The Beem family took charge. Confiding in a customer they believed to be in contact with the resistance, they found a man who "hated the Germans and understood we [the couples] wanted to go to Switzerland. He did not want to earn much from our misery."[5] Two more Jews from Rotterdam joined the group, and the customer put them in contact with a passeur who took them over the French border.

Switzerland lay but one border away. From an anti-Nazi bookseller in Brussels whom Max and Bram knew and had visited while seeking a way out of Belgium, they had got an address in Besançon, about twenty-five miles from the Swiss border. According to the bookseller, that contact would not turn Jews away, but his group aimed primarily to support anti-German activities. A *cheminot* (railway worker), he used his position to move people clandestinely over the armistice demarcation line, hiding anti-Nazi agents and refugees in the coal tenders of trains to unoccupied France. He did not work on trains to Switzerland. But these people needed help, and the cheminot proved an experienced and generous host. He found a passeur to accompany them on a train to a town near the Swiss border, offered them a warm dinner, and lodged them in a hotel occupied by Germans where, he believed, they would be safest. He was correct. The Germans mounted *razzias* (dragnets) throughout Besançon and arrested all foreign and stateless Jews in the city the next day. They did not bother to search the hotel in which they themselves were quartered.

The passeur brought the six Jews to the town of Morteau, three miles from Switzerland. It was pouring. The passeur accompanied them on foot to a spot near the border. He would go no farther; the Germans shot anyone in that strip. They had two options, he explained. One path went from farm to farm, inhabited by people prepared to help, and moved between France and Switzerland. The other path, more arduous, traversed an open plain and ascended the Jura; the border ran across the top.

The two Jews from Rotterdam chose the less daunting route. The others learned later that an informer had betrayed the farmers. Arrested at the third house, the refugees were sent to Drancy and then to Auschwitz.

The Gans and Horodisch couples ran for their lives across the open field, glad of the rain because it prevented the guard dogs from picking up their scent, impeded the sentries' view, and muffled the noise they made as they crashed through the meadow. Safe on the other side, they climbed the mountain and walked into Switzerland. Welcomed by a local farmer who organized a car for them, they went on to Max and Jenny's business associate, Jean Louis[6] in Chaux-de-Fonds. When he had been their guest in the Netherlands in 1940, Jean Louis had invited them to visit and to stay for a month. Now he asked to see their papers. Learning they had none, he demanded they leave his home immediately. Past midnight. In the rain. Holding himself a law-abiding citizen, Jean Louis drove them to a cheap hotel in utter silence.

The policeman who interrogated them the next day was more sympathetic. Jenny's shoes had fallen apart in the sodden climb, and he took her to buy a new pair before he dealt with their legal problems. He also told the shop clerk to bill Jean Louis for the purchase. Still, the four Jews were "illegals," and they were committed to prison in Neuchâtel on 20 July. Jenny and Max were transferred to a reception camp in Summiswald, then to another camp in Leysin on 30 July, and finally into the custody of the Dutch envoy in Bern on 13 August. Through the Dutch consulate in Geneva, they received new passports and a guarantee of financial support while in the forced residence imposed on them by the Swiss government. Diplomatic and consular protection thus prevented the worse option of internment. Alice and Bram, stateless Jews from Germany, enjoyed no such protection. They remained in prison for two months and then were interned in a convent in Fribourg.

Still, the two couples had managed to cross all three borders and,

Crossing the Alps in September 1943, Jewish refugees escape from the formerly Italian-occupied zone of France to Italy after the latter signed an armistice with the allies.

once in Switzerland, the authorities did not send them back. They enjoyed luck, fortuitous circumstances, links to a sufficient number of trustworthy people, and timing. They entered Switzerland a mere month before it became impossible to do so. The very day (16 July 1942) that the cheminot welcomed the Ganses and Horodisches at his door in Besançon—not because he was committed to undermining the Nazis' racist policies, but because he was engaged in an effort to combat the Nazi regime—the Swiss army intelligence service reported what it considered alarming news. Increasing numbers of Jewish refugees from the Netherlands and Belgium were stealing into Switzerland. "All of these people leave their countries for the same reason: to escape the work camps to which they are sent by the occupation power," the agents stated flatly. "After analyzing the transcripts of witness interrogations we conclude that regularly established organizations, paid considerable sums of money, take these people to Swiss territory. We see it as urgent to take measures to prevent the arrival of whole groups, which has become a usual occurrence recently."[7]

The Swiss leadership had no illusions about the nature of those work camps, as an internal memo (30 July) by Robert Jezler, deputy to Heinrich Rothmund, head of the Fremdenpolizei and chief of the police department, revealed. All information "about the nature of and the manner in which the deportations are conducted, and about the conditions in the Jewish districts in the East is so horrible that one can understand the refugees' desperate attempts to escape such a fate, and one is hard pressed to take responsibility for rejection,"[8] Jezler acknowledged. Noting that the local people in the border strip felt sympathetic toward the asylum seekers, he agreed with the principle that motivated their stance: "protection of a critically endangered refugee is a basic assumption of our political system." Yet, he argued, Switzerland was in a struggle for its existence. "One cannot be squeamish. We therefore have ordered the ruthless expulsion of refugees" except those "at risk of life or limb."[9] Cantonal authorities too often ignored the federal council decree of 17 October 1939 to expel illegal refugees, and that had to stop, he admonished. Not only were aliens arriving in numbers, but smuggling people had become an organized activity. According to informants in the pay of the Swiss police, French passeurs earned tidy sums to bring people across the Swiss border. "The names of the 'passeurs' are known in Belgium," the informants reported. "The 'passeur' gathers people at night into small groups of five or ten and travels to the Swiss border with them." The operation was fraught with risk, they acknowledged, "as there are a lot of German soldiers in [the border town] Pontarlier and patrols are sent out day and night which must be avoided."[10]

Roused by the numbers and, as the federal council put it, the "character" of infiltration—"more and more organized" and "coordinated by professional 'passeurs'"—the government demanded action.[11] Rothmund promptly called (4 August) for the strict enforcement of the 1939 decree. "In future, the rejection of foreign civilian refugees will take place on a larger scale, even when the foreigners who are involved will incur serious disadvantage (risk of life and limb)."[12] If no one had known what the ultimate consequence of *refoulement* (driving back) would be in the years since the Swiss had closed the border to refugees in August 1938, now they did. And so the government simply shifted ground. This did not constitute refusal of asylum, Rothmund's political boss Federal Councillor Eduard von Steiger contended. It was merely a justifiable measure against criminal activity, "the dirty métier" of "smuggling emigrants."[13]

Rothmund traveled to the border on 13 August to see the situation for himself. Moved by the plight of "two lovely children" among the "Polish and Belgian Jews, all from Brussels," who had smuggled in that day, he did not order the police to expel them on the spot.[14] The immediacy of their tragedy faded upon his return to Bern. "Political refugees" could stay, but "refugees on the basis of racial grounds, Jews for example, do not count as political refugees."[15] He reasoned that his draconian orders would reverberate in Belgium and Holland, and the flow would cease. "Thus I decided," he admitted upon his retirement twelve years later, "with a heavy heart, to take responsibility for the total closure of the border."[16] Alas for sad Rothmund.

Over and over again, clandestine passage turned on timing. Timing in terms of the progress of the war: as the tide turned against Germany, neutral nations became more hospitable toward refugees. Timing with regard to the season and increased difficulty in traversing terrain in inclement weather. The timing of running across a field during the interval of the sentries' rounds. Luck and fortuitous circumstances loomed large, and links to helpers and passeurs were critical. But timing too was key. Luck, fortuitous circumstance, and linkages were with Simon and Laja Sonabend and their children Charles and Sabine. Their timing was wrong.[17]

When Sabine got called up for forced labor in Poland, her family promptly left their home in Brussels on 9 August. Her father Simon, a watch wholesaler, had good contacts in Switzerland and, like Max and

Jenny, he expected their support. He also had a Swiss bank account of 200,000 Swiss francs, a sufficient sum to see them comfortably through the war. They carried considerable resources: $5,000 in cash and $7,000 in checks, 65,000 French francs (FF), and valuable jewelry. They needed it. The Sonabends used professional passeurs to cross into France and then Switzerland and paid FF125,000 for these services, a decade's earnings for a French laborer. They entered Switzerland on 12 August and stayed in a small house in a forest for two days, expecting someone to collect them. While they waited, Rothmund ordered the cantonal police forces to seal the border and strengthen controls at all the railway stations. The Sonabends went to Bienne (Biel), where Simon's business partner Ernest Schneeberger, director of the Freco watch factory, welcomed them warmly. The Sonabends were relieved and felt safe.

None of them knew then that Rothmund had ordered police to enforce the 1939 law ruthlessly. When the Sonabends' friends tried to register them officially, the Bern cantonal authorities responded by arresting them. Obeying Rothmund's instructions of 13 August, district commander Sergeant Choffat took the decision to return the Sonabends to the border that very evening. Schneeberger jumped to their rescue, persuading district judge Alfred Ribeaud, a well-known conservative, and Colonel Ali Rebetez, an equally well-known liberal, to contact Choffat in a bipartisan effort on behalf of the Sonabends. He also got Paul Graber, a social democratic member of parliament and chief editor of the *Sentinelle*, to call.

Choffat refused to reconsider. At 9:00 p.m. he collected Simon and Laja, who began to scream that this meant her death. Passersby heard her, and some fifty people surrounded Choffat's car. "Overcome by pity," Choffat reported, "the public protested the refoulement by the police."[18] In order to prevent a riot, Choffat took the Sonabends to prison. Theirs was a short reprieve. Police dressed in civilian clothes collected the family and, unimpeded by the public, brought them to the border by taxi and pushed them across at 10:30 p.m. on 17 August. "The border crossing went well," Choffat reported to his superior the next morning. "The costs of the taxi and the escort were paid by the party concerned [the Sonabend family]."[19]

For the Sonabends, refoulement spelled the end. Caught by German patrols, they were brought to Belfort, where parents and children were separated. Simon and Laja were sent to Drancy on 23 August and put on a train number 23 to Auschwitz the next day. Laja was gassed upon arrival; Simon soon after. The Germans sent Charles and Sabine to an orphanage run by the French Jewish Council, the UGIF (*Union Générale des Israélites de France*). Drancy was full, so the children, who were slated for future deportation, survived.

The refoulement of the Sonabends also spelled the end of Rothmund's harsh policy. Graber and his fellow MP Paul Billeux mounted a campaign in the press and in parliament reminding their countrymen of the basic humanitarian principles at stake. Walter Rüthli, a popular minister, joined them.[20] Clergymen and liberals around the country laid bare the country's bad conscience, and hardliners began to look for ways to soothe their own. In early September Rothmund instructed police to admit elderly refugees and family members of earlier asylum seekers. On 26 September he added ill people, pregnant women, unaccompanied children under the age of sixteen, and parents with their own children.[21]

Unofficially, another policy took hold: refugees who emerged at least seven miles into Switzerland were not deported either. This prompted a new genre of passeurs: Swiss citizens who helped clandestine entrants move out of the border zone into the interior. Swiss Jews took the lead in this activity, organizing *réseaux* (networks) to help their endangered coreligionists. The military police uncovered one such réseau in November 1942. "Jewish families resident in Switzerland and who live in the Bernese Jura, namely the families Spira, Rérat, Schoppig, Picard and others, have received refugees after they have passed the border and helped to move them by means of contacts into the interior of the country to ensure that the authorities could not expel them,"[22] a military court concluded. This particular network had gained currency in Brussels, where it originated in the homes of Irène Rérat and Marcel Riat. They organized the first leg of the trip to Porrentruy. Armand Spira took over from there, arranging travel by private car or taxis to friends in Delémont or Bienne. Safely outside the border zone, refugees registered with the police. These interior passeurs operated within a technical loophole. While legislation passed in

September 1942 criminalized helping refugees enter Switzerland illegally, no law forbade assistance once the refugees were in the country. Passeurs were exposed and put under surveillance but not imprisoned.[23]

If the informal change in policy gave rise to réseaux within the country, the September hardship allowances prompted initiatives outside the Alpine state to spirit Jews to safety. Swiss officials noticed a new pattern in illicit crossing in early 1943: groups of children. By April this configuration had become so common that Robert Jezler determined to investigate. "According to reports by the relevant military offices, a remarkable stream of refugee children aged five to sixteen has appeared near Geneva for the past three days," he reported on 21 April 1943. "The children arrive in groups of as many as 32 per day. As they are not accompanied by adults, it is clear that an organization takes them to the Swiss border."[24]

Believing that the French Red Cross was responsible, the Swiss government contacted its representative in Vichy, Walter Stucki. The French foreign office had looked into the matter, he responded (28 May), but the best it could offer was that there was some evidence that an organization named OSE was involved. Unfortunately, Stucki concluded, neither the French foreign office nor he knew anything about OSE.[25]

That they did not was sheer luck for everyone in the OSE operation. The officials had no reason for ignorance: OSE, a legal philanthropic organization, had operated in France for a decade by that point. Initially a charitable health care organization, OSE (*Obsczestvo Sdravochraneniya Eryeyev*, or Society for the Health of the Jewish Population), was founded by Jewish physicians in Russia in 1912. After the revolution its headquarters moved to Berlin and, following the election of Hitler in 1933, to Paris. It was there that the society took the name *Oeuvre de Secours aux Enfants* (Children's Aid Organization). Responding to the deteriorating situation in Europe, OSE began to focus on protecting Jewish children. The fall of France in June 1940 and division of the country into the northern occupied zone and the southern free zone under the collaborationist government of Marshal Pétain in Vichy forced OSE to move quickly.[26] In the midst of the occupation of Paris and the mass exodus to the south, OSE emptied its orphanages in the Parisian suburbs and fled to the south. OSE-Sud became responsible for the activities carried out in the unoccupied zone. Two officers, Falk Walk and Eugène Minkovski, carried on in Paris and kept the OSE office at 92 Champs-Elysées open throughout the war. How the French foreign office failed to find an organization with a Champs-Elysées address remains a mystery.

SOON REALIZING THAT FOREIGN JEWS were at greater risk than their French-born coreligionists, OSE-Nord turned to smuggling central and eastern European children across the demarcation line. OSE-Sud, in turn, began to develop a legal network of services. It undertook clandestine activities later, in the wake of the August 1942 dragnets, still maintaining its legal structure of children's homes and health care centers, which also served as a screen to organize secret border crossings and laboratories to produce false identity papers and to hide those in imminent danger of arrest. The German occupation of the free zone in November 1942 meant that fewer resources could be wasted on legal work. At a meeting in Lyon on 16 January 1943 the OSE directorate decided on "the systematic camouflage of children sheltered in the various children's homes." They had become too obvious and too vulnerable a target and had to be hidden.[27] Those who could not go underground (due to religious practice, inability to speak French, or too "Jewish" an appearance) needed to be smuggled over the border, primarily into Switzerland but also into Spain.[28]

Dr Joseph Weill, medical director of OSE, proposed that Georges Garel, an OSE co-worker, develop a network to hide Jewish children who could "pass" as gentiles. Andrée Salomon was tasked with looking after those who could not "pass."[29] And as Georges Loinger recalled it, Weill's instruction to him amounted to one sentence: "'You, Georges, I charge you with developing a network, a way to escape to Switzerland."[30]

Weill reckoned that Loinger, an Alsatian like himself, spoke German as flawlessly as French, which would prove useful. Then too, he had good contacts in the Zionist movement (he had joined an Alsatian variant of the German Zionist organization Blau-Weiss in his youth) and with the *Eclaireurs Israélites* (EI, or Jewish Scouts), which meant that he enjoyed a wide network of connections. Loinger had earned a degree in engineering but, passionate about teaching and sport, he had used his training to support a second degree as a physical education instructor, and he was healthy and fit. Equally important, he had impressive military discharge papers stating that he had served, been taken prisoner, and had escaped from a POW camp. His job as supervisor-in-chief of the *Compagnons de France* for the Vichy region provided another set of useful documents. The Compagnons was the first of some sixty organizations for young people to spring up by March 1941 in the new nationalistic climate of Pétain's regime in the south. Jewish youth organizations had been permitted to continue, and a few Jews, like Georges, worked for the new national youth movements. Designed for young people aged fifteen to twenty, the Compagnons was subsidized by Vichy.[31] "That served me well, because I had official papers from the Vichy state. It was a very important cover for me that served me throughout all the rest that I did." What Weill probably did not know was that Georges also had joined the national resistance organization some months earlier and was attached to the réseau Bourgogne. This too helped him develop a successful escape route.[32]

"I chose Annemasse as the departure point of the transit line for OSE children," he explained decades later. Located at the end of a railway line, near the Swiss border, Annemasse had long been a choice location for vacation groups. It had facilities to accommodate large numbers, and the townspeople were used to seeing lots of children come and go. Annemasse also had "a tradition of traffic between France and Switzerland; it had an established contraband system." By chance, Georges got to know Eugène Balthazar, the director of a *Secours National* (National Aid) center in Annemasse, and that "became my rendezvous point." Chatting with Balthazar, Georges realized that he supported Charles de Gaulle and the Free French movement, and Georges, in turn, explained his mission. Balthazar "agreed to host my groups for a night or two."[33]

The "key to my organization," however, was the mayor of Annemasse, Jean Deffaugt, who had come to Georges's attention through the réseau Bourgogne. Deffaugt gave him the names of two passeurs. Feeling his way forward, Georges entered into discussion with them and at the same time organized his own plan. "Furnished with official Compagnons

Jewish refugee children received by passeurs on the French-Swiss border in 1943.

de France papers that allowed me to travel and with work orders for a sports event with the reception centers in Annemasse . . . I took my first group of about twenty EI youngsters from Moissac [the Scouts' children's home]." Sympathetic railway workers helped Georges and the children avoid German patrols at the Annemasse station exits by posting an "Exit for Camp Groups" sign over one door. Georges took the children to a sports ground right next to the border, where they played soccer until "the propitious moment. Then the children went six by six up to the previously loosened wire." They were to be met by OSE Swiss on the other side. He learned from this experience: those over sixteen were refoulés. He managed to collect them and brought them back to Moissac, where they got new papers with adjusted ages. And he decided to use professional passeurs.[34]

Georges chose "the son of an innkeeper in a small village outside Annemasse who undoubtedly had been a contraband runner before the war." The cost at the time ran between three and five thousand francs per child. Georges met the children in Aix-les-Bains and took them by train to Annemasse. They exited through the specially marked door and went directly to the Secours National center, which "offered the advantage of being an official institution, above all suspicion." The children remained there for two nights. At 10:00 p.m., after curfew, they lined up silently, two by two, an older child holding a younger by the hand, and filed out with the passeur. Passeurs "don't like others to know their transit spots," Georges observed. "They must be prudent and above all keep their secrets to themselves in order to make themselves indispensable; that's the foundation of their business. That's the reason why I couldn't accompany the children to the crossing point." If the passeurs wanted to keep their secrets, Georges sought to maintain his. "I ordered the children never to say the word 'OSE,' but to talk about the Red Cross."[35] Perhaps this is why the Swiss believed the Red Cross was responsible for the organized crossings.

Georges paid the passeurs after the fact, when all had gone well. The costs were high. Through his resistance network he got into contact with passeurs who were "a little less greedy than the others." And they, knowing his maquis connections, did not abandon the children halfway or try to dupe him. Still, the cost ranged between twenty-five hundred and three thousand French francs. By spring 1944, no amount of money sufficed. "At the end, they were afraid. The Germans had reinforced their border patrols, and [the passeurs] just didn't want to chance it, even for more money." As Georges knew the route, "I myself took the children."[36]

By that time a number of OSE operatives were taking children to the border. Elisabeth (Böszi) Hirsch had come to Paris from her native Romania in 1929, when she was sixteen years old. When the war erupted, she became an *interne volontaire* (voluntary social worker) in the French internment camp of Gurs and, in 1943, she got involved in hiding children in France or spiriting them out of the country.[37] Jewish, Romanian, and speaking accented French, Böszi guided children to the Swiss border. Occasionally, older people joined these convoys, and it was they who posed the greatest problems for her. "Once, after a day's march crossing the frontier, a physician said that he wanted to turn back. The passeurs promptly responded, 'If you turn back, we will throw you down the mountain.' And they would have done it, because he would have put the whole group in danger. It was sheer misery to see the adults trailing along; they simply could not walk well. When the passeurs left us near the border, the older folk got lost in the fog. We saw that there were people who could not keep up with the group."[38]

Böszi typically accompanied the children to the frontier but did not cross herself. In August 1944, however, Andrée Salomon asked her to take a Palestine-bound group over the Pyrenees to Spain. The whole company consisted of a dozen eight- to fourteen-year-olds, five adults, and six guides.[39] The terrain grew difficult. Despite their sweaters and scarves, the icy temperatures gnawed at them, and they took the wrong path for some hours. Yet they persevered and crossed with the entire group intact. First interrogated by Spanish border guards, then welcomed by the American Jewish Joint Distribution Committee (JDC) in Barcelona, the refugees moved on to Lisbon in October, members of a larger group destined for Palestine on a chartered Portuguese boat. Spanish authorities kept Böszi in Barcelona until November. Perhaps they wished to ensure her immobility. In any case, it was OSE's last run to Spain.[40]

OSE was but one of the Jewish organizations to develop clandestine routes to Switzerland and Spain. Although Vichy police had made many arrests, the incidents appeared to be unrelated. The officials could draw but one conclusion: "obviously many rings are involved."[41] The Eclaireurs and a broadband Zionist organization, the *Mouvement de Jeunesse Sioniste* (MJS) in conjunction with the Jewish armed resistance movement *L'Organisation de Combat*, for example, ran active clandestine operations. At war's end, the MJS reported that two thousand children and many hundreds of families had crossed into Switzerland through its networks, and that it had organized a route to Spain for hundreds of young people to join the allies.[42] The Eclaireurs reckoned that its routes had served about five hundred in all.[43] The JDC credited OSE with smuggling two thousand children into Switzerland as well; it is probable that Georges Loinger alone was responsible for half that number.[44]

WE KNOW OF PASSEURS such as Böszi Hirsch and Georges Loinger because they belonged to organizations that wished to tell their history and the history of the people they had served or tried to serve. We know little about the "professional" passeurs, who had smuggled goods before the war, people during the occupation, and went back to contraband after the surrender. At best, police reports explained that passeurs "live near the frontier and recruit above all (for the Spanish border) among Spanish subjects and among guides for the Swiss border. They are almost all notorious contraband runners, ready for any type of job. They don't hesitate for a moment to turn over the people who have put themselves under their protection to the French or Spanish police." A typical individual entry yields little but a name: "PEREZ Jose, who may be the same as PEREZ Victor, born 10 September 1901 in FLIX (Spain) was domiciled in 1941 at Prades 8 rue Voltaire."[45] We know even less about the thousands of people who helped Jews like the Gans and Horodisch couples or the Sonabend family. It is probable that most Jews did not flee through an organized underground. They sought their way on their own and, if they found trustworthy people to help them and luck, fortuitous circumstance, and timing was with them, they succeeded. Isabelle Silberg-Riff and her sister Charlotte were among them, but we will never know the passeurs whose efforts saved the lives of these young girls.

Isabelle was born on Christmas Day 1932 in Antwerp. Her Czech-born, Yiddish-speaking father was part owner of a diamond cutting and polishing business; her Hungarian mother was a housewife. The business did well, and "I remember in 1937 we moved to a flat. It was great event to move from a terraced house into a modern flat with central heating [and] modern furniture." When "my father would come home on a Shabbat afternoon and he wanted to put his feet on the new chair, [my mother] ran quickly to get a paper to put under his shoes; it shouldn't

Jewish refugee boys living in Hôme de la Fôrêt, run by the Swiss branch of OSE, stand at the source of the Rhine with one foot on either shore, July 1945.

spoil the new chair. And that was 1937; 1940 the war broke out, and we left everything, the new chairs, the new chandeliers, whatever was fashionable in those days, we left it."

Isabelle, her two-year-old sister Charlotte, and their parents sought safety in the south of France. They landed in Béziers, where they lived off the sale of valuables they had brought with them, help from OSE, and the generosity of strangers. Refugee life, precarious at best, teetered on the edge of disaster. When Vichy, in collaboration with the Germans, unrolled dragnet operations targeting foreign and stateless Jews in the summer of 1942, her parents recognized their peril. The girls were to be smuggled out of the country. The last time Isabelle and Charlotte saw their parents during the war, Isabelle recalled, "my mother had a new dress for each of us. She had new shoes for us. And I remember her giving me a comb, and she said to me from now on I must comb my sister's hair. I must wash her, I must clean her, I must look after her. And that we were going to Switzerland; I had another uncle who lived in Switzerland then, and that he will be there to receive us. How we would get to Switzerland, or who would take us, she did not know. I remember we had a meal together, and then our parents kissed us good-bye."

One of Isabelle's many uncles was a university student in Montpellier. His friend, a young woman and fellow student, brought the girls false papers. Posing as their mother, she accompanied them by train to her home in Montpellier. Well after midnight another student came to fetch the children from her house. The girls were told to follow him but were forbidden to speak to him or acknowledge his presence. Traveling again by train, they went to Lyon and on to Thonon-les-Bains, a small resort town on the French side of Lake Geneva. The student booked himself and the two girls into a hotel. "We were there for two weeks in that beautiful town. It was absolutely breathtaking. And for me to live in a hotel and eat what they brought to the table—that was nonkosher food! For me that was an experience. I could not understand it. And my parents had said, and *everybody* had said, 'Whatever they give you, you eat. Whatever they tell you to do, you do.' We were there in this hotel, and he was trying to contact a smuggler to take us over to Switzerland. He could not find the smuggler."

One day, when the town was entranced with a troupe of traveling artistes and their performing dogs, bear, and clown, the young man telephoned the girls' uncle in Montpellier: what should he do? "No sooner had he put the phone down than there was a raid on the hotel. The Germans came, and they were looking for us. I took my sister and we mingled amongst the people standing in the street watching the performance."

Neither the girls nor the student were found, but he had to disappear and they had to move on. "I was told there would be a lady with a bicycle. We followed her; we did not walk with her through the streets. She took us to her father's house." He was the local Protestant parson. The girls were safe for a week before another raid drove them out once more. The minister's daughter took the girls high up into the mountains, to an orphanage she directed. "And she told us, 'There are some staff who are with the French, and there are some who are collaborators with the Germans.'"

Isabelle's spirits flagged and her health deteriorated. "I was violently sick; this was tension. I could not eat by then. I was already beginning to become desperate, because we were handed from people to people whom I never knew. I had never seen them before and I will never see them again. But they were very kind. Otherwise we would not have survived."

One Sunday in September when the children of the orphanage went out to collect mushrooms, Isabelle and her sister, with baskets on their arms, walked away from the group deeper into the woods. The director of the orphanage pointed the way. "My sister's shoes were torn by then, those new shoes which my mother had prepared in the flat. The sole had curled off; it was made from paper. And I remember I had to put on my sister those torn shoes. We left the group of children and we walked."

This time they were successful. They were met by a smuggler carrying a lunch box filled with "real Swiss chocolate." Persuading her sister to walk by tempting her with candy, they crossed the border. "It was beautiful—the taste of that chocolate I have never found again."[46]

CAUGHT IN
INTERNMENT CAMPS

F EW JEWS SOUGHT ASYLUM IN THE USSR BEFORE THE OUTBREAK OF war. The Soviets gave them little reason to do so. Moscow had not cooperated with the high commission established by the League of Nations, participated in the Evian conference, or sent delegates to the Inter-Governmental Committee established in the wake of that conference. Furious that the League had protected White Russians with its Nansen passport, the Soviets refused to recognize these documents or to issue or hold as valid the later *certificats*. Except for officially invited visitors, the Soviet Union admitted no one.

The German invasion of Poland and the Molotov-Ribbentrop pact changed the situation on the ground. Hearing about German atrocities against Jews in Czestochowa and other towns, some 300,000 Jewish refugees from western and central Poland fled east, joining the 1.2 million Jews who lived in Soviet-occupied Poland.[1] At the same time, many young Zionists left for Romania in the hope of traveling on to Palestine but, unable to cross the border, found themselves stranded in the Soviet part of Poland.[2] Soldiers in the Polish army either had been detailed to the east or, following orders, relocated east of the Vistula, and they too fell under Soviet authority. Jerzy Kagan's father, for example, a physician called up in the Polish army, "never came back to Lublin," where his family lived. "My father found himself in the eastern part of Poland which the Russians occupied," Jerzy recalled decades later. "When he saw what was happening, he went to Bialystok and stayed with his relatives."[3] The German-Soviet treaty of 28 September set the partition line, and the Soviets accepted everyone who had lived in their part of Poland before the outbreak of war, as well as those who had fled there.

Describing the situation in German-occupied Poland, Jewish Joint Distribution Committee (JDC or Joint) officials cabled: "Physical, spiritual suffering exceed all previous experience. November tenth [1938] reports paling in comparison. Impossible convey actual situation." Throughout September, men "fled east, thousands crossing into Russian territory daily"; they planned to situate themselves before sending for their families.[4] A mass exodus continued throughout the autumn and visibly affected Jewish communities on both sides of the border. "There is no end to the 'flight' of the Jews to the Führer's 'friends,'" Warsaw resident and educator Chaim Kaplan confided to his diary on 15 November 1939. He saw it as nothing less than salvation. "Our sages' words were justified: 'The Almighty prepares the remedy before the sickness.' Were it not for Soviet Russia we would be strangled to death."[5]

Forced flight swelled the refugee stream. Once the demarcation line was established, Berlin saw an opportunity. Jews were "expelled by Germans without notice, unable to take clothing, any belongings whatsoever, Russian aid at present limited one meal daily which not all able get regularly," a Joint cable reported. "Half million people without winter clothing and impossible obtain Russia."[6]

The Soviet attitude changed by the end of October. They had secured the territory, and they were overwhelmed by refugees. "Formerly received hospitably now encountering dificulty," Joint workers observed on 1 November.[7] Germans continued to push Jews over the border, but the Soviets now barred entry. Caught between German gun barrels and Soviet threats, the Jews sat in a no-man's-land. The weather grew "bitterly cold and many froze to death," reported a Jew who adopted the pseudonym David Grodner for self-protection as his accounts were smuggled abroad. "Thousands eventually gathered in these no-man's lands. Nazi guards would have 'fun' with them, and their cries would be heard on both sides of the boundary." For Grodner, as for the JDC workers, language failed. "It is impossible to describe the appearance of these refugees, hungry, starved, ill, and dressed in rags." Their situation deteriorated daily. "When finally the refugees had reached a point of desperation, they stampeded past the Soviet guards. Several were shot, but most of them got across after overpowering the sentries by their sheer weight of numbers. Sometimes red soldiers who sympathized with these unfortunates disregarded the orders of their superiors."[8]

The Soviets lodged protest after protest against the expulsions with the German foreign office. On one occasion, for example, Vladimir Potemkin, deputy commissar of foreign affairs, handed German Ambassador Friedrich von Schulenburg a memo detailing blatant incidents between 10 November and 12 December in which a total of 23,275 Jews had been forced over the demarcation line.[9] The Soviets might have been more inclined to accept them had the Germans not followed their established practice of depredation before expulsion. The Reich's refusal to allow Jews to emigrate with their property had proved a major obstacle to immigration to other countries, and it remained a deal breaker now.[10]

The Germans pushed Jews over the Lithuanian border too, and the Lithuanians followed the Soviet example. Jewish refugees had fled into the Suwalki district in an effort to escape the German advance, and in the hope of reaching Lithuania which still had connections with the outside world.[11] From there, perhaps immigration to Palestine or the United States might be organized. According to a report by Moses Beckelman, vice chairman of the Joint's executive council, there were fifteen thousand Jews in the district when the Germans annexed it to the Reich and unrolled a new expulsion action at the end of October. Announcing that Jews were to go to Lithuania and Germans in Lithuania were to come to Suwalki, Nazi authorities ordered Jews to "pack immediately (immediately varying from twenty minutes to two hours) and leave. They were escorted to the frontier and when the Lit guards refused to admit them they were told to make their own way over the frontier as best they could but not to return to German Poland under penalty of death. All papers, passports, etc. were taken from them and destroyed." Lithuania was in a bind. Beckelman quoted Vice Premier Bizauakas's observation that "while Lithuania could perfectly well admit 500 or even 1000 such refugees this would simply constitute an invitation to the Germans to send in thousands more which would swamp the country." Still, several hundred made their way into the country, and "about a thousand were scattered at various points on the frontier" in no-man's-land by 2 November. Asked to send aid, the Lithuanian Red Cross declined "on the grounds that these were not Lithuanian citizens and were not on Lithuanian territory." At the same time, Lithuanian frontier guards refused to allow Jews from the area to "bring food, clothing, and blankets to the refugees in the field."[12]

Beckelman struggled to convey the work of the local Lithuanian Jewish communities. "It is impossible to overemphasize the devotion and sacrifice of these small Jewish communities," he wrote. "In a town of fifty Jewish families every home has seven or eight refugees who were being housed and fed." Comparing their activities to "an underground railway" of the Civil War era, Beckelman explained that "the actual work of smuggling refugees over the frontier was carried by Jewish young people" intent upon rescuing their coreligionists. The "railway" continued in Lithuania. "Elaborate patrol systems were worked out for meeting refugees along various roads and guiding them to prearranged houses where they would be sheltered until morning and then passed on." Beckelman admired the participants' dedication. "Young men go out to the frontier night after night and remain on duty waiting for people to come through." In the east as in the west, border crossing also rested in the hands of "professional smugglers who ran the frontier with refugees purely as a business proposition." The Joint official worried about them as "a source of danger and blackmail but," he acknowledged, "their knowledge of the territory and of the frontier guards was useful."[13]

Jerzy Kagan's family, like so many others, depended upon just such Jewish and gentile smugglers. They turned to them to send and receive letters and parcels because the mail service no longer functioned,[14] and they relied on them to reunite their families. "We were with the Germans from September seventeenth when they marched into Lublin until the twenty-ninth of November 1939. My father [Leon] told us [by] a letter smuggled by someone that he was going to send a smuggler for us. They were Polish peasants who were smugglers of human cargo. He [the peasant] would smuggle us to Soviet-occupied Poland. We departed Lublin on the twenty-ninth of November, and on the first of December—which was my birthday, I was thirteen; this was my bar mitzvah—for my bar mitzvah gift I got an arrival in the Soviet zone of Poland, which wasn't a bad gift." Jerzy remembered that carrying just one small bag apiece, he and his mother Rywka "walked part of the way, and then we traveled in a horse and buggy part of the way. Eventually we got to the Bug river." They waited until it grew dark. "At night, this peasant got us into a little boat and paddled. He was either skilled or lucky because we didn't run into Germans and we didn't run into Soviets. We got to this place on the border, and that's where my father met us." If Jerzy at age thirteen took these events more or less in his stride, his father did not share that nonchalance. "My father met us, and I was very surprised that he was crying." Together, they joined Leon's family in Bialystok.[15]

The Kagans were fortunate to have relatives in the city. Bialystok and Lvov quickly became two main magnets for refugees, and the population swelled far beyond the capacity of the Jewish community to offer aid. "Thousands of refugees had nowhere to sleep," a refugee from Warsaw observed. "Many of them spent their nights loitering outdoors, slumbering on park benches, standing in some gateway, or leaning against a wall. At dawn, they queued up for the beds of people who had found a place to sleep that night."[16] Ideologically opposed to philanthropy, the Soviets forbade Jewish relief agencies to raise funds and shut down the spontaneously organized soup kitchens that had opened in an attempt to meet the refugees' needs. And they dismantled Jewish communal governing boards (*Kehillot*), the body that would have addressed such problems.[17] Allowed to function, synagogues became foci of relief efforts, and refugees sheltered in every corner of these buildings. As Joseph Ceder, whose family fled from Lodz to Warsaw to Bialystok, recalled, "all those refugees were put up in synagogues." In Grodno too, his family's next stop, "That's where we slept, it was freezing cold, people . . . were rich and poor and beggars and representatives of all the classes of people who fled the German occupation. Most of them had nothing."[18]

Refugees needed work to survive. Leon Kagan secured a job as a physician in a hospital. The Ceder family too was "doing a little bit better after a while, because my brother was working in a restaurant, my mother was working in the kitchen which was feeding the refugees, and Papa was also doing some kind of work." But few found employment. The Soviets, for their part, wanted to put the refugees to work. With hundreds of thousands of uprooted people on their hands, they wished to regulate the situation. And they worried about the economy. Adopting an official policy of Ukrainization and Belorussification, the Soviets offered employment in the Ukraine and Belorussia to refugee doctors, nurses, pharmacists, and teachers who spoke Ukrainian or Belorussian; this promoted their plan to expand the local health and education systems. The introduction of communism also brought bureaucracy, which opened opportunities for clerks, accountants, and economists.[19]

Few Jews knew these languages, however, and the Soviets offered them jobs in the USSR proper. Enticed by free transportation, advance payment, and employment in their profession or trade, tens of thousands of refugees registered to work in large factory towns like Magnitogorsk in the Urals or in orange plantations in the Crimea or in peach plantations in Uzbekistan. They soon discovered how poor conditions were: put to work as unskilled laborers, they received starvation wages and primitive housing. Many left their jobs without permission and returned to Bialystok where they were promptly arrested. Departure without official approval was a punishable offense in the USSR.[20]

Tension quickly mounted. Exasperated, the Soviets saw the refugees as ingrates. The refugees feared the Soviets as tyrants. And indeed: intent upon absolute control of everyone within their borders, the Soviets offered the refugees citizenship. At a time when no other country offered citizenship to émigrés, the Soviet Union adopted a policy of mass naturalization. They envisioned it as an effective framework of Sovietization for a population that proved reluctant to adapt to new conditions.

The Soviets extended their citizenship law to their annexed part of Poland on 29 November 1939. All Polish citizens who found themselves in Soviet territory on 1 and 2 November (when Belorussia and the Ukraine were incorporated into the USSR) were invited to become citizens. Those who had arrived after those dates were offered citizenship on easy terms. The Soviets simply did not want stateless people on their hands or people with Polish citizenship, which had no value since partition.

If the Soviets saw their offer as a gift, for the vast majority of Jewish refugees it posed a cruel dilemma. They wanted to regularize their situation but, hoping for family reunification and repatriation to western and central Poland, they were loath to take a new nationality. To accept Soviet citizenship meant formally and finally to give up on the idea of return to home and family or emigration abroad. Dora Huze, a refugee from Lodz via Warsaw, attended a teacher training school run by the Soviets in Grodno where "I get bread, I get a soup, I can eat in the dining [room] that was beautiful! The best." But when "they asked to register," she declined. "I was thinking the war would be over soon, I would go back to my family. And if I take citizenship, I could never leave Russia." "We turned them down," Jerzy declared. His mother's family had remained

Refugees in the Soviet Union (note the Cyrillic letters CCCP *[in English:* USSR*] and hammer and sickle) board a deportation train composed of freight cars for labor camps in Siberia sometime between 1939 and 1941.*

in Lublin, and his father was too great a Polish patriot to accept such a proposal. "The result of this was that about two months later, on the thirtieth of June 1940, about four in the morning, three in the morning, there was a knock on the door, and there were seven soldiers giving us the invitation to join them in northern Russia. And this started the trip to Soviet Russia."[21] A journey Dora Huze, her husband, and at least two hundred thousand other Jews were forced to take. "They didn't beat us," Dora hastened to clarify. "They didn't do any harm to us. No. They only told us to go. And we have to obey orders."[22]

The Soviets were determined to put the refugees to work: they needed the newcomers' labor and, xenophobic to the core, they were highly suspicious of those who refused citizenship. Newspapers referred to such refugees as "garbage to be swept out,"[23] and action soon followed propaganda. Deportation of refugees started in June, and those caught were not unduly alarmed. They believed (correctly, as it happened) that this relocation would be temporary. They imagined working deep in the Soviet Union and waiting for the collapse of the Third Reich. Some refugees actively sought transport to the east. "'We cannot stay [in Grodno]; we're too close to the Germans,'" Joseph Ceder reported his father saying. "'Those two [Russians and Germans] cannot get along . . . and we have to see somehow to get deeper into Russia. This thing will not stay this way.' And he did all that was in his power to try to register for work deep into Russia." Neither Reb Ceder nor anyone else imagined how harsh life would be.[24]

Experienced in deporting large populations, the Soviets picked up and packed off over two hundred thousand refugees in a few days.[25] "They brought us to the railway station in Bialystok. There were thousands and thousands of people," Jerzy remembered. "The station was surrounded by NKVD [Soviet secret police]. They were assisted by units of the border guard in their blue and grassy green hats." Like Dora, Jerzy specified, "I do not recall seeing any physical violence." And he continued, "We were loaded into cargo trains, which had some kind of multitier shelves which were used for lying down. The mode of transport was primitive, but bearable."[26] This meant that "there was a stove in the middle of the car. I think there was a bucket, but I also remember that at every stop, people went to relieve themselves. Women one way, men the other."[27] Evidently, the Soviets did not worry that the deportees would attempt to escape. "Security was not all that strict, and once we left the centers of population often the doors to the cars were open."[28]

Oddly, no one—not Jews who accepted Soviet citizenship or those who declined—was sent to Birobidzhan, the autonomous Jewish region in Siberia. Jews were transported to mining areas, to regions where the Soviet Union needed roads, railways, and canals to provide connections to the Arctic Sea (Germany controlled all routes out of Russia in the west), and to logging sites. Birobidzhan boasted none of these. Jews ended up in the Arctic region of European Russia, Siberia, or the Soviet republics of central Asia, where work of strategic importance to the Soviet war effort lay. Most were detailed to internment camps and collective farms. Some, infinitely less fortunate, were formally convicted of a convenient crime (like lack of valid papers) and shunted off to a prison camp.

The Kagan family's transport went to an internment camp in the Arctic. Passing through Kargopol (Political Prisoners' Town) around 7 July, they proceeded for another two and a half weeks by foot, horse-and-buggy, and horse-drawn railway on log tracks to a settlement called Poy-aminka, arriving on 26 July 1940. Situated in a clearing in the woods, "the camp consisted of some barracks and a few houses. There was no fence and though there were watchtowers, they were unmanned."[29] Like many other Jews deported to such internment camps, Jerzy stressed the harsh-ness of the climate, the tasks, and the daily work quota, not human brutal-ity. "The whole guard was maybe two or three soldiers for the whole camp because there was nowhere to run away. . . . There was no show of arms. . . . It was not really like a prison in a way. It was a camp. We were there, and there was no place to go." The deportees—all of whom in Jerzy's memory were Jews—were put to work felling trees. "There was no physi-cal maltreatment. The major problem was the weather and the food."[30]

Once again the Kagan family enjoyed good fortune. "We were very lucky because my father turned out to be the only doctor in the train. So he became the camp doctor, which was a big thing because even the NKVD needed a doctor. Our conditions, by camp standards, were very luxurious. First of all he had a little hospital; there were two or three or four beds. Then we were given a separate house." The Kagan family inhabited one room, a nurse and her husband a second; a dispensary occupied the third. The kitchen consisted of a stove in the middle of the hut. "Obviously there was no bathroom, just an outhouse. In the winter that was a bit of a problem, with forty degrees below centigrade. And there was no bathroom in terms of washing yourself." The "hospital" served three camps, but "there were no supplies or anything," not even suturing materials to stitch wounds, a common occupational hazard.[31]

Leon Kagan's position as a physician spared him the life-threatening ordeal of the Soviet work quota. Rywka, a dentist, worked with her husband. Just about everyone else over the age of fourteen felled trees, including physicians and dentists who arrived on later transports. Food rations depended upon the degree to which a laborer fulfilled the work norm. No one did, and hunger raged. Even Jerzy's family, protected from the daily caloric expenditure of hard manual labor, needed to supplement the internment camp diet. Many, including the Kagans, survived on food parcels sent by friends and relatives until Germany attacked Russia in June 1941.[32]

The work quota, Julius Margolin, a Jewish inmate of a prison camp explained, was based on the "full labor potential of a healthy Russian peasant." Margolin had fled from Lodz, declined a Soviet passport, and was arrested and deported to northern Russia, where he ended up in a camp known as 48 square. He was a committed Zionist, whose training framed his analysis of the Soviet system. In his view, Zionists understood the difficulty of transforming middle class people into laborers, and their program involved training and idealism. "We created a complex system for our youth to initiate them in manual work," which included hachshara and, later, support "by our organization in Palestine. Furthermore, these young people were imbued with an ideal. They were enthusiastic, convinced of their historic mission, and their role as a national avant garde." By contrast, "the Soviet government sent masses of those who belonged to the intelligentsia and semi-intelligentsia, employees, merchants, traders, Jewish small artisans into the camps. And they were told: 'You have three weeks to learn to work.'"[33]

The intense cold without proper clothing or heating; the hunger, body lice and bedbugs inside, and biting flies and bloodthirsty mosquitoes outside; and the backbreaking, unending labor quotas, shape former inmates' recollections. "We have to work in the forest. And the condition was terrible!" Dora Huze remembered. We can't survive there in those conditions. And we can't leave there."[34] Joseph Ceder's father had registered the family for work in the interior, and "we were accepted to go to work in a town called Nizhny Tagil," in the Ural mountains, a center of railroad car production. "We arrived on May 1, 1940. We opened the doors. We are in woods. Snowing. May first, snowing, woods as far as the eye could see. . . . We got out, looked around us—this is it. We lay down to sleep. The next day we got instructions that we're going to be building a railroad. . . . After one day of rest, we went out to work. Everybody worked. Everybody worked."[35]

Many died. Many more suffered from scurvy and lost their teeth. Even greater numbers endured typhoid, tuberculosis, dysentery, malaria, and accidents on the job. At the same time, as Dora put it, "It was not like the German camps. We were not beaten. There were no ovens. . . . We adjust ourselves to the condition . . . we start living. And we make the best of what is possible."[36] "In retrospect, they saved us," Jerzy concluded. "But this was not their intention. This was not the intention." The fate of his uncle's family elaborates this observation. Jerzy's uncle fled with them to Bialystok, where the Soviets charged him with counterrevolutionary activities and sent him to a prison camp. His wife and daughter remained in Poland; they had planned to join him when he had got settled. The uncle survived and returned to Poland after the war. "He didn't find his wife and daughter because they were killed in the Holocaust. He came back, but in very poor health. He lost all his teeth; he had scurvy."[37]

THE GERMANS INVADED THE SOVIET UNION on 22 June 1941, and some 10 percent of the Jewish population in eastern Poland fled before the Nazi onslaught. The German attack also changed the deportees' status. The Soviet Union promptly joined the Allied camp. This called for a rapprochement with Poland—which the Soviets had invaded two years before. Moscow established diplomatic relations with the Polish government-in-exile in London on 30 July and, consequently, officially recognized Polish deportees, including refugees who had not accepted Soviet passports in 1939–40, as Polish nationals under Polish diplomatic protection. Such niceties counted, even in 1941 Europe. An official amnesty soon followed (12 August 1941), and Poles (including Jews) who had been shipped off were now free to leave the collective farms and internment and prison camps. Word trickled slowly to the far north, Siberia, and central Asia, and some local Soviet officials were loath to

Polish-Jewish refugees in the Soviet Union bake matzah for Passover, c. 1945.

give up the inmate labor. Nearly two years later (April 1943), the Russians still had not released everyone. But continued diplomatic pressure by the Polish ambassador meant that the deportees had a champion, and they knew they had not been forgotten.[38]

WHILE INTERNMENT CAMPS IN THE SOVIET UNION permitted a chance for survival, internment camps in France conduced to death. And while Jews had harbored few illusions with regard to Russia's hospitality, they fled to France after the Nazis' rise to power, believing it offered asylum. France had a long tradition of hospitality. Most recently it had absorbed large numbers of White Russians in 1919. Targets of the Nazi regime followed in 1933. And the collapse of Republican Spain in 1939 sent hundreds of thousands of refugees into France. Nearly as many refugees left Spain for France in the first two months of 1939 as left Germany, Austria, Bohemia, and Moravia from 1933 until 1941: 465,000 as compared with 475,000.[39] The French government responded to this crisis by erecting three large tent camps on the Roussillon beaches and dumping 43,000 refugees at Argelès, 70,000 at Barcarès, and 30,000 at St. Cyprien. More camps followed, such as Gurs and Le Vernet in the foothills of the Pyrenees and, farther from the border, Septfonds and Agde.[40] Intended to be temporary, they soon became fixed, miserable institutions.

These centers secured government control and offered little to the refugees. Not even the legal protections afforded prison inmates applied to camp inmates. They did not get food, clothing, or shelter as specified by penal code, and they lost their civil liberties. "Hundreds of thousands of women, children, old people, soldiers, and intellectuals have been driven like cattle into camps surrounded by barbed wire," Alfred Kantorowicz, a German-Jewish refugee who had served in the International Brigade until 1938, wrote in his diary on 20 February 1939. "No food, nothing to drink, no huts, no barracks, no bandages. The wounded and ill die in their own blood and shit. The others lie on the bare ground through the winter nights. Children cry of hunger. Men suffering from nervous breakdowns fight for a scrap of bread, or a blanket."[41]

When Spaniards began to return to their homes at the end of 1939, the French government found a new use for these incarceration facilities: enemy aliens, stateless persons, and people "under suspicion" arrested after the outbreak of war. With so many foreigners detained the state opened eighty new camps.[42] Socialist deputy Marius Moutet blasted the mass arrests of refugees in the Chamber of Deputies. "It is unacceptable that those who escaped the Hitler camps are now interned in French camps," he thundered. "This is too great an injustice, too cruel for words. These people must be released immediately."[43] But few followed his lead. "A tide of xenophobia swept over France with morbid rapidity," Arthur Koestler observed in his 1941 memoir.[44] A refugee legally residing in France since 1933, Koestler was arrested on 2 October 1939 and sent to Le Vernet. His "first impression on approaching it was of a mess of barbed wire and more barbed wire," he recalled. "There was no stove during the winter of 1939, no lighting, and there were no blankets. The camp had no refectory for meals, not a single table or stool in the hutments; it didn't provide spoons, or forks to eat with, nor soap to wash with. A fraction of its population could afford to buy those things; the others were reduced to a Stone Age level."[45] Thanks to outside interventions, Koestler and fifty others were released in the next few months; the rest, at least two thousand people, remained.

More arrived when the Germans attacked the Netherlands, Belgium, Luxembourg, and France. Fearing a fifth column, French authorities now called on all men between fifteen and fifty-five and all unmarried or childless women of German nationality or who had come from Germany, to report to collection camps.[46] Arrest and internment were the order of the day. The camps bulged with people who had fled to France to escape the Nazis. But when France fell, officials did not open the gates to give them a chance to escape. Worse: according to the armistice signed on 22 June, the French betrayed the principle of asylum, agreeing "to surrender upon demand all Germans named by the German Government in France as well as in French territories."[47] Varian Fry, head of an American initiative, the Emergency Rescue Committee (ERC), explained the situation on the ground to the home office in New York. "The French are being pushed," he observed from the ERC office in Marseille. "They have nothing against the refugees (though they will do nothing for them), but they somehow do not see that the honor of their country is involved if they arrest their former guests and turn them over to the Germans to be executed. Or if they do vaguely realize that the question is one of honor, they evidently prefer dishonor to defiance."[48]

It was sheer luck for refugee Jews in France that the Germans did not want them.[49] The Nazi government had gleefully bid them farewell in the 1930s, and they continued to do so in 1940. Now unoccupied France would serve as a fine dumping ground. Within days of the armistice, the Germans arrested three thousand Jews in Alsace, which was to be annexed to the Reich, and transported them to the free zone. A month later (August 1940), the German authorities in Bordeaux pushed fourteen hundred Jews over the demarcation line, and the French authorities interned them in St. Cyprien. The Germans' forced expulsion of Jews was both opportunistic and part of a larger plan to transport all of Europe's Jews to Madagascar. With the collapse of France, this idea, bruited in Berlin throughout the 1930s, appeared possible. Parking Jews in the unoccupied zone brought them nearer a departure point.

The Nazi leaders of Baden and Saar-Palatinate saw an opportunity to make their districts *Judenrein* (cleared of Jews).[50] They too would send their Jews on their way to Madagascar via Vichy. Hitler approved the plan, Heydrich organized it, and Eichmann got the trains over the line in October by telling "the stationmaster at the last station in the occupied zone that these were Wehrmacht troop trains." Of course, "after that, there were difficulties with the French government in Vichy, but the Foreign Office had to straighten them out."[51] Too cowed to send them back, the French classified those expelled as refugees, promptly arrested them, and sent them to internment camps in the south, with Gurs receiving the majority.

These events unfolded under the scrutiny of outside observers. "Reich Jews Sent to South France: 10,000 Reported Put into Camps," ran a *New York Times* headline of 9 November 1940.[52] "Gurs Camp Shocks Red Cross Officer," an article announced a month later. "Some 12,000 Jews, including 6,000 Jews uprooted on one hour's notice from their German homes, are existing on rations sufficient for only 8,000 to 9,000 persons in the big French concentration camp at Gurs, in the Pyrenees mountains, near the Spanish border," the reporter recounted.[53]

Women prisoners in front of a barracks in section M in Gurs internment camp, April–May 1941.

Many of these refugees had obtained quota numbers for the United States through the consulate in Stuttgart. Now they would have to get new visas and affidavits.[54] A significant number of other inmates struggled with the same difficulties, and all were stuck. Imprisoned in internment camps, the refugees could not queue up at consulate offices and police stations in pursuit of entry and exit papers. Acknowledging their predicament, the Jewish philanthropic organization HICEM adopted a new principle: "If a refugee cannot come to HICEM, HICEM will go to him."[55] Established in 1927 through a merger of the New York–based Hebrew Immigrant Aid Society (HIAS), the Paris-based Jewish Colonization Society (ICA), and the Berlin-based Emigdirect, HICEM aimed to help European Jews negotiate their way to the new world. By 1940 it had a lot of experience seeking immigration possibilities, assisting Jewish migrants, intervening with consular and other officials, arranging passage, providing hostels upon arrival, and negotiating employment opportunities.[56] This stood HICEM in good stead after the fall of France. Supported by the Joint, HICEM moved its French office to Marseille and focused on the interned refugees. Negotiating bureaucratic labyrinths, HICEM saw to it that visa application dossiers were moved from the consulates where they had been initiated (like Stuttgart for the Baden-Palatinate expellees) to the consulate in Marseille; organized for new affidavits to be obtained, submitted, and approved (as the validity of previously approved affidavits had lapsed); and sought exit visas from France and transit visas through Portugal or Morocco.

The organization shouldered an enormous workload. In 1941 HICEM staff sent 120,000 letters and cables, made 60,000 calls on officials, and mediated between applicants and consular and national authorities on 12,000 occasions. These efforts enabled the emigration of 3,221 refugees that year and cost the organization $1,250,000, an average of $400 per case, while expending only $27,000 on administration, or $8.38 per case.[57]

Still, HICEM faced great disappointments. It held high hopes of mass immigration to Sosúa in the Dominican Republic at the beginning of 1941, but this came to little. Then the state department closed all consulates in Germany, Italy, and Nazi-occupied countries on 15 July 1941, and the consulate in Marseille lost the authority to determine immigration status. All cases were henceforth considered in Washington, D.C., and the Marseille consulate became a postbox. After the United States entered the war in December 1941, the consulate remained open because America was not at war with Vichy France, but the visa procedure in Washington became even more cumbersome. Applications wound their way through the bureaucracy at an average rate of six months, with few approvals at the end. In September 1942, for example, only 276 of 1,108 passed.[58]

OBSTACLES TO EMIGRATION MOUNTED, and conditions in the camps declined. Vichy authorities permitted social work teams from philanthropic organizations (such as OSE, the American Friends Service Committee [AFSC], Unitarian Service, Eclaireurs Israélite, and *Secours Suisse*, among others) to live in the camp on a voluntary basis.[59] They provided food, medication, and clothing and organized medical and dental clinics, kindergartens, and schools. Most important, they functioned as a link with the outside world, a sign that the refugees were not forgotten. As Vivette Samuel-Hermann who, during what should have been her student years, served as an OSE internée volontaire in Rivesaltes put it, her role was "to be present." Just to be visible was significant.[60] Refugees hoped that the information voluntary interns passed to reporters and officials might press their case. And perhaps Vichy too trusted such news to open doors elsewhere.

The social workers reported regularly to their home offices in France, Switzerland, and America. According to an account from Gurs in early 1941, the camp quartered ten thousand inmates: fifty-eight hundred Jews from Baden and Saar-Palatinate, three thousand from Belgium, and the remainder interned in France since the beginning of the war. One-quarter of the population was sixty or older, and one-fifth of all inmates were sick. The camp had no medicine or medical instruments. Vermin infested, severely malnourished, and at risk for infectious diseases, six hundred inmates had died in three months. With little hope of emigration, "there follows a discouragement which borders on despair."[61]

Vichy's decision to allocate Rivesaltes to shelter refugees heartened social workers. Built by the army to house twenty thousand soldiers, Rivesaltes "offers great possibilities as a refuge for a large number of unfortunates scattered in various camps, provided careful planning is done in advance of placing them there. If this is not done it will soon become just another place of misery and squalor," D. E. Wright, a Quaker worker, reported.[62]

No such planning occurred. Rivesaltes had showers, "but too few for such a large population," a May 1941 OSE report noted. "The wash basins are too small, the water closets cannot be cleaned and, at Rivesaltes, they are not always attached to drainage pipes." The result was filth, and "infection with lice was endemic."[63] These conditions posed grave risks most especially for the thousands of children housed in Rivesaltes who had been moved from other camps. By May 1941 Gurs counted fifty-nine children, Argelès three hundred, and Rivesaltes thirty-two hundred.

Supplemental food rations and other measures would help, but hope lay in emigration. The American Friends Service Committee teamed up with the United States Committee for the Care of European Children (USCOM), which enjoyed the support of Eleanor Roosevelt, to sponsor a group of one hundred children.[64] In the meantime, OSE managed to obtain the release of a number of youngsters from internment camps and sheltered them in its children's homes. OSE officials in Montpellier worried about the oldest of these children. In their case, as so often in the refugee experience, time loomed as a key factor. "The adolescents on whose behalf we now appeal to you," OSE wrote to its Quaker colleagues, deserved special consideration. "According to regulations issued in respect of alien subjects living in France, the child is considered an adult as soon as he or she reaches the age of 15." Worse: "this situation becomes more and more tragical as the child draws near the fatal age of 17—when he may be re-interned in a concentration camp."[65]

The question of whom to choose riddled the process, while the difficulties of securing all the necessary permissions slowed the project. The first group left France in June 1941 accompanied by Isaac Chomski and his wife. They met the children in the AFSC office in Marseille. "Ragged and disheveled, each child carried a small untidy bundle and a battered valise. The white numbered cards which hung from their necks made them look like so much live baggage."[66]

When children left on youth aliyah after Hitler came to power in 1933, their parents smiled and waved. Fewer parents accompanied their children to the kindertransports in 1938–9; many fathers had been arrested and imprisoned in concentration camps. Fewer still were alive and in France to say good-bye now. None was at a child's side as the group walked to the station in Marseille.

Chomski handed the children their food ration of three thin slices of bread as the locomotive crawled through southern France. The youngsters knew the train had a scheduled stop at the small station of Oloron close to Gurs, and that OSE had persuaded the camp authorities to allow interned kin to go to Oloron to bid them farewell. In anticipation, a "youngster timidly displays a photograph of a sweet, comely, young woman. 'Minna,' he explains [to Chomski], 'my sister. She took care of me.' The snapshot was taken only a year ago. Today, she too is in Gurs."[67]

The children rushed to the windows as the train reached Oloron. "A loud cry, more piercing than any mechanical noise, suddenly rends the air. From the train comes the answering call of over a hundred shrill voices. Mothers, fathers, and kin, with the last few ounces of strength in their frail bodies, suddenly tear through the cordon of gendarmes and dash to the doors of the train." Chomski observed the reunion. "As the children pour out of the train, their parents and relatives hug them tightly. . . . The train leaves in three minutes. These moments will never again return." Minna was there too. "Minna, comely Minna, is now a living corpse. Thin as a lathe, sallow-faced, she has no strength for words. Instead, she immediately falls upon her little brother's neck and smothers him with kisses."

The children offered their loved ones the currency of the day: bread. "'Father, take this—take this, mama—please take.' Bewildered, the parents look at the bread and then at the children. Their eyes seem to ask many questions. They also tell a tale of hunger. But they refuse to take the bread. 'My child, you'll have nothing left,' one mother after another declares. The children are persistent. Again and again they cry, 'Please take . . . please take.'" Chomski recognized the enormity of the youngsters' gift. "Children of eight and ten, themselves terribly hungry, are giving their own precious bits of bread to strange fathers and mothers." So did the parents. "As the realization of the children's sacrifice begins to dawn upon them, a heart-rending wail bursts from their throats. The hardened gendarmes lose control of themselves and begin to weep. The cry of the internees is long and pitiful, a cry of mingled shame and despair." Touched, the French commanding officer allowed the train to remain in the station for an extra few minutes. Then "the train begins to move, the clatter of the wheels drowning out the cries of farewell. Through the doors and windows, the children wave their hands to the group of living dead. The shriveled faces slowly grow less distinct, become distant specks, and then are seen no more."[68] Traveling through Lisbon, the children arrived in New York on the SS *Mouzinho* chartered by HICEM.

USCOM, OSE, and AFSC workers pressed forward with additional transports. The bureaucratic difficulties did not abate, nor did discussion of selection criteria. Writing (18 July 1941) from the Friends home office

Jewish refugee children on the first USCOM transport wait at a pier in Lisbon on 10 June 1941 to board the SS Mouzhino, *chartered by HICEM to take them to the United States.*

in Philadelphia to her colleague Allen Bonnell in Marseille, Margaret Frawley cautioned that non-Jews would not support the rescue of Jewish children. "Some non-Jewish children strengthens the United States Committee position as a non-sectarian group and will enable it to make its financial appeals to a larger group," she explained. "If you send only

Jewish children, it is more than likely that the appeals for funds will meet response only from individuals who will thereby be compelled to reduce their contributions to the Jewish refugee agencies."[69] Frawley also stressed age as a factor. If OSE pressed to include older children, as they were at greater risk for internment and deportation, she argued that "younger children have a better opportunity to identify themselves with life here and in the minds of the public the program is identified with the younger children."[70] This fostered the future of the operation.

Preparing the fourth transport, Marjorie McClelland of the AFSC office in Marseille reflected upon the criteria she applied in a letter (22 April 1942) to Margaret Frawley. "When making the actual selection of the children, I had in mind two basic considerations—the necessity for emigration and the desirability of immigration, of each child. I wished to satisfy myself (in so far as was possible under the circumstances) of the child's desirability as an immigrant to America—that he was a normal, at least averagely intelligent, adaptable child, who would be able to fit into an American family without too much difficulty." But life on the ground in Europe carried weight too. "I also took into consideration the situation of the child here in France, for obviously not all cases were similar. I considered the children who had lost one or more parents, children whose parents had remained in Germany, or had been deported to Poland, children who were all alone without any family, have less future here and therefore have greater need for emigration to America than children of families who are all here."[71]

McClelland sent short biographies of each of the fifty children selected for the convoy that left Marseille on 14 May 1942. Child #47: "STEUER Antoinette (called 'Toni')," five years old, Polish by nationality, German by birth, "is entirely alone in the world. Her mother, Marie Steuer, is thought to be either dead or to have gone insane, and her father, Max Steuer, was put into the concentration camp of Dachau in Germany, and has never been seen since."[72] Henri and Miriam Mass (children #26 and 27), aged six and eight respectively, also Polish by nationality, were born in Antwerp, where their parents owned a small restaurant. The family had fled to the south of France after the Germans had occupied the Low Countries in May 1940. The father, Samuel, was put to forced labor in January 1941, and the mother, Regina, and children were interned in Rivesaltes; McClelland met them there. Regina Mass "seemed like a very nice, simple, earnest woman, very much concerned over her children. I thought it remarkable that she was so clean in the midst of the camp where cleanliness is so unbelievably difficult to achieve."[73]

"Refugees Reach Land of Freedom from the Prison That Is Europe" ran a *New York Herald Tribune* headline on 26 June 1942. A picture of eight happy children, smiling, waving, and hanging over the railing of the *Serta Pinto*, accompanied the article. Antoinette Steuer "was too busy trying to eat an orange and suck on a chocolate milk shake through straws to answer questions," the reporter chortled. The past behind her, she turned to the good things America had to offer. "Whether the queries were put to her in French or Polish, 'Toni' had just one response. Tucking her orange under her arm, she would hold up two fingers V-wise and then return to her double task. Since 1939 she has been an inmate of orphanages and 'children's colonies.'"[74]

A FIFTH TRANSPORT LEFT FOR THE UNITED STATES before Vichy granted Germany permission on 4 July to deport foreign Jews from the unoccupied zone. The Holocaust had arrived in western Europe, including France. Berlin drew up a plan in June to deport forty thousand Jews from France: thirty-six thousand from the occupied zone and "only" four thousand from the free zone. Half would be French nationals, half foreigners. To save face by protecting its own (French) Jews, Vichy offered to increase the unoccupied zone quota with foreign Jews. The Germans accepted happily. Less work for them: fewer Jews to arrest and process in the occupied zone. The French did not shoulder much extra work either; internment camps offered a ready supply of alien Jews. Pure opportunism on the part of the French thus turned a camp system that never had been intended to serve the "Final Solution" into an immediate and— as it proved—convenient anteroom to Auschwitz. Officials sorted and selected inmates in a matter of weeks.

The aid organizations sought to lay themselves down across the train tracks to the east. They moved strenuously on two fronts: to intervene

American Friends Service Committee worker Marjorie McClelland with Antoinette Steuer in May 1942.

with the Vichy government and to accelerate the emigration of refugees. Tracy Strong, general secretary of the World's Alliance of the YMCA, secured an appointment with Pétain on 4 August and emphasized that deportations would have a negative effect on American public opinion. But Strong "had the impression that the matter failed to register with the Marshal."[75] Donald Lowrie, a Quaker who worked for the YMCA and had joined forces with Strong on this matter, obtained an audience with Pétain and his secretary Jean Jardelle a few days later. Lowrie stressed that the Quakers and YMCA had operated in unoccupied France for two years and had helped ten thousand refugees to emigrate. "We are willing to continue this service, but we are now greatly concerned about the present measures being taken against certain foreign refugees." Seeking to put Lowrie off, Pétain asked whether he would "be in Vichy for a week or ten days to have a reply." "Monsieur le Maréchal, the first train is leaving today," Lowrie shot back. "Well, then, I will speak to Laval this afternoon and you may telephone M. Jardelle tomorrow morning for my reply." Laval, in the meantime, had got the same representations from AFSC officials Ross McClelland and Lindsley Noble. All to no avail. When McClelland phoned Jardelle, the secretary told him that there was no reply because Laval had been called to Paris, "and the Marshal was very busy."[76] As these events unfolded, the first deportation train left for the east.

The aid workers did not give up. A concerted effort by representatives of USCOM, the AFSC, and the JDC pushed the state department to grant a thousand visas for children.[77] By this time the trains rolled regularly. Emigration had become rescue. The American consulate in Marseille prepared to issue fifty visas per day, and the AFSC grew confident that the thousand visas would be increased to five thousand. Utterly intrepid, the Friends in France carried on without regard for their own safety, as a new arrival from the United States, Burrit Hiatt, observed. His colleagues in Marseille "have for so long found life an affair of being frightened rather than being hurt that they have become inured to the danger of a situation that alarms me," Hiatt admitted in his logbook at the end of his first day (11 October 1942). "They have an unconcern about French officials and about the power behind the French officials that I have not learned."[78]

The aid workers faced old dilemmas—which children were eligible and how to determine selection?—and new ones—who would escort the children? Logistical problems beset them. With their eyes on the clock, they planned processing schedules against the calendar. How long would it take to bring the children to Marseille, photograph them, see to their medical examinations, and obtain American visas, Spanish and Portuguese transit visas, and French exit visas? How many children could the organization handle per day?[79]

Vichy officials raised the ante when they suddenly insisted that "only real orphans" might leave.[80] Undaunted, the aid workers refused to quit. The first group of children arrived in Marseille on 8 November. But as so often in the history of refugee initiatives, time was not with them. American and British forces launched Operation Torch that very day, invading Vichy-controlled Morocco. Vichy and Washington broke diplomatic relations. "All exit visas were cancelled and the frontiers closed," Hiatt lamented in his diary. Yet the Friends staff continued to move forward until the German army occupied the free zone on 11 November and all Americans were ordered to leave the department Bouches-du-Rhône by 5:00 p.m.[81]

"Possibilities departure from unoccupied France practically non-existent now," a JDC representative in Lisbon cabled USCOM in New York the next day. "All emigration from France to the United States has now stopped and children will not be permitted to leave," a cable of 13 November announced. "Have cancelled all transportation arrangements." Later that day: "all telephone communication with Marseille now suspended."[82] The trap had closed. Internment camps no longer quartered refugees. Now they functioned as transit camps, holding pens for Jews slated for death in the east.

THE OUTBREAK OF WAR added internment to the history of Jewish refugees, and in the Soviet Union and France it shaped their fate. Deportation in 1940 of refugee Jews to the interior of the Soviet Union in Jerzy Kagan's words "saved us," although "this was not their intention." Internment claimed many lives; Jews, like others, died because the demands upon them and the resources allocated to them, determined by officials in Moscow, held little relation to human abilities and needs. This gap between abstract thinking (fundamentally flawed from the start) and the complex reality of human life proved lethal for thousands and debilitating for many more. And yet, deported in 1940, the internees did not face the German onslaught of 1941 and after.

The Soviets proceeded with a plan: abstract, inhumane, unaccommodating. The French improvised step by step: reactive, opportunistic. In Koestler's words, "a mixture of ignominy, corruption, and *laisser-faire* so typical of French administration."[83] The French authorities just wanted the refugee problem to go away and, for the most part, happily released internees when they organized visas and passage elsewhere. If the refugees in Soviet camps suffered because of central planning, refugees in

French camps suffered from no planning at all. In 1942 this became fatal for inmates who had not secured transit overseas or got smuggled into Switzerland or Spain. To satisfy the German appetite for victims, Vichy readily traded refugees for Jews of French origin. Giving up their own citizens—even if they were Jews—undermined Vichy's authority as a sovereign state. The refugees' fate had been of little interest to the government while they were interned. It remained of little interest, except that the inmates numbered shippable bodies. Thus, internment camps proved a harsh blessing for those who escaped to the Soviet Union and an unintended trap for those who escaped to France.

LOVED ONES
BECOME LETTERS

WILHELM AND ADELE HALBERSTAM FOUND REFUGE IN THE NETH-
erlands in April 1939, joining their three grandchildren, Klaus, Ernst, and
Lore, who had arrived with a kindertransport in February that year and
their son Albert, who had fled when the Nazis came to power in 1933.
The children's parents, Käthe Hepner-Halberstam and Heinrich Hepner, remained in Berlin. Heinrich had been arrested during the November pogrom; released from Sachsenhausen six weeks later, he was not
well enough to travel, and his children and their grandparents emigrated
while he recuperated. He and his wife joined the rest of the family in
May and promptly moved on to Britain with their children. It was the
first leg of a journey to Cuba, thanks to visas Käthe had bought from
(happily) corrupt Cuban consular officials. Wilhelm and Adele chose
not to emigrate. They stayed in Amsterdam with Albert and thus began
their long-distance relationship with their daughter and grandchildren
that depended upon letters. "Do not spare us your news, even when it
is not 100 percent happy; we are prepared for that," Wilhelm wrote five
days after their departure. "We do not know how long it will take letters to travel, and how often they may go, but we seek to remain close

to you—to share your life as much as possible. Sadly, we now belong to those we pitied, whose children became letters."[1]

Remaining in Amsterdam, the Halberstams also became a conduit for letters between friends in Germany and their families in England, France, and Poland when war began in September 1939. Correspondence between belligerent or occupied nations ceased just when friends and kin became ever more concerned about each other's welfare. Many turned to people they knew in neutral nations who could serve as go-between; the Halberstams, for example, forwarded letters sent to them in Amsterdam from friends in Berlin to the intended recipients: loved ones in England. And vice versa.

This came to an end when Germany invaded the Netherlands on 10 May 1940. Writing to his daughter that day, Wilhelm lamented the outbreak of war, the end of Dutch neutrality, and the effects of both on communication lines. His task as a go-between had ended, and he regretted it. "The mediation of these [letters] for friends and acquaintances might have been expensive and time-consuming, but gave us much pleasure."[2] Worse: invasion threatened his own contact with his daughter and her family. In his first letter after the Dutch army's surrender Wilhelm did not mention a word about it. Instead, he wrote, of all that had transpired, "the lack of news from you to us and us to you was for *Mutti* [Mom] and me the most heavy to bear."[3] From this point forward, the irregular schedule of and changing route for their letters continued to worry the Halberstams.

In this breach, a middle-aged (born 1888), single woman from neutral Switzerland stepped forward to connect German-Jewish refugees with their families. Living on a small, inherited income in an attic apartment in Stäfa near Zurich, Elisabeth Luz undertook an extensive postal service from 1939 to 1945. She took the project one step farther than, for example, the Halberstams had done when Holland had been neutral. Parents in Germany sent a letter to her, *Tante* (aunt) Elisabeth in Stäfa, as if she were the intended recipient. Keeping the original, she copied each letter, sending it on to the real addressee, officially her "nephew" or "niece." Every country censored mail, and Elisabeth's time-consuming and laborious system fooled the censors.

News about the aunt who forwarded letters spread quickly among anxious parents in Germany and children in Britain and France. Before long Tante Elisabeth gained dozens of "nephews" and "nieces." She soon became a counselor and confidante, although nearly none ever met her. Genteel poor herself, she nevertheless sent writing paper, envelopes, and International Reply Coupons (IRCs) to youngsters in children's homes in Vichy France. Created by the Universal Postal Union (which organized the interface between national mail services) in 1906, an IRC was purchased

Elisabeth Luz, 29 August 1965.

at any post office in one country and enclosed in an international letter; the recipient exchanged it locally for postage to send a letter in return. A variation of the IRC, which Elisabeth also used, was an international *carte postale avec réponse payée* (reply-paid postcard): two attached postcards, one written and one blank, with postage for both paid by the purchaser. IRCs and reply-paid postcards helped Tante Elisabeth support contact—against all odds—between utterly impoverished refugees and their families. More than three thousand letters passed through her hands.

While the technical problems of sending letters from one country to another plagued refugees, USCOM children and their parents faced an institutional barrier as well. Discouraging contact between the youngsters they had brought to America and family members in Europe, USCOM did not furnish parents with their children's new addresses. Marjorie McClelland, who worked closely with these families, objected. "While I

Jewish refugee children on the first USCOM transport write letters to family members, many of whom are interned in France, to tell them of their safe arrival in Lisbon in May 1941.

can understand quite well that it is probably psychologically easier on the children to break the ties with the Old World completely, and to identify themselves entirely with their American life, I think that it is not right to discount parents completely," she wrote to Margaret Frawley at Friends' headquarters in May 1942. "We must remember that the fathers and mothers of these children have the same feelings about them that parents everywhere have for their children, and that it is only because they are living under condition of the utmost misery and despair that they will sacrifice themselves to the extent of letting their children go."

Letting go was one thing; cutting ties another, she admonished. It is "too much to ask," she advised, "that they never hear from them again, that they do not know where, in the broad expanse of America they are, or under what conditions they are living."

Parents were desperate for news of their children. They had sent away their youngsters in the belief that they were acting in their children's best interest. They had never visited the country to which their children immigrated; they did not know the people with whom they lived, the language they now spoke, or the circumstances in which their children found themselves. Powerless to help them further, the parents nourished hope that they had made the right choice. Marjorie McClelland understood all that. "A letter from the child saying he is happy, that he is gaining weight, that he likes his new family, repays them for the sacrifice they have made and gives them hope at least for their children." Her work in the French internment camps had taught her a great deal. Realizing that her colleagues in America might not be able to imagine what she saw on a daily basis, she tried to convey her insights. "We, who know the parents, who read their pathetic letters begging for news of their children, cannot believe that it is right to keep the whereabouts of the children from them, for that is to neglect to consider them and their fundamental needs as human beings."

Illustrating her point, McClelland wrote of Regina Mass. Two of her children had been included in an USCOM transport, while OSE had placed the youngest, four-year-old Hélène, with a French family in Montpellier. McClelland recounted a moment of intimacy with Regina. "She brought forth from her handbag her most precious possession to show me, a well-worn letter written by the father of the family in which little Helene was living, telling her that the little girl was well and happy that they loved her as one of their own children, and would not neglect to advise her if the child was ill or if there was any change of circumstances. This one small letter is a veritable treasure of comfort and reassurance to this mother."[4]

Frawley forwarded McClelland's letter to Robert Lang, executive director of USCOM. Her observations touched a raw nerve, and he proposed that USCOM prepare a report on the condition of each child twice a year and send it to the Friends in Marseille to pass on to the parents.[5] Even this miserly solution came to naught; many of the parents were deported before any such report was sent.

MCCLELLAND HAD IDENTIFIED A KEY ISSUE: the importance of information about daily life to separated family members. Severed apart, neither could follow or comprehend fully the situation of the other. Yet they yearned to understand and to be understood. Refugees experienced radical changes of circumstance and environment from one day to the next; the framework of their lives shifted, and their loved ones knew nothing of the new context and its rules. All of this needed to be communicated, letter by letter.

The Halberstams sought to build up their mental picture of their daughter and her family's situation. The Hepners had embarked from Liverpool for Cuba on 18 May on the *Orduña*. Arriving in Havana on 28 May, a day after the *St. Louis*,[6] *Orduña* passengers who had obtained visas in Berlin were not allowed to land. For six weeks the captain tried to unload his passengers in South American ports as he steered the ship to the Pacific through the Panama Canal. The Halberstams, anxious and impotent, followed the journey from their apartment in Amsterdam. "Have you landed in Balboa on orders of the shipping line, or has Panama offered to take you in?" Adele asked her daughter. "Is the quarantine site just a way station to a permanent sojourn in the city itself, or must you move on again the moment Cuba or another country offers to let you in?" Truly ignorant of her loved ones' situation, she asked practical questions. "How is the climate? Do you need some sort of inoculations, against malaria for example? How do you live there? Are you interned or are you able to move around freely?" Begging her daughter to write at least once a week, she reminded her, "I really live from letter to letter."[7]

Through the good offices of a Chilean diplomat the Hepners had met aboard the *Orduña*, they were allowed to disembark in Valparaiso on 12 July and take up residence. Relieved, Wilhelm wrote (20 July), "Please instruct us untaught Europeans how the seasons compare to ours, and how many of the hours of the day are light and dark. You are always with us in our thoughts, so we really would like to know. Do you get up early and finish early, or the other way around? What is the main diet? Is the population light or dark? These questions I ask not only because I am simply curious, but out of a lively interest."[8]

As the Halberstams and Hepners tried to fill in the white spots on their canvas of knowledge, others found that circumstances changed too quickly and too radically to track. "My sister and those who are close to us certainly worry a lot about us. Often I think: our beloved fret more than necessary, and at other times I think the opposite, that no one can imagine what our life is like," Martha Levi wrote from the Gurs internment camp to Tante Elisabeth on 8 February 1941.[9] Elisabeth had served as a conduit between Martha's sister Betty Levi-Frank and Betty's children and nephew, and Betty turned to her when her sister Martha and brother-in-law Leopold were expelled suddenly in the Baden-Palatinate action. Would Elisabeth help her establish contact with Martha and Leopold? Elisabeth responded immediately, and thus her communication between the sisters began.

Martha awaited an affidavit from a brother in America and for passage to be organized. She was not so sanguine two months later, she confessed to Elisabeth on 29 April. Her brother and sister-in-law had written that affidavits would be sent shortly to the Marseille consulate but, as no berths were available, he had not yet paid for tickets. Martha worried that if no places were found, the affidavits would not remain valid. And could Elisabeth stress to Betty that packages from the family were very welcome?[10]

Their correspondence continued until Elisabeth sent a carte postale avec réponse payée to Martha on 6 September 1942, asking if she should send a package of reading material to the usual address. "One reads so much about rapid changes of residence in these past days," she wrote, referring to the deportations from the internment camps that had begun a month earlier and had swollen the refugee flood so much that they had led to Rothmund's closure of the border on 13 August. And she added, "I haven't heard anything from Betty." Elisabeth heard nothing more from Martha either. Her card—not the expected prepaid reply card—

came back a few weeks later with the address "Frau Martha Levi, Ilôt M, Baraque 7, Camp de Gurs, Basses Pyrenées, France," crossed out. Stamped on top: "Return to Sender."[11]

Fearing just such loss of contact, separated spouses, siblings, lovers, and parents and children wrote repeatedly of their affection for each other. They sought to weave a web of letters to hold each other tightly and to assure each other that notwithstanding the pressures of their radically changed circumstances, their relationship endured. And each wished to feel reassured.[12]

Heinrich Blücher, a German political refugee, was arrested and interned shortly after the outbreak of the war, first in the forty-five-thousand-seat Olympic stadium in Colombes near Paris and after that in the internment camp at Villemard. He had been living in France since 1934, and with Hannah Arendt since 1936 (they married immediately after his release from Villemard in January 1940). A packet of letters Arendt had sent to the Olympic stadium caught up with Blücher in Villemard. "My darling," he wrote in response on 6 November 1939, "I have suddenly received, all together, the letters and cards you had sent to Colombes, and I read them many times over with such emotion!" He delighted in the reiteration of her love. "In one of these old letters," he noted, "you pointed out that love letters always have, to some extent, a monotony about them. This is true, but what an incredible monotony! A monotony like the sound of the sea. The more one hears it, the more one wants to hear it."[13]

Love takes many shapes in families, and letters written between refugees and kin expressed a myriad of forms. At one point in October 1939 the elderly Halberstams believed they might be able to obtain visas for Chile, and Adele's longing for her daughter spilled onto the page. "The thought, the prospect, the possibility that my most deeply desired wish to see you again, to remain with you, might be fulfilled is too beautiful to become true."[14] Children pined for their parents, just as parents hungered for their children, as the letters that passed through Tante Elisabeth reveal. Eva and Susi Guttmann were among the 130 youngsters who came to France on a kindertransport in late 1938 and were housed in Baron Robert de Rothschild's castle La Guette in Villeneuve St. Denis.

Elisabeth established contact between the girls and their parents in February 1940; the children's first letter written on fine paper reflects their luxurious circumstances.[15] Evacuated as the Germans approached in 1940, the La Guette youngsters were sent to Hôtel d'Anglais, an OSE home run by Flore Loinger (wife of Georges Loinger) in the small spa town of La Bourboule in the Massif Central. Susi promptly wrote a postcard—now a cheap affair—to Elisabeth, asking her to tell her parents about the move and to assure them that she was safe.[16] A month later she wrote asking Elisabeth to tell her parents that "I think about them *all the time*, and I have just one hope: to see them again."[17]

In this card of 19 July 1940, Susi also mentioned Fée Beyth, with whom she shared a room. Could Elisabeth perhaps establish contact with Fée's father, Walter Beyth in Berlin? Thus Elisabeth became the connection between Fée and her father Walter, who was blind and cared for by his sister Käthe Hollaender-Beyth. Just as Susi introduced her friend Fée, Walter introduced his friend Ernst Matzdorff in turn. Matzdorff had married a gentile woman named Herta who, pressed by her prospective father-in-law, had converted to Judaism. Herta left for London just before the war; the Matzdorff children, Werner and Ursel, got stuck in France. Tante Elisabeth maintained contact between all of them and became a steady confidante for the lonely Matzdorff in Germany. He wrote her long letters in which he detailed his trepidations and repeated his single greatest wish: to be with his children again. He had hoped as a father to shape his children's character, he explained to Elisabeth. "If there were even a glimmer of such a happy reunion, they probably will not be children any more,

Fée and her father Walter Beyth.

but already rather grown-up people." Still, "one can accept all that so long as they maintain the love and affection for their parents that, to my inexpressible delight, speaks from the lines they write. It goes without saying that this single fact is the sole support which one still finds in these times." Like others, they set their sights on family unification, "even though the obstacles are so great that no one can see how one could possibly overcome them. But thinking of this single, great goal keeps one strong, and it must happen one day."[18]

THE GOAL OF FAMILY UNIFICATION occupied all parties, and letters were key to their efforts. As the writer Carl Zuckmayer, who had escaped Austria shortly after the Anschluss and, with journalist Dorothy Thompson's help, had entered the United States on a tourist visa, observed after the war: "When émigrés wrote each other letters, especially between the years 1938 and 1945, it always concerned the rescue of friends and colleagues who had not yet escaped mortal danger."[19] Zuckmayer identified but one strand. The letter-ladder to asylum included official correspondence with consulates to shipping companies and private correspondence with all who might help.

Letters, in short, formed the primary medium through which aid was requested and provided. Writing to little Susi Neuwalder's father a few months after the child had come from Vienna on a kindertransport, Phyllis Shepherd (who, with her husband, had provided her guarantee of support) reported on his daughter's adjustment. In closing, she asked, "Will you remember that we should very <u>very</u> much like you and Frau Neuwalder to come and stay with us for a little while."[20] Dr Neuwalder, a Jew, had fled to Italy by that time; his wife, born Catholic, had remained in Vienna to wind up their affairs. In his reply he attended first to matters pertaining to Susi; then he addressed his own situation. "You are so exceedingly kind to invite my wife and me for some time in your house. But the political events in the meanwhile render it impossible," he noted, referring to the start of the war in September. "If you know anybody in America who could make an affidavit for my wife and for me I would be very grateful to you. I have been writing to many committees on such a purpose, but without any success." Dr Neuwalder needed to move quickly: "My Italian permit is ending in February 1940."[21]

"How greatly we wish we could help," Mrs Shepherd answered on 9 January 1940. "We certainly do send you a most hearty invitation to come and stay with us as soon as you are able—both you and your wife." She understood the significance of the deadline he faced. "So if, when your permit ends, there is any chance of your coming to England, you will let us know, won't you? . . . Or is there anything we can send you, that would be of any use?"[22]

Herbert Neuwalder ran out of money before his permit expired. As his letter of 25 January 1940 revealed, he needed assistance desperately. To his shame, this formerly middle class physician had "not been able to pay my lodging-rent for January and I have to leave my lodging on Feb. 1st if I am not paying for two months together." The sum due: "Lira 625—or about £8-. I am so sorry to tell you all that, but I really do not know what to do."[23] "Can you leave Italy and come to England, if traveling expenses are found for you?" Phyllis Shepherd asked in reply, repeating her offer of home hospitality. And if not: "Can we send money to you?" Most important, "whatever happens <u>do not lose touch with us.</u>"[24]

Phyllis Shepherd sought to do what she could for the Neuwalders. Tante Elisabeth sought to do *more* than she could. She accrued ever more correspondents and, writing on average at least two letters a day, she aimed to assist every one of them. "Please pardon us that we write you without having asked permission to do so," two boys wrote her. "Our names are Adolf and Robert Hess. Adolf is 12 years old and I am 14 years. We live in Hôtel des Anglais in La Bourboule." They had been selected for an USCOM transport to America. "We write to you because we would like to write to our mother and have no other possibility. Please write our mother that she can write us via you. We must ask our mother for permission to travel to America." Faced with the prospect of departure they had another request: "Can you also send us a photo of her?" Providing their mother's address in Vienna, their own address, and a photo of themselves, they concluded, "Thank you so much for sending our letter onward. . . . Please answer us!"[25] She did not disappoint, and they were included among the twenty-two children from La Bourboule on the transport.

Heinz Pfützner was too. In a letter posted on 10 June he explained that they had "traveled from La Bourboule to the American consulate in Marseille to get our papers ready and to get our visa." And he asked, "Can you inform my parents about my departure and write them all that is necessary? He planned to "write my parents from Lisbon," but he wanted them to know his movements as quickly as possible.[26]

Elisabeth Luz's letters reveal that her willingness to provide assistance extended to clandestine activities in addition to deceiving the censors. In early October 1942, Elisabeth received a letter in code from France written by a J. Bingen mentioning that she (or he) had received a letter meant for Ursel, but was unable to pass it on to her. "Ursel left a few days ago," Bingen wrote, indicating s/he had hidden her, "and attempts—with hope of success—to visit an aunt who mailed her Goethe's famous words: *Sei du im Leben wie im Wissen durchaus der reinen Fahrt beflissen* [Always be assiduous in life and in the pursuit of knowledge]."[27] Bingen trusted Elisabeth to turn to Goethe's poem and to understand that Ursel had embarked upon a perilous journey—she had set out to cross the frontier—and that she had chosen to do so believing this was the most promising way to survive.

Hinting at her (his?) own role, Bingen explained, "Ursel stayed for some time at my place because her family had left for other destinations. I have no doubt that Ursel will communicate the remaining lines of the Goethe poem to me as soon as she can."[28] Elisabeth understood that she was the aunt and Ursel aimed to cross the border. As it happened, Ursel's efforts proved successful and she had already written to Elisabeth from the refugee camp Münchwilen on 12 September 1942.[29] Elisabeth happily continued their correspondence and, when Christmas approached, she asked and received permission for Ursel to stay with her.[30] In the meantime, Flore Loinger too wrote a letter in code. "I cannot answer all your questions but it is probable that Hanna, Ernest, and Minnie will spend some weeks of holiday in your area," she alerted Elisabeth. "They certainly will give you all news." Indicating that she knew Ursel's plans and knew too that Elisabeth stood ready to help, she concluded, "Please congratulate Ursula on my behalf and send my greetings; many of her friends are spending their holidays in the same manner over there."[31]

Many Jews caught in occupied Europe as well as those, like J. Bingen, who helped them resorted to code in correspondence with the outside world. Many more fell silent. As mail connections became increasingly tenuous, a sense that the ever greater dimensions of the tragedy endured by those who remained behind could not or must not be entrusted to paper shadowed each letter. Correspondents struggled with what they should write or say. If eyewitnesses found that words failed to convey what they wished to report, correspondence between refugees abroad and family and friends left behind was burdened by the power of words and thus a desire not to utter them.

"Out of consideration for you, I do not allow my pen to overflow with what fills my heart. Why should you become as sad as I am?" Adele wrote to her daughter Käthe on 2 July 1940.[32] Her self-censorship marked her first step away from communication, an admission that the changing circumstances in the Netherlands challenged the mutual understanding the Halberstams and their daughter had so painstakingly rebuilt after their separation a year earlier. As the occupation continued and with it the elderly couple's financial impoverishment, social isolation, and daily humiliation, their trust that they could maintain a common reality collapsed. They grew ever more silent about the tightening screws. When a fact slipped in—usually in Adele's letters—like a friend's suicide, or the May 1942 order to wear a yellow star, Wilhelm sought to undermine the gravity with irony. But he nevertheless allowed his daughter to read between the lines. "The sun shines as if it were May, and the winds rage like in November; only the barometer behaves like April! We turned off the heat yesterday, but don't think it is warm here. At this moment, the weather is also 'forbidden' here, and it shares this fate with the parks, promenades, pleasure grounds, benches, theaters, concerts, cinemas, restaurants and cafés. And the same with cars!"[33] Similarly, when Adele wrote that she was busy sewing yellow stars on all their garments, Wilhelm added, "The yellow stars that Mutti mentioned are not to be confused with the 'Yellow Stars' in the clothing industry, which was the name for models who were particularly beautifully built (waist 42 centimeters, but still everything there!) They were of all religious backgrounds and very much desired by adolescent and somewhat older young men."[34] No mention of the fear the star decree generated; not one word about the humiliation they endured.

Ultimately, events overwhelmed silence. Adele wrote that their maid Hertha Oppenheimer had been called up for work in the east. Their friends too. "Of the L[ehmanns], for example, Marianne and Franz have left; the transport has, according to the information of the responsible office, already reached Kattowitz. The age-group included those 16 to 40 years old, but will certainly expand."[35] In fact the train had reached not only Kattowitz but nearby Auschwitz. Hertha Oppenheimer and Marianne and Franz Lehmann were murdered on 18 July 1942.

Fearing the deportation of their parents still in Germany, the children who wrote to Tante Elisabeth from France did not know what to say or how to express their anguish. Norbert Roth wrote to Elisabeth (2 January 1942) from an OSE children's home. He wanted to reach his parents Richard Roth and Regina Roth-Kaczinsky in Bad Freienwalde (Oder)—although, as he apologized, he did not have any money to buy IRCs.[36] Elisabeth established a connection. None too soon: his parents were about to be deported, he wrote Elisabeth on 13 April. Would she mail his letter immediately—"minutes may prevent the arrival of my letter [in time]." And he confessed, "I am completely agitated, and must control myself in order not to show this to my loved ones. Who knows when or even if I will see them again. I have already heard so many things that I am totally broken."[37]

Regina and Richard were shipped to the Warsaw ghetto, where they resumed correspondence with Norbert and his two siblings through Elisabeth. Norbert acknowledged his worries to her but not to his parents. "I recently read the *Schweizer Israelitische Familienblatt*, and saw with horror how the people live in Poland. They have almost nothing to eat, and in the winter they chopped up doors, window frames, furniture etc. to have fuel to heat. Many thousands starve to death, and many thousands from typhus. In every family there are victims. Shouldn't I be afraid?"[38] Similarly, his mother spoke only of her yearning for children and not of the horror she experienced. Her last letter, written on 1 November 1942, said not a word about the mass deportations to Treblinka that had just assailed the ghetto. "I am so unhappy to have received no lines from you lately," she began. "I hope you are healthy, which, thank God, I can report about us as well." And she continued, "We have our 21st wedding anniversary this month (on the 20th). The most beautiful present would be a few lines from you all."[39] But by then Norbert had been arrested in an OSE home and deported to the east.

DEPORTATION. DEATH. How, all parties wondered, to transmit such information? Walter Beyth struggled with this in a letter to Elisabeth. Ten days earlier, on 17 February 1941, he had written a long letter to his daughter Fée in which he had tried to tell her "in a gentle manner" about the death of her seventeen-year-old brother Reinhard. "Do you believe, dear Miss Luz, that she accepted the sad facts in the way I intended?"[40] A mentally retarded boy who also suffered from epilepsy, Reinhard had been admitted to an asylum in 1939 and murdered toward the end of 1940 in the gas chamber of the prison of Brandenburg/Havel, victim to the Nazis' T4 program to kill the mentally ill and the physically "defective."

Fée, for her part, worried about her blind father and the aunt who looked after him, but she too discussed these fears with Elisabeth and not with her kin. Her trepidations grew stronger as the noose tightened. "Even if they exempt a blind man and do not send him to Poland, they certainly will not spare Aunt Käthe," she wrote a year later. "And father without Aunt Käthe . . . is completely helpless! I just worry how all of this will turn out."[41] She would learn later that Walter committed suicide the evening before he was to be deported. In the meanwhile, Fée also wondered what happened to her mother, Irma Beyth-Lichtenstein, who had fled to Shanghai. Finally, she exulted to Elisabeth in May, "after a delay of almost a year, I received a card from my mother today, and I would very much like to send a short message through the Red Cross. Could I ask you to send the message below to Geneva."[42] Shaped by silence, her text to "Mrs Irma Beyth, General Post Office, Poste Restante, Shanghai" read: "Received your card. Am in good health. Passed hotel examination, was on stage. Still at Laguette. Details will follow! What is your work? Affectionate kisses. Fée."[43]

As 1942 wore on, letters accrued their final and most essential function: they served as a sign of life. No one cared *what* was said, so long as one received word *at all*. Mail took longer and longer to travel to and from war-torn Europe until all ordinary services ceased at the end of that year. Red Cross letters of twenty-five words or less written on Form 61 became the standard means of communication. Introduced during World War I and developed during the Spanish Civil War, these letters allowed civilians separated by war to exchange information of "a strictly personal nature" to family members, "wherever they may be." One side of the reply-paid Form 61 carried the name and address of sender and receiver and a message of twenty-five words. The recipient wrote a reply on the back. This system grew rapidly during World War II, with 23.5 million such messages passed from one side to the other via Geneva. Restrictions imposed by the belligerent nations limited communication to fourteen languages and one form per family per month.[44]

The Halberstams turned to the Red Cross system when regular postal connection between German-ruled Europe and neutral Chile ceased in early 1943. They continued to use it after they were deported from Amsterdam to the Dutch transit camp Westerbork. Mail delays grew so long that they continually wondered whether their letters got through at all. Still, they persevered in the hope that ultimately and eventually word would arrive in both directions. The pattern of Adele's messages remained consistent: little discussion of hardship, humiliation, or fear, and always an emphasis on family ties, love, and longing. "Since 20 June here," Adele explained in a letter of 8 August (which arrived in Chile nearly a year later). "That's enough. Received from Albert forwarded letters of October and January. Sign of life from Helene. Congratulate Klaus and Heinrich. Greetings full of longing."[45]

Inevitably in Nazi Europe, inexorably, ineluctably, letters brought news of death. Sometimes, as in Adele's Red Cross letter of 5 October 1943, this message was explicit. "Last night Father passed away unexpectedly due heart attack. Albert here since 4 days, of course great happiness for me. Inform Fischers. Letter follows. Unspeakably sad."[46] More often, it foreshadowed what the recipient knew then or learned later was the fate of two-thirds of Europe's Jews during the Nazi era. Adele's last letter, dated 31 October, read: "Mother and Albert greet wishing very best. Mary also here without child. I function as an automaton, no purpose in life. In love and longing."[47] Adele and Albert were deported to Auschwitz on 16 November 1943. They arrived on the seventeenth, and Adele was murdered that day. Albert survived until 31 March 1944.

Tante Elisabeth was well aware that death loured. Through the course of 1942 into 1943 she saw her efforts to pull her correspondents out of the Nazi net—pleading their case for entry into Switzerland with the authorities; writing repeatedly to the Aide aux Emigrés and the Swiss aid branch of the Confessing Church in Germany; sending along letters to advance individual immigration plans; and simply linking people together—fail. Letter by letter, over and over again.

Elisabeth helped Hanna-Ruth Klopstock, one of the children in La Guette, correspond with her mother Frieda and brother Werner in Germany. When Hanna-Ruth did not hear from them for some time, she wrote to Elisabeth, expressing her yearning for a sign of life from them. "Every day I tell myself: 'Today I will certainly receive a letter from Mutti,'" she explained. "And still nothing. I do not know what to think about this silence. Maybe the letters have been lost like the letter from Aunt Fischer. I hope so!"[48]

Hanna-Ruth's fears were well founded. By the end of 1942 Frieda could not imagine a happy end to the tragedy they lived. She bade farewell to her son Werner, who had been sent to a forced labor camp in Germany, detailed to heavy agricultural work, and wrote to Elisabeth on 21 December. "I foresee nothing good and must hold myself together." Frieda thanked her for everything she had done and penned a last request: "Please help my child, the only one left to me, Hanna-Ruth, and console her when this heavy fate will touch me also."[49]

Frieda was deported to Auschwitz some six weeks later, on 3 February 1943. It fell to Werner to relate the news to Elisabeth and Hanna-Ruth. "As you see I alone must write this letter because, as I just heard, Mutti has not been at home for the past week."[50] According to Werner, she had expected deportation for some time. Werner followed less than a month later, as Tante Elisabeth soon learned. A postcard she had written to him on 23 February was returned with the address crossed out, and the words in German *"Zurück"* and French *"Retour, parti."*[51]

Remarkably, this was not the last sign of life from Werner. On 2 August of that year the mailman in Stäfa delivered a standard postcard from him written in a "labor camp" in Upper Silesia on 18 July and mailed in Berlin. The sender was "Werner Klopstock, Arbeitslager Jawischowitz, Haus III, Oberschlesien." Oddly this information was not filled out in the section at the left bottom of the address side with blank lines marked "sender," "street," and "place," but above, in the message space. Oddly too, a big stamp instructed the recipient (Elisabeth) to: "Reply only via the Reichsvereinigung der Juden in Deuschland Berlin-Charlottenburg 2, Kantstr. 158." We do not know what Tante Elisabeth thought about these directions. Perhaps she wondered why she should not reply directly to Werner, as his return address was right there on the card. We also do not know if she examined the card carefully and noted that the postage stamp—a fifteen-pfennig stamp picturing Hitler's profile—had not been canceled in Jawischowitz or the adjacent town of Auschwitz, but in Berlin. The card, in other words, had traveled the first leg of its journey from Werner's lager in Upper Silesia by a courier of sorts, not by the Reichspost. Did she pursue this thought to its logical conclusion: if she wrote to the Berlin address (as the stamped instructions dictated) that meant that the same courier would be required for her reply to reach Werner. In short: Wherever Werner might be, he was beyond the reach of public postal services.

Tante Elisabeth knew a lot about what was happening in eastern Europe. She did not know about crematoria and gas chambers, but by 1943 Auschwitz had acquired its reputation as a deadly concentration camp. But even if she had surmised that Arbeitslager Jawischowitz was a subcamp of Auschwitz, we will never know if the evidence offered by the postcard signaled to her that this was not an ordinary concentration camp; Werner was not an ordinary inmate; and the card no ordinary card.

Ordinary cards abounded in the 1930s and early 1940s. Sent by concentration camp inmates, they followed an invariable pattern: the address side carried a printed extract from the camp rules that covered correspondence. Typically: the inmate may receive two letters or cards containing fifteen or ten lines of text, respectively. Prisoners could enclose up to five postage stamps, but no money. And "packages may not be sent because the inmates can buy everything in the camp." The prisoner number and birth date, and stamps by the barrack leader and camp censor adorned every piece of concentration camp mail.

Werner's card carried none of these markers. All the rules and visible control mechanisms that severely constricted what was still a "normal" traffic of letters between the world of the camps and the world outside were absent. Apparently so ordinary, Werner's postcard was in fact extraordinary.[52] Written in block letters, his message ran:

DEAR TANTE ELISABETH AND DEAR HANNA RUTH,
I INFORM YOU TODAY THAT I AM HEALTHY
AND REMAIN HERE FOR THE FUTURE. SADLY I HAVE
NO NEWS FROM YOU. BUT I HOPE
YOU ARE WELL. FOR TODAY
VERY HEARTY GREETINGS FROM
WERNER.[53]

Six lines—not the ten permitted.

No other postcards followed. What we know now, but Elisabeth would not have realized then, was that the Nazis too recognized the importance of letters. Indeed, they unrolled a special project, the *Briefaktion der RSHA* (Letter Program of the Reich Security Main Office) to deploy letters to their benefit: cards as camouflage. From time to time, the Auschwitz SS forced inmates to write cards "home" to soothe the anxiety of those left behind and counter rumors of mass killing in the camps. According to Dieter Wisliceny's testimony in the Nuremberg trials, the Briefaktion was one of his boss Eichmann's inventions. "He had thought out a special system of post cards and letters, whereby he believed he could mislead the public. The Jews brought to Auschwitz or to other extermination camps were forced, prior to being murdered, to write post cards. These post cards—there were always several for each person— were then mailed at long intervals, in order to make it appear as though these persons were still alive."[54]

And thus letters that seemed signs of life served as markers of death.

LIFE AS A
REFUGEE

THE AUSTRIAN-JEWISH WRITER STEFAN ZWEIG ENJOYED GREAT FAME and wealth in 1933. With books published in every European language, he counted on an enormous reading public to shield him from political adversity.[1] When the Nazis included his work in their book burning extravaganzas (10 May 1933), Zweig was shocked to the core. This assault, and the failure of his regime-approved colleagues to speak up, prompted him to distance himself physically and psychologically from the life he had built with such care: a gorgeous Salzburg mansion equipped with a magnificent library and the world's richest collection of autographs and musical manuscripts. "I am mentally prepared to leave," he wrote to his friend the French pacifist author Romain Rolland the day of the book pyres. "Mentally, I have already said good-bye to my house, my collection, my books. Let whomever take the lot. I don't care." Zweig determined to see this as an opportunity: "One becomes younger when one leads a new life."[2]

Zweig's optimism soon waned. "You will understand my hesitation," he wrote to Rolland a month later. "After thirty years of hard work, it is truly difficult to arrive in a country as a refugee, as an outcast."[3] Zweig

wavered until October, when he left for London and rented an apartment on Portland Place. His Austrian-Catholic wife Friderike remained
in Salzburg to sell up and move out. She, for her part, did not want to
emigrate, and Zweig could not quite make up his mind to settle in London. The socialist uprising of February 1934, triggered by a government
attempt to disarm the party's militia, found him back in Salzburg. In
a public display of evenhandedness (Zweig was no socialist), the police
searched his house for weapons.[4] Zweig promptly returned to London,
once again leaving Friderike to deal with their affairs. Responsible too
for her husband's welfare in England, she secured a secretary for him, a
young Jewish refugee she knew named Charlotte Elisabeth Altmann.

Zweig had chosen exile before it was forced upon him, as other refugees with fewer options or resources noted. "In Ostende, he was envied
warmly by many poor, unimportant refugees," the German émigré novelist Irmgard Keun reported in 1936. "He knew and was friends with the
most famous men in every country. He faced no closed borders, or passport or visa difficulties. He could live where and how he liked."[5] And he
did, embarking upon a lecture tour in Brazil that year. Accorded great
respect, Zweig found the country and its people enchanting.

Upon his return to England, he moved to regularize his uprooted
life. Friderike still had not sold their Salzburg home, nor had she joined
her husband in exile. Their disparate desires highlight the remarkable
unanimity found among other refugee couples. Even if they differed
about the need to flee, when one spouse left before the other—Jewish or
gentile—it was with the agreement that the second would follow. Friderike did not. She did not wish to give up her social position and the cultural life she enjoyed. Then too, she had two adult daughters by a former
marriage, neither of whom had a husband or home of her own. Perhaps
her sense of her responsibility as a mother outweighed her idea of her
duty as a wife. Whatever the reason: Friderike felt free to make an independent decision, and that independence—choosing what was best for
her as an individual rather than what was best for the two as a couple—
illuminates the dominant norm. In that time and place, many could
have felt that the old rules did not apply; that each had to decide what
was best for himself or herself. That they did not, that they sought, often

desperately, to emigrate together, says much about the strength of family relationships and the ways in which the family—and not the community, or the party, or other units of civic society—remained the bedrock social unit.

Pressed by Stefan, Friderike finally sold their mansion. But this did not alter the course of their separation. In Salzburg to oversee the final packing and disposition of his belongings in May 1937, Stefan and Friderike initiated divorce proceedings. Measured by any scale, the distance between them was too great to reconcile. He could not face problems at home in addition to those of an exile, he explained.[6]

Notwithstanding his foresight, resources, and connections, Zweig was ill equipped to face problems of any kind. When his Austrian passport ceased to be valid after the Anschluss in March 1938, the British granted him an identity certificate. But Zweig remained *déraciné*, uprooted. "Since the day when I had to depend upon identity papers or passports that were indeed alien, I ceased to feel as if I quite belonged to myself," he observed in his autobiography.[7] The ravages of his inner turmoil showed ever more clearly. The German émigré novelist Klaus Mann saw Zweig in New York while the latter was on a two-month lecture tour. Passing him on Fifth Avenue, "I looked at him, the stubble-chin and the unfocused, gloomy eyes, and I thought, 'Oops! What is wrong with him?' Then I approached him. 'Where are you going? And why so hurried?' He shrank, like a sleepwalker who hears his name. A second later he had got hold of himself, and he could smile again, chat, joke, engaging, energetic as before: the cosmopolitan and elegant, a bit too smooth, a bit too kind 'man of letters.'"[8]

Perhaps because Zweig—like many people separated from their partners—felt lonely, but possibly driven by a deeper sense of disconnectedness peculiar to the refugee, to the exile, he'd been having an affair with Charlotte for some years. Extramarital affairs abound under ordinary circumstances, and thus its prevalence among refugees should not be particularly noteworthy. In the exiles' case, however, the social structures that had maintained stable relations had fallen away, replaced not simply by absence but, often, by a deep yearning for human connection or for proof of esteem shown in the sexual desire manifested by the new lover. "Under the pressure of emigration, long-standing marriages broke apart in a surprising number of cases," observed Käthe Frankenthal, a refugee psychiatrist who had fled to Paris. The bonds of marriage that had held fast as husband and wife fled broke with the strain of refugee life. Reduced in the estimation of the society in which they now lived, and ashamed of their diminished selves in the eyes of their spouse, many sought comfort in extramarital relationships. "I'm almost tempted to say that I know few emigrants whose family life remained completely intact," Frankenthal continued. It was an "emigration psychosis." "The complete readjustment demanded by emigrant life requires a parallel readjustment of all one's habitual notions."[9]

Zweig and the much younger Charlotte Altmann married in September 1939. He acquired British citizenship and bought a house in Bath. But much as he understood that he had to renounce his former status and possessions, he proved unable to do so. Remembering the comfort he enjoyed in Brazil, he and Charlotte applied for permanent residence there. Far from Europe, he sought once again to adapt to his new circumstances. "The thing is to survive this era," he wrote in September 1941 to his ex-wife, with whom he maintained close contact. "News from France and, indeed, everywhere highlights the fact that eating and sleeping are great achievements. You simply have to reduce your standards to absolute zero, forget who you were, what you wanted; to be utterly modest in your demands."[10]

Zweig could not forget. Despite his fame, he felt isolated. "I do not like to talk now, because nobody can understand our position," he explained to his ex-wife. And despite his comfortable home in Brazil, he felt unable to work because he had no ready access to the libraries, art, and music he needed. He had enjoyed being alone when surrounded by his books. Now, as he wrote in his last letter to Friderike, "I liked Petropolis very much, but I did not have the books I wanted, and the solitude which had such a soothing effect at first became oppressive." Zweig did not manage the readjustment of his "habitual notions," to use Käthe Frankenthal's term. He committed suicide on 22 February 1942. "I was too tired for all that," he wrote to Friderike that day.[11] Charlotte did not leave him; she too drank the Veronal.[12]

. . .

SPEAKING ABOUT ZWEIG IN A LECTURE presented in Paris in spring 1939, Jules Romains praised his novelist colleague's perspicacity and planning. "He was clearer-visioned than many statesmen and was convinced, soon after the assassination of Chancellor Dollfuss, that the fall of Austria was inevitable in the form of a Nazi *Anschluss*," Romains observed. "Instead of waiting, as so many others did . . . instead of passively allowing himself to be engulfed . . . Zweig took the necessary steps slowly and carefully."[13]

It availed him naught. Zweig's history is a riposte to the oft-adduced arguments: if only those who sought to emigrate had had more money; if only they'd had greater insight. If only they'd planned ahead. The underlying assumption: if people got out of danger, they would cope and even prosper in their new environment. Many did not. And as they failed, they left little trace for the historian to follow. Zweig's suicide brings that failure to cope into the public realm.

Suicide rates peaked in Germany among Jews after the 1 April 1933 boycott and among the Jews of Greater Germany following the Anschluss in March 1938 and the November pogrom that year. Evidence suggests that it was not persecution itself that drove Jews to despair, but the concomitant sense of isolation, marginalization, and loss of esteem in the public realm. They simply did not count any longer. The rates spiked again during the deportations of 1942 and 1943. Notes by Jews who killed themselves rather than face relocation to an "unknown destination" explained that they preferred to end their lives rather than face an opaque and terrifying future. Age too seems to have figured largely in the decision to commit suicide, with the average possibly somewhere between sixty and seventy years old.[14]

Refugees confronted similar difficulties, and some made the same choice. Writing in 1943, Hannah Arendt observed that "suicides occur not only among the panic-stricken [Jews] in Berlin and Vienna, in Bucharest or Paris, but in New York and Los Angeles, in Buenos Aires and Montevideo." She had survived internment in Gurs; safely landed in New York by then, she explained: "[O]nce we were somebodies about whom people cared, we were loved by friends, and even known by landlords as paying our rent regularly. Once we could buy our food and ride in the subway without being told we were undesirable." For a small number, the pain and the bewilderment of their déraciné and déclassé existence in a new land proved too great. As Arendt put it, "Theirs is a quiet and modest way of vanishing; they seem to apologize for the violent solution they have found for their personal problems."[15] Fragmentary evidence suggests that among refugees too, age proved a factor. A young person has hope, a future, credit in the bank of life, the Austrian-Jewish essayist and refugee Jean Améry pointed out much later. "But the credit of the person who is aging depletes. His horizon pressed in on him, his tomorrow and day-after-tomorrow have no vigor and no certainty."[16] For elderly refugees, the future even in a safe land was too insecure, too frightening. They simply did not have the material or emotional resources to brave the challenges.

Nearly all refugees faced tremendous difficulties. Downward mobility and social isolation framed their lives. As we have seen, only a tiny fraction of refugee professionals such as physicians, lawyers, and dentists found employment in their field. This was not due solely or even primarily to the political agenda of government officials. On the contrary. The restrictions on posts reflected the wishes of the refugees' professional colleagues. The rejection operated on a social level. If it had been a question of marginalization by the government alone, the asylum seekers would not have experienced such profound isolation. But they were spurned by their professional peers whose attitude was: I didn't want you to come here to practice; I will not accord you recognition as a colleague (who alas is not permitted to work by government regulation). You are just about lucky enough to be my butler.

Indeed, at a meeting between the British home secretary and representatives of the medical profession a few months after the Anschluss, Secretary of State Samuel Hoare began the conversation by clarifying the competing interests the home office sought to balance. "On the one hand, we are very anxious here to do nothing that would injure the medical profession in this country," he explained. "On the other hand we are very anxious to do what we can to help in difficult international crises and to do something in the interests of humanity generally." At issue was the number of refugee doctors from Austria the medical profession was prepared to accept.

Robert Hutchison, president of the Royal College of Physicians (RCP), jumped in immediately to set the tone of the discussion. Avoiding "the question of competition"—"I would rather not say anything about that"—Hutchison moved to the point he believed would prevail: "the ethical standards of Austrian refugee doctors are not ours. . . . [A]fter meeting some of these gentlemen," he told all assembled, "I begin to sympathise with Hitler, and I constantly hear that view expressed."

Not everyone got on board with Hutchison. Perhaps because he was Regius Professor at Cambridge, John Ryle (who was also a member of the RCP) addressed the "question of students. Many of our professional colleagues in Vienna have sons who are just embarking on the medical profession." He did not have anything grander in mind than "a quota as a gesture of sympathy," but he reminded everyone of the human disaster then unfolding. "I had in my house yesterday a refugee from Vienna, and they have just had a round-up of doctors there and packed them out to Dachau." His Viennese colleague sought to "get two sons into this country. . . . At present there are only two alternatives, one is for them to be taken prisoner, and the other is to commit suicide, and one cannot listen to that sort of thing without feeling that we cannot have too absolute an attitude about keeping the foreign Jews out." Still, if Sir Samuel had any hope that his suggestion that the profession set an admission quota of 1 percent of the number of currently registered physicians (fifty thousand), or five hundred foreign doctors, it evaporated in minutes. The final figure was set at fifty, ten of whom would be students, and none of whom was welcome in London or any other major metropolitan area.[17]

Hertha Nathorff and her husband Erich, both physicians, were not among the fifty. They entered England on the strength of a quota number for the United States. Arriving in Britain in May 1939, they were reunited with their son Heinz who had left Germany on a kindertransport two months earlier. The Nathorffs' six-month visa fell due in November, but January 1940 found them still waiting for their number to be called. "We sit here and wait, my husband and I, silent, in anguish and despair, since the beginning of May. This having to wait has cost us all the earthly goods we still owned. Our tickets have become void, our money in Germany has not been transferred, our lift [shipment of furniture] in Holland has been lost." They did not fear deportation—the outbreak of war in September saved them from that—yet they had no resources or prospect of temporary employment. "We depend upon the help and goodness of strangers for our simple meals and housing," Hertha despaired to her diary.[18]

The Nathorff family sailed to America on the *Volendam* the following month, but life did not improve for Hertha. Her uncle Carl Lämmle, founder of Universal Pictures and guarantor for the family's visa application, had died, and she received no help from his estate. Her husband studied single-mindedly to pass the medical licensing exams. She worked as a private and summer camp nurse to earn money for the family. Within a year, Erich enjoyed success. "He cannot believe it and I cannot grasp it either. To have passed the exam, doctor again, soon with a practice," she exulted in her diary on 20 December 1940. And then she confessed her own ambition. "I dream, dream, that perhaps I also . . . no, I ought not write that down."[19]

Hertha soon began to study but, as Erich did not support her aspirations, she did so in secret and with a wavering spirit. "I have lost my courage once again," she confessed. Like so many refugee couples that had accessed all their emotional, physical, and financial resources to pull each other out of danger, Hertha and Erich grew apart once they had gained safe harbor. They too suffered from the "emigration psychosis" that Käthe Frankenthal observed in Paris. "The glass wall is there again," Hertha observed of her marriage, "and there is a tense silence between us."[20] She persevered nevertheless, passing the language exam in May 1941. Now she faced the state medical exam. Caught between her desires and her husband's disapproval, she found it impossible to study openly and equally impossible to give up. "I have again lost my courage. I try now to work secretly toward the state exam. But my husband does not like it." She had supported him financially and emotionally when he studied, yet he undermined her efforts. "'Please help me,' I have asked him a few times when I did not understand something. 'Everyone knows that, of course' was his answer, and I was ashamed of my ignorance."

Hertha grew so despondent that "I left one evening, and stood at the edge of the water; the Hudson river water tempted, tempted. . . . I took off my shoes, my thin coat and hat, and put everything including my handbag on a bench nearby, and I walked on and on, approaching the water—and there a hand grabbed me, roughly and firmly." Her suicide attempt was cut short by a fellow German-speaking refugee who assured her that "'it was not yet time to die.'" Accompanying her to her door, he wrote his telephone number "on a scrap of paper and made me promise that I would call him the next morning to tell him that I was still alive."[21]

Hertha recognized that her husband's attitude was not completely new; the problems they now experienced had been expressed in Germany too. "Already over there he was somewhat pained that his wife worked, earned money." Erich carried that attitude and his sense of family standing with him to the new world. "He cannot let go of the fact that he is the son of a *Geheimrat* [privy councillor]; he cannot let go of his background, of his pride, his stupid pride, that he must be the provider of the family and that he will be so in the future." Perhaps having lost so much, Erich held on to his ability to provide for his family to maintain his self-esteem. And perhaps Hertha's loss of the support by family and friends that had enabled her to complete her medical studies in Germany left her without the structure she needed to move forward in America. Whatever the case, she turned to the man who had "saved" her. Speaking of her relationship with him, she confided, "It may be playing with fire, but it will not burn me, this fire. It warms a soul that has gone cold."[22]

Martin Gumpert, a German-Jewish dermatologist and writer who, like the Nathorffs, immigrated to America via London, noted that many refugees felt despondent and analyzed the possible causes. "Ignorance of the simplest customs and formalities, the difficulties of communication, uncertainty as to one's own situation and worry about those for whom one is responsible—all these only serve to heighten the state

Cartoon of a Jewish refugee, drawn by Dutch-Jewish artist Jo Spier, and published by the Dutch daily De Telegraaf, *March 1940. The captions under the ten repeated images capture the dilemma refugees faced: nothing they did met with approval.*

Here he sits in front of the "Café de la Paix" in Paris; the "Métropole" in Brussels; "Américain" in Amsterdam; "Esplanade" in Lisbon; Café "Wiwex" in Copenhagen.

If he drinks a small cup of coffee, they say: "He's taking up the best place, and is drinking only a small cup of coffee."

If he drinks a bottle of champagne, they say: "Look at him. Now I understand why they wanted to get rid of him."

If he eats a local speciality like *boerenkool* [kale], they say: "Look at him trying to fit in."

If he orders German fare like *Eisbein* [pork knuckle] with sauerkraut, they say: "They'll never learn how to fit in."

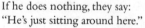

If he opens a café himself, they say: "He's taking our jobs."

If he does nothing, they say: "He's just sitting around here."

If he applies for an American visa, they say: "There he goes. The moment things get dangerous here, he runs away."

And if he doesn't apply for an American visa, they say: "We'll never get rid of him."

He is "a refugee."

of confusion," he explained. Framing his analysis in medical terms, he described the adjustment process: "The mind reacts with apathy to the excess of stimulus and tension. Time and again this initial depression can be observed, especially in people who were once accustomed to definite bourgeois security."[23] He himself responded differently, ready to jettison the furniture and shed the clothes brought from Europe. He embraced the "mysterious metamorphosis that penetrates into every pore of one's being—until at last, after a long period of contemplation and readjustment, one makes up one's mind to buy an American tie. He who can manage to wear an American tie is a citizen beyond doubt."[24] Reveling in "the tremendous stimulus brought on by emigration," Gumpert nevertheless acknowledged that his experience spoke for few.[25]

If some refugees like Gumpert donned an American tie, acculturated, a small elite of artists and intellectuals brought their culture with them and had a great impact on laboratory science, the practice of medicine, literature, philosophy, and film. Famous and influential, they loom deceptively large in popular perceptions of the refugee experience.[26] Most refugees did not fall into that category. As Gumpert put it, "Unless one happens to be an Einstein, one is deprived of all one's marks of rank and left only with the opportunity to regain them under completely changed circumstances."[27]

Often that opportunity failed to materialize. And even when it did, the gains could slip away again, as Hugo Spiel learned to his great dismay. A chemist who worked on the production of artificial rubber and who held important patents, Spiel, an Austrian-Jewish refugee to Britain, should have been well positioned to pursue his career; the war industry required artificial rubber. Spiel cleared ruins in London until the ministry of supply recognized his work and appointed him supervisor of a laboratory in Leeds. His daughter Hilde de Mendelssohn-Spiel and her husband Peter de Mendelssohn had organized the immigration of Hugo and his wife Marie shortly after they themselves arrived in England, and Hilde reflected upon Hugo's history years later. "Finally they took note of his method to create artificial rubber and used him in this field. For some time he was on his way up. The famous Professor J. D. Bernal had taken him under his wing, and even wanted to nominate him for a membership in the Royal Society." But the war took another turn. "The rubber plantations in the far East were conquered back, and one did not need his rubber anymore, and simply sent the fifty-eight-year-old away." Back he went to clearing ruins and died shortly thereafter. In Hilde's view, "exile had killed him."[28]

Menial jobs were the rule, not the exception. As we have seen, people took whatever work they could find to gain a toehold in their adopted land. And they hoped that their employment as maids, butlers, artisans, and laborers would lead to security and further opportunities. This philosophy prevailed among refugees who had escaped occupied Europe and settled across the globe in England, America, South Africa, South America.

IN PALESTINE, HOWEVER, ZIONIST IDEOLOGY valorized manual labor. Contrary to social values elsewhere, the culture that prevailed in Palestine honored those who built up the Jewish state with their hands. Arie Eflel (born Appel) was a member of the first group of young people to leave Germany for Palestine with the youth aliyah movement Recha Freier and Henrietta Szold set in motion in 1933. Reflecting upon his experiences nearly half a century later, he focused on work and its significance. "Work came first in importance," he explained. Most of the sixty youngsters in his group undertook farm work. "In farming, work was regarded as an educational tool of primary importance, and the most fruitful hours of the day were devoted to it." Far from trivial or unimportant, this labor was imbued with transcendent significance. "Work was the highest expression of the fact that there was no other way to redeem the land except by tending it." The land rooted the people and, as the people developed the land, they grew the nation; this was their mission. "The nation could only be rebuilt by manual labor, and the reshaping of the Jew as a hard-working man."[29]

Marie Syrkin, an active Labor Zionist in America, focused on the importance of this creed when she visited (January 1941) the agricultural settlement of Sosúa in the Dominican Republic and emphasized the role of ideology in shaping daily experience. "A refugee, whom I met in Ciudad Trujillo, the capital of the Dominican Republic, said to me: *siedeln muss man mit Begeisterung* (one must colonize with inspiration)." She found his observation on point. "Experience has shown this to be more than a phrase. Colonization, like genius, may be nine-tenths perspiration but without that final one-tenth of 'inspiration' the whole does not function." Comparing the refugees' experience in Sosúa with their counterpart in Palestine, Syrkin reflected, "I could not help remembering the rapture with which a girl in a small kvutza [another word for kibbutz at the time] in the Emek once brought me a radish, saying, 'These are our first radishes,' as though this radish sprung from Palestine earth were something unique and precious. This high sense of purpose, of exaltation, I felt at no moment, neither while at Sosúa, nor while discussing the project with many people in the Dominican Republic." Syrkin did not propose that "every human being must live in an idealistic fervor." But she recognized ideology as key to commitment and dedication. Sosúa "does not pretend to solve the Jewish problem or to build a Jewish future," she noted.[30] The Zionist project drew its strength from precisely that premise. "We know that when Hitler is defeated, and the world resumes a human aspect, immigration to Palestine will proceed with even greater impetus," she concluded. "The drive, beyond the immediate exigency, is there."[31]

Not everyone found fulfillment in manual labor. Not even all the youngsters of the youth aliyah movement, as Otto Suschny's history illustrates. Then fifteen years old, Otto sailed from Trieste on the *Galileo* chartered by the Jewish Agency in November 1939. Like the rest of his group, formed and trained in Vienna, he was imbued with Zionist ideals and accepted the basic premise that "a normal people should have a fair share of farmers and a fair share of factory workers." The instruction they had received had taken root. They had been schooled to look to each other for support and affection, and in Palestine "our group really was a family for all of us. Within the kibbutz we were one family." They readily accepted their assigned work; Otto trained as a carpenter. At the same time, "we organized a group for self-learning . . . everybody was a teacher and also a pupil of the others." By the end of his two-year apprenticeship on the kibbutz, Otto acknowledged that "I didn't like it too much in the kibbutz. I didn't want to work in agriculture." And he burned easily. "I never liked working outdoors: I have fair skin." Still, Zionist ideology had helped him. Ensconced in the social norms of Palestine, he did not experience manual labor as shameful downward mobility. He simply did not enjoy it.[32]

Ideology proved a powerful elixir for young refugees elsewhere as well, helping them cope with their new lives and manage their longing for and worries about family. Gerda Geiringer, who had gone to England on a kindertransport in December 1938, found solace in the British-based Young Austria organization. Arriving in England, Gerda's transport went to Dovercourt Bay, where she and another girl were chosen to live in a British home. But this was just Gerda's first stop. The woman who had taken them in could not manage their care. Shortly after her sixteenth birthday on 2 June 1940, Gerda and ten other émigré girls went to Manchester. "We sat in a park, there in Manchester, spinning plans, and then someone said, 'We've got to stay somewhere tonight.' We went to an estate agent which we had seen, and asked if they had a house with at least ten rooms and empty? 'But the trouble is that we don't have any money, but we promise that if you don't get your pay for the first week by the end of the week, then we'll move out again.' He looked at us, he laughed, and said, 'Yes, I've got something like that, fourteen rooms, will that do you?' Within three days half of us had jobs (I worked at Marks and Spencer's), and we were able to pay the rent by the end of the week."[33]

This independently organized group home served a vital social and, ultimately, political function in these girls' lives. As Gerda explained, "That house became an institution for Manchester." With the start of war in 1939, refugees had become enemy aliens and a number were incarcerated; the government embarked upon a policy of mass internment of male refugees in May 1940. According to Gerda, "By the time we had set up that house, the first people came back from the internment camps because they had been cleared. The main internment camp was on the Isle of Man, and when the men came over onto the mainland and left the restricted coastal area, the first place they came to was Manchester. They had to have a roof over their heads, and we always had two rooms ready for people just to pass a few days or so." Many of the young men had joined Young Austria while interned, and they influenced Gerda and her housemates. "That was the turning point. The turning point was not the internment and not the house, but the people we met by it. Suddenly we realized that we weren't the only Austrians in Manchester; there were others. We met with others, and we found out that there was a little organization for Austrian youth which we all joined."[34]

Established in England in 1939 on the first anniversary of the Anschluss, Young Austria remained in existence until 1947. As the youth arm of the Free Austria Movement, officially it had no specific religious or political affiliation. In fact, it was a communist organization that aimed to attract adolescent refugees. By the middle of the war Young Austria counted thirteen hundred members who frequented fifteen different centers in Great Britain, and published five hundred copies of a monthly, also called *Young Austria*. The declared ideological line held that Austria remained the true national home of the émigrés, that Austria fell as Hitler's first victim, and that another Austria, which resisted Hitler, existed. "It was important for us not only to be beaten refugees, but to stand for something, to find or recover our own identity," Erich Fried, then the librarian of Young Austria in London, explained. "And there [in Young Austria], we helped each other very much." It proved a bulwark against the social isolation and loneliness that a great many émigrés experienced. And it gave them an aim, a goal. "We stood for our own future, and against Hitlerism and fascism. That was good for us, and it was important. But it was also for a better Austria."[35]

Young Austria provided a place for refugees to meet each other, to pursue cultural interests, and to participate in sports activities. But as Gerda explained, "Behind the lines it was very different than the front appearance. The front appearance was that we got together to read, to sing, to dance, to have fun—play chess and other games. Then, slowly but surely, little groups of people got together to learn things. We took a subject and learned about it, and more and more Marxism was mixed in. Before I realized what was in the back of it, quite a few months went by. By then I was not only in Young Austria, but also in what we called symp groups, groups of sympathizers."[36]

Georg Eisler arrived in England in March 1939 at age ten. Within a year or two he too found his way to the Young Austria group in Manchester. He went to school, he learned English, "and I was also learning how to be a refugee. The political refugees, to which we belonged, had a certain cohesion. We had this communist organization, the Austrian communist organization, which went on throughout England, and whatever its drawbacks, at least it had a certain discipline which prevented this self-pity which is the greatest danger to any refugee." Georg appreciated the structure Young Austria provided and the ideological insistence upon looking to the future of the whole Austrian nation. "This phenomenon of rigid discipline saved a lot of lives—whatever its intention was. Perhaps I put this overdramatically. It prevented people from becoming too introspective. They were kept busy the whole time with political education, organizational forms, a study of the most ridiculous Stalinist compendium called *A Short History of the Communist Party*. It's bullshit, but at the time people believed it, and in any case, to take up this study matter kept people going."[37]

The majority of young people who attended Young Austria meetings probably did so only for fun; still, a significant proportion sooner or later belonged to a symp group. This was, according to Gerda, "because the people who went to Young Austria, *and stayed there*, always had the idea at the back of their minds to return to Austria, and that was channeled, politically channeled."[38]

As Robert Rosner, who had become involved with communist youth activities when he was interned by the British as an enemy alien, put it, "In Vienna we had the fascists, and we did not know what to do. Then, in England, I met the Austrian communists, and they said, 'We'll make great changes. We'll fight back.'"[39]

The ideologically committed members of Young Austria knew what they would do when the war ended: it was their job to bring communism to Austria. "We believed," Robert recalled, "that all Austrians would become communists, and we were quite certain of a socialist-communist world. The question was, how could we convince people that they should go back? It was no longer a question of whether I should go back, but how I could convince others."[40]

·   ·   ·

WHILE ROBERT, GERDA, GEORG, and their comrades dreamed about a communist Austria, the three hundred thousand Jews who had fled primarily from Poland to the east lived in a fully communist Soviet Union. Their experience reveals that ideology served merely as fuel to propel a refugee forward or as glue to cement a group together; it did not protect against loneliness or despair. Young Austria offered companionship and prevented social isolation. Its communist ideology provided an attractive rationale for cohesion, but it was that cohesion rather than the ideology that helped the refugees.

Lena Jedwab learned the distinction between the two from experience. Born in Bialystok in 1924, Lena and her family did not flee, nor were they deported east when the Soviets occupied the city in 1939. Lena joined the communist youth organization, and the German attack on the Soviet Union in June 1941 found her working as a counselor in a Young Pioneers summer camp in Druskenik, a Lithuanian health resort. Evacuated en masse to an orphanage in the Autonomous Soviet Republic of Udmurtia, the group reestablished itself, and Lena sought to adjust. "Did I ever dream that I would be so far from home, in a remote village in Udmertia? That I would be the ward of a children's home, part of a collective of children who are strangers to me, all alone in a foreign land?" she wondered in her diary on 8 October 1941. Her days, she confided, passed "in unending sorrow and yearning for home." Turning to her immediate surroundings, she exclaimed, "Is home really a cot in a communal dormitory, my satchel, notebooks, and books that lie orphaned, waiting for the school year to start? No! My home is there—on the other side of the front, in Bialystok!"[41]

Living on two levels simultaneously, Lena acculturated to her new environment and, at the same time, held fast to her family and her Jewish identity. "I miss my home more than ever," she recounted a month later (16 November). "In class I'm not very attentive." Still, she noticed a curious phenomenon: "That doesn't prevent me from answering the questions that are put to me and even from getting good reports. What will be in the future? When will the war end? When will I finally be able to go home? When will I be able to see my parents, my family, my friends?"[42]

Lena adapted. She wrote her most private thoughts, her diary entries, in Yiddish. Yet when she and her friend Genya had their photograph taken, she "automatically inscribed it in Russian." She surprised herself. "I have truly changed. I am ashamed to say it, but sometimes I think in Russian—against my will." Negotiating between conforming to expectations and maintaining her own sense of self, she fit into the children's home as she pursued an exit strategy from it. She aimed to study at a university and asked to be released from communal work in order to prepare for the required exams. The director of the children's home agreed, but the war intervened. "Who can make plans for the future at such a time?" she anguished on 21 July 1942. She was, she said, in "a deep depression. Not only has nothing come of my plans, but I feel the ground crumbling beneath my feet—the whole country is being destroyed." Depression gave way to a sense of isolation. "Now I know what it feels like to be lonely," she acknowledged some six months later.[43]

These feelings grew when she found work in the tractor driver department on a collective farm in June 1943. "My life working in the fields is becoming more stressful by the day," Lena admitted on 9 July. First, the drivers did not value her tasks as real work. "Second, it's because I'm Jewish. (Who says there is no anti-Semitism here?)" Then too, her habits differed. She washed her hands before eating and, the greatest offense of all, "I won't let them embrace me." Within a fortnight, the fact that she was a Jew elided the others. "The tractor drivers pick on me because I am Jewish. They say openly to me that the Jews are the worst people in the world, and that Hitler is right to oppress them." But Lena embraced the communist creed and interpreted her experiences through an ideological lens. "Is it really their fault?" she asked rhetorically, "when their lives are so hard and cruel?" Their behavior and beliefs flowed from their economic situation. "When I consider [their] circumstances, I forgive them everything. Forgive them even for persecuting me as a Jew."[44]

If communist ideology helped her to understand and ignore the abuse she endured, it did not protect her from isolation and loneliness. It did not help her feel at home. "I want to wholly adapt to them," she confessed. But, she recognized, "Unfortunately, I haven't succeeded. Their needs can in no way satisfy me—on the contrary." The external habits she adopted—"we eat together from the same bowl, scooping honey with a spoon, crumbling bread into the milk"—remained superficial markers.[45] She coped, but she did not belong.

Like refugees in the capitalist west, Lena adjusted, adapted, conformed. But home was somewhere else. She achieved her ambition and got to study in Moscow. Yet she remained isolated. "There is no one who loves me," she grieved in September 1943. "Nobody worries about me, thinks about me. I'm all alone in a city of five million people." She diagnosed her own condition, "the loneliness that chills and hardens your heart." And she knew the cure: "I long for a sincere, warm word, for some hope, for my mother!" That sat at the heart of her woe. "After two and a half years as an orphan, I hope and yearn. I will never ever have a home, or find a kindred spirit." In short, she asked herself in May 1944, as the war began to end, "What should I do with myself and my loneliness?"[46]

Stefan Zweig had asked himself precisely this question.

PART IV

1946

Holocaust survivor Abram Zylbersztajn (center) with two other young Jewish survivors, Buchenwald, April 1945.

HOLOCAUST

THE ENTRY OF THE UNITED STATES ON THE ALLIES' SIDE IN DECEM-ber 1941 cemented the Germans' decision to murder the Jews of Europe, and Hitler announced that his prophecy of their annihilation would be fulfilled. For his subordinates, the sole questions were who carried responsibility and how this mission was to be accomplished.

These matters were soon settled. The Wannsee conference (20 January 1942) consolidated and formalized Himmler's SS and Heydrich's Reich Security Main Office (RSHA) authority over what had already become a program of systematic genocide. And after trying a number of methods of mass killing, the Germans settled on the establishment of specially built annihilation camps equipped with gas chambers. Construction of three such installations near the Polish villages of Belzec, Sobibor, and Treblinka began in early 1942. Located along railway lines, these camps came into operation in the summer of that year.

The SS also allocated four new crematoria equipped with gas chambers to Auschwitz, a concentration camp that had been established in April 1940 adjacent to the town of Oswiecim. Operated by Jewish slave laborers, these gas chambers with incinerators (capacity: 4,416 people per day) provided a thoroughly modern and technologically sophisticated solution to the problem of mass murder. It introduced an anonymity of procedure in which the act of killing became invisible and personal responsibility diffused to such an extent that SS doctors conducting selections of arriving deportees could convince themselves that they were not accomplices in an enormous crime, but saviors of those whom they assigned to slave labor.

Organized and coordinated by the same Adolf Eichmann who had streamlined expropriation and emigration in post-Anschluss Vienna, trains filled with Jews from ghettos in the east and collection points and transit camps in the west rolled into these camps. "Emigration" had become "deportation." From July 1942 until Himmler closed the last remaining killing installations in October 1944, between 2.7 and 3 million Jews were gassed, and another 150,000 died in camps where they served as slave laborers.

An utterly new development in history, annihilation camps were literally unimaginable to the outside world. Still, reports that Jews deported to an "unknown destination" faced death trickled into Allied capitals in late 1942,[1] and the Polish government-in-exile reiterated this information in a special note to each of the allies. Persuaded of the veracity of the reports, the British issued a declaration on behalf of eleven Allied governments and the French National Committee in the House of Commons on 17 December. The Germans, British Foreign Secretary Anthony Eden announced, "are now carrying into effect Hitler's oft-repeated intention to exterminate the Jewish people in Europe."[2]

Tragically, by the time the allies understood that the Germans were systematically, eagerly, and energetically obliterating the Jews from the face of Europe, they had established principles to guide their joint conduct of the war that they refused to abandon. Each of these axioms obstructed rescue efforts. First, the allies were adamant that there were to be no negotiations with the Germans that might be construed as possibly leading to a separate peace or a negotiated peace. To win the war, the allies had to cooperate closely, raising mutual trust and minimizing mutual suspicion. Churchill and Roosevelt on the one side, and Stalin on the other, suspected the other secretly wished to conclude a separate peace with their common enemy. Thus, no negotiations of any kind were permitted—including negotiations about Jews in German clutches.

Then too, the British blockade of the continent destroyed any chance to trade Jews for goods or for cash.[3] And finally, the allies refused to help the Germans and their collaborators achieve a "Judenrein" Europe by removing the Jews for them. Despite much evidence of mass murder, they held fast to the old policy of standing firm against "blackmail." The allies wished only to win the war. "The only real remedy for the consistent Nazi policy of racial and religious persecution lies in an Allied victory; every resource must be bent towards this supreme object," British Deputy Prime Minister Clement Attlee insisted.[4]

Nevertheless, public clamor for rescue initiatives prompted the Anglo-American Bermuda conference of April 1943.[5] Delegates to the conference knew the horrible truth—and yet did nothing. As they dithered, the Warsaw ghetto went up in flames. A thousand emaciated ghetto inhabitants, untrained in military matters, defiantly resisted over two thousand German soldiers and officers while Bermuda conferees shut the matter away. Richard Law, one of the British participants at Bermuda, remarked twenty years later, "We said the results of the conference were confidential, but in fact there were no results that I can recall."[6] No program of rescue, no sanctuaries, no agreement to relax immigration rules to the United States or Palestine—nothing. An ad in the *New York Times* summed up the story. "Bermuda was a mockery, and a cruel jest."[7]

Five months later Danes and Swedes showed that not all thought of rescue was a mockery. The small Danish-Jewish community of five thousand and the fifteen hundred German Jews who had found refuge in Denmark had survived unscathed until the summer of 1943. The Danes had surrendered quickly to the Germans in 1940; King Christian had stayed on the throne, national sovereignty had remained undisturbed, and most aspects of pre-war civilian life had remained intact for nearly three and a half years. By August 1943 the Danes had had enough of collaboration. Faced with popular unrest, the Germans declared martial law, and the government resigned.

Direct German rule gave the Gestapo an opportunity to deport the Jews. But German plenipotentiary Werner Best realized that it would make future Danish-German collaboration impossible. He leaked the date of the *Aktion* (2 October) to his aide Georg Duckwitz and sent him to Sweden to make sure Jews would be permitted to land.

Sweden had admitted only two thousand German-Jewish refugees before the war. When, however, the Germans set out to deport Norwegian Jews—whom the Swedes considered fellow Scandinavians—Stockholm offered (3 December 1942) to accept "all remaining Jews in Norway."[8] The German government refused to discuss the matter, and the Swedish consul general in Oslo promptly renaturalized Norwegian Jews who had been Swedish citizens and naturalized all Jews with any Swedish connection. Danish Jews were also fellow Scandinavians. Then too, by October 1943 neutral Sweden recognized that the Wehrmacht had no reserves left to threaten Sweden's security and that Germany was bound to lose the war. The Swedish government publicly broadcast (1 October) its willingness "to accept all Danish Jews in Sweden."[9] Indeed, *all* Jews who reached Swedish shores would be given asylum, the Swedish envoy in Copenhagen assured his Danish colleagues.

Working together, Swedish and Danish officials, the Danish resistance movement, the Danish-Jewish community, and ordinary Danes—housewives, fishermen, students, professional and working people—rescued the Jews in Denmark. While the German navy did not interfere, and Best tried to rein in the Gestapo and military police, the rescuers faced many Gestapo officials who were dedicated to deporting Jews. The exodus was perilous and frightening, undertaken at mortal risk under cover of darkness. The Gestapo never lost its zeal for catching Jews, but it had to do so without the support so plentiful elsewhere, and its effectiveness plummeted. It shipped some 6 percent of the Jewish population, 477 people, to Theresienstadt. The rescuers had prevailed. Close to 6,000 Jews, 1,300 "part-Jews," and 686 non-Jewish spouses had been ferried to refuge in Sweden.[10]

The rescue of Danish Jewry was an exceptional event in a tragedy that continued to unfold, albeit at a slower pace in 1943. At least 1.1 million Jews had been killed in 1941 and 2.7 million in 1942. The number of victims dropped to 500,000 in 1943; the Germans had run out of Jews to kill. In German-ruled Europe, few Jews remained, and they were in hiding or protected by marriage to a gentile. The 750,000

Jews of Hungary constituted the last major Jewish community, and their turn came in 1944.

By May 1945 the total number of Jews murdered by the Germans and their collaborators had reached between five and six million. What this figure signified was presented in photos and films to an astonished world when the Allied forces reached the camps. In Stockholm, Peter Weiss, a twenty-eight-year-old German-Jewish refugee, watched newsreels replete with images. "On the dazzlingly bright screen I saw the places for which I had been destined, the figures to whom I should have belonged. We sat in the seclusion of a darkened room and saw what had up to this moment been inconceivable. . . . There in front of us, amongst the mountains of corpses, cowered the shapes of utter humiliation in their striped rags. Their movements were interminably slow, they reeled around, bundles of bones, blind to one another in a world of shadows. These eyes in the skeletal skulls did not seem to grasp that the gates had been opened."

Knowing that he would have been one of the corpses or the living dead dressed in rags had he not fled, he asked: "To whom did I now belong, as a living person, as a survivor?"[11]

SHERIT HAPLEITA: THE SURVIVING REMNANT

WITH VICTORY ACHIEVED, OUR FIRST CONCERN MUST BE FOR THOSE whose sufferings have been almost beyond human endurance," U.S. Secretary of State Cordell Hull declared in a worldwide broadcast aired on 23 July 1942. "When the armies of our enemies are beaten, the people of many countries will be starving and without means of procuring food, homeless and without means of building shelter, their fields scorched, their cattle slaughtered, their tools gone, their factories and mines destroyed, their roads and transport wrecked. Unknown millions will be far from their homes, prisoners of war, inmates of concentration camps, forced laborers in alien lands, refugees from battle, from cruelty, from starvation . . . victory must be followed by swift and effective action to meet these pressing needs."[1] Hull recognized that the allies would face an enormous problem resettling displaced persons, and he worried about what to do with these refugee masses—including Jews— after the war. Perhaps humanitarian sentiment prompted him to address this issue. Tackling the matter early surely would prove advantageous to postwar refugees. Or perhaps he was animated by the same antisemitism that had shaped his department's practice of preventing Jewish refugees from entering the United States before the war. Advance planning would allow the government time to decide whom to admit and whom to exclude. Possibly he was simply a pragmatist; he foresaw a problem and positioned his department to deal with it.

Whatever the case, Hull was not alone. Many politicians looked to the postwar problems the victors would face. At the behest of their governments, the Inter-Allied Committee on Post-War Requirements and the United Nations (as the allies called themselves) Office for Foreign Relief and Rehabilitation Operations prepared studies throughout 1942 and 1943 on the challenges ahead. Clearly, a new body would be needed, and on 9 November 1943 the allies established the United Nations Relief and Rehabilitation Administration (UNRRA).[2] According to the preamble of the agreement between the nations, the main purpose of this new organization was to ensure that upon the liberation of Nazi-occupied territories and in close collaboration with the Allied occupation forces, "the population thereof shall receive aid and relief from their sufferings." In addition to dealing with the basic necessities—food, clothing, shelter—the covenant stipulated that "preparation and arrangements shall be made for the return of prisoners and exiles to their homes."[3] UNRRA's program envisioned four main stages of assistance: rescue, relief, rehabilitation, and reconstruction. Its architects imagined that rescue would dominate UNRRA's work until the end of hostilities. With Germany's capitulation, relief efforts in war-ravaged areas would take center stage. Rehabilitation, enabling people to help themselves, was to follow. Long-range reconstruction projects formed the final phase of the agenda.

The allies harbored no illusions about the dimensions of the problem they faced. Estimates at the time put the number of displaced persons (DPs) in Europe requiring repatriation at somewhere between twenty-one and thirty million. As the International Labor Office put it in 1943, "The political, economic and social reconstruction of the liberated countries cannot be contemplated until some degree of order has been restored among this confusion of peoples."[4] Returning the nationals of each country required an unprecedented international collaborative effort.[5]

A task of enormous proportions, it could be negotiated if the repatriants wished to return and their governments accepted them. Absent such a wish or acceptance, however, where were the DPs to go? Looking to the future, a number of political leaders predicted a human and diplomatic nightmare even worse than the refugee problem of the late 1930s. The international organization charged with solving such problems, the Inter-Governmental Committee on Refugees created in Evian, inspired little confidence. Its first director, George Rublee, had negotiated vigorously but fruitlessly with Helmuth Wohlthat to transfer abroad some portion of German-Jewish property. His successor, Sir Herbert Emerson, had run an organization that existed only on paper and had not managed to actualize any practical activities to relieve the plight of refugees.[6] Forced into idleness, Emerson turned to the refugee situation in postwar Europe. He foresaw a distinction between short-term refugees, displaced people who wished to return to their homes and had the opportunity to do so, and a "residuum" of others. "Some will be unable to return for reasons other than physical—either because their governments will not be prepared to receive them or because they themselves will refuse, in view of past events, to incur the fresh risks that might be involved," Emerson explained in January 1943. Such nonrepatriable "persons will be true refugees."[7]

Jewish observers realized that most, if not all, western and central European Jews would be nonrepatriable. Jewish communities had suffered total annihilation. Writing in the summer of 1943, the American Zionist thinker and leader Ben Halpern saw clearly that "the ruin of the Jews is complete. There is no sound stock left in Belgium, The Netherlands, Denmark, Norway, Germany, Austria, Czechoslovakia, Poland, the Baltic countries, or Rumania upon which to graft the stricken members."[8]

Families, the basic social unit of those communities, had been annihilated. Comparing the assault on gentile and Jewish households, Halpern observed that "only a fraction of the non-Jews of Europe have been taken away by the Germans: a son or two, or a daughter or a father to each stricken family. In Western and Central Europe, except in Italy and France, practically all the Jews have already been deported; virtually no families still have a foothold in the sheer physical sense." If repatriation aimed at family unification, surviving Jews would not be served by returning home. Their kin might be "in Kazakhstan or in Shanghai, in Palestine or in New York." Justice and logic demanded that, for Jews, "repatriation" included the opportunity to join relatives in other countries or to move to Palestine to join a Jewish community.[9]

Where the unrepatriable would go took second place to a more fundamental question in 1943: what body would be responsible for them? Not UNRRA, the subcommittee that dealt with displaced persons maintained. UNRRA would provide immediate relief "for a reasonable period" to DPs who "cannot or do not desire to be repatriated." After that, they were to become the wards of another organization. Emerson had suggested a new entity, but the delegates to the first UNRRA Council session (November 1943) charged Emerson's IGC "to remove them to new places of settlement."[10] Furthermore, UNRRA took responsibility solely for the allies' nationals. As a World Jewish Congress (WJC) delegation reminded the UNRRA Council, this policy excluded what they estimated would be 150,000 Hungarian, Romanian, and Bulgarian Jewish DPs in areas liberated and occupied by the allies. They urged the inclusion of "non-nationals of United Nations who have been obliged to leave their homes or places of de facto residence for reasons of race, religion or political belief."[11] This proposal spoke to a legal conundrum that plagued most refugee Jews in Allied countries since the outbreak of war: their status as stateless persons or (on paper) nationals of belligerent countries and thus "enemy aliens." Not recognized as nationals by their own governments (Germany and its allies), however, they did not enjoy any legal protections. As Hannah Arendt observed in 1944, this lack of rights had reduced refugees to "something utterly inhuman."[12] The WJC proposal to treat Jewish DPs who were stateless or of enemy nationality *as if* they were Allied nationals aimed to help them practically *and* to remove them from a political no-man's-land.

No decision was taken at the time. This worried Zorach Warhaftig, a member of the WJC executive board, whose job it was to plan the postwar rescue and rehabilitation of survivors. Education, insight, and experience trained Warhaftig for his task. An ordained rabbi and practicing lawyer in Warsaw before the war, Warhaftig had fled to Lithuania in September 1939. As a refugee in Kovno, he urged his coreligionists to make their way to Palestine immediately, and he sought other escape routes. Building upon the good will of the honorary Dutch consul in Kovno, Jan Zwartendijk, Warhaftig suggested a legal ploy to identify the Dutch colonies in America (Surinam, Curaçao, and five smaller islands) as a destination for refugee Jews. Zwartendijk entered an official declaration authenticated by a consular stamp in Jews' passports to the effect that they did not need a visa to enter these Dutch colonies. No one mentioned that the Dutch governors of these colonies had the power to refuse admission to any foreigner and certainly would have barred Jewish refugees. On the strength of Zwartendijk's phantom visa and, like his colleague, motivated by compassion, the Japanese consul Chiune Sugihara provided Jews with transit visas for Japan, which in turn enabled them to obtain a transit visa for the Soviet Union. At least two thousand Jews were saved in this manner, including Warhaftig himself, who reached the United States.[13]

Warhaftig's legal acumen had served Jews in 1940, and it served them again in 1944. He predicted that most survivors would have no wish to be repatriated, and he was certain that the IGC would not have a clue as to how to help them. Poorly funded, with limited personnel and scant political support in the world's capitals, the IGC could not possibly provide the practical assistance refugees required. "The Intergovernmental Committee on Refugees has always been looked upon either as an expression of the charitable feeling of its members, or as a protector against the flood of refugees to various countries," he argued. UNRRA, by contrast, "is an organization set up by all the United Nations in order to redress some of the wrongs caused by the war which are regarded as common tasks to be dealt with by all the member governments." An arm of the allies, "UNRRA is not merely a relief organization but rather an expression of the common will of the United Nations to win both the war and the peace."[14] Warhaftig saw but one solution: UNRRA should take care of the unrepatriable as well.

His call to increase the scope of UNRRA's responsibilities came at the wrong time. In November 1944, UNRRA officials realized that they were hardly prepared for the tasks with which they were charged. The new estimate of 9 million displaced Allied nationals (of which 8.7 million were in Greater Germany) stood lower than feared, but the ongoing destruction of cities and infrastructure and rapidly deteriorating civilian conditions dramatically increased UNRRA's burden. It hardly needed an additional mission that required extensive diplomatic infrastructure.

UNRRA did not extend its scope to resettle unrepatriable DPs but, thanks to Warhaftig, it did proffer services to Jews who were or had been enemy nationals. Analyzing the decisions taken by the first UNRRA Council meeting, Warhaftig realized that the organization had unwittingly bound itself to care for such Jewish DPs. The report of Committee IV, Subcommittee 4 on Policies with Respect to Assistance to Displaced Persons addressed the division of labor between UNRRA and the IGC.[15] And the report stated that "UNRRA has to assist in the care and repatriation of all persons who come within the scope of the activity of the Inter-Governmental Committee on Refugees, provided only that they can and wish to return to their countries."[16] This insight led Warhaftig to scrutinize the minutes of the Evian and Bermuda meetings. He concluded that "UNRRA, which is obliged to assist all victims of persecution who are within the jurisdiction of the Intergovernmental Committee, cannot discriminate against such enemy nationals as may be victims of racial, religious, or political persecution." Driving his point home, he emphasized: "Indeed, the Committee was established for the specific purpose of caring for enemy nationals (from Germany and Austria); and in its present setup it is obliged to help victims of persecution from all countries *regardless of their nationality*."[17] Months of negotiation followed. But by April 1945, when the Allied armies marched into Bergen-Belsen, Buchenwald, and other camps, the matter had been sufficiently settled: all displaced persons who had been persecuted for racial, religious, or political reasons were eligible for UNRRA assistance.

As PREDICTED IN 1943 and planned for in 1944, Allied forces freed a staggering number of people in spring 1945 who fell under the definition of "displaced persons." According to an UNRRA report, "During April, displaced persons were liberated in greatly increased numbers. Most of them were found in deplorable physical and mental condition, particularly those who had managed to survive the horrors of the Nazi concentration camps." By the end of that month some 1,750,000 had been freed, and by the end of May "the total number liberated had reached 3,500,000, of which 90 percent were accommodated in camps or repatriated." Round repatriation figures stood at 140,000 in April and 849,000 in May, "the bulk of them being West Europeans." Soviet citizens were soon sent home as well. Following a meeting with the Soviet High Command on 17 May, a comprehensive plan for repatriation led to the return of 1,600,000 Soviets in just two months. "By August there were less than 500 Soviet citizens left in the U.K., U.S., and French areas." In sum, "as of 1 August, over 4,000,000 United Nations displaced persons had been repatriated. It was estimated that by 1 September the only displaced persons remaining would be those who were either stateless or for one reason or another could not be immediately repatriated."[18]

Jews fell into this group, of course. They amounted to a tiny fraction of liberated persons: only some twenty-five thousand Jewish survivors were counted in Germany and Austria immediately after VE Day. But they were the most vulnerable. No one knew what to do with them. Unlike other nationals (like Poles or Belgians), their identity as "Jews" held no official political status; no Jewish government existed to call for immediate action on their behalf. While the decision to treat all Jewish displaced persons *as if* they were United Nations nationals had given all European Jews rights within the DP camps system, it had not created a political body with the power to extend diplomatic protection or to ensure their rights through bilateral or multilateral negotiations. The Jewish Agency had no governmental standing in relation to the DPs and could not intervene on their behalf. Lacking such political protection and posing a practical problem, Jews dropped to the last action item on the military authority and UNRRA agenda. Without malice aforethought, but also without giving the matter any thought at all, the occupation authority herded Jews into DP camps already filled with antisemitic east European nationals. Nor were the latter the worst; that title went to General George S. Patton, commander of the Third Army which occupied southern Germany where most Jewish DPs were located, an unabashed antisemite and admirer of Germany and Germans, who thought it perfectly reasonable to lock Jewish DPs in camps surrounded by barbed wire and guarded by armed soldiers.

Eager to find their loved ones and attempt life anew, Jewish survivors in DP camps felt both baffled and betrayed by the lack of action on their behalf—if not by secular authorities then at least by their coreligionists. "We, the surviving Jews of Europe, appeal to you as the central agency of the Jewish people," the Lithuanian-Jewish physician Zalman Grinberg, the German-Jewish legal scholar and journalist Samuel Gringauz, and

DP camp inmates protest conditions in Linz (in the American sector of Austria), winter 1945–6. From a farewell gift album created by inmates in Bad Gastein DP camp and presented on 28 March 1946 to American army chaplain Rabbi Eli Bohnen in appreciation for his work on their behalf.

an A. Bergmann wrote from their displaced persons quarters in Bavaria to the World Jewish Congress in New York on 31 May 1945. "Four weeks have passed since our liberation and no single representative of any Jewish organization has come to speak to us concerning what has happened to us in the most horrible persecution that has ever transpired; to give us comfort, to alleviate our need or to bring us aid. We have had to help ourselves with our poor strength. This has been our first great disappointment since our liberation and it is a fact which we cannot understand." Most particularly: "Two questions torment us: Each of us burns with the wish to find out the tragic facts about his own family. We ask you therefore to send us as speedily as possible lists of the Jewish survivors in the Soviet Union and the German occupied territories. We must know for whom to say Kaddish. The second question is: What will become of us? Where will they send us? Where will we have to continue our misery?"[19]

What Grinberg and Gringauz did not know was that the WJC had been negotiating with UNRRA, the State Department, and the IGC for months, pleading the need for Jewish representatives in the camps to care for Jewish DPs and offering to fund this effort. To no avail. Each Allied nation appointed liaison officers responsible for repatriation, but they paid little attention to their Jewish nationals who did not wish to be repatriated. And no one attended to Jewish enemy nationals.

American Jewish army chaplains stepped into this vacuum, although it was not their job and notwithstanding anti-fraternization rules that prohibited them from speaking with enemy nationals. Ernst M. Lorge, one such chaplain, took the matter into the public arena, describing how poorly Jewish DPs were served in comparison with others: "You enter a camp, and immediately you will find officers in the uniforms of practically all European nations running around and giving orders. They drive in beautiful sedans with a large sign 'Liaison Officer,' and the name of the country they represent." These liaison officers had vast resources at their disposal to dispense on behalf of their nationals. No such situation obtained for the Jews. "The Jewish group, alone, runs around, disorganized and bewildered." Yet no one required help more urgently than these Jewish DPs. They had, he emphasized, "suffered still more than the others. All of the Jews were in concentration camps and extinction camps, while most of the others suffered a much less severe fate as slave workers. Their families have been slaughtered, while most of the others are reunited with a large part of their families." What worried him most was that "their mental state deteriorates from day to day, as they find that the dreams of liberty and the future, dreamt for so many years of abject misery, are not coming true. Instead, they find themselves to be the only completely forgotten of the earth."[20] Lorge and other Jewish chaplains sought to help but, lacking authority, their efforts were stymied. "In his capacity as ambassador to the suffering of his people, he is self-appointed and without any official backing,"[21] Lorge observed. And as their primary responsibility was the soldiers under their care, when their units moved to other assignments the chaplains left with them.

Private conversations bolstered public calls for action. Nahum Goldmann and Stephen Wise of the WJC and Secretary of the Treasury Henry Morgenthau approached the state department. Morgenthau suggested that Earl G. Harrison, former U.S. commissioner of immigration and naturalization and the newly appointed American representative on the IGC, conduct a special study of the DP situation as it then stood. Acting Secretary of State Joseph C. Grew approved the idea and observed to President Truman that his explicit endorsement of Harrison's mission to inquire into the condition and needs of the displaced persons, "particularly the Jews," would be helpful. Truman obliged, and thus Harrison came to conduct his mission with presidential support.[22] Recognizing that a multiperson task force would lend greater validity to his final report, Harrison invited Joseph Schwartz, director of the Joint in Europe, Patrick M. Malin, vice director of the IGC, and Herbert Katzki of the War Refugee Board to accompany him.

As Harrison and his group toured the DP camps, Grinberg, Gringauz, and other survivors organized the Association of Surviving Jews in the American Zone of Occupation. To the outside world they came to be known as "surviving Jews," but to themselves they were not "survivors," or "displaced persons," or even "refugees." At the suggestion of army chaplain Abraham J. Klausner, they drew upon a term in the Book of Chronicles referring to those who had survived the Assyrian destruction of the Kingdom of Israel: Sherit Hapleita (the saved remnant).[23] The term implied a prophetic world vision. They had survived suffering and loss of biblical proportions, and they saw their destiny as part of what they believed to be the ordained mission of the Jewish people: to found the Jewish state and to root the people of Israel in it. Fervent Zionists, the Jews who affiliated with Sherit Hapleita demanded "the opening of the gates for immigration to Palestine to all Jews who want to immigrate there and the creation of the groundwork for the proclamation and establishment of a Jewish State in Palestine."[24] No repatriation; no immigration to the United States or other countries overseas. There was only one solution to the predicament of Sherit Hapleita: Palestine.

Appalled by conditions in the DP camps, Harrison came to a similar if less rigid conclusion. He opened his report with an indictment. "Three months after V-E Day . . . many Jewish displaced persons and other possibly non-repatriables are living under guard behind barbed-wire fences, in camps of several descriptions (built by the Germans for slave-laborers and Jews) including some of the most notorious concentration camps, amidst crowded, frequently unsanitary and generally grim conditions, in complete idleness, with no opportunity, except surreptitiously, to communicate with the outside world, waiting, hoping for some word of encouragement and action in their behalf."[25] Urging the allies to recognize the sustained assault Jewish survivors had endured, he pressed for recognition of them as "a separate group with greater needs."[26] The help they needed did not "come within any reasonable interpretation of privileged treatment" but was "required by considerations of justice and humanity."[27]

Help was one thing; home quite another. Now that the great majority of other DPs had been repatriated, the time had come to attend to the future of Jewish survivors. Like Sherit Hapleita, Harrison saw that future primarily in Palestine. He recommended that the American government endorse the Jewish Agency petition to the British for an additional one hundred thousand immigration certificates for Palestine.[28] But on his tour of the DP camps he had heard also from Jews with family in America, and in his report he sought permission for these DPs to join their families.

Harrison urged this course because he recognized the Jews as a distinct people with attendant political rights, including the right to go to their old-new homeland. And he urged this course because he realized that the treatment and settlement of the DPs served as a civics lesson for the Germans. In the most famous paragraph of his report, Harrison shone a searing light on a question that lingered since the 1930s: the difference between the Nazis' position with regard to the Jews, and that of the western democracies. "As matters now stand, we appear to be treating the Jews as the Nazis treated them except that we do not exterminate them," he contended. "They are in concentration camps in large numbers under our military guard instead of S.S. troops." His point: "One is led to wonder whether the German people, seeing this, are not supposing that we are following or at least condoning Nazi policy."[29] Harrison well knew that the Germans had ample reason to believe this to be the case. The Nazis had trumpeted the flaccid response of other governments at the Evian conference to the urgent pleas of desperate Jews.[30] As the German émigré writer Raimund Pretzel (writing under the pseudonym Sebastian Haffner) put it in 1941, "If the Nazis have ever had a propagandist success in Germany even among their sworn enemies, it was their advertisement of this attitude of the Western Governments, who offered the suppliant fugitives nothing but vague prospects of being sent, later on, to New Guinea—of course not all at once—while they were being tortured to death in the concentration camps."[31] If the allies were to establish their moral authority, the treatment of the Jews stood as the litmus test.

Harrison submitted his report in August. Truman responded immediately, sending it on with a stern letter to General Eisenhower. Quoting Harrison's direct parallel between the Nazi and American conduct toward the Jews, Truman held that even the perception of such a similarity was intolerable. The United States bore a particular responsibility to victims of persecution, Truman insisted, and Americans had to show by word and deed that they "thoroughly abhor the Nazi policies of hatred and destruction. We have no better opportunity to demonstrate this than by the manner in which we actually treat the survivors remaining in Germany."[32]

Eisenhower had already taken action to improve the situation of Jew-

ish survivors before Harrison had submitted his report and thus before
he got Truman's reproof. Perhaps because his military experience had
trained him to see people in groups (divisions, battalions, armies) or perhaps because he had honed his political instincts and skills (he was chosen to run the war in the west because he was the only American general
who could deal with his British counterparts), Eisenhower had come to
see the Jews as a distinct people. At the end of July he had begun to relocate Jewish DPs in camps exclusively for them. He reiterated this policy
on 22 August. If the Nazi camps had defined Jews as a special nation
slated for death, Eisenhower's Jewish DP camps affirmed the Jews as a
nation slated for life.

His response to Truman redounds to his credit. Holding himself
responsible, he expressed great readiness to confront the situation. "I
am very much concerned by your letter of August 31st on the Harrison
Report," he cabled Truman on 14 September, "and I am today starting
a personal tour of inspection of Jewish Displaced Persons installations."

*General Dwight Eisenhower leaving the synagogue on a tour of Neu Freimann
displaced persons camp in fall 1945.*

He had just received a positive report from the Joint, he added, "as it has recognized that all matters mentioned in Harrison's Report are being remedied with the utmost speed consistent with the difficulties of the situation."[33] Accompanied by Patton, the person culpable for conditions in southern Germany, Eisenhower set off to review Jewish DP camps.

However sanguine the Joint may have been, Eisenhower's visit taught him otherwise. In his preliminary report to Truman on 18 September, he acknowledged serious problems. The key issue was the future. DPs worried about where they were to settle, and he understood that most wished to go to Palestine. On this point he felt powerless. Neither he nor the American army could move that forward. "There is nothing whatsoever that I or my subordinates would be justified in promising or intimating." Skeptical that the British would throw open the gates to Jerusalem, Eisenhower noted that "the matter draws practical importance for us out of the possibility that caring for displaced persons may be a longtime job."[34] In the meantime, he instituted what changes he could to improve life in the camps. Reminding his generals that helping DPs was "a primary military mission," he removed American guards from the camp perimeters, increased the daily ration for victims of racial and religious persecution from twenty to twenty-five hundred calories, and assigned many more UNRRA workers to the Jewish displaced persons camps.[35] Most important, he got rid of Patton, relieving the most successful warrior in the American forces of his command of the Third Army and detailing him to head "the Theater Board studying lessons of our late campaigns."[36] Few Jews—or in Patton's words, "a sub-human species"[37]—there.

Patton transferred on 7 October, and Eisenhower submitted a full report "on matters pertaining to the care and welfare of the Jewish victims of Nazi persecution within the United States Zone of Germany" the next day. The issue of Jewish DPs claimed front-page coverage in the United States by then. When Pennsylvania Avenue knew that Eisenhower had taken control of the situation, the White House released (29 September) the Harrison report and Truman's letter of 31 August. A week later the administration released Eisenhower's report. This appeared to wrap up the last threads of the war. Everyone was looked after or on the way home. The relocation of displaced persons (except for the Jews) shone bright on paper. The Allied armies and UNRRA had repatriated over 5 million DPs in one hundred days. By 7 October, when Eisenhower submitted his report, the average had dropped from 1.5 million repatriants per month to fewer than 200,000 per month. When the White House unrolled its public relations coup at the end of September, UNRRA sent out a press statement proclaiming its accomplishment of "5,163,000 displaced persons" repatriated. It boasted too that it was negotiating with military authorities about a new arrangement for care of the 1 million remaining displaced persons, "the non-repatriables and stateless as well as those who for one reason or another cannot be repatriated in the near future."[38]

IF THE FUTURE OF JEWISH DPS reached headline status, it also became a serious political matter. At just about the same time, on 24 September, the Zionist leader Chaim Weizmann called attention to the British government's offer of only fifteen hundred Palestine certificates (the balance permitted by the 1939 White Paper)—a far cry from the hundred thousand the Jewish Agency requested and Harrison recommended. This enraged many in Palestine and in the United States. After the systematic slaughter European Jews had suffered for the past six years, the best the British could do was to offer survivors what remained of the original seventy-five thousand certificates? Didn't the Holocaust demand a reconsideration of the White Paper?

Many embraced the cause of the "100,000." As one writer observed at the time, "the urgency of the Jewish problem has taken concrete shape in the form of 'the 100,000 Jewish DPs.'" Indeed, "friend and foe of Jews alike are talking in terms of 100,000." In his view, "such a conception of the problem makes it more concrete, more visual than the more ambiguous 'Jewish problem in Europe.'"[39] The "100,000"—and the problem they represented—triggered acts of sabotage in Palestine and the beginning of an undeclared war between yishuv Jews and the British empire, as well as massive anti-British demonstrations in the United States. Prompted by such public displays of dissatisfaction, the British cabinet met on 4 Octo-

Bad Gastein DP camp workshop, late 1945–early 1946. From a farewell gift album created by inmates in Bad Gastein DP camp and presented on 28 March 1946 to American army chaplain Rabbi Eli Bohnen in appreciation for his work on their behalf.

ber and confirmed its adherence to set policy. Admission of one hundred thousand "would lead to an explosion in the Middle East [and] would not solve the problem of the Jews in Europe," it concluded. Seeking a politically expedient solution, Foreign Secretary Ernest Bevin proposed "a fresh approach to the problem": a new committee. He suggested the appointment of an Anglo-American commission to investigate the situation of the Jews in Europe and possibilities for immigration, including to Palestine as well as UNRRA camps in North Africa. The cabinet happily accepted Bevin's proposal, as did Truman.[40]

Concerned that the Anglo-American Committee of Enquiry regarding the Problems of European Jewry and Palestine (AAC) might be nothing more than a "time-saving device, a camouflage to conceal a cruel and brutal policy of do-nothing,"[41] as appointee Bartley Crum put it, the members insisted upon public hearings and an explicit undertaking by the British and American governments to effect unanimous recommendations. With these conditions in place, the AAC tackled its first problem: discerning the number of Jewish refugees and displaced persons in Europe. Analyzing various data, it concluded that of the 9.9 million Jews in Europe in 1939, only 4.2 million still lived in 1946. Of these, 3.8 million remained in their countries of origin (including 2.5 million Russian Jews), and 391,000 were "refugee and displaced." This last figure counted 152,500 refugees and displaced Jews in countries subjected to the persecution of the Nazis and their allies, and who were "survivors" in the strictest sense. In addition, a total of 238,500 Jews had found refuge and were still in the United Kingdom (50,000 German and Austrian Jews), the Soviet Union (165,000 Polish Jews), and the neutral countries of Spain, Portugal, Sweden, and Switzerland (23,500).[42] While the official figure of "refugee and displaced" Jews thus ran to 400,000, the AAC assumed that a significant percentage of Jews in Poland, Hungary, and Romania would join that number as soon as they possibly could, and therefore 500,000 actual or future refugees and displaced persons was a more realistic figure.

Satisfied that it had ascertained the true dimensions of the problem, the committee focused on the political repercussions of relaxing the quota on Jewish immigration into Palestine to accommodate some portion of the refugees. It then turned to its most difficult task: formulating recommendations and achieving unanimity. The Americans, who had no mandate in Palestine, pressed for the immediate immigration of one hundred thousand DPs. The British, by contrast, disagreed both with the Americans and among themselves. Philip Baker, now minister of state for foreign affairs, flew to Lausanne where the AAC met to urge his countrymen to develop common ground and to seek it with the Americans; only a unanimous report would carry weight.[43]

Deliberations continued for three weeks in April 1946. Finally, the British MP Richard Crossman persuaded his countrymen that endorsing the immigration of one hundred thousand Jewish DPs was a politically astute move. Crossman saw immigration to Palestine as a fact of east European Jewish life. "Zionism, whether we liked it or not, was a bare necessity for the existence of eastern European Jewry," he observed. Jews faced a stark choice: emigrate or perish, and they had nowhere to go but Palestine. "Nothing could stop this movement to Palestine, though it could be halted for a moment. It was not the product of Zionist organization, but the expression of the most primitive urge: the urge for survival." Furthermore, if Zionism was a vital necessity for DPs, it had become a moral necessity for British and American Jews, who would do everything to support the immigration of Jewish DPs to Palestine. The debacle of British policies in Ireland framed Crossman's analysis of the Jews and Palestine. American Jews, he predicted, "would fight as passionately for the existence of the national home as the American Irish, or the American Poles had fought for the rights of the Irish and Polish nations."[44]

Crossman also argued that agreeing to an immediate immigration of one hundred thousand DPs would put the Jewish Agency "on the spot," forcing the shadow Jewish government to collaborate with the British, suppress terrorism and illegal immigration, and restore law and order. In a stroke, the admission of the hundred thousand would restore British prestige and authority in Palestine, pull the Jews in line, and pressure Arabs to accept partition. All of these conduced to the ultimate goal of partition and independent Jewish and Arab states in Palestine by 1948 or 1949, which, he pointed out, trumped the "horrid prospect of fifty years of British Trusteeship."[45]

The British and American delegates joined forces and submitted their final report on 20 April 1946. They recommended that the British government grant one hundred thousand immigration certificates to Palestine immediately. In addition to all the reasons Crossman had adduced in discussion with his colleagues, the committee presented what it saw as another positive outcome of this step. Rapid emigration of the hundred thousand, it contended, would allow the allies to close "the Jewish displaced persons centres and thereby discourage the further migration of Jews in Europe." The very existence of the camps had encouraged Jews elsewhere, especially in the east, to leave their homes and begin a journey "from centre to centre, zone to zone, and country to country." Noting the difficulties that "such movements" imposed on the Allied authorities, the committee concluded that "stabilisation will give sympathetic governments a better opportunity of implementing national schemes of resettlement and will encourage the Jews themselves to give more careful consideration to such opportunities."[46]

Crossman did not prevail on the two-state solution. The AAC supported a bi-national state in which "Jew shall not dominate Arab and Arab shall not dominate Jew." Bitterly disappointed, the Zionists recognized that the certificates were bought at the price of a sovereign Jewish state. Such support as existed in the yishuv for continued cooperation with the British evaporated. In the end, Whitehall did not issue the certificates either. Faced with Arab strikes and demonstrations, and speculation that the Soviet Union might support the neighboring states against the British in Palestine, London and Washington abandoned the plan.

The Zionists did not. Starting in April 1945, even before VE Day (8 May), the Jewish Agency pressed SHAEF (Supreme Headquarters Allied Expeditionary Force) for permission to send high-level representatives to the DP camps. To no avail. Frustrated that Salomon Adler-Rudel, who had served on the Reichsvertretung until the Nazis expelled him from Germany in 1936 and then had worked arduously in London on behalf of refugees, could not obtain travel papers, Chaim Weizmann complained to Secretary of State of War Sir James Grigg. "We are constantly receiving requests from the different camps to send a representative to Germany," he wrote on 21 June, after waiting for two months, "and I am afraid that the impression which these refugees must be getting is that the non-arrival of an Agency representative is due to neglect on our part rather than to the fact that we have so far not been able to obtain the necessary permission from the military authorities."[47] It took until August before Adler-Rudel set sail, and still, no major political figure from Palestine was admitted.

The leaders of the yishuv felt responsible for the Jewish DPs, and they also recognized that the European Jews were a key political factor in the demand for a Jewish state. At the same time, they worried about how to care for the survivors and whether the immigration of even five thousand DPs would turn Palestine into "one big madhouse."[48] Were the survivors physically and emotionally able to take on the task of pioneers? And was Palestine stable enough to absorb them?

Zionist leader David Ben Gurion chats with Major Irving Heymont, an American Jewish serviceman, during a visit to Landsberg displaced persons camp. U.S. army chaplain Abraham Klausner stands to the left of Heymont, nearest the viewer.
PHOTOGRAPHER: GEORGE KADISH / ZVI KADUSHIN.

Ben Gurion finally wrested permission from the Americans to enter their zone in Germany (the British refused entry), where he was met (19 October 1945) by Judah Nadich, chief of the Jewish chaplains in the American forces in Europe. Nadich took him to the DP camp in Zeilsheim. The inmates had not been told that Ben Gurion was to visit.

Nearly a decade later Nadich recalled his arrival vividly. "Suddenly, one of the Jews . . . happened to peer into my automobile and, recognizing the strong face and white shock of hair, suddenly screamed in an unearthly voice, 'Ben Gurion! Ben Gurion!'" His cries electrified the camp. "Like one man, the entire group turned toward the car and began shrieking, shouting the name of the man who was accepted by all of them as their own political leader." Nadich implored them to assemble in the camp auditorium. "In a few minutes I led Ben Gurion into the large jammed hall, all the seats occupied, all the aisles filled, every inch of space packed, those unable to enter, standing near the doors and leaning across the window-sills. As I led Ben Gurion into the hall, the people spontaneously burst into song, 'Hatikvah,' the hope that had never died, the hope that was unquenchable in their breasts, the hope that had kept them alive. As Ben Gurion stood on the platform before them, the people broke forth into cheers, into song and, finally, into weeping." Ben Gurion wept too. Everyone recognized the significance of that moment: it held the past and the future. As Nadich put it, "For the incredible was true; the impossible had happened. Ben Gurion was in their midst and they had lived despite Hitler, the Nazis, and all their collaborators with all the diabolical instruments of destruction at their command—they had lived despite them all to this day when they could welcome Ben Gurion!"[49]

Ben Gurion traveled to Landsberg and Feldafing; he addressed camp inmates and met with the Zionist leadership. He told the DPs how arduous their lives in Palestine would be, and he sought to assess the sincerity of their Zionist aspirations. If he was not entirely persuaded that the DPs would make the best immigrants, he was utterly convinced that Palestine was the best option for them. "We will have troubles," he declared upon his return, "but at least the troubles will come from Jews."[50]

Ben Gurion's visit yielded another significant result. Forging a relationship with Eisenhower and his chief of staff, General Walter Bedell Smith, the Zionist leader pled the case for the admission to DP camps of Jewish refugees in addition to those liberated in April and May. Smith secured Eisenhower's approval: Jews arriving at the gates of American displaced persons camps would be admitted—no questions asked.

Ben Gurion had his eye on the fifty thousand survivors in Poland

Concentration camp survivor Shmuel Rakowski (seated in the center) and Jewish DPs whom he, working with the Bricha *(Escape) movement, had guided clandestinely out of Poland and into Germany.*

and the more than two hundred thousand refugees in eastern Europe who had been included in the general amnesty of 1941 and had survived imprisonment or internment in the Soviet Union. The Soviets allowed all Polish citizens (as of 1939) of Polish or Jewish ethnicity to repatriate to Poland in 1945, even if they had accepted Soviet citizenship. This included the Polish-Jewish refugees who had flocked into Soviet-annexed Poland in 1939 and had fled or been shipped farther east. Few of these Jews had homes to which to return, and they followed the path taken by many of the 50,000 Jews who had survived the war in Poland. These survivors found little welcome in a country with few resources and even fewer people willing to give up the Jewish property and possessions they had appropriated. Five years of Nazi antisemitic propaganda had sharpened pre-war prejudices. "Still alive?" "Didn't the Nazis kill you?" "Still so many Jews?"[51] The murder of 350 Jews in a series of pogroms put paid to all hopes. Anxious to leave Poland and eager to gain entrance to Palestine or the United States, survivors fled to American DP camps in Germany. By the beginning of 1946 some 25,000 Polish Jewish survivors had crossed into the American zone in Germany. Postwar refugees, they—in the terminology of the time—"infiltrated" into the DP population.[52]

Abraham Klausner, the American Jewish chaplain with great organizational skills who had coined the term "Sherit Hapleita" for the DPs and who championed survivors' needs and rights, witnessed their arrival. "The few Jews returning to Poland from years of horror in the concentration camps and the numbered Jewish partisans coming out of the woods after their heroic escapades are met by waves of anti-Semitic pogroms. As more and more Jews are killed by Polish terrorists, the panic-stricken remnant seeks protection by escaping to the only available area—the American Zone in Germany. Thousands have arrived." Desperate, they fled by whatever means available. "They come by foot, by car and by train. They come as a driven people. This week three hundred arrived in box cars in which they had been traveling for weeks."[53]

Jewish leaders assumed more were on the way. Testifying before the AAC that same month, Dr Joseph J. Schwartz, head of the Joint in Europe, predicted that 250,000 Jews were likely to leave. He minced no words. "The great majority of the Jews in Poland are sitting on their valises. They are all packed and ready to go." And he hastened to add: "Everybody knows, including the Polish government, that these people are leaving Poland. Everybody knows the reason why."[54]

Seeking to understand the entire sweep of the problem, the AAC used the term "refugee and displaced" to describe the postwar status of nonrepatriable European Jews. This included Jews in former Nazi Europe, as well as those who had fled to the east, had crossed legally or clandestinely into Spain, Switzerland, and Portugal, and those who had made their way to Britain and Sweden. All had been displaced, and all were now counted as postwar refugees.

WHERE NOW?

THE END OF THE WAR AND THE COLLAPSE OF THE THIRD REICH raised a question for all European Jews who had survived the Holocaust: where now? Host countries had accepted refugees on the premise that they would go home when the Nazi regime fell, or they would move on in due course. But war's end found few, in either DP camps or safe havens, prepared to return. Jews from west European countries such as the Netherlands, Belgium, and France proved an exception to this general rule. The Dutch government, for example, welcomed survivors, including refugees, restored political and civil rights immediately, without discussion, and as a matter of course, and promised to institute a process of restitution for material losses. Of the 140,000 Jews in the Netherlands in 1940, only 30,000 lived to make this choice in 1945, and the sheer weight of the loss might have given them pause. Yet nearly all returned, including Jenny and Max Gans who, from their refuge in neutral Switzerland, had carried on writing to their family and friends; from the latter they learned their loved ones had been deported to the east. Receiving this news in 1943, they held little hope of finding them alive in 1945.

They found that their community had been destroyed and nearly all of their family had been killed; Max's in Sobibor; Jenny's in Auschwitz. Yet the Ganses felt deeply rooted in Dutch soil. Jews to be sure. And

Dutch. In any case, eager to empty the country of its wartime refugees, Swiss Chief of Police in the Ministry of Justice Heinrich Rothmund terminated their right to stay. Jenny, Max, and a young refugee girl they had taken in as a foster child boarded an Amsterdam-bound train in Basel on 27 August 1945. Rothmund wanted them out, and they wished to go: they saw their future in the Netherlands. Perhaps their wartime correspondence with gentile neighbors and friends, that they had learned of their families' fate from them, facilitated their vision of possibility. As Jenny put it, "We had survived the war. Our main objective was not to be refugees any more, but citizens of the Netherlands."[1] Like their coreligionists who had survived the war in hiding, in concentration camps, or as refugees abroad, they agreed with the perspective articulated by survivor Abel J. Herzberg that "the persecution of the Jews in the Netherlands, even if it happened on Dutch soil, is not properly Dutch history." In his view, "It did not arise from Dutch circumstances. One can even say with certainty that it could not have arisen from it."[2]

German and Austrian Jews could not hold such sentiments, yet some felt so attached to their homeland that they sought to recover the landscape, culture, and language robbed from them years before. Ernst Lothar found himself in the grip of just such feelings. Director of the famous Josefstadt Theater, Ernst, his wife, the actress Adrienne Geiringer, and their daughter Hansi had left Austria soon after the Anschluss. The Nazi daily *Völkischer Beobachter* had identified "the Jew Lothar" as the cause for the "Jewification" of Viennese theater on 18 March 1938,[3] and direct threats followed. The Lothars needed no further invitation to pack up and leave in their recently purchased car, which they thought to sell when they crossed the border. A great plan, but it did not work. They were stopped thirty miles from Switzerland by SA men who forced Ernst to give up the automobile "voluntarily" and "for national purposes" in exchange for an escort to the border town of Feldkirch, where the Lothar family continued their journey by train. For Ernst, that "last piece of road, one of the most beautiful in the world," became a journey of dissolution. His sense of "connectedness"—to the landscape, to the country—"fell into pieces" with each passing mile.[4]

Bereft as Ernst felt, his luck held. The Swiss had not yet instituted

a visa requirement for Austrians and admitted the family. They proceeded to France where, after a mere nine months, they received American immigration papers. Ernst found work teaching theater criticism at
Colorado College; Adrienne began to rebuild her career on Broadway.
Ernst admired what America offered and recognized that his countrymen had abandoned him. Unlike the Ganses, Ernst did not hear from his
former gentile friends. "No one had had that little bit of courage to write
a line or to send a message to say we think of you, how are you doing?
Not one," he recalled twenty years later. "And so many had sworn their
loyalty."[5]

Yet he could not stop longing for the country that did not want him.
"Homesickness is an overlooked disease," he observed. He feared that he,
like his friend Stefan Zweig, would "succumb to the lethal disease of emigration."[6] Caroming between head and heart, Ernst applied, successfully,
for American citizenship as soon as he was eligible. And when the war
ended he applied, again successfully, for a new state department position,
"Theater and Music Officer," whose job it was to oversee the denazifica-
tion of the arts in the American zone in Austria.

The Lothars thus returned to Austria in spring 1946. When they
stopped in Zurich on their way, news caught up with Ernst about his
older brother Robert: a victim of the Holocaust, he had been deported
from Vienna and murdered in Riga. Yet as their train pulled into Salzburg and Ernst saw the church towers and domes, he felt "the miracle of
return and survival even more wonderful than I had believed possible."[7]
When his appointment ended, he and his wife did not hesitate. Expressing their gratitude for the refuge America had offered them, they handed
in their naturalization papers and passports to the American consul in
Vienna. Stateless for the second time in their lives, they applied, successfully, for restoration of their Austrian nationality.[8]

ERNST AND ADRIENNE FELT CONFIDENT TO SAY, "I belong in my *Heimat* [homeland]." Other refugees felt equal confidence that they did not
belong in the country where they had found asylum. "I don't belong *here*"
expressed the sentiments of those who had fled to Shanghai. It had served

as a waiting room for almost a decade by the time the war ended, and most refugees had eked out an existence marked by poverty and constrained circumstances. Many had been incarcerated in a ghetto area in 1943, but even those who had lived beyond those precincts, who had managed to maintain what under the circumstances passed for a middle class life, did not feel rooted in the Chinese city.

Armin and Edith Gruber had arrived with little but each other in May 1939. Armin had been packed off to Dachau shortly after the November pogrom, and detailed to hard labor. Edith sought his release and, with passport (issued 17 February 1939) and ship tickets to Shanghai, Armin was set free. Fortunately for this young couple, soon after their arrival they met Mr and Mrs Kikoin, Russian Jews who had come twenty years earlier. The Kikoins, by then in their fifties, were in the retail garment business. Edith had expertise in dress design, and the Kikoins wanted help with their enterprise. Edith and Mrs Kikoin signed a lease on 4 August 1939 for premises in the French concession at 1017 Avenue Joffre. Armin obtained work too, and the couple found an apartment. As their son (born in Shanghai in September 1946) explained sixty years later, his parents' accounts of their experience emphasized the importance of earning a living, finding housing, avoiding the many tropical illnesses that swept the city, and helping to organize events such as concerts to enable other refugees to work. Both parents stressed how lucky they were, finding it a responsibility to help others. At the same time, they always worried about Edith's parents and Armin's mother left behind in Vienna.[9]

Weathering the war in Shanghai, the Grubers, like other refugees, celebrated its end. But it was clear that there was no future for Jews in China. The old extraterritoriality had been abolished. The Nationalist Chinese government invited Europeans to remain and offered them citizenship. The refugees, however, saw communism on the horizon which, they believed, did not augur well for them. In any case, most wished to return to the west. They had not habituated to the climate, the infectious diseases, or the rudimentary hygiene.

According to an UNRRA report, Shanghai had sheltered 16,300 refugees: 7,380 had held German nationality; 4,298 Austrian; and 1,265 Polish; 87 percent of all of these refugees were Jews.[10] Exhausted by their experience of the Shanghai ghetto, a number did not have the energy to start anew in yet a third location. The elderly especially yearned for the known world and, as it remained difficult to enter the United States where many had kin, chose to repatriate. This suited UNRRA, which was dedicated to the project of repatriation, and it was convenient for the Joint. Thus, 650 German and Austrian refugees left Shanghai in July 1947 on an American troopship called the *Marine Lynx*. Arriving in Naples, half continued on a special train to Berlin; they constituted the largest single group of refugees to repatriate to their former Heimat.[11]

Uncertainty gloomed their return. Germany stood in ruins. Life was harsh for everyone, including repatriates, gentile or Jewish. Still, German Jews suffered additional burdens. They had been stateless since November 1941, and in 1947 there was no German state to restore their citizenship; this legal problem disappeared only in May 1949 under the new Federal Republic of Germany. Then too, the repatriates en route to Berlin had no idea if and how their property would be returned to them. Attempts by the Allied governments to develop a unified restitution law across all occupation zones had failed because the Soviet military government refused to permit restoration of property to individual owners. The American, English, and French military governments would soon enact restitution laws (by early 1948) for their respective zones, but in an economy in which cigarettes circulated as the currency of choice, the prospect of more durable financial arrangements remained dim.[12]

The Austrians moved more quickly but to no happier effect. The government in Vienna passed a Nullity Law voiding all legal acts from the Anschluss in March 1938 until May 1945.[13] A series of restitution laws followed. Yet there was little political will to give these acts muscle. Unlike Germany, the Austrian state felt no need to prove its democratic credentials, holding that it had been a victim of Nazi Germany. And in postwar democratic politics, there were few votes to gain and a lot to lose by pressing wide-scale restitutions; too many voters had profited.

Jewish refugees in Shanghai may not have known these particulars, but the general message reached them even in their outpost in China. The great majority did not wish to return to the countries they had fled. Again, the Grubers were lucky. Edith's brother had emigrated from

Vienna and had made his way first to New York and then Louisville, Kentucky. He provided an affidavit of support for his sister and her family, and their application for admission to the United States was approved. Their deposition papers, signed by American vice consul Elizabeth Engdahl, show that they traveled without a passport because they were stateless, yet they counted toward the Austrian quota.

Edith and Armin tied up loose ends in May 1947. A testimonial obtained from Siegmund Fischel, president of the Jewish community in Shanghai (12 May), explained "to whom it may concern" that "in the year 1944 Mr. GRUBER served in the directing board of the Communal association of Central European Jews managing the Department for cultural and press affairs with great discretion." Fischel went on to say that "being a religious Jew, Mr. GRUBER always has supported the religious, cultural, and social institutions of this organization." In business as well he held the esteem of his contemporaries: "As a merchant Mr. GRUBER enjoys a city-wide reputation for his correct dealing as well as for his modest and amiable manners."[14] With their immigration visas (issued 24 May) and smallpox vaccination papers (reinoculated 31 May), the Grubers were prepared to depart. They set sail on 15 July and arrived in San Francisco a fortnight later. Edith's brother had crossed the continent to meet them at the pier and to take them home to Louisville with him.

The situation worsened for the refugee community the Grubers had left in Shanghai. The Chinese government ordered all foreigners to leave the country in 1947, but where were they to go? Conditions in the city deteriorated as Nationalist forces lost to the communists in 1948, and Shanghai Jews became increasingly anxious.[15] With the founding of the state of Israel on 14 May, three thousand refugees chose to go there. A fledgling country in a precarious situation with its neighbors, Israel offered little security or material comfort, but for those refugees it appeared a better prospect than Shanghai. Jews who remained searched the globe anew but could not generate interest by western governments in their fate until the communist armies approached the city late that year. "Save the Shanghai Refugees," ran the headline of the 19 November issue of the New York–based German-Jewish newspaper *Aufbau*. The newspaper sought to publicize the inequity of the June 1948 DP act that des-

Herman Auslander, a seventy-five-year-old Jewish refugee from Shanghai,
conducts a service on board a sealed train from San Francisco to Ellis Island, via
Jersey City, c. January 1949. The refugees were sent on to Israel.

ignated as DPs Jews who had reached Germany, Austria, or Italy by 22
December 1945, thus barring Shanghai refugees from that status and eli-
gibility to enter the United States. Prompted by the crisis and its importance to the people in his district, Representative Emanuel Celler of New
York introduced an amendment to the act that, although unsuccessful,
focused attention on the problem.

Israel remained the sole alternative to repatriation for most Jews in
Shanghai. The International Refugee Organization (IRO; the successor to UNRRA) began to evacuate Jewish refugees systematically in fall
1948. Like HICEM in 1941, the IRO chartered ships to transport refugees. Those with American visas disembarked in San Francisco. Cana-
dian visa holders proceeded directly to Canada. The rest, which claimed

the majority, traveled in a sealed train to New Jersey, were interned in Ellis Island, and proceeded from there to either Europe or Israel. Thus, for example, the former troopship SS *General Gordon* docked in San Francisco on 23 February 1949. Of the 648 Jewish refugees on board, 137 held visas for the United States, 44 were Europe-bound, and the remaining 467 were to travel on to Israel. They were not Zionists. They had no relatives in Israel. On the contrary. They had children and parents, brothers and sisters in America—but they did not have the visas they needed to reunite their families. Acknowledging the bitterness of their situation, the Israeli consul general in Los Angeles, Reuben Dafni, cheered the refugees: "You are now going where you are wanted and where we wait for you."[16]

The crisis continued into 1949. "4,000 Jews in the trap of Shanghai," *Aufbau* reported on 6 May. The city was about to fall. Communist authorities had given European refugees exit visas,[17] but they lacked transport out. A week later *Aufbau* noted that five airplanes had been chartered for an evacuation operation and that America and Canada had agreed to fast-track visa procedures for Shanghai refugees.[18] No such acceleration occurred, and when the Joint closed its Shanghai office a year later, over a hundred of the city's refugee Jews sat in an IRO refugee camp near Bremerhaven, waiting for their U.S. visas to join their kin in America.[19]

If refugee Jews could not see a place for themselves in postwar China, most Polish Jews who had survived camps, or by hiding, or now returned from the Soviet Union soon saw that they did not belong in their native land. "[T]he same story I heard over and over again," an American journalist, Isidor F. Stone, observed. "Jews returned from concentration camps in Germany or from service in Russia; they very rarely located a relative or a friend alive; they found whole Jewish communities destroyed; and they felt themselves unwelcome, despised, and hated in an atmosphere of virulent anti-Semitism." Jews did not describe the government as antisemitic; the Polish people held that title. According to Stone, Jews on the run again told him, " 'The government's hold is weak. Conditions are lawless. Life is dangerous. The government is trying its best to establish new colonies and homes for the Jews, but the task is hopeless. We have no future in Poland. We see only more pogroms ahead.' "[20]

*Jewish refugees in the Soviet Union leave Bukhara (Uzbekistan) for Poland on
1 June 1946.*

Lena Jedwab returned to Poland later than most Jews who had fled
to the Soviet Union. She had written to her family in Bialystok at the end
of July 1944 "with the first mail after the liberation of the city. My letters
were the first! That's what the girl in the post office told me," she confided to her diary. Devastating news came in return. 6 September: "The
pain of waiting has ended with greater pain: all the many letters that I
sent to Bialystok have been returned with the notation that the address-
ees are absent. The horror is clear: they all perished as martyrs." With
nothing and no one awaiting her in her homeland, Lena remained in the
Soviet Union until September 1947, when attacks against Jewish intellectuals and leaders prompted her to seek greater safety in Lodz. She did

not find it. Lena, her husband Sholem (whom she met shortly after her arrival and soon married), and her brother-in-law Ksyl crossed the Polish border clandestinely in August 1948 and made their way to Paris.[21]

ANTISEMITISM IN POLAND AND COMMUNISM in Shanghai shaped the postwar actions of Jewish survivors. For many refugees, social and political circumstances did not send such a neon signal, and war's end found them without a clear sense of where they belonged. Hilde Spiel, who had fled from Vienna to England with her husband Peter Mendelssohn returned to visit in 1946. A naturalized British citizen since 1941, she had gained a modest but secure foothold in British life. Yet the disappointments and humiliations her father Hugo Spiel had suffered in England followed by his death immediately after VE Day challenged her sense of assimilation. "Where did we belong?" she asked. "Now that the continent was open to us again, exiles faced the choice of whether to return to their place of origin and once again tear up the roots they had put down, or grow them deeper into the soil of their second Heimat."[22]

A war correspondent for the *New Statesman*, Hilde took the opportunity to travel to Austria in January 1946. "I am returning to my origins, estranged by the long absence, steeled by some of the losses and ready for a hard, presumably painful experience," she confided to her diary.[23] Her prediction proved correct. Entering the former center of her social life, Café Herrenhof, she found herself face-to-face with Herr Hnatek, the waiter who had served her years before. With no understanding of her ordeals, Herr Hnatek, "full of self pity," rushed "to complain about his fate and the fate of Vienna whose dust I so successfully have shaken from my shoes. 'Frau Doctor did the right thing by going away. The bombings alone—three times they set the entire city in flames.'"[24] This was no homecoming. Ernst Lothar valued geography and architecture more than inhabitants. For Hilde Spiel, people carried far greater weight.

Herr Hnatek spoke for many: ordinary citizens and officials alike. The allies declared that Austria had been "Hitler's first victim," and the new Austrian government seized that line to rewrite history.[25] State rhetoric and social discourse sent a clear signal to returnees that neither public nor private recognition of their travails and losses would be forth-coming. Reentry, if desired, came at the price of silence.[26] At that point in her life, the cost was too great for Hilde Spiel. She returned to London at the conclusion of her assignment.

Spiel chose to go to Austria in the British uniform of a war corre-spondent. A significant number of German- and Austrian-Jewish refu-gees found themselves in their homelands as soldiers in the American army. Second Lieutenant Stefan Heym (formerly Helmut Flieg) had escaped from Germany to Prague where he lived until 1935 when he went to the United States on a student visa sponsored by a fraternity at the University of Chicago. There he had become the editor of *Deutsches Volksecho*, a German-language anti-fascist weekly. Drafted into the army in 1943, he worked in a publicity and psychological warfare unit, pro-ducing German-language broadcasts and leaflets to demoralize German soldiers. After VE Day, Heym was in charge of publishing American-sponsored newspapers in occupied Germany.

As Heym traveled through Germany and spoke to its citizens, he found that no one had known about the camps. When he reminded them that the regime had depended upon them to do their part, "their contrite look, which was obligatory at the beginning of such a conversa-tion, changed to a blotched, angry expression: 'It's easy for you to speak, Herr Lieutenant, you weren't here, you have no idea what it was like, the pressures under which we have lived for all those years.'"[27] No one had wanted the war "and of course neither that with the Jews." They had not wished to harm anyone, and they had suffered greatly. And they asked: "'Herr Lieutenant, what would you have thought, what would you have done?'"[28] Perhaps they had a point, Heym reflected. Had he not been a Jew, had he not been a known anti-Nazi and thus forced to flee, he might have behaved as they did. This insight did not diminish Heym's disgust with the moral cowardice of the Germans he met, but it allowed him to return to East Germany some years later when the anti-communist hyste-ria triggered by the Cold War and exploited by Senator Joseph McCarthy made the United States uncomfortable for the socialist writer.

Spiel left London for Vienna when her marriage dissolved in 1963. Heym, prompted by the McCarthy-era political environment, moved to

East Germany, the part of the country in which he had grown up and the German state with which he had greater sympathy. Ludwig Marcuse, whose wife Sascha had prevailed at the American consulate in Marseille in 1938, tested a homecoming by using a sabbatical from the University of Southern California for a visit to Germany in 1949. "I do not feel so lonely anywhere as in the city in which I was born,"[29] he wrote from Berlin. "I have not found anything that belongs to my past. . . . Memory tries to hold on, but reality cannot be held on."[30] Reflecting upon his experiences a decade later, Marcuse identified what he saw as the key components of his identity. "I am an American. I am a writer. I am a professor. Where do I belong? I have Sascha, who was my home in all of my places of exile."[31] Indeed, his home had been, remained, and was to be his wife Sascha.

WERE REFUGEES WHO WISHED TO RETURN welcome in Germany? If Austrians hid behind the fiction that they were the first victims and thus refugee returnees were no worse off and in fact in a better situation because they had left, what position did Germans take with regard to the émigrés? A radio broadcast by Germany's most famous exile, Thomas Mann, elicited a clear answer to this question. Shaken by news reports about the concentration camps, Mann spoke about "this overwhelming shame"[32] and the Office of War Information carried his broadcast on VE Day. "Everything German, everyone who speaks German, writes German, has lived according to German customs, is implicated," he declared. "It was not a small group of criminals, but hundreds of thousands who belonged to the so-called German elite, men, young men and dehumanized women, who, with diseased desire, committed these crimes under the influence of crazed teachings."[33] No German who had remained in Germany was guiltless, Mann concluded. His speech was carried in all the German-language newspapers published by Stefan Heym's publicity unit in Germany.[34]

Frank Thiess, a popular writer who had not joined the party or openly supported Nazi positions—but did nothing to oppose the regime either—took umbrage. He had negotiated his way by making the compromises necessary to ensure his own survival and prosperity.[35] His ability to adapt did not abate: after the regime collapsed, he proved adept at recasting those compromises into a history of resistance. Thiess introduced the concept of "inner emigration" or "inner exile." When the Nazis had burned some of his books in 1933, he had chosen an "inner emigration;" he had created "an inner space, which Hitler failed to conquer despite all his efforts," he explained. "I have often been asked why I did not emigrate, and I had but one response: if I were to manage to survive this horrible period (the duration of which we certainly all underestimated), my spiritual and human development would gain much more, and I would come out of that richer in knowledge and experience, than if I watched this German tragedy from the theater boxes and stalls abroad."[36] Thiess claimed that those who had chosen "inner emigration" understood the situation better, and implied that they were more principled, more honorable, than those who had left. The latter, he contended, had not shared their countrymen's suffering; indeed, they had not suffered at all, spending the war as they had in comfort abroad. His argument stuck. His countrymen embraced it with relish. Everyone, it seemed, had been AWOL at home.

The Austrians loved it too and adapted it to fit their national fiction. As they were the true victims, the refugees owed *them* help. The New York–based *Austro American Tribune* printed (November 1945) a letter written by Viktor Matejka, a city councillor of Vienna. Addressed "to the Austrian artists and scientists in the USA," Matejka wrote about the restoration of cultural life. Any help they cared to offer was welcome, especially books. He wanted material goods, not human resources; he did not suggest that refugees return.[37]

Requests for all manner of commodities, especially food, flew fast. "Not a single day passes when I do not receive letters from dear friends from the old Heimat, letters replete with affection, full of information about what they suffered, descriptions of the ruins, hunger, afflictions," Robert Rie wrote to the Austrian federal chancellor in an open letter published (September 1946) in the *Austro American Tribune*. "These letters rarely end without suggesting the possibility of dispatching care packages to the writer. Help for Austria, Mr Chancellor, is freely demanded. But what about help from Austria?"[38] Rie, a lawyer and, later, professor of German language, and a friend of Stefan and Friderike Zweig, had fled Austria after the Anschluss. When he got to America, he had worked as a porter in a railway station, at times dependent on food donations from black fellow workers. Neither then nor at any other time had anyone from Austria ever sent a care package. "Our former compatriots should not ask for food packages, but for our return," he declared. "Addresses should not be given to us to which we ought to send care packages; rather we should be informed about laws with which the federal government intends to make good the damage done to us."[39]

No such luck. On the contrary. Intelligence personnel of the Office of the Military Government of Bavaria (OMGB) asked postwar opinion leaders, "democrats" with a clean past, if exiles who had been prominent in 1933 should "return and participate in the reeducation and rehabilitation of Germany?"[40] No question about ordinary neighbors forced to leave was asked, nor was the word "Jew" mentioned. The answers conveyed the same message as in Austria: Jews might return if they recognized that Germans were the victims. As one Anton Ott, a prominent Catholic youth leader in Augsburg put it, "They must first reintegrate, and learn what the German people were forced to accept and endure not only during the war, but since the summer of 1933."[41] Or as the composer Carl Orff, who had continued to work happily throughout the Third Reich explained, the Jews could return because they would do him good. "For a period in my life I was on friendly terms with many Jews. In other words, at that time it was of no consequence: this one is a Jew and that one not. That perspective sneaked in from the outside later. I was often with them because they understood me and because they stimulated me, and I would be happy if it could be once again as it used to be."[42]

Arthur Koestler wanted none of this. Like many others, he did not see it as his job to make Germans feel good about themselves or to serve as their inspiration. Koestler had been on the road since the 1920s, when he spent some years in Palestine. Returning to Europe, he had sought refuge in France. He had never felt at home. "During my seven years as a refugee in France, I lived entirely in the company of fellow-refugees and continued to write and think in German," he reflected in 1954. He fled across the Channel in 1940, and "from the moment when, in 1940, I settled in England, I began to write in English, moved among English friends and ceased to be a refugee."[43] For him, the refugee "homesickness" that many had noted was "not focused on persons and places, but a rather diffuse nostalgia for a specific human climate." After years of harsh treatment on the continent, "I have found the human climate of England particularly congenial and soothing—a kind of Davos for internally bruised veterans of the totalitarian age. Its atmosphere contains fewer germs of aggression and brutality per cubic foot in a crowded bus, pub, queue or street than in any other country in which I have lived."[44] England had become home for him, as America had become home for Martin Gumpert. For Gumpert there was no return either, and for the same reason: Germany could not offer the human climate he valued. "The cobweb of barbed wire will long hang in the air, and it will be a ghostly reconstruction, with the moans of the tortured and slain dinning into all ears," he predicted. "I have not yet struck roots here," he wrote after living in America for five years, "but it is becoming clearer and clearer that I can never go back over there."[45]

If refugees like Martin Gumpert and Arthur Koestler knew with utter clarity that they had no wish to return because the human climate they valued could not possibly exist in their homelands, others wished to reemigrate in order to create it. Imbued with communist ideology, they went to build a new Germany, a new Austria. While no welcome was extended to Jewish former citizens by socialist, Christian, or nationalist Austrian politicians, the communist party invited them to return. And many young people who had become politically engaged during their refugee years heeded the call. Robert Rosner, Gerda Geiringer, and Georg Eisler were but three of more than one thousand Austrians who returned to their homeland from Britain after the war, and all of these by then young adults joined the party. "I didn't realize that the Austrians were really in the forefront of the German killing machine until much later," Gerda explained. "I bought the line that Austria was Hitler's first victim. And when I returned to Austria in September 1946, I was very quickly disabused. . . . I didn't think that we would be greeted at the Westbahnhof with cheers. I didn't think the communists would have a big following. I was one of the most realistic people. But coming to Vienna, I was more than surprised. I mean I was horrified and surprised. . . . I can show you photos I took in the fifties, in the *fifties,* which look exactly like the photos you could see in '38 on public streets or on shop-windows: *Juden Raus* [out with the Jews]. Of course I had a shock."[46]

Robert Rosner came to political life because of antisemitism, and he believed that communism would be the end of antisemitism. "I thought the communists had found a way, and we had to make the Austrians communists, and then there would be no antisemitism. And I didn't feel much antisemitism in Austria after the war. I honestly didn't feel it. I was so closed in in the communist party, it was so much my family and I was so happy to find here a *big* family, that I didn't see or feel any antisemitism."[47]

THE EXISTENTIAL QUESTIONS OF RETURN posed by Ernst Lothar, Hilde Spiel, and Stefan Heym would have appeared fantastic and perhaps self-indulgent to the vast majority of Jewish refugees, had they been aware of these discussions. And the conviction held by the Young Austrian youth and communists who returned to Austria and the Soviet sector of Germany, respectively, to build up a new state would have seemed utterly foolish and naïve. By the end of 1946 most of the refugees still in DP camps had experienced the Soviet system firsthand and had left the USSR at war's end. They had survived, and they remained grateful to the Soviet Union, but they held no illusions about civil liberties or quality of life under the Soviet system.

The Jews who filled DP camps in Europe and who had survived the war in Shanghai faced a world as closed to them as it had been to Jewish refugees in 1938. With no other options, and inspired by the ideological commitment of survivors who took on leadership roles in many camps, DPs embraced Zionism. The dream of Palestine, the prospect of building their own Jewish state, imbued them with optimism for the future. "To judge from the stories they tell, to many of them all hope remaining and Zionism were identical things," Ernst Lorge, Jewish chaplain in the American army, observed.[48]

David Ben Gurion's visit to the DP camps camps in October 1945 had strengthened the DPs' zeal and the authority of the Zionist leadership. An UNRRA survey in early 1946, taken to help the Anglo-American Committee, revealed that 18,072 of the 19,311 DPs questioned identified Palestine as their first choice of destination; 393 wished to go to the United States, 95 to a west European country, and 13 desired to stay in Germany.[49] "We did not accept these figures without exhaustive questioning of our own," Bartley Crum noted in his account of his work on the AAC. "We asked: Why was Palestine so predominantly the first choice?" As the AAC members questioned DPs, "the faint sound of marching feet came to our ears. We looked out of the window. Men and women were marching three and four abreast, toward us. . . . They carried a Jewish flag and banner reading, 'Open the Gates of Palestine!' It began to rain." Undeterred, "the men and women stood outside to attention, heads up, silent, the rain beating down on them."[50]

Zalman Grinberg, one of the Zionist leaders, summarized the DPs' situation for Crum: "A bitter, terrible yesterday, an impossible today, and an undetermined tomorrow."[51] A survivor told him bluntly: "My uncle in the United States wrote me a letter saying 'I can send you money.' My sisters in Palestine wrote me, 'Come to us.'"[52] Richard Crossman, another member of the AAC, heard the same message. "Even if there had not been a single foreign Zionist or a trace of Zionist propaganda in the camps these people would have opted for Palestine. Nine months had passed since V-E day and their British and American liberators had made no move to accept them in their own countries. They had gathered them into centres in Germany, fed them and clothed them, and then apparently believed that their Christian duty had been accomplished," he recounted. "They knew that they were not wanted by the western democracies." And, in sharp contrast, "they knew that far away in Palestine there was a national home willing and eager to receive them and to give them a chance of rebuilding their lives, not as aliens in a foreign state but as Hebrews in their own country."[53]

The Zionism that inspired postwar DPs differed from pre-war Zionism. The hothouse of the DP camps and the politics of immigration gave birth to a militant and even prophetic form of Zionism, a biblical Zionism that was homegrown but also encouraged from without. When Ben

Gurion had visited, he had suggested a variation on the biblical exodus from Egypt. According to Judah Nadich, chief of the Jewish chaplains in the American forces in Europe, at a meeting in Frankfurt with a group of DP Zionist leaders, Ben Gurion laid out "a plan which envisaged the organized exodus of all the Jews from all of the DP camps on a certain day when they would begin a march on foot, if need be, to move solidly across Germany, across its frontiers, across Italy and France to Mediterranean ports." Ben Gurion explained that this was meant as "an act of desperation to be used only as a last resort and it was hoped that no power on earth would be able to stop the march of 50,000 or more desperate people who had nothing to lose and who had already tasted of the worst that man could do." And he asked the DP leaders: "Would the Jews in the camps agree to participate in such a grim plan fraught with all kinds of possible dangers, even to life itself?"[54] The answer resounded: ready and willing.

The arrivals from eastern Europe readily absorbed the DP Palestinocentric view. As they streamed in, they far outnumbered survivors who had gone through the German camps by the end of 1946, but the latter's politics shaped the DP agenda. As Samuel Gringauz observed in 1947, "the experiences of concentration camp prisoners and partisans were decisive in creating the ideology of the Jewish DP's; even those Polish Jews who during the war took refuge in Siberia and later came across Poland to Germany have in the course of time adopted it."[55] Their Zionism took little interest in the political divisions and economic objectives of the pre-war movement. Theirs was an emotional Zionism supercharged with overwhelming tragedy, a historical-philosophical Zionism conceived, in Gringauz's words, as "a debt to the dead, as a retribution toward the enemy, and as a duty to the living."

A visionary, Gringauz preached a radical, emotionally laden Zionism that absolutely refused to admit to any Jewish future in Europe. Reaching from the perdition of Auschwitz to the redemption of Palestine, this Zionism provided a closed but comprehensible universe. Crucial as this ideology proved to the spiritual salvation of the DPs, it came at a price. Gringauz and his colleagues forged DP unity by systematically silencing non-Zionists, Bundists, and communists, and by sabotaging efforts by

The emblem of the Sherit Hapleita adorns the program cover of the third Conference of Liberated Jews in the U.S. zone in Germany, held in Bad Reichenhall on 30 March–2 April 1948. Note the felled tree with a small live branch framing a white map of the U.N.-endorsed Jewish state to be established in Palestine.

HIAS and the Joint to register refugees for immigration to the United States. A poster published by the Central Committee of Liberated Jews spoke volumes: a Jewish DP turns his back on a city of skyscrapers and directs his steps toward a land of palm trees.[56]

The United Nations Special Committee on Palestine (UNSCOP), formed in 1947 when Great Britain handed over its Mandate for Palestine to the United Nations, was as suspicious of the apparent uniform DP position as the AAC had been a year earlier. And an UNSCOP subcommittee went to Germany to ask the very same questions. According to an account by the Guatamalan representative, Jorge García-Granados, they got the same answer. The commissioners queried children at Indersdorf, a camp for Jewish orphans; all of them expressed their desire to go to

Palestine.[57] They met with members of the Central Committee in Pasing, who expressed the identical wish.[58] Moving on to Landsdorf, which held 5,000 DPs at that time, "we chose our witnesses at random, but used great care not to pick anyone who appeared eager for questioning or who asked to be questioned, on the ground that such persons might be primed for us or might not be truly representative of the rank and file," Granados reported. "The results, nevertheless, were the same. No matter to whom we spoke, in whatever language—German, Russian, Polish, Rumanian, Hungarian, Yiddish—the desire was one: to go to Palestine and only to Palestine."[59]

THE EMOTIONAL ZIONISM OF SHERIT HAPLEITA, like other passions, depended upon circumstances. Clandestine immigration to Palestine in 1946 and early 1947 continued to fan the flames of Zionist enthusiasm. Run by Zionist organizations like the survivor-based Bricha and the yishuv-based *Ha'mossad Le'aliyah Bet* (literally: "The Institute of B-Immigration"; "A-Immigration" indicated official entry with Palestine certificates), "illegal" immigration offered adventure for a sacred cause.[60] Survivors relished the prospect of making their way to the Promised Land by crossing the green borders by foot and embarking on leaky ships in Italy or France to run a blockade imposed by the most prestigious navy in the world. It was exciting to disembark in the middle of the night on a beach in Palestine. And it was empowering to be the agent of one's own destiny, a hero in an epic tale that arced from death in the ghettos and camps to the birth of the homeland. Compared to that, the memory of Jews lining up anxiously in front of consular offices or the local Palestine Office waiting for a visa or a certificate, or imprisoned on ships traveling from port to port in search of an opportunity to disembark, burned shameful.

The La Spezia affair, in which an intercepted convoy of refugees was kept on a small ship in the Italian port of La Spezia, or the journey of SS *President Warfield*, renamed SS *Exodus 1947* when it set sail for Palestine with forty-five hundred refugees on board, were morality plays staged for the world press in the no-man's-land of the sea, between a continent of loss and the shores of salvation.[61] These spectacles recalled, reframed, and redeemed the sad story of the *St. Louis*. They changed public opinion, and they inspired DPs in Germany and Austria, as Granados and his UNSCOP colleagues learned. They found a makeshift memorial in Indersdorf dedicated to a Zwi Jacobowitz: "Our Brother and Friend, Who Fell Victim at the Door of Palestine. We Shall Follow in His Footsteps." Granados asked the children about Jacobowitz. He was one of seventy youngsters in the camp who had shipped on the *Exodus*, they reported proudly. And he had been killed when the British boarded in Haifa. Who could resist the call of such passionate Zionism? So many had been murdered for nothing; here an opportunity offered to risk life for *something*.

The circumstances that fueled this stripe of Zionism changed, however. The British transferred the surviving *Exodus* passengers from Haifa to British internment camps in Germany, and journalists lost interest in a story that promised neither a heroic nor a happy ending. As the months collected into years and the gates remained closed, Palestine lost some of its allure. DPs began to investigate other options for emigration. By March 1948 estimates held that two-thirds of the Jewish DPs wished to move to a Jewish state.[62] Still a majority, but not so universal as a year earlier. In the meantime, British family reunification schemes, which allowed entry to close kin—children, parents, and spouses—of refugees settled in that country, had taken effect. And soon after the establishment of the state of Israel in May 1948, the American Displaced Persons Act (July 1948) reinforced the Truman directive of 1946 and cracked open the door to the United States.[63] In the end, of the 250,000 DPs, 142,000 (56 percent) settled in Palestine and Israel, 72,000 (28 percent) in the United States, 16,000 (6 percent) in Canada, and 20,000 in other countries. Of the 142,000, around half went to Palestine illegally, and of these, 42,000 were caught by the British and interned in camps in Cyprus.

The groundswell of Zionism of 1946 was not realized. Indeed: the most prominent leaders of the Central Committee of Liberated Jews who had shaped the Zionism of Sherit Hapleita—men like Grinberg and Gringauz—emigrated to the United States. As Abraham Hyman, who served as legal consultant to a number of advisers on Jewish affairs

A Hebrew class in Zeilsheim displaced persons camp, sometime between 1945 and 1948. The girl's sentence reads: "The Jews will immigrate to the Land of Israel."
PHOTOGRAPHER: E. M. ROBINSON.

to the U.S. commands in Germany and Austria from 1946 to 1949, put it, "When the moment of decision arrived," DPs weighed the pull of the Jewish state against "the influence exerted by considerations of family ties, relative security and relative economic opportunities."[64] Many remained Zionists, but they followed the "normal" Zionist model of the majority of those who had preceded them. They "joined the ranks of the countless Zionists in the Diaspora who year in and year out recite the prayer *'Leshana Haba'a bi-yerusahalayim'* (Next year in Jerusalem)," Hyman scoffed. "Next year, but not this."[65]

Hyman had little cause for derision. The yishuv's own attitude toward the DPs influenced this outcome significantly. The skepticism with which old-style Zionists had greeted the Zionism of Sherit Hapleita in 1945 remained alive and well in 1948. "The Jewish State, in the prevailing terrific situation, will have to take care for itself, not for the refugees," Nahum Goldmann announced a week before the proclamation of

Israeli independence. "It can use, under the dictate of *sacro egoismo*, only young people who can shoot. It cannot be interested in this time in youth aliyah, in children, families and old people." To ensure absolute clarity, Goldmann declared, "The DPs, in general, do not represent the human material Eretz Yisroel needs today." Nor were they useful as an international bargaining chip. "The DPs represent no political argument for Palestine any more either. This angle does not make any impression on General Marshall any more; it is therefore a politically irrelevant thing from the point of view of the Jewish State. We have reached the brutal phase where the interests of the State count alone."[66]

Goldmann's position did not prevail in the end. But the calculus of decision making shifted for DPs. Family ties took center stage. Ultimately, the personal weighed more heavily than the political; survivors yearned to reestablish family more than to establish a state. Especially when there were intimations that perhaps that state no longer welcomed them.

SARA GROSSMAN-WEIL SURVIVED THE LODZ GHETTO, Auschwitz, and a string of other camps. Liberated in Bergen-Belsen, she sought her loved ones. "In the beginning, no one knew about anyone who I cared and wanted and hoped to find. But as more people were coming into Bergen-Belsen more and more familiar faces did I see. And at one time, a young man approached me, and he said, 'Sarenko, I heard, I hope it's true, that [your husband] Menek is alive." It was very hard for me to believe, but this was the best news I ever heard. And I was hanging on to this thought, and I was proclaiming all over this camp, that someone heard that Menek Grossman is alive.

"I began to ask anyone and everyone who came into the camp if they saw him, if they know him, or know about him. . . . Meanwhile, our names were taken and written up in books, just the names—first, middle, and last name—and these books were sent out to different places, so that these people who are searching anyone, maybe they can find a familiar name. And we, in turn, were given some sheets with names too. . . .

"The rumors that I heard about Manny came closer and closer. Suddenly, I heard that he was liberated, and he had been in Hungary where he was working with young people to transport them from Hungary to Israel. The other rumors I heard about Manny were that he was in Lodz, living with some of his friends in one apartment, and that he was working for the Zionist movement, and trying to organize young people who wanted to go to Israel. Another rumor that came to me is that he is alive, and that his friends saw my name on one of the lists that arrived in Lodz. And I was told that since they found out that I am alive, they will get in touch with him wherever he is.

"What happened is that they sent a messenger from Lodz to Hungary to let Manny know that I am alive. He was about to assist a transport of young people going to Israel. When he heard the news, he immediately sent the people with another leader (and when I say sent them, they had to be traveling on false papers, because the English did not let anyone in unless you had papers). . . .

"It's hard for me to describe my feelings when I saw him alive and whole and right near me. It was a miracle for me, and I am sure for him too. . . . I was overwhelmed. I was the happiest young woman on earth. But I also felt very bad that my sister-in-law Esther did not find her husband."

Sara, Menek, their sister-in-law Esther, and Esther's daughter Regina whom she had adopted in Lodz ghetto, moved to Fulda, a small town near Bergen-Belsen. "My brother-in-law Favek, [his wife] Ruska, and [their baby] Tikva [born after the war] just came from Russia and they joined us."

Manny opened a textile shop that prospered. "We began to buy clothes and items and flowers for the house, anything that really was not extravagant but was considered a luxury. But we decided to leave Germany, and we were very serious about going to Israel. I began to buy some items that could be sent to Israel, like a washing machine, dishes, and a sewing machine." At the same time, "I began to receive letters from my uncle [her mother's sister's husband] who lived in the United States, in Brooklyn, New York, in which he wrote that he heard that I am alive. He heard that I am married and he would like for us to come.

"I said no, I want, because my husband wants, to go to Israel, and I do want this too. This is just a continuity of what we always wanted to do." They had been Zionists before the war, and they remained so afterward. "He wrote back to me, and he said, 'I don't have a daughter, and I loved your mother.' Which he really did. 'I want you to come, and I promise you that after a short while I will take care of your passage from the United States to Israel.' . . . The letters were coming back and forth in which I wrote no. And he kept on begging and promising that as soon as we decide to leave, he's the first one to take care of it. All he wants is to see us. I was talking to Manny about it, and he was very reluctant, but finally he said, 'Since this is your mother's sister, and they are pleading with us, and if you say we will go and from there continue to Israel, OK. I will do it for you.' Meanwhile, we had sent away all our belongings to Israel."[67]

Sara and Menek Grossman arrived in New York on 14 May 1949. In time, they got an apartment right above Sara's aunt Helen and uncle Benny. They never joined their belongings in Israel.

Then again, they never joined Menek's brother Favek, his wife Ruska, and their children either. With no relatives in America to draw them there, that family immigrated to Israel, certain that Sara and Menek would arrive in due course. Ironically, Menek had been an ardent Zionist before the war; Favek less so. The conversation continued across continents. Would the Israeli Grossmans join the New York Grossmans? In the end, when their third child was born, they named him Jacob (for the biblical Jacob, renamed Israel by the angel with which he wrestled) and pledged their future to the new Jewish state. Thus, the war and its aftermath separated these two survivor brothers.

LISTS OF
THE LIVING

REFUGEES HAD ENDEAVORED TO MAINTAIN CONTACT WITH THEIR families in Nazi Europe throughout Hitler's reign. In the wake of massive deportations, cut communications and, finally, news of mass murders, millions of people searched for loved ones. Where were they? What had happened to them?

Individuals created lists; organizations created lists. Lists of those found alive; lists of those known to be dead. Decades before photocopy machines, let alone fax, computer, database, and Internet technology, creating comprehensive lists and circulating them posed great difficulties.

The indefatigable letter writer Elisabeth Luz updated her address book carefully during the war years in a continuous quest to keep refugees and their families connected through mail. Her correspondents helped her by sending her news of the movements—both life-threatening and life-saving—of others. She got help too from Lotti Rosenfeld, a young Czech refugee in Zurich. A high school student in 1943, Lotti systematically listed all the people she knew at home in Bohemia and Moravia and tried to keep track of them. Elisabeth and Lotti made contact, and together they formed a tracing service of two. They shared the information they gathered with the Committee for Relief of the War-Stricken Jewish Population in Geneva, which kept its own records.[1]

Elisabeth's role took on a new cast toward the end of the war, as she participated in an urgent search for her correspondents and their kin. Lotti wrote her electrifying news: she had read in the newspapers that the Germans had released twelve hundred Theresienstadt inmates, and they were on their way to Switzerland. The report was correct. Himmler's masseur Dr Kersten had got his patient to agree to send a number of Jews to Switzerland, and a deal was struck with its former president, Jean-Marie Musy.[2] Selection of those to be released began on 3 February: no one famous and no one with relatives deported to Auschwitz. A passenger train left Theresienstadt on 5 February and arrived in Zurich the next day. Lotti "stayed out of school today [8 February] and made lists of all the people I know in Theresienstadt, or about whom we have heard nothing. The result was a very long list," she wrote to Elisabeth. "If you

Jewish refugees in Shanghai scrutinize lists of survivors posted on the wall of a bicycle repair shop owned by a Jew, 1946.

too are willing to make a list with more names and addresses, then you can send it to Rabbi Dr. Lothar Rothschild, St. Gallen, Linsebühslstrasse 25a," she suggested. "They may possibly send that list around, but I am not sure of that."[3]

Lotti followed up with Elisabeth a week later. "This morning, I was at the Jewish community, Lavaterstrasse 57, Zurich 2 (tel. 244655) where there are lists of the new arrivals." Hoping Elisabeth would find someone she knew, she urged her to "create an alphabetical list of your people and to send it to the address noted above with a message that you are ill, and that you kept connection via letter with those people, and that you are unable to come to Zurich. One of the gentlemen there will certainly take care of your list." Lotti was not so lucky. "Of my own people, I have found no one on the list."[4]

Elisabeth wrote to the Jewish community at once, asking for a copy of its register of Theresienstadt Jews. Her reputation stood her in good stead. "In response to your letter of 14 February 1945, we send you, as a great exception, the enclosed list of refugees who, coming from Theresienstadt, have arrived in Switzerland," the Swiss Organization for Jewish Refugee Aid answered a fortnight later. "We ask you <u>urgently</u> to <u>return</u> this list after inspection because we only have a few copies left." The significance of the document was on everyone's mind: "We hope that you will find the persons you are seeking on the list."[5]

Throughout 1945 Elisabeth queried every organization that might possibly have information about her correspondents. She usually received a pre-printed card in return.

> *In response to your query of **** we inform you that the person(s) you are searching does/do not appear on the lists that have reached us until now.*
>
> > *Sincerely,*
> > *World Jewish Congress*
> > *Geneva Office.*[6]

While she sent out letters in search of information, a number of contacts during the war turned to her once again for counsel and help.

Heinz Pfutzner, one of the kindertransport children harbored in La Guette and La Bourboule, had corresponded with his mother through her. Heinz had been included in a 1941 USCOM transport to the United States, where he had moved to Santa Barbara and adopted the name William H. Forster. "Dear Mrs. Luz," he wrote in English on 12 January 1945. "Again I am writing to you to supplement one of my previous letters which I hope you received alright. It is only the anxiety for the fate of my family of whom I have lost contact since the middle of 1941 that prompts me to make every effort toward a renewal of contact and an exchange of letters. I am sure that you can understand my plight because you have aided us from La Guette many a time for which we are very obliged to you." He lived near a few of the other young people who had corresponded with their families through Elisabeth, and "none of us has heard from any of our relatives for a long time and all of us are worried as to their welfare." William/Heinz turned to her for help. "I know that you can send my message to my mother who, I am sure will be grateful for any news from me. So I beg you to aid me once more in communicating with her so that both of us can rest with the knowledge of the safety of each other."[7] He enclosed a letter to his mother, written in German.

Dearest Mother,

It is so long since I last wrote to you that I have no idea where you are and how you are doing. I read the letters that you wrote to me a few years ago, and my heart is with you. So much time has passed and as a result I am unable to write German very well. I must use the typewriter to be sure you can read the writing. I am safe and healthy; my greatest hope is that you are also content and healthy. I cannot write too much because I don't have much paper. My worry is that I do not know what has happened in the time I did not hear from you. Oh, Mom, we will see each other again soon and the whole family will be reunited. Uncle Leo and Aunt Grete send you their warmest greetings and hope that you will be able to write. Pardon my mistakes, but it is a long time since I used the language. I just want to be with you and to show you that I have made great progress since we saw each other the last time. I am engaged to the most lovely girl in the world and I would like to bring her to you. All these years have passed by so quickly, and I am older, 19 years, and the only thing I want is to help you and to pay you back for the love and care you have given me when I was young. I love you so much and I am sure that one day I will embrace you again and give you all the kisses I missed out on. Be assured, little mother, my love is with you every day. Please write me how you are and what you do. Where is father and how is he doing? How is Aunt Ella and the people I used to know?

> I must end the letter now to send it immediately.
> Many kisses and a million greetings from your loving son, Heinz.[8]

Elisabeth's efforts to amass information yielded results. Heinz heard from her some weeks later. "I hasten to answer your letter of the 5th of February which indeed brought sad tidings to me, that of the death of my beloved mother," he wrote on 7 April. The news was terrible, but he took comfort that finally he knew. "I am so grateful to you for clearing up all the uncertainty that had been eating at my heart all this time. It was a hard blow but I had been steeling myself for just a thing like that." And he did not give up on his dream of a family reunion. "I am still hoping that my father will be able to get in touch with you again, or the other way around."[9]

Now functioning as a tracing service, Elisabeth labored under the burden of grim news. The reunion of Ludwig (Lutz) Scheucher and his mother was a rare pleasure. Lutz had gone on a kindertransport to France in 1938. From La Guette he went to a technical school to train as a mechanic, and it was from there that he reestablished contact with his parents Alexander Scheucher and Agnes Scheucher-Fränkel through Tante Elisabeth.[10] Arrested in 1942, Lutz was sent to a number of concentration camps. His skill saved him: he ended up working as a slave worker in a rayon factory in Hirschberg. Liberated in Buchenwald, Lutz was repatriated to France, where he contracted typhus.[11]

Alexander and Agnes Scheucher were deported to Riga ghetto in January 1942. When the ghetto was liquidated, Agnes was separated from her husband, who was sent to Auschwitz. She went to a camp in Riga and, in October 1944, to another camp in Libau (today Liepaja), where she fell very ill. In February 1945 Agnes was shipped to Hamburg, where she was put in jail. Force-marched to Kiel in April, she was shoved into yet another camp. Finally released to the Danish Red Cross on 1 May, Agnes was brought to Sweden, where she was interned in a refugee camp in the town of Smålandsstenar.[12] She cabled Elisabeth from there (22 May 1945): "Request address of Ludwig Scheucher. Warm greetings. Agnes Scheucher."[13]

Elisabeth did not know Lutz's whereabouts, she confessed to Agnes, but she would do her best to find him. She turned to OSE, under whose care Lutz had been at the technical school, and received an answer a few days later from its headquarters in Geneva. "I hasten to give you a very good piece of news: Luwig [*sic*] Scheucher (Lutz) of La Guette, deported in 1942 from the school in Brive, has returned to Paris. He is not yet in good health, but doctors are confident that he will soon regain his strength and that he will be able to return to regular life."[14] Wonderful news indeed. Not knowing precisely where he was, headquarters telegraphed OSE in France to find Lutz and tell him his mother had survived.[15] In the meantime, Agnes, who did not yet know that Lutz had been found, replied to Elisabeth's first letter in despair. "Now I am totally alone. My husband gone, totally impoverished. If I am unable to find my son, I will not continue to live. It is simply not worth it."[16] Receiving the letter from OSE, Elisabeth promptly cabled Agnes. And Agnes cabled back: "Am beyond happy that Ludwig Paris hoping soon address 1000 thanks."

Lutz wrote to Tante Elisabeth from an OSE orphanage in France on 7 July; it was their first direct contact since his arrest in 1942. "Now everything has passed, save revenge! I hope that I will be able to see Mama again soon; that would be so beautiful. We have been separated more than six years, always with the hope that one day. . . . Dear Tante

Elisabeth, maybe you can send me Mama's address?"[17] And thus she reestablished contact between mother and son.

When he was sufficiently recovered, Lutz traveled to Sweden. "You may imagine how great our happiness is finally to be together again," he rejoiced from Stockholm (25 January 1946). "Yes, if I just could remain here. My visa is valid for only two months, but I will attempt to get a residency permit. But I have little hope that I will succeed."[18] Agnes too sounded the twin notes of elation and long-term anxiety. "Finally, finally, the boy is here, and I cannot describe to you the feeling of happiness. Through you, we were able to find each other so quickly, and now I wish that you could have been a witness to our happiness." She had left a young boy and was reunited with a young man. "Lutz has grown a head taller than I, and often pulls my leg. He is smart and thoughtful and very neat." She was grateful that they got on well and understood that "it could have been so different, and it would not have been a surprise after the difficult years in a concentration camp." Yet she worried about their long-term prospects. "I hope that he will be able to remain here; otherwise this period of happiness will end." And she also worried about how to manage going forward. "To begin a new life is very difficult for those of our generation."[19] The United States provided a haven. Lutz moved two years later to America, where he began a new life with a new name: Louis Scott. Agnes joined him there.

Eager to find their loved ones and to be found, survivors in Europe developed their own means of communication. Like Elisabeth Luz and Lotti Rosenfeld, each operated individually, and their efforts reflect independent agency. Elisabeth, Lotti, and thousands upon thousands of survivors did not wait for an organization to take charge. Each did what she or he could to effect reunion. The office of the Central Committee of Liberated Jews in Bavaria, located in the bombed-out German Museum, emerged as one such site of individual action. Much trafficked, it was a logical location to look for information. "In this hall of dank corridors where the Committee began its work, a Jew appeared one day and wrote his name on the white wall," American army chaplain Abraham Klausner recalled. "Four months later the wall was black with the names of those who had come and gone in search of husband or a wife."[20] No one by then, the summer of 1945, harbored hope for children.

Such graffiti walls sprang up in many locations, each a sign and symbol of survivors' yearning and determination. Traveling with a group of haluzim from Poland to the west in spring 1946, the American journalist Isidor F. Stone reached an UNRRA repatriation center in Bratislava. It was housed in the former residence of a Slovak nobleman. "An ancient staircase of stone curved upwards in a magnificent spiral just inside the grand entrance, but the steps were chipped and broken," Stone observed. Serving as a key place to leave a sign of life, "the stairway walls were scrawled over with handwriting." Sites such as this provided an important tool for survivors to establish contact. "One saw this kind of scrawl in every reception center in Europe and along the stairs in every building housing a Jewish organization," he reported. "Refugees wrote their names and hometowns on every wall they came to with the hope that some friend or relative might see them." There, in Bratislava, the refugees with whom he traveled, "having rid themselves of their baggage, went immediately to read the names, each trying to find someone he used to know, or perhaps a relative." Poignantly, "even those who knew they had no one left joined with the others in reading along the walls— just in case; who knows? The age of miracles had not yet passed." The reunion of one elated all. "It was thrilling to be there when a familiar name was discovered." An all too rare occurrence: "None of our group found any names that morning."[21]

Stone, a journalist, reported on such initiatives. Klausner, an army chaplain, viewed them through another lens and saw a crucial piece of postwar identity formation. "Are we not, each of us, defined by our relationships with parents, clan, and country?" he asked rhetorically.[22] Klausner was sent to Dachau on a special one-month tour of duty with the 116th Evacuation Hospital. His official task was to care for Jewish servicemen, but Judah Nadich, who had dispatched him, anticipated that he would succor Jewish survivors in the camp. "Chaplain Klausner went immediately to Dachau and at once started what proved to be a superb piece of work," Nadich recalled a few years later. " 'Red tape' and 'channels' provided no obstacles for him. He cut through them, across them or forgot that they existed."[23]

The 116th Evacuation Hospital dealt with the emergency situation in Dachau and moved on. Klausner did not. He became, in his fellow serviceman Abraham Hyman's words, a "roving rabbi in uniform, who somehow exempted himself from Army discipline and became accountable only to himself."[24] He had found his mission: "If I brought brothers together and nothing more, I would have achieved some small measure of significance in my life."[25] Thus, Klausner counseled and comforted Jewish DPs, but his signal contribution to DP well-being was his survivor list project. "I suggested that our first response to liberation would be to determine who was alive, to take a census of those in Dachau, listing them by name, age, and place of birth," he recalled decades later.[26] Collecting paper, pencils, and typewriters, he brought the lot to the camp inmates and asked them to join forces with him to prepare a comprehensive register of the Jews in Dachau: name, year of birth, last place of residence, present whereabouts. Fanning farther afield, Klausner organized residents of other DP camps in Bavaria such as Landsberg and Feldafing to compile similar lists and to send them to him in Dachau, where Jewish inmates integrated the information and alphabetized the names.

He realized the full importance of these rosters when he encountered a group of Hungarian-Jewish women in a one-barrack DP camp close to the Brenner Pass. Offering them a copy, "they fell upon the pages, moaning and crying as they searched for a name that would link them to the living."[27] Once again, survivor response pointed the way for Klausner. Clearly, the lists needed to be published and disseminated. He promptly found a printer and ordered a thousand copies, although printing for nonmilitary purposes was forbidden. He chose the name *Sharit Ha-Platah*, the saved remnant, for the published register. His thinking on this influenced Grinberg, Gringauz, and the Association of Surviving Jews in the American Zone of Occupation, and (as we have seen) they, too, opted for that name.

"In these pages are contained a portion of the names of the 'Remnant of Israel' now scattered throughout the camps in Bavaria," Klaus-

Workers at the UNRRA Central Tracing Bureau search the master card file in 1947.

ner explained in the foreword to the first volume, published in July 1945. "Haste took precedence over perfection. Consequently the lists have not been systematized," he cautioned. "They are for the most part arranged alphabetically according to camps and to divisions within the respective camps" and, he pointed out, "this list covers only the region of Bavaria." Most important, more volumes were forthcoming. "Since this collection has gone to print, additional lists have been made." The second volume of *Sharit Ha-Platah* was published on 20 July; the third on 1 August. Volumes four and five followed, and they included lists of DPs in the rest of Germany, Austria, and of survivors in Sweden, England, and

Australia. These volumes gained such stature that the U.S. army published Klausner's consolidated edition of all the names in volumes one
through five, some thirty thousand in total, in December 1945.[28] The
title announced its purpose: *Sharit Ha-Platah: An Extensive List of Survivors of Nazi Tyranny, Published So That the Lost May Be Found and the
Dead May Be Brought Back to Life.*

Klausner's registers were supplemented by other efforts. The World
Jewish Congress published lists of survivors in individual countries.
And the Joint, which like the WJC had representatives on the ground
throughout Europe, created an important tracing service in Berlin. That
initiative began in the Jewish chaplain's office also, and the survivors of
the Berlin Jewish community constituted its initial database. The Berlin
office tracked Jews in other areas in the Soviet occupation zone, where
the Red Army had no tracing service and UNRRA did not operate.[29]

THE NEW YORK WEEKLY *Aufbau/Reconstruction* developed into a key
source of information. A newspaper, *Aufbau* was already published and
distributed; its new function as a clearinghouse grew out of its original
mandate. Established in December 1934 as an organ for the German
Jewish Club (a social center for refugees) in New York, *Aufbau* provided
information for club members. It became a regular monthly magazine
in 1936 and took off when Manfred George became editor in chief in
April 1939. A successful writer in Germany, George fled to Prague over
the green border in 1933 and after the Munich pact (1938) moved on
to Hungary, Italy, Switzerland, France and, finally, the United States.
George transformed *Aufbau* from a small monthly magazine directed
to German Jews living in New York to a serious weekly paper for German exiles everywhere, persuading illustrious refugee writers to contrib-
ute: Thomas Mann, Stefan Zweig, Lion Feuchtwanger, Hannah Arendt,
Ludwig Marcuse, Ernst Lothar, Carl Zuckmayer, and many others.[30]
Every issue addressed matters vital to the refugees. One article, for example, explained the intricacies of the American quota system and noted
the expected time interval between placement on the waiting list at various consulates and receipt of a visa—for instance, someone registered in

1939 at the Stuttgart consulate with number eighteen thousand could look forward to a visa in July 1942.[31] A regular column entitled "Say It in English" gave readers sentences like "I hope you will succeed to make the examination" to correct.[32]

George soon introduced (May 1939) a special advertising section "Es Suchen" (seeking), reflecting his vision of *Aufbau*'s global reach and his grasp of a key refugee dilemma: maintaining contact with far-flung family and friends.[33] Desperate to emigrate after the November pogrom, Jews left Greater Germany the moment an opportunity opened, and many lost track of each other. The *Aufbau* "In Search Of" column provided space for refugees and others to post queries and state their own addresses. By November 1942 the editors realized they needed to publish another genre of list. Introducing this new section listing refugees deported to "an unknown location," they wrote, "We accept this sad responsibility because we believe that the certainty that is gained by this means is preferable to waiting without consolation for a message from your beloved ones." The editors lamented their own inability to do more. "We cannot do anything else but publish these names. We do not know anything about the location of these unhappy people, and we have no information about the fate of individuals. We therefore urgently beg our readers to desist from making fruitless calls or sending futile letters to the editors."[34] Lists of those known to have been deported from internment camps in southern France followed, as well as Red Cross rosters of people that organization sought to find.[35] None too soon. The *New York Times* reported later that month (25 November) that the Germans had already killed two million Jews in the east.

More lists appeared in *Aufbau* in early 1943. A short introduction to the first of a few lists of Jews buried in Vienna in the summer of 1942 noted that "the percentage of double-suicides is considerable."[36] In April 1943 the Union of Russian Jews began to publish registers of Jewish refugees in the Soviet Union who, after their release from internment, had found refuge in Kazakhstan, Uzbekistan, and other Soviet republics in the south, and who sought contact with family members in the United States.[37] From time to time, ads appeared announcing the death of a family member in occupied Europe.

A short time ago information reached us that our dear father and father-in-law

Bernhard Hausner

(formerly Munich)

has died at the age of 91 in Theresienstadt. Those who knew his cheerful disposition and his noble character will share our pain.

Ernesto Hausner

Djin Lillie Hausner

Buenos Aires, Calle Peru 490

Mary Hausner

Location at this time not known.[38]

After the war Ernesto would discover that by the time he placed the ad his sister had already been murdered in Riga.

Such death announcements of people killed by the Germans appeared irregularly during the war and multiplied ferociously at its end. Framed by heavy black lines, boxes of announcements filled almost two pages of the 24 August 1945 issue. Ludwig Allmayer's family posted a large notice (two columns wide, three inches high):

Only now we received the sad news that our beloved husband, father, brother, brother-in-law and uncle

Ludwig Allmayer

(formerly from Idar on the Nahe, Luxembourg)

died as a result of illness in January 1945 in the Flossenburg Camp in Bavaria, where he worked as a nurse. In deep mourning:

FANNY ALLMAYER, **née Weil, and children,** Sornac, Corrèze, France

ADOLPH ALLMAYER **and family,** 1263 W. Leland Ave., Chicago 40, Ill.

ALBERT & ELLA MANN, **née Allmayer, and children,** Buenos Aires, Argentina

ROSALIE HIRSCH, **née Allmayer, and children,** Buenos Aires, Argentina

SIMONE ALLMAYER, **née Behr**

KURT ALLMAYER, Lugano Paradiso, Ticino, Switzerland
ARTHUR & META ALLMAYER, **née Berg and child,** labor camp Hed-
ingen near Zürich, Switzerland
JULIUS & JOHANNA ALLMAYER, **née Koehler,** location unknown
LEO & LISEL ALLMAYER, **née Baum,** location unknown.[39]

The Allmayer family did not yet know that the last four had been murdered as well: Julius Allmayer in Auschwitz and his wife Johanna in Maj-
danek; Leo Allmayer in Auschwitz and Lisel (Alice) in Theresienstadt.

Ida Wittner's family ran a slightly smaller announcement (two columns wide, two inches high).

Our most dearly beloved mother, grandmother and mother-in-law
IDA WITTNER, née Pollak
(formerly Breslau)
has died in Theresienstadt.
Ernst Unger and **wife Helene, née Wittner,** Kfar Sava P.O.B. 17,
Palestine
Dr. Leo Berlinger and **wife Hertha, née Wittner** (location
unknown)
Dr. Heinz L. Wittner and **wife Raia, née Gurewitsch,** 210 Riverside Drive, N.Y.C.
Helmuth L. Wittner and **wife Carla, née Weinberg,** 125 West
96th St., N.Y.C.
and three grandsons.[40]

Announcements one column wide were available too. The surviving
family of Benjamin Wolff, formerly of Ockenheim in Rheinhessen, thus
reported his death in Theresienstadt. Among the listed relatives was
Benjamin's grandson, Staff Sergeant Gunter Wolf and wife, U.S. army
in Germany.[41]

Aufbau published rolls of the living as well. Sent by diverse sources,
these pertained to a range of groups. "Jews in Munich" presented the
names of survivors found in that city by the American army. "Without
exception, this list concerns Jews who lived in mixed-marriages here."

The same page carried "returnees—third list. Destination: Munich."
"We begin today with printing the third list of returnees from Theresienstadt," the editors explained. "This time we publish a partial list of
those on their way to Munich or who have already arrived there." Comprised of birth dates and maiden names of married women, "the list was
made available to us by the Czechoslovak Jewish Committee, affiliated
with the World Jewish Congress, 1834 Broadway. Further information
can be obtained only there."[42] Another list of returnees from Theresienstadt "was sent to us by a soldier," the paper noted. It covered Jews with
names starting with *W* and *Z* who had returned or were about to return
to Vienna. The editors added: "Correct addresses of those concerned
cannot be obtained yet and at this time it is not possible to contact these
people."[43] And then there was a list of German-Jewish refugees deported
from Belgium and France who returned to Belgium, as well as a con-
tinuation of a list entitled "Jews in Berlin," few of whom were "so-called
'full Jews.' . . . The list with addresses can be consulted at [the] *Aufbau*
[offices]. No information by telephone."[44]

Recognizing that not every survivor's name would find its way to
a list, *Aufbau* instituted a "First Signs of Life" section. It recorded "the
names of those saved" who "have not been able to establish any contact
with relatives abroad." Taking on the function of an agency, the editors
offered: "When no address is listed, we ask the person searched to contact us, and we will do whatever is possible to make the connection."[45]
Typically, survivors searched for family members who had fled in time.
Feodor Pochert, for example, sought relatives who had got to Argentina,
Palestine, and England:

> **Feodor Pochert** (formerly Berlin-Pankow),Vilshofen, Hoerdtstrasse
> 14, seeks **Walter and Melitta Bernfeld,** née **Zippert** (formerly Ber-
> lin, now Buenos Aires); Wolf **Zippert** (Haifa); Dr. **Max Lowen-
> stein** (formerly Berlin W., Budapesterstrasse, now London).[46]

Richard Schlesinger sought kin in America.

> **Richard Schlesinger** (Procurator of the Wiener Bankverein),
> Vienna IV/50, Operngasse 32/18, seeks **Emil Schlesinger,** USA.[47]

And what of those whose fate was unknown? The "In Search Of" section, inaugurated by Manfred George in May 1939, claimed increasing columns of newsprint.

I am looking for my mother
Ida Loewenstein
née Meyer
Born 8-11-1868, formerly Bocholt in Westphalia, since 1939 Holland, Hilversum, Amsterdam, latest Westerbork.
Hannah Plaut
930 Sixth Street, S.W.
Massillon, Ohio.[48]

Hannah Plaut would not find her mother. Ida Loewenstein was deported in March 1943 to Sobibor, where she was murdered. Nor would Berthold Gumpel find his wife and children:

Grateful for any news about my wife
Gertrud Gumpel, née Koppel
And three children
Kurt, Felicitas, Thomas
Formerly Hamburg, Antwerps, Brussels, then **Camp de Lalande, France,** all deported from there, probably to Poland.
Berthold Gumpel
24 State Street
New York 4 N.Y.[49]

Gertrud, Kurt, Felicitas, and Thomas had been murdered in Auschwitz.

Aufbau published lists created in europe and, given the geography of loss, tracing service efforts grew and developed there. Indeed, bracing for war during the Munich crisis in September 1938, the International Committee of the Red Cross (ICRC) prepared to expand upon the service it had offered during and after World War I. Established in 1914, the ICRC's *Agence Centrale des Prisonniers de Guerre* (International Prisoners of War

Joe Dziubak, a survivor of Lodz ghetto, Auschwitz, and Buchenwald, asks, "Where are our parents?" on a children's transport train from Buchenwald to France in June 1945.

Agency) included a tracing office. A small operation in September 1914, the bureau had grown to a massive effort employing more than a thousand people by December that year.[50] Visiting its headquarters in the Rath museum in Geneva, Stefan Zweig appreciated its crucial humanitarian role. "Outside, from the one end to the other of our world, the crucified body of Europe bleeds from countless wounds. But here its heart still beats."[51] If the Great War had reduced people to mere numbers and the dead to cold statistics, they regained their individuality in those offices. "This is the raw material of a great epic of humanity."[52] In Zweig's view, the Rath museum was a locus of hope amid the madness and destruction of war.

When hostilities loured on the horizon in 1938, the ICRC strength-ened its tracing service with the latest technology: radios, photocopiers, telegram capability, and the new electromagnetic IBM sorting and fil-ing machines. And when Germany invaded Poland in September 1939, the ICRC obtained the use of the Palais du Conseil Général in Geneva that at 50,000 square feet was four times larger than the Rath museum. By the end of the war additional buildings had been rented to house the operation, and four thousand people employed to run it. Divided into departments, the ICRC included civilians interned as enemy nation-als. These included, for example, German-Jewish and Austrian-Jewish refugees interned in France and Great Britain, which cooperated by sending information to Geneva. The ICRC tried to obtain information about civilians of Axis states or German-occupied countries interned or deported by the Germans. But they, like political detainees in concentra-tion camps, did not fall under any international agreement, and Berlin refused to comply. The ICRC therefore turned to receipts for parcels sent to concentration camps to gather data that yielded over a hundred thou-sand names of concentration camp inmates.

Recognizing that stateless people and Jews were especially at risk, and realizing that it was almost impossible to obtain any information about them, the ICRC created two special sections to tackle this prob-lem. The *Civils Internés Diverse* (Civilian Internees Section) sought par-ticulars about people who had been arrested and interned, who did not benefit from treaty protection and who, unlike detained enemy aliens, had no protecting state. "They were refugees of various origin, mostly Jewish fugitives, but they also included men who had survived from the International Brigades which had fought in Spain," the official report on the activities of the ICRC during World War II explained. The fate of German- and Austrian-Jewish refugees and stateless people became a central focus of the CID section. But, as a 1948 report admitted, the sec-tion had not met with success. "The data on which the Section worked were inevitably very vague," the authors noted. "Almost the whole of its work was concerned with Jews, and it is common knowledge that nei-ther Germany, nor countries under German control, would give any information on these people."[53]

The ICRC also set up an *Immigration en Palestine* (Immigration to

Palestine Section, or IMPA) tracing service under its umbrella. Established in December 1943, IMPA tried to delay the deportation of Jews by negotiating with the Palestine Office and the Jewish Agency and by officially registering Jews in German-controlled Europe for emigration to Palestine. Those on the list were provided with a future date of admission to Palestine, a guarantee of Palestinian nationality upon arrival, and a guarantee of transit visas for all countries crossed en route. "Unhappily, as it might have been feared, the results did not correspond to the exertions made," the 1948 report acknowledged with regret. "Although the IMPA Section sent out many tens of thousands of immigration certificate numbers, only 285 people to their knowledge were able to benefit by these in practice."[54] It was no more successful in 1945, when it instituted a special service to trace everyone who had been placed on the Palestine lists or for whom it had tried to obtain a passport of a South American or Central American state. "Since the people who were the subject of the enquiry had, in practically all these cases, disappeared without leaving any clue, the results proved of course sadly disappointing," the authors observed. "Cases of deported children were very numerous and especially distressing."[55]

Charged with a new function in 1945, IMPA began to compile rolls of concentration camp survivors, obtaining names from other sections of the agency and from external sources: Jewish communities, World Jewish Congress, the Joint.[56] IMPA amalgamated these and forwarded them to the ICRC broadcasting section, created in March 1945. With the help of Swiss federal broadcasting authorities, the ICRC began to read out lists of names. "The period of these broadcasts was extended by degrees to twelve hours a day, Saturdays and Sundays included," the 1948 report noted. At its peak, "the lists of names and the messages being sent out were read in turn by two speakers, a man and a woman, in the language of those whose names or messages were broadcast, at an average rate of 150 names an hour, or in a day of 12 hours' transmission, about 1,800 names."[57] From 1 May 1945 to 30 June 1947, when the broadcasts ceased, the ICRC had been on air a total of 4,868 hours, and 570,000 names were read.[58]

Many Jews listened to the radio transmissions. Others heard the Red Cross lists read aloud. Decades later, Karola Siegel (who came to be known as Ruth Westheimer, or Dr Ruth) recalled those sessions vividly. After her father had been arrested in the November pogrom, her mother obtained a place for her on a kindertransport (5 January 1939) from their native city of Frankfurt to Switzerland where she was sent to a children's home called *Wartheim* (Waiting Home). Irma Siegel planned for her daughter, then ten years old, to stay for six months while she organized emigration papers and obtained her husband's release.[59] Luck was not with her; she did not obtain the papers she needed in six months. The Swiss renewed Karola's permission to stay for another half year. But her parents were trapped. Karola received a last letter from her parents in September 1941. A month later she got a note from family friends. "They wrote that my dear parents and my grandma emigrated," Karola confided to her diary. "I don't know where to. I hope they weren't deported. I hope they are well. All I can do now is hope."[60]

Like virtually all children separated from their parents, Karola yearned for reunification. And again like virtually all survivor children, she was to be bitterly disappointed at war's end. "Reality was far different from the gleeful celebration I had envisioned," Dr Ruth explained at a distance of some four decades. "Instead of rejoicing and reunion, there was more waiting. I should have expected it—this was Wartheim after all. The main thing we were waiting for was news of our relatives and loved ones."

All the children in Wartheim held out hope. In Dr Ruth's view, the orphanage staff handled the situation poorly. They may well have thought their system would serve the youngsters but, lacking insight into their wards' needs, they exacerbated an already terrible situation. "Every week the Red Cross published lists of people who had survived the concentration camps. And instead of first reading the list themselves and then privately calling in any child with a relative on it, they made us all gather together and they read us the entire list. This may have been in case a relative or friend was on the list whose name they didn't recognize, but they needn't have bothered. No parent's or relative's name was ever read." Her diary entry of 18 May 1945 records her loss and desolation. "It is a terrible feeling to read these lists, looking for two or three names, holding your breath—and then, finished—nothing. Cold and empty."[61]

ADJUSTMENT

Aᴛ ᴡᴀʀ's ᴇɴᴅ ᴛʜᴇ ꜱᴡɪꜱꜱ ɢᴏᴠᴇʀɴᴍᴇɴᴛ ᴄᴏᴜʟᴅ ɴᴏᴛ ᴏᴜꜱᴛ ɪᴛꜱ ʀᴇꜰ-ugee Jews fast enough, filling international trains with the former asylum seekers throughout the summer of 1945. As we have seen, some, like Jenny and Max Gans, returned willingly to their country of origin (in their case, the Netherlands). Others, like Karola Siegel, had no intention of repatriating (in her case, Germany). Nor did Karola wish to stay in Switzerland. Six years of applying every six months for permission to remain had underlined the message: she did not belong. Palestine appealed to her imagination, and off she went on youth aliyah in August. Interned in the Atlit camp upon arrival, she "waited while the British sorted out who was to go where, who had papers and who didn't."[1] Fortunately, her documents passed muster, and she went on to Kibbutz Ayonot, where she slept in a tent because there was no more durable shelter to be had.

This lack of accommodation signaled a significant move away from the pre-war Zionist stance on absorption. Clearly, while infrastructure lagged behind need, the Palestine authority sought to find a place for as many refugees from Europe as the British admitted or as slipped through the Mandate's patrols. This policy grew deep roots after the Proclamation of the State of Israel on 14 May 1948, and the immediate repeal of the White Paper of 1939 that had all but closed Palestine to Jewish immigrants. Articulated in the Declaration of Independence, the principle of unlimited admission of Jews to Israel was confirmed by the Law of Return (July 1950), which gave every Jew the right to immigrate and to immediate citizenship.[2] The existence of Israel did not mean there would be no Jewish refugees in the future. But it did mean that if at some future date Jews found themselves refugees, they had a place to go.

Equally important, they had a purpose: to build up the Jewish Home. The establishment of the new state provided a narrative that inspired. Part practical necessity (the new state needed people and skills), part political ideology (a shared dream to fuel action), the narrative of a great project, the building of the new state in the Promised Land, and of participation through aliyah, proved compelling. All Jews were welcome to join. For decades, mainstream Zionist policy had been to build the yishuv as quickly as possible, but as slowly as necessary to ensure organic development. The Holocaust ended objections to unrestricted immigration of endangered Jews; as Max Nordau had predicted, the alternative had been devastatingly worse. Immigration policy now rested on the concept of *Kibbutz ha-galuyot*, ingathering of the exiles. Paradoxically, while the establishment of Israel resolved future Jewish refugee problems, it also triggered an immediate refugee flood from Muslim countries in the near east and north Africa.

Until the postwar period, the history of Jewish refugees focused on Europe (from whence they came and where many received temporary asylum), Palestine, the United States, and other overseas countries, where many found a permanent home. The Jewish communities in the middle east and north Africa (save Palestine) did not figure in the history of Jewish refugees from Nazi and postwar Europe. They neither generated refugees nor constituted a destination. The governments of Arab countries did not welcome such asylum seekers, nor were local Jewish communities in a position to absorb and help them. According to a study by the American Jewish Committee (1947–8), in the Muslim world a few rich Jews and a small number of middle class Jews "enjoy the amenities and comforts that favor decent health and living standards. Many Jews live in a lamentable state of ignorance, poverty and disease in dirty mean quarters."[3]

Largely Arabicized, the Mizrachi Jews were an indigenous presence in Arab and Muslim societies. The communities of Iraq, Yemen, and Egypt dated to biblical times and, in general, were relatively well integrated. Second-class citizens under Muslim rule and subject to lesser or greater economic restrictions, Mizrachi Jews nevertheless enjoyed a measure of socioeconomic stability and physical security as recognized minorities. In their history there were no parallels to the great expulsions of the middle ages, the massacres of the seventeenth century, the antisemitic hysteria of the nineteenth century, and the racist, annihilatory antisemitism of the mid-twentieth century.[4] They managed the constant pressure of daily restriction rather than waves of violent persecution, serving in the words of the Iraqi Jewish writer Naim Kattan an "apprenticeship of injustice," which was "the price one had to pay for being different."[5]

A coup d'état on 1 April 1941 against the pro-British government of Regent Abdul al-Ilah by a group of pro-Nazi officers shattered the status quo that had obtained in Iraq. Inspired by the pro-Nazi Mufti of Jerusalem, Haj Muhammad Amin al-Husseini (who had sought refuge in Baghdad in 1939 after the Mandatory government in Jerusalem had issued a warrant for his arrest on terrorist charges), the new junta saw an opportunity to expel the unpopular British whom they perceived as all too influential in their country's affairs, and to align Iraq and its enormous oil wealth with the Axis. Al-Husseini offered the Germans the support of the Arab world if they, in turn, would allow the Arabs to liquidate the yishuv and annul the promise of a Jewish National Home in Palestine. The German foreign office accepted his proposal in March and promised military support to a pro-German Iraq.[6] The rapprochement between Berlin and Baghdad caused anxiety among Iraqi Jews, who were well informed about Nazi antisemitism. Kattan recalled "my brother, my uncle, our neighbors, spoke of the Germans in low voices and cautiously, as of an imminent catastrophe."[7]

The junta moved quickly and on 30 April enclosed a British air base fifty-five miles west of Baghdad. Iraq and Britain were now officially at war. Germany sent a squadron of Heinkel bombers and another of Messerschmitt fighters via Vichy-controlled Syria to attack the base. Overwhelmed by superior force, Britain's position in Iraq appeared untenable.

But the British-led Arab Legion, stationed in Jordan, turned the tide, arriving on the outskirts of Baghdad a fortnight later. The junta fled to Iran, bringing the Thirty-Day War to what Iraqi nationalists saw as an ignoble end.[8]

Using the radio as a genocidal weapon, the Mufti blamed this humiliating defeat on the Jews. Claiming that they worked as spies for the British, he called for their death. In the power vacuum between the demise of the junta and the return of Regent Abdul al-Ilah, mobs of soldiers, fascists, and Bedouins murdered 180 Jews and injured and mutilated several hundred more, desecrated synagogues, and destroyed property belonging to Jews. Only the entry of the Arab Legion brought an end to it.

For many Iraqi Jews, the *farhud* (great pogrom) in Baghdad spelled the end of an era. "The Jews of Baghdad, the most influential and well-established single element in the city, were shocked, terrorized, and demoralized," Nissim Rejwam, a poet, journalist, and literary critic, recalled many years later. "It was those events that made the Jews of Iraq receptive of Zionist teachings and ideology, an ideology that had failed to take root because most of them could not reconcile it with their seemingly complete integration into Baghdad life."[9] Many Jews sought to leave the country, Kattan recalled. "Every morning hundreds of families besieged the passport office." In a country without established registries or birth certificates, obtaining a passport posed special difficulties. "An army of professional witnesses offered their services," Kattan explained. "Officials closed their eyes to certain anomalies. The man who declared officially that he had been present at my father's birth was ten years younger than him."[10]

Few actually left, but making arrangements to flee their country in 1941 prepared Iraqi Jews to act when their government promulgated a series of antisemitic decrees immediately after Israel was founded. Indeed, it prepared some to act before the British Mandate expired, fearing violence and closed borders. Aliza emmi-Mnashee was one such person. Born in Basra in 1909, Aliza emmi-Mnashee was orphaned at a young age and married at sixteen to a nineteen-year-old tobacco merchant, Salem abu-Mnashee.[11] Aliza refused to accept the confined life of a conventional Iraqi-Jewish wife. Believing passionately in the dawn of a new, modern age, she began her battle at home. When, for example, she failed to persuade Salem to shed his robes in favor of western shirts and trousers, she gave away his clothing and left a few suits waiting for him. The family story is that he grumbled but, a good-natured man who adored his wife, he accepted the fait accompli with grace, as he did all decisions she took unilaterally.[12]

Living in Basra, Aliza and her family did not suffer in the farhud. Nevertheless, she embraced the Zionism that quickly took root in its wake. For many women, and for young people, it offered an answer to the conservative Iraqi-Jewish establishment and to the growing antisemitism among their Muslim neighbors.[13] When son Mnashee fell ill in 1942, Aliza took him (and five of her by now seven children) to Jerusalem for treatment. In the yishuv she discovered the world she had envisioned, in which women were equal to men and were fully engaged in public life. Returning to Iraq in 1943, she moved the family to Baghdad, and their home became a center of Zionist activity and Hebrew instruction. Fulfilled in one way, Aliza suffered greatly in another. Mnashee's condition worsened and he died in 1944. Her eighth and last child, born in 1947, carries his name.

Aliza's individual and communal experience of political constraints, antisemitic violence, her ambition for equality and safety, as well as her experience of the fragility of life, prompted her to move swiftly in early 1948. She believed that the moment the Jews of Palestine proclaimed an independent state, life for Iraqi Jews would become impossible. For her, the farhud served as a harbinger of further pogroms—perhaps even the annihilation of the Iraqi-Jewish community. Obtaining false passports and exit visas for her family, she planned an escape before the end of the Mandate, when an inevitable war would close national borders. But Salem refused to leave Iraq so precipitately. He agreed to the departure of his wife and children but insisted upon remaining to wind up his tobacco business.

In early May, a week before the Mandate ended, Aliza and the children went to Baghdad airport and boarded a private plane she had chartered to take her and the children to Cairo for a short holiday. That was the official story given to the police and written in the flight plan submit-

*Emmi-Mnashee family, Basra, 1942. From left to right: Viola, Aaron, Marlyn,
Aliza, Mnashee, Salem, Samira, Hilda, Frayin.*

ted to Iraqi air traffic control. As the plane entered Palestinian airspace,
however, Aliza instructed (and, one supposes, bribed) the pilot to land
at Lydda airport. In the history of aliyah bet, which had seen beaten-
up ships ready for the scrapheap beached on the shores of Palestine, the
arrival of Aliza emmi-Mnashee and her children was unique. It certainly
stunned the British official who, in the last week of his official assignment before returning to Britain, granted all of them a visitor's visa in
their forged Iraqi passports.

Salem did not wind up his affairs soon enough, and the Iraqi police
arrested him in early 1949. The charges were serious: as of 10 August
1948 all Jews who had left Iraq for Palestine, either legally or clandestinely, and who had not returned were considered criminals as they had
defected to the enemy and were to be tried in absentia by emergency military tribunals. Death by hanging and massive fines and/or confiscation
of all property awaited the victims. Aliza and the children were indicted,

with Salem as an accessory. He surely would have been summarily convicted and executed were it not for Muslim friends who bribed officials
and got his trial repeatedly postponed until martial law was lifted (17
December 1949). With regular courts back into operation, illegal departure became a less onerous offense. At his trial, Salem asserted that he
had known nothing about his wife's plans. The long history of his marriage and his wife's independent actions, starting with throwing out his
robes, stood him in good stead. The judge acquitted him and convicted
Aliza and her daughters in absentia, sentencing them to six years of jail
with hard labor.

Released, Salem was not free to join his family; the Iraqi government
at that time forbade immigration to Israel to prevent strengthening the
Jewish state. Thus thousands of Iraqi Jews, including Salem, turned to
an underground organization that smuggled them into Iran. "In accordance with the tradition of tolerance, stamped deep into the Iranian
nation for six thousand years, the policy of an open door to political and
religious refugees will be continued," Iran's prime minister Muhammad
Said Maragai declared in February 1950.[14] Salem traveled to the Kurdish
province of Iraq and, with the help of local passeurs, crossed into Iran.
Received by people from the Iraqi-Jewish underground, he was brought
to Teheran and sent on to Israel. The family settled in Jerusalem, where
Salem opened a small shop selling nuts.

Shortly after Salem fled Iraq, Baghdad changed policy once again.
In March 1950 the Iraqi government passed a Denaturalization Law,
valid for one year, that deprived of citizenship Jews who left Iraq for
good, or who left or attempted to leave illegally, but allowed them to take
a limited amount of cash and goods.[15] A ploy to allow Jews to emigrate
without loss of face for Baghdad, the law worked on both counts. The
Iraqis estimated that ten thousand Jews would take this opportunity to
emigrate with some resources; assets in Iraq would remain theirs, managed by an Iraqi citizen. Israel, by contrast, assumed the arrival of eighty
thousand. How to absorb them? By then one hundred thousand immigrants (including Karola Siegel) were living in tents.[16]

Within two weeks twenty-three thousand Jews had registered, and
within four months the figure ballooned to seventy thousand. Practical

difficulties plagued their transfer from Baghdad: scarce aircraft; no direct flights (at Baghdad's request); absorption capacity. The Israeli government watched the clock anxiously as the country burst at the seams with no homes or jobs for the new arrivals. In Iraq, denaturalizations proceeded at the rate of five hundred Jews per day, creating an ever-growing body of stateless Jews in that country. By the end of the year Israeli authorities worried that fifty thousand stateless Jews would remain in Iraq when the law lapsed and, as they had renounced their citizenship voluntarily, the Iraqi government would not hesitate to persecute them. A grenade explosion in the Mas'uda Shemtov synagogue on 14 January 1951, killing three and injuring twenty, underscored the desperate position of the Jews as the March deadline drew near. The law lapsed while the operation was still in progress, and the Iraqi state appropriated all assets. The richest Jewish community in the middle east twelve years earlier was now stateless and destitute. The Israeli government carried on and, as the Jews continued to leave in a massive airlift, the Iraqis did not unleash a massacre. By year's end the Iraqi-Jewish community, which had existed for twenty-five hundred years, and which had given the world the great treasure of the Babylonian Talmud, had ceased to exist on its native soil.

The actions of both the Israeli authorities and the Iraqi Jews reflect post-Holocaust adjustment. The Zionist leadership did not give up the principle of absorption capacity, but the staggering losses of the Nazi era reframed their focus and shaped their decisions. And it was these losses too that prompted Iraqi Jews to flee. The traditional response of Jews to local violence had been to hang on and hold out, to negotiate for better conditions and to make do with worse. By 1948 Jews had abandoned that policy and practice as bankrupt; worse: as leading to genocide. Iraqi Jews had experienced the farhud of 1941; when the possibility of a Jewish state made newspaper headlines after the war, most read contemporary events with greater insight than their European coreligionists fifteen years earlier. "The newspapers raged against 'Zionists' who were plotting, in obscurity and mystery, the theft of an Arab country," Kattan recalled. "Protests of patriotism, professions of nationalist faith, did not calm those who, in greater numbers every day, questioned our loyalty to the Arab nation."[17] In light of the Holocaust, Iraqi Jews harbored no illusions; there was no future for them in their homeland. According to Kattan, after the panic of the farhud had passed, Jews had believed that life would return more or less to normal; they would go on as before. But after 1945, "catastrophe was being traced against a calm horizon. It was before us, and the future concealed the worst misfortunes. Everywhere we read bad omens."[18] After Auschwitz, a new coding process prevailed. Jews interpreted the world in which they lived differently. A profound post-Holocaust adjustment.[19]

ADJUSTMENT TO THE ANNIHILATION OF TWO-THIRDS of Europe's Jews and the culture they had created occurred on a communal level and in the private sphere. The ideology of the ingathering of the exiles provided a collective and socially accepted meaning for refugees who chose to settle in Israel. As we have seen, others embraced the social narrative of communism. For most, this ultimately proved a far less successful credo than the ingathering story for Jews returning to their ancestral homeland. Austrian Jews who had spent the war in Great Britain and had chosen to return to Austria to regenerate their nation through the political power of communism ended up disillusioned with the party and with their countrymen. While in England they had underestimated the deep-rooted antisemitism, anti-Marxism, and national chauvinism of Austrians. Having defended their country's reputation for six years, they returned to find that their idealized portrait was just that. "It was a kind of brainwashing; it *was* brainwashing," Robert Rosner reflected. "The communists had a lot of literature about 'the rest of Austria' and how 'the Austrians are fighting.' Of course we knew about the Civil War of 1934. I gave lots of lectures about what a happy country Austria was until the Germans came. I believed it. I did believe it. We all just kept forgetting the things that happened in between 1934 and 1938."[20]

Communism too was not what they had hoped—far from it. Stalin's purges, the violent Soviet action in Hungary in 1956 and Czechoslovakia in 1968, and the party's position on the 1967 war in the middle east depleted the Austrian communist party and the communist youth organization of its Jewish membership in successive waves. As Otto Suschny, who had repatriated to Austria from Palestine put it, "I finally broke with them in '56. Hungary really was it. All my friends said at one point that they had had enough. Hungary was one of these turning points. Czechoslovakia was another. Israel in '67 was another."[21] One of only about half a dozen of his initial youth aliyah group to leave Palestine (of whom three or four returned to Vienna), Otto had become a member of the Free Austria Movement in Tel Aviv, joined the British army in 1943, and arranged to serve in Europe rather than north Africa.

Otto had not adapted to Palestine and, at that point in his life, communism resonated with him more than Zionism. Then too, he wished "to get closer to my family," about whom he knew nothing. "In Israel, people were beginning to become apprehensive about what was happening. Some news leaked out, so we knew a little bit about the camps. It was a rumor; it wasn't a certainty, but one was already afraid. Still, I hoped to find my family. . . . At that time, I didn't quite rationalize that my family probably wasn't alive anymore. There were some rumors, but I still had hopes."[22]

Like most of his fellow repatriates, Otto did not find his family and was disappointed by his fellow citizens. In the late 1980s this group of refugees whose lives had been shaped by politics faced the Waldheim affair. When he ran for president of Austria, former Secretary-General of the United Nations Kurt Waldheim's wartime history came to light. He had served as an intelligence officer in the German army unit that committed mass murder in western Bosnia, for which he earned a place on the Wehrmacht's "honor list." And he had reviewed and approved antisemitic propaganda leaflets to be dropped behind Russian lines, one of which read, "enough of the Jewish war, kill the Jews, come over."[23] Yet the Austrians went to the polls and voted for him. Once again Jewish reémigrés were confronted with the antisemitism of their countrymen, and this time communism offered no comfort.

So where and to whom do they belong? In a fundamental way, Gerda Geiringer spoke for all. "Austria is my country. I feel myself deeply Austrian; Viennese, really Viennese, not Austrian. Yes, I feel at home here in Vienna. I am quintessentially a central European, and that is where I locate myself—as a central European. And would you please send all the other central Europeans away? They're not quite my style anymore."[24]

German Jews who returned to build the communist state in East Germany found similar disillusionment. Alfred Kantorowicz had joined the party in 1931, believing it the only force that could stop the Nazis. He fled to Paris in 1933, fought in the Spanish Civil War, returned to France only to be interned in 1939, and reached the United States in June 1941. Kantorowicz repatriated to the Soviet occupation zone of Germany in 1946, eager to build a communist society. "I was interested not in the resurgence of Judaism in Germany, but in the rebirth of democracy," he explained twenty years later. "Besides, I believed in Germany. I thought that Nazism was an episode in German history, not the end product of that history. Now a new chapter was beginning. I could help in writing it."[25]

Appointed professor of contemporary German literature at the Humboldt University in East Berlin, Kantorowicz received many honors. But he felt decreasingly at home in the socialist state. In the wake of the bloody suppression of riots in 1953, he entered his own version of "inner exile," and when the authorities asked him to write a defense of the Soviet suppression of the Hungarian uprising in 1956, he refused and fled to West Germany. Welcomed as a distinguished refugee from communism, he was soon asked to denounce the Soviets in particular and communism in general. Again he refused, and Bonn began to make life difficult for him. He remained in West Germany but, an outcast once more, he discovered a Jewish identity. "Today, my being Jewish has become a point of reference. Mine was once a large family, but I am the only one who remains. The rest died in Auschwitz and Theresienstadt because they were Jews. I am part of them, as I am part of all the other Jews who died for just being Jews. Just as I am part of the other millions who died because of the Nazis."[26] If Kantorowicz's postwar life history was both more privileged and more turbulent than his fellow Jewish communist repatriates to Germany, he nevertheless spoke for many by the late 1960s.

THE QUESTION OF WHERE AND TO WHOM refugees belonged loomed large in 1946 and beyond. Inspired by neither communism nor the ingathering of the exiles, the majority who repatriated, or stayed in European countries of refuge, or immigrated to countries overseas had no narrative to endow their experience with meaning. They had to resolve the emotional difficulties, practical problems, and existential questions attached to starting life anew without the support of a communal goal.

Family matters dominated postwar adjustment and, perhaps counterintuitively, even those who had the good fortune of finding kin had great difficulties knitting the family together again. Most particularly, many children separated from their parents for years could not quite reestablish their pre-war ties of affection and familiarity. Susi Neuwalder had gone on a kindertransport to England in the summer of 1939. Initially taken in by the Shepherds, she was moved within a year to Phyllis Shepherd's maiden aunts, and then to Phyllis's elderly parents, and finally to her younger sister Mary. "To my intense astonishment and joy, Auntie Mary showed up to pick me up. She was recently married and had no children of her own yet at the time," Susanne recalled half a century later. "She took me in and I was their first child."[27] News of Susi's father came to Mary, as a letter she wrote to him on 29 April 1944 explains. "I have recently heard from the Red Cross that you are still at Cosenza since the Allied occupation. We have heard nothing from you for over a year and we are rather worried."[28] With communication reestablished with Dr Neuwalder, attention turned to Susi's mother, who had remained in Vienna. "You must be very anxious about your wife," Mary commiserated with Herbert Neuwalder (15 November), "but you won't have very long to wait now."[29] "Have you heard from Mother yet?" Susi asked her father in a letter of 16 January 1945.[30] Communication was not reestablished until the end of the year. "Today I received a letter of my wife at Vienna," he exulted (4 December 1945). "The short letter has been coming not directly but in a private way over the Czechoslovakia. It is the much beautiful present for me and the children. The letter is dated August 20th, 45."[31]

The entire family of four had survived. But by that point, "that family and I had nothing to do; it was as though my past didn't exist." Practical complications prevented Susi's parents from coming to England to fetch her, and she was sent to join them in Italy in June 1948, nine years after she had last seen them. "I knew I was leaving and it was just very, very painful and I couldn't bear it. So my aunt took me on a train to London, and I remember sitting on the train and saying to her, 'Every time the wheels turn, I go further and further away from my home.'"[32] Susi flew to Rome, where her father met her at the airport. "I was so embarrassed I just didn't know what to do. . . . I wanted to run away. . . . I didn't know what to do with my father, so I didn't do anything." They no longer had a language in common, and they did not recognize each other. "I still remember, I didn't want to be there. I didn't want him to hold my hand. I didn't want him to be my father. And I wanted to go home." At the same time, "I felt guilty. This man is my father. I'm supposed to love him."[33]

The parents did their best, and Susi and her brother (who had gone to Italy six months earlier) did their best. The Neuwalders immigrated to New York. Dr Neuwalder requalified as a physician and worked in his profession again. "But the thing the war did, it really did destroy that family. Even though all the family all got back together again. And we were a family in a certain way, but the feelings were never the same." She believed her parents felt similarly. "They lost us when we were four and five. They didn't see us again until we were thirteen and fourteen. By then I was an awkward teenager going through my own teenage development. They had lost their children. And even though they found them again, they weren't quite their children. That was lost."[34]

Isabelle Riff and her sister were separated from their parents for a far shorter period than Susi and her brother from theirs, but they too suffered profound postwar dislocation. Isabelle and her sister had crossed clandestinely in fall 1942 into Switzerland, where they were offered a home by the Hildesheimer family, who had volunteered to take one refugee child but, faced with the two sisters, accepted both warmly. Isabelle's parents, Gisela and Herman Riff, had tried to follow their daughters over the border. Arrested, they were sent to Rivesaltes and Gurs. Liberated in 1944, they returned to Belgium when it was safe to do so to find a flat and make a home to which their children could return.

Gisela went to fetch the girls in Switzerland in 1945; they had been separated for three and a half years. "I recognized her, but her voice I didn't recognize," Isabelle recalled decades later. "I remember that quite clearly. Her voice was different to what I had remembered. But she was also out of concentration camp, very thin, and emaciated, and older-looking. And we also, we didn't look as we looked when she had left us. It was quite traumatic." Isabelle and her sister were not emotionally prepared to leave. "We were so happy in that family; I would have stayed on with that family, for my part, I would rather have stayed with that family in their house than going back with my mother, who to me was a stranger at the time."[35] At that age, Isabelle reflected, "after three and a half years, one gets integrated into a family. And it was a very secure and happy home. We were happy there. . . . They had three children, older than we were. They had a daughter and two sons. And we participated in whatever they did." In part it was a question of stability. "That security I felt—when you are a child who has been handed to so many strange people, the one thing you want above all is security. And I felt if I go back to Antwerp where I knew that my parents were fighting for a flat and were fighting for work and to reestablish themselves, everything had been lost."[36]

Her apprehensions proved correct. "When we came back, it was quite difficult. There was a lot of tension. I had to cope myself and overcome it myself, even as a child. With me, it demonstrated itself in that Monday, Tuesday, Wednesday, I went to school. But Thursday I had a temperature already. By Friday I was in bed. This went on for quite a while." Hermann built up his diamond cutting business again. Gisela made a home for them. Both girls went to school. But, she said, "I don't think that one ever becomes normal again. It's a very long, long time, and it lingers in your subconscious, but it's there, and what happened during the war years is even more vivid than what happens every day."[37]

There was no "solution" to the problem of knitting back together, resuming family life, just as there was no "solution" to the ragged finality of death. Eva and Susi Guttmann were among the 130 youngsters who came to France on a kindertransport in late 1938 and were in contact with Elisabeth Luz. Through her they maintained communication with their parents for a time. Then silence followed. Their parents did not return. And the sisters, separated during the war, did not know where the other was. Fortunately, they found each other a few months after liberation. Eva was in Paris, she wrote to Tante Elisabeth on 10 September 1945; Susi had reached Palestine in July 1945 and was living on a kibbutz near Haifa. "My joy is immense. When I received her message I cried with happiness—I have never been so happy in my life," Eva bubbled to

Elisabeth.[38] Susi married Shimon Sachs, who had gone from Berlin to Palestine with youth aliyah in 1938, and in December 1946 gave birth to their daughter. Eva joined her sister in Palestine the following year.

Communication lagged between Elisabeth and the two sisters for a decade. But then Susi began to feel poorly. Her health had deteriorated, she admitted to Elisabeth in April 1958.[39] While objectively she was doing well and appeared content, she was suffering from all kinds of psychosomatic problems, she explained a month later. "Probably the burden of those years of suffering never really passed, and now it erupts violently."[40] Her situation did not improve. Wartime experiences threw tentacles around her, trapping her in the past. "Most likely the war years and everything that is connected to it left deep scars. I thought that I had overcome all of that, yet old experiences, the losses and much darkness, remain deep in my soul. That is how I understand my illness."[41] Hospitalized with what she called a "breakdown" in April 1959, Susi realized that she had to attend to her problems. Throughout all of this turbulence, Elisabeth offered stability and continuity. She wrote letters and sent packages, thus reminding Susi that someone of her parents' generation had cared about her since 1938; she was not utterly bereft in that regard.

Believing that a new environment would be beneficial, Susi, Shimon, and their family left the kibbutz with its emotional demands of collective life, for the youth village of Ben Shemen. A well known educator, Shimon had been offered the directorship of the agricultural school. Eva and her husband joined them. Susi took comfort from her children's happiness, the absence of the intrapersonal tensions inherent to a kibbutz, and the greater material comfort they now enjoyed. Her health still was not good, she confessed to Elisabeth, but she counted her blessings after such a difficult life. Still, the past was ever present, and she now faced the task of passing that history to the next generation. "Last night, it was Friday, the whole family sat together and we were looking at family pictures, and then Chagai [her son] saw pictures of Shimon's and my own parents. We explained to him that those were his grandparents, and he asked where they were now, and then we explained that difficult, evil time to him. He has a good head on his shoulders and he understood perfectly."[42] Like so many others, Susi married, had children, worked. She, like they, created a productive and meaningful life for herself. For all of them, adjustment meant learning to live with their memories, not moving forward as if they had none.

PRE- AND POSTWAR REFUGEES FACED great practical challenges as well as emotional difficulties. The situation of Susi and Eva's friend Hanna-Ruth Klopstock reflected the economic conditions of many European Jews. The sole survivor of her nuclear family, Hanna-Ruth remained in France after the war. She wrote to Elisabeth in May 1946 to say that she was pregnant, and while she loved the baby's father, he did not wish to marry her or to take on the role of a father. In order to provide for her child, she had secured a position in an OSE home in Savoy. Gisela was born at the end of August.

A single mother with a full-time job, Hanna-Ruth had little time to write letters and gradually lost touch with Elisabeth until 1954. "Now I will tell you about myself," she announced. "In general nothing has changed. Life continues. Sadly, the conditions in which I find myself are not such as to make life easier. Just this week in Paris we celebrate the tenth anniversary of the Liberation. Who would have thought in 1944 that 1954 would be as it has turned out to be?" A devoted mother, "my happiness is my child. I enclose a photo. She is a lovely girl." They managed in rather straitened circumstances. "We lived in a children's home until last year, I as a cook." Housing was simply beyond her reach. "A one-room place goes for one million francs [around thirty thousand dollars in 2008]." She sublet a small room in her friends' apartment. "As you see, not everything is as we imagined it 10 years ago," she concluded. "But apart from that, things are OK. The hope, yes the certainty of better times, is still alive."[43] Better times did not come. Two years later, Hanna-Ruth, then working as a cook in a vocational school, had been forced to separate from Gisela. "We still don't have a home. She is in a children's home near Paris. Gisela visits me every Sunday. She comes by herself, as she is very bright."[44]

Hanna-Ruth's predicament was not extraordinary. Of the approximately forty thousand Jewish refugees in France in 1940, some eight thousand had survived the war in that country. Those of working age and older had absolutely nothing: no clothing, linens, personal possessions, or housing. Without exception, all who had flats or houses when the Germans invaded had been denied repossession in 1945, and because of the chronic postwar housing shortage they were unable to obtain any accommodation other than hotel rooms. Such lodgings often absorbed half of their meager earnings, which meant that even those who worked lived in poverty. Then too, many refugees were aging, and marked by the betrayal they had experienced in the 1940s. "Even now elderly people will contact French authorities only with anxiously beating hearts," a survey of German-Jewish refugees in 1955 observed. "Thus elderly people will not claim the relief to which they are entitled, for fear that this might have adverse consequences, in particular: for fear that they might be expelled because they have lived on public funds. This deprives those most in need of a modest addition to their income." The report also noted that the various French-Jewish organizations, "unfamiliar as they are with the psychological after-effects which years of persecution have had on this group," failed to serve these elderly refugees.[45]

Refugees in Great Britain fared little better economically. Werner Rosenstock, who had been a lawyer for the Centralverein and who became a leader of the German-Jewish refugee community in Britain, observed in 1955 that while they had been spared the persecution to which refugees in France had been subjected, and while their legal situation was stable as most of them had been naturalized, their circumstances remained rather marginal. "It cannot be said that the refugees have been absorbed in British economic life. There is one shadow which hovers over most of them—old age. Even though the majority are employed, their income is not sufficient to allow them savings of any considerable size." Whatever they had put by in Germany had been lost, and their wages in Britain had not afforded them the opportunity to recoup. "Only very few of them can think of retiring and they dread the day when a slump would make them the first victims among the employees of their English firms, or when a breakdown in health would force them to give up their positions."[46] And, like survivors everywhere, they had little family to turn to for help. Those essential networks of mutual assistance and care had been destroyed.

Notwithstanding the commonly held idea that pre- and postwar refugees constituted a singular American success story, and notwithstanding the enormous economic strength of the United States after the war—especially in comparison with Britain or France—a parallel narrative was the case for many. If older refugees might have accepted their loss of profession and status as the price they paid for safety, a lot of younger people who believed that the future would be theirs were disappointed. Mariánka Zadikow's history plots this story. Mariánka had fled to Czechoslovakia from her native Germany in 1933 and had taken five courses offered by the Jewish community in Prague to prepare for immigration before she was deported to Theresienstadt. Her father Arnold died there; she and her mother lived to see the Germans flee at the end of April 1945. The International Red Cross took the camp under its protection and, when they were strong enough, Mariánka and her mother returned to Prague.

Hanna-Ruth Klopstock and her daughter Gisela, La Chaumière, France, 26 September 1946.

It would be comforting to imagine that now all was well. Or at least, as well as it could be for Mariánka and her mother, without Arnold. The allies had won the war; Hilda and Mariánka were free. But Mariánka and her mother returned to little: family, Jewish community, national identity—all destroyed. For years she had dreamed of liberation, but what she experienced had nothing in common with those fantasies. "I was very close to suicide in 1945. The war was ended. In Prague. Where you saw nothing but empty windows of people who were dead." Stateless—

the Nazis had stripped all German Jews of citizenship on 25 November 1941—she inhabited a kind of no-man's-land. "At that time, I was nothing. I was not a citizen." Scorned for her German birth, she was also the object of suspicion simply because she was alive. "[People] asked me, 'Did you help them in order to survive? How come you made it?'"[47]

Mariánka asked for help at the Jewish community offices in Prague to change her legal status. In her memory, the officials were too few and too frightened to do anything for her. Overwhelmed by survivors' needs, or traumatized from their own experiences and loath to confront the Czech authorities about the question of national identity, they shrank from helping her. Ultimately, Jewish community administrators "who at first refused to help me [asked], 'Would you consider helping us here?'" She accepted. "I needed an employment of some kind, even a barely paid one." For two years, from October 1945 until she immigrated as a displaced person to the United States in 1947, Mariánka worked in the legal department of the Jewish Community Center in Prague. She undertook general office work, and she served as a translator and support for transient Jews in Prague who wanted to move on but did not have an exit visa. Mariánka helped them negotiate the numerous government offices and forms required to obtain the papers they needed. "I loved it. I loved what I did there."[48]

Her plan, at the time, was to obtain an education and to immigrate to Israel. Neither worked out. Hilda, who was not a Zionist, ended up in Israel for two and a half years, while Mariánka left for the United States. It was the only period in their lives when they were separated. And Mariánka never got an education. Not in Czechoslovakia and not in America. "I wanted help just to go to high school and have a diploma. There was no such thing. I never had another chance for schooling." She brought her mother to the United States; she married; she had two daughters. All of these enriched her life. But "some of us know that under other circumstances we would have done better. . . . I was interested in the medical field. I might have become a nurse practitioner or a researcher in a laboratory. And I definitely would have had to do with people." She and her husband had a chicken farm. "I had to do with nothing but chickens. For seventeen years, no people, never. Seven days a week. Later, five days a

week." After her husband died, Mariánka, the person who had lit the fires
and cleaned the toilets in the notions factory in Theresienstadt, became a
custodian in the public schools. "And the next eleven years, I had again no
people because I was cleaning classrooms and bathrooms and throwing
away garbage and having absolutely nothing to do with people."[49]

Mariánka's sense of isolation flowed from the jobs she held. For
the essayist and public intellectual Jean Améry (Hans Maier), it was an
intrinsic concomitant of forced exile. Améry had fled from Vienna first to
France and then to Belgium in 1938. Arrested by the Germans in 1943, he
was tortured for his participation in resistance activities and deported to
Auschwitz for being a Jew. Returning to Brussels after the war, he found
that he did not quite belong anywhere or to anyone. In an essay on "How
Much Home Does a Person Need?" Améry addressed the problems of
adjustment. "We" refugees "had not lost our country, but had to realize
that it had never been ours," he observed bitterly. "What we believed to
have been our first love was, as they said there, racial disgrace."[50]

His view admitted to no happy end. In the decades after the war, the
refugee discovered that departure, flight, or expulsion "was not a wound
that was inflicted upon him, one that will scar over with the ticking
of time, but rather that he is suffering from an insidious disease that is
growing worse with the years." This illness was rooted in the refusal of
their past to take on the contours of a comfortable "once upon a time"
life narrative. And as refugees could never fully come to peace with their
history, they could not come to own it, and thus they were doomed to
"remain unrecognizable in the ruins of the years 1933 to 1945." Evidence
for this abounded. For Améry this was clearly reflected in a quick and
marked shift in the refugees' behavior. Arriving in their ports of safety in
the 1930s, they had boasted of their fortunes, careers, or positions "back
home." But they soon fell silent. "Their past as a social phenomenon had
been retracted by society; thus it was impossible to retain it as a subjective, psychological possession." Time offered no solace. Quite the contrary. "The older they grew, the harder their loss became."[51] Certainly
this proved true for Améry: he committed suicide in 1978.

.   .   .

The history of pre- and postwar refugees resists a triumphalist conclusion. There is no silver lining to this story. One cannot say, "They lost their homes, language, families, roots, and sense of belonging to their native land, *but* they survived, went on, made lives for themselves." What one can say is: "They lost their homes, language, families, roots, and sense of belonging to their native land, *and* they survived, went on, made lives for themselves." At the same time. It is a history characterized by adjustment and adaptation, and marked by loss and a thread of loneliness. Constructive lives, and lives slightly apart. Never quite at home.

NOTES

Please note that all translations (texts, oral histories, letters, archive documents) have been done by the authors unless otherwise identified. Please note too that survivors' names in the text are as they were at the time, with the insertion of women's married names if used. (Thus, Susanne Harris-Neuwalder should be read: Susanne Harris née Neuwalder.) The corresponding notes reflect current names and spelling.

The following abbreviations have been used:

AFSC	American Friends Service Committee (Philadelphia)
CBF	Central British Fund (London)
CDJC	Centre de Documentation Juive Contemporaine (Paris)
ICH	Institute of Contemporary History (London)
JDC	American Jewish Joint Distribution Committee (New York)
PRO	Public Records Office (London)
	CAB: Cabinet
	FO: Foreign Office
	HO: Home Office
	MH: Ministry of Health
USHMM	United States Holocaust Memorial Museum (Washington, DC)

INTRODUCTION

1. Micha Wertheim, "Anne Frank," *Het Parool*, 3 October 2004; for Anne Frank's own view of her nationality and her refugee status, see Anne Frank, *The Diary*

of Anne Frank: The Critical Edition, ed. David Barnouw and Gerrold van der Stroom, trans. Arnold J. Pomerans and B. M. Mooyart-Doubleday (New York: Doubleday, 1989), 274, 601, and 656f.

2. See Jacob Presser, *Ashes in the Wind: The Destruction of Dutch Jewry*, trans. Arnold J. Pomerans (Detroit: Wayne State University Press, 1988), 221ff.; Presser notes that until July 1942, German and Austrian Jewish refugees had no representation at all in the Jewish Council. This contributed to their sense of special vulnerability.

3. We thank Debórah's colleague Nina Kushner for this insight.

4. In the notes to the chapters that follow, we have conformed to standard academic practice and included sources for quotations and key texts that informed our argument. As the structure of our book precluded some subjects, a number of important works on refugee Jews were not captured in the notes. The books listed below are of singular significance for further study.

Points of departure for any study of refugees in the 1930s and 1940s: Tony Kushner and Katherine Knox, *Refugees in an Age of Genocide: Global, National and Local Perspectives During the Twentieth Century* (London and Portland, OR: Frank Cass, 1999); Michael Marrus, *The Unwanted: European Refugees in the Twentieth Century* (New York and Oxford: Oxford University Press, 1985); Malcolm Jarvis Proudfoot, *European Refugees, 1939–1952: A Study in Forced Population Movement* (London: Faber and Faber, 1957); John Hope Simpson, *The Refugee Problem: Report of a Survey* (London: Royal Institute of International Affairs, 1939); Jacques Vernant, *The Refugee in the Post-War World* (London: Allen & Unwin, 1953).

On the flight of anti-Nazi artists, intellectuals, and political opponents, see Jean-Michel Palmier, *Weimar in Exile: The Antifascist Emigration in Europe and America* (London and New York: Verso, 2006).

Useful general studies from the period that focus specifically on refugee Jews include: Arieh Tartakower and Kurt R. Grossmann, *The Jewish Refugee* (New York: Institute of Jewish Affairs, 1944); Mark Wischnitzer, *To Dwell in Safety: The Story of Jewish Migration Since 1800* (Philadelphia: Jewish Publication Society of America, 1948).

German scholars have developed a large literature on refugees from Nazi Germany, both Jewish and gentile. Important anthologies include: Ernst Loewy, ed., *Exil: Literarische und politische Texte aus dem deutschen Exil, 1933–1945* (Stuttgart: Metzler, 1979); Egon Schwarz and Matthias Wegner, eds., *Verbannung: Aufzeichnungen deutscher Schriftsteller im Exil* (Hamburg; Christian Wegner, 1964). For studies of particular importance, see inter alia: Wolfgang Benz, ed., *Das Exil der kleinen Leute* (Munich: Beck, 1991); Wolfgang Benz and Marion Neiss, eds., *Deutsch-jüdisches Exil: das Ende der Assimilation?* (Berlin: Metropol, 1994); Kurt R. Grossmann, *Emigration: Die Geschichte der Hit-ler-Flüchtlinge 1933–1945* (Frankfurt: Europäische Verlagsanstalt, 1969); Claus Dieter Krohn a.o., eds., *Handbuch der deutschsprachigen Emigration, 1933–1945* (Darmstadt: Primus Verlag, 1998). K. G. Saur has published a number of important encyclopedic and bibliographic works reviewing various aspects of the history of refugees from Nazism. See for example: Harald Hagemann and Claus Dieter Krohn, *Biographisches Handbuch der deutschsprachigen wirtschaftswissenschaftlichen Emigration nach 1933* (Munich: Saur, 1999); Werner Röder a.o., *International Biographical Dictionary of Central European Emigrés 1933–1945*, 3 vols.; John C. Spalek, Konrad Feilchenfeld, and Sandra H. Hawrylchak, *Deutschsprachige Exilliteratur seit 1933*, 4 vols. in 8 parts (Munich: Saur, 1976–2003); John C. Spalek with Sandra H. Hawrylchak, *Guide to the Archival Materials of the German-speaking Emigration to the United States After 1933*, 3 vols. (Munich: Saur, 1991–6); Herbert A. Strauss, *Jewish Immigrants of the Nazi Period in the USA*, 6 vols. (Munich: Saur, 1993); Frithjof Trapp a.o., *Handbuch des deutschsprachigen Exiltheaters 1933–1945*, 2 vols. (Munich: Saur, 1999); Horst Weber, *Sources Relating to the History of Emigré Musicians, 1933–1950* (Munich: Saur, 2003); Ulrike Wendland, *Biographisches Handbuch deutsprachiger Kunsthistoriker im Exil* (Munich: Saur, 1998).

A number of scholars have researched government asylum and immigration policies, and we too discuss aspects of these matters. Studies that did not find a place in our notes include Irving Abella and Harold Troper, *None Is Too Many: Canada and the Jews of Europe 1933–1948* (New York: Random House, 1983); Richard Breitman and Alan M. Kraut, *American Refugee Policy and European Jewry, 1933–1945* (Bloomington: Indiana University Press, 1987); Haim Genizi, *America's Fair Share: The Admission and Resettlement of Displaced Persons, 1945–1952* (Detroit: Wayne State University Press, 1993); Monty Noam Penkower, *The Jews Were Expendable: Free World Diplomacy and the Holocaust* (Detroit: Wayne State University Press, 1988); David S. Wyman, *Paper Walls: America and the Refugee Crisis, 1938–1941* (Amherst: University of Massachusetts Press, 1968); David S. Wyman, *The Abandonment of the Jews* (New York: Pantheon, 1984).

The internment of refugees as enemy aliens in Great Britain in 1940 has emerged as a subject of special interest. See: Miriam Kochan, *Britain's Internees in the Second World War* (London: Macmillan, 1983); Alexander Ramah, *Barbed Wire on the Isle of Man* (New York and London: Harcourt Brace Jovanovich, 1980); Austin Stevens, *The Dispossessed: German Refugees in Britain* (London: Barrie and Jenkins, 1975).

The adjustment of Jewish refugees in the United States has generated a large literature too. See inter alia: Lewis A. Coser, *Refugee Scholars in America:*

Their Impact and Their Experiences (New Haven: Yale University Press, 1984); Maurice R. Davie, *Refugees in America: Report of the Committee for the Study of Recent Immigration from Europe* (New York and London: Harper & Brothers, 1947); Donald Peterson Kent, *The Refugee Intellectual: The Americanization of Immigrants of 1933–1941* (New York: Columbia University Press, 1953); Ruth Neubauer, "Differential Adjustment of Adult Immigrants and Their Children to American Groups: The Americanization of a Selected Group of Jewish Immigrants of 1933–1944" (Ph.D. thesis, Columbia University, New York, 1966); Sibylle Quack, *Zuflucht Amerika: Zur Sozialgeschichte der Emigration deutsch-jüdischer Frauen in die USA 1933–1945* (Bonn: Dietz, 1995); Gerhart Saenger, *Today's Refugees, Tomorrow's Citizens: A Story of Americanization* (New York and London: Harper & Brothers, 1941).

Finally, we urge readers to note the memoir literature. The following are merely a few key titles. Desider Furst and Lilian R. Furst, *Home Is Somewhere Else* (Albany: State University of New York Press, 1994); Karen Gershon, *We Came as Children* (New York: Harcourt, Brace & World, 1966); Ernest G. Heppner, *Shanghai Refuge: A Memoir of the World War II Jewish Ghetto* (Lincoln and London: University of Nebraska Press, 1994); Leo Spitzer, *Hotel Bolivia: The Culture of Memory in a Refugee from Nazism* (New York: Hill and Wang, 1998). Anthologies of shorter pieces: Mark M. Anderson, *Hitler's Exiles: Personal Stories of the Flight from Nazi Germany to America* (New York: New Press, 1998); Dorit Bader Whiteman, *The Uprooted: A Hitler Legacy* (New York: Insight Books, 1993); and Ruth E. Wolman, *Crossing Over: An Oral History of Refugees from Hitler's Reich* (New York: Twayne, 1996).

5. See inter alia: Nicholas Balabkins, *West German Reparations to Israel* (New Brunswick, NJ: Rutgers University Press, 1971); Inge Deutschkron, *Bonn and Jerusalem: The Strange Coalition* (Philadelphia, New York, and London: Chilton Book Company, 1970); Marilyn Henry, *Confronting the Perpetrators: A History of the Claims Conference* (London and Portland, OR: Vallentine Mitchell, 2007); Nana Sagi, *German Reparations: A History of the Negotiations* (Jerusalem: Magnes Press, 1980); Rolf Vogel, ed., *The German Path to Israel: A Documentation* (London: Oswald Wolff, 1969); Ronald W. Zweig, *German Reparations and the Jewish World: A History of the Claims Conference*, 2nd edition (London and Portland, OR: Frank Cass, 2001).

6. Julian Barnes, *A History of the World in 10½ Chapters* (New York: Knopf, 1989), 181–8.

7. See Lisa Fittko, *Escape Through the Pyrenees*, trans. David Koblick (Evanston: Northwestern University Press, 1991), 103–15; Lisa Fittko, "The Story of Old Benjamin," in Walter Benjamin, *The Arcades Project*, trans. Howard Eiland and Kevin McLaughlin (Cambridge, MA: Belknap Press, 1999), 946–54.

8. Benjamin mentioned that he traveled on a Certificat d'Identité des Réfugiés Provenant d'Allemagne in a letter to Gershom Scholem, 8 April 1939, in Walter Benjamin, *The Correspondence of Walter Benjamin and Gershom Scholem*, ed. Gershom Scholem, trans. Gary Smith and André Lefevere (New York: Schocken, 1989), 252.

9. Lisa Fittko, *Escape Through the Pyrenees*, 106.

10. Ingrid Scheuermann, *Neue Dokumente zum Tode Walter Benjamins* (Bonn: Thiele & Schwartz, 1992); Wilfried F. Schoeller, *Deutschland vor Ort: Geschichte, Mythen, Erinnerungen* (Munich and Vienna: Carl Hanser, 2005), 273ff.

11. Hannah Arendt, *Men in Dark Times* (New York: Harcourt, Brace & World, 1968), 171. For an eyewitness account of the situation at Port Bou the day after Benjamin's suicide, see Elisabeth Freundlich, *The Traveling Years*, trans. Elizabeth Pennebaker (Riverside, CA: Ariadne Press, 1999), 84f.

12. On the monument in Port Bou, see Christopher Rollason, "Border Crossing, Resting Place: Portbou and Walter Benjamin," *Lingua Franca* (Brussels), vol. 5, no. 8 (2002), 4–9; Dani Karavan, *Homage to Walter Benjamin. "Passages," Place of Remembrance at Portbou*, ed. Ingrid and Konrad Scheurmann (Mainz: Verlag Philipp von Zabern, 1995); Michael Taussig, *Walter Benjamin's Grave* (Chicago and London: University of Chicago Press, 2006), 3–30. The path that Benjamin took from France to Spain has become a popular pilgrimage route. See Rebecca Solnit, "Hatred at One End, Rejection at the Other: A Writer Retraces Philosopher Walter Benjamin's Failed Walk to Freedom," *Los Angeles Times*, 1 August 2004; Michael D. Jackson, "In the Footsteps of Walter Benjamin," *Harvard Divinity Bulletin*, vol. 34, no. 2 (Spring 2006), 42–57.

13. Original text in Walter Benjamin, *Gesammelte Schriften*, ed. Rolf Tiedemann and Hermann Schweppenhäuser, 9 vols. in 16 parts (Frankfurt: Suhrkamp, 1972–89), vol. 1, 1241; English translation in Walter Benjamin, "Paralipomena to 'On the Concept of History,'" in Walter Benjamin, *Selected Writings Volume 4, 1938–1940*, ed. Howard Eiland and Michael W. Jennings (Cambridge, MA.: Belknap Press, 2003), 406; Les Back, "Homage in Ruins: A Visit to Walter Benjamin's Grave," in *Street Signs* (Spring 2007), 15.

1933: THE END OF AN ERA

1. Quoted in Max Domarus, Hitler: *Speeches and Proclamations, 1932–1945*, 4 vols. (Wauconda, IL: Bolchazy-Carducci, 1990–7), vol. 1, 232ff.

2. Gerd Rühle, ed., *Das Dritte Reich: Dokumentarische Darstellung des Aufbaues der Nation: Das erste Jahr, 1933* (Berlin: Hummelverlag, 1934), 17ff.

3. Ibid., 20ff.

4. Anthony Kauders, "Legally Citizens: Jewish Exclusion from the Weimar

Polity," in Wolfgang Benz, Arnold Paucker, and Peter Pulzer, eds., *Jüdisches Leben in der Weimarer Republik/Jews in the Weimar Republic* (Tübingen: Mohr Siebeck, 1998), 160ff.; also Peter Pulzer, "Between Hope and Fear: Jews and the Weimar Republic," ibid., 271f.

5. Wladimir Wolf Kaplun-Kogan, *Die jüdischen Wanderbewegungen in der neuesten Zeit (1880–1914)*, diss. Breslau University, 1919 (Bonn: A. Marcus & E. Webers Verlag, 1919), 8.

6. Mark Wischnitzer, *To Dwell in Safety: The Story of Jewish Migration Since 1800* (Philadelphia: Jewish Publication Society of America, 1948), 100ff.

7. Quoted in Kauders, "Legally Citizens: Jewish Exclusion from the Weimar Polity," 171.

8. Peter Pulzer, "Between Hope and Fear: Jews and the Weimar Republic," in Benz a.o., *Jüdisches Leben in der Weimarer Republik/Jews in the Weimar Republic*, 278; Arnold Paucker, "Der jüdische Abwehrkampf," in Werner E. Mosse, ed., *Entscheidungsjahr 1932: Zur Judenfrage in der Endphase der Weimarer Republik* (Tübingen: J. C. B. Mohr [Paul Siebeck], 1965), 442ff.

9. On the number of Ostjuden in the Weimar Republic, see Trude Maurer, *Ostjuden in Deutschland, 1918–1933* (Hamburg: Hans Christians Verlag, 1986), 72ff.

10. "Vor den Entscheidungen," *Centralverein Zeitung* (20 May 1932), as quoted in Donald L. Niewyck, *The Jews in Weimar Germany* (Baton Rouge and London: Louisiana State University Press, 1980), 83.

11. As quoted in David Bronsen, *Joseph Roth: Eine Biographie* (Cologne: Kiepenhauer & Witsch, 1974), 422.

12. See Henry Ashby Turner, Jr., *Hitler's Thirty Days to Power: January 1933* (Reading, MA: Addison-Wesley, 1996).

13. "Die neue Regierung," *Centralverein Zeitung* (2 February 1933), as quoted in Niewyck, *The Jews in Weimar Germany*, 83.

14. Manès Sperber, *The Unheeded Warning, 1918–1933*, trans. Harry Zohn (New York and London: Holmes & Meier, 1991), 190.

PEOPLE: THE FIRST TO FLEE

1. Friedrich Katz, oral history conducted by Debórah Dwork, Chicago, 14 November 1987, transcript, 4f.

2. Alfred Döblin, "Abschied und Wiederkehr," *Schriften zu Leben und Werk* (Olten and Freiburg im Breisgau: Walter-Verlag, 1986), 265f.

3. Ibid., 266. Who set the fire has been disputed for seventy-five years. In support of the view that van der Lubbe was responsible, see Fritz Tobias, *The Reichstag Fire* (New York: G. P. Putnam's Sons, 1964); Hans Mommsen, Martin Broszat, and others agreed. Their analysis has been challenged recently in Alexander Bahar and Wilfried Kugel, *Der Reichstagbrand: Wie Geschichte*

gemacht wird (Berlin: edition q, 2001) and Hans Schneider, *Neues vom Reichstagbrand?* (Berlin: Berliner Wissenschafts-Verlag, 2004). For earlier works holding the Nazis to blame, see *Braunbuch über Reichstagbrand und Hitler-Terror* (Basel: Universum, 1933) and Internationale Komitee Luxemburg, *Der Reichstagbrand* (Luxembourg: Der Freundenkreis, 1978). We believe the Nazis were responsible.

4. Käthe Frankenthal, *Der dreifache Fluch: Jüdin, Intellektuelle, Sozialistin* (Frankfurt and New York: Campus Verlag, 1981), 197ff.

5. Stefan Heym, *Nachruf* (Munich: Bertelsmann, 1988), 76. In exile in Prague, Helmut Flieg adopted the alias of Stefan Heym so he could correspond with his parents. Later this became his pen name, under which he became famous.

6. Hirschberg in Silesia, Germany, is Jelenia Góra in the Polish province of Slask today, while Spindlerbaude is Spindlerova Bouda.

7. Stefan Heym, *Nachruf*, 78.

8. Ibid., 83f.

9. See Herbert E. Tutas, *Nationalsozialismus und Exil: Die Politik des Dritten Reiches gegenüber der deutschen politischen Emigration 1933–1939* (Munich and Vienna: Carl Hanser Verlag, 1975) and Herbert E. Tutas, *NS-Propaganda und deutsches Exil, 1933–1939* (Worms: Georg Heintz, 1973).

10. PRO, FO 371/16740, 10676, 333–5.

11. Quoted in Max Domarus, *Hitler: Speeches and Proclamations, 1932–1945*, 4 vols. (Wauconda, IL: Bolchazy-Carducci, 1990–7), vol. 1, 299f.

12. Sebastian Haffner, *Defying Hitler: A Memoir*, trans. Oliver Pretzel (New York: Farrar, Straus and Giroux, 2002), 142.

13. Bertha Kahn-Rosenthal, oral history conducted by Debórah Dwork, New Haven, CT, 6 and 13 March 1992, transcript, 20; 1f.; 20; 28.

14. Ibid., 26ff.

15. From April 1933 to September 1935, when the Nuremberg Laws were proclaimed, the term "non-Aryan" referred to Jews who were members of a Christian church. The Nuremberg Laws did not make any distinction between Jews who adhered to Judaism, Jews who were Christians, or Jews who were secular.

16. CBF Archives, reel 154, 3ff; Hildegard Feidel-Mertz, "Integration and Formation of Identity: Exile Schools in Great Britain," *Shofar*, vol. 23, no. 1 (2004), 71–84; Amy Zahl Gottlieb, *Men of Vision* (London: Weidenfeld and Nicolson, 1998), 99f.

17. Harry Pape, ". . . Originally from Frankfurt-am-Main," in Anne Frank, *The Diary of Anne Frank: The Critical Edition*, ed. David Barnouw and Gerrold van der Stroom, trans. Arnold J. Pomerans and B. M. Mooyart-Doubleday (New York: Doubleday, 1989), 3ff.

18. The *Frankfurter Zeitung* reported (7 December 1933) a figure of sixty thou-

sand refugees who had left Germany in 1933, of whom fifty thousand were Jews. This number was adopted as authoritative in 1934 by the high commissioner for refugees (Jewish and other) and was adduced in the 1939 report sponsored by the Royal Institute of International Affairs. Of these sixty thousand refugees, some ten thousand returned to Germany within a year. Jews were among the repatriants; thus the total number of Jewish refugees who left in 1933 and remained abroad was probably between forty and forty-five thousand. After the war, researchers such as Werner Rosenstock and Herbert A. Strauss estimated the total number of Jews who fled Germany in 1933 and did not return at thirty-seven thousand. See Norman Bentwich, *The Refugees from Germany, April 1933 to December 1935* (London: George Allen & Unwin, 1936), 33; John Hope Simpson, *The Refugee Problem: Report of a Survey* (London: Oxford University Press, 1939), 140; 148; 562; Werner Rosenstock, "Jewish Emigration from Germany," *Leo Baeck Institute Year Book*, vol. 1 (1956), 377; Herbert A. Strauss, "Jewish Emigration from Germany: Nazi Policies and Jewish Responses (1)," in *Leo Baeck Institute Year Book*, vol. 25 (1980), 326.

19. Bentwich, *The Refugees from Germany*, 36.

20. The *Reichsfluchtsteuer* (Reich flight tax) came into law in December 1931 to help stabilize the German currency by preventing the export of capital abroad. Germans who emigrated—with the exception of those who had less capital than two hundred thousand Reichsmark or an annual income of less than twenty thousand Reichsmark and with the exception of those who went temporarily abroad while being employed by a German company—had to pay a tax of 25 percent of their assets. See *Reichsgesetzblatt*, 9 December 1931, 731ff.

21. Bentwich, *The Refugees from Germany*, 38. In her study of French refugee policy, Vicki Caron puts the figure at twenty-five thousand, of whom 85 percent were Jews. Vicki Caron, *Uneasy Asylum: France and the Jewish Refugee Crisis, 1933–1942* (Stanford, CA: Stanford University Press, 1999), 14.

22. Bentwich, *The Refugees from Germany*, 44ff. Even if the number of refugees who remained in Czechoslovakia remained relatively small, the democratic regime and the presence of a German-language press allowed Prague to become a center of the left-wing German political establishment in exile. See Kurt R. Grossmann, *Emigration: Geschichte der Hitler-Flüchtlinge 1933–1945* (Frankfurt: Europäische Verlagsanstalt, 1969), 34ff.

23. The standard work on Jewish refugees in the Netherlands is Bob Moore, *Refugees from Nazi Germany in the Netherlands, 1933–1940* (Dordrecht, Boston, and Lancaster: Martinus Nijhoff, 1986); important also: David Cohen, *Zwervend en Dolend: De joodsche vluchtelingen in Nederland in de jaren 1933–1940* (Haar-

lem: De Erven F. Bohn, 1955), and J. Baert, *De vluchteling in Nederland, met een overzicht van het aantal en de aard der vluchtelingencomité's* (Assen: van Gorcum, 1938).

24. See Theodor Verweyen, *Bücherverbrennungen: Eine Vorlesung aus Anlass des 65. Jahrestages der "Aktion wider den undeutschen Geist"* (Heidelberg: Universitätsverlag Winter, 2000); Ulrich Walberer, ed., *Zehnter Mai 1933: Bücherverbrennung in Deutschland und die Folgen* (Frankfurt: Fischer, 1983).

25. "Undeutsches Schrifttum auf dem Scheiterhaufen," *Völkischer Beobachter*, 12 May 1933.

26. The quote is from Heinrich Heine, *Almansor*; available on the web through the freie digitale Bibliothek (Dig.Bib) at www.digbib.org/Heinrich_Heine_1797/ Almansor. For an analysis of the use and abuse of Heine's quote, see Verweyen, *Bücherverbrennungen*, 1ff.

27. On the history of the library, see inter alia: J. B. Trapp, "Aby Warburg, His Library and the Warburg Institute," *Theoretische Geschiedenis*, vol. 13 (1986), 169–86; Tilmann von Stockhausen, *Die Kulturwissenschaftliche Bibliothek Warburg: Architektur, Einrichtung und Organisation* (Hamburg: Dölling und Galitz Verlag, 1992); Hans Michael Schäfer, *Die Kulturwissenschaftliche Bibliothek Warburg: Geschichte und Persönlichkeiten der Bibliothek Warburg mit Berücksichtigung der Bibliothekslandschaft und der Stadtsituation der Freien und Hansestadt Hamburg zu Beginn des 20. Jahrhunderts* (Berlin: Logos-Verlag, 2003).

28. Bernhard Buschendorf, "Auf dem Weg nach England: Edgar Wind und die Emigration der Bibliothek Warburg," in Michael Diers, ed., *Porträt aus Büchern: Bibliothek Warburg und Warburg Institute, Hamburg 1933 London* (Hamburg: Döling und Galitz Verlag, 1993), 94.

29. Michael Diers, "Porträt aus Büchern: Stichworte zur Einführung," in Diers, ed., *Porträt aus Büchern*, 10.

30. Buschendorf, "Auf dem Weg nach England," 96ff.

31. The Emergency Committee in Aid of Displaced German Scholars, *Report of January 1, 1934* (New York: 1934), 13f.

32. Caron, *Uneasy Asylum*, 17f.; Henry Feingold, *The Politics of Rescue* (New York: Holocaust Library, 1970), 138; Anthony Heilbut, *Exiled in Paradise* (Berkeley and Los Angeles: University of California Press, 1997), 80; Eugen Weber, *The Hollow Years* (New York: Norton, 1994), 106.

33. "Wissenschaftsemigration: Einleitung," in Claus-Dieter Krohn a.o., *Handbuch der deutschsprachigen Emigration 1933–1945* (Darmstadt: Primus Verlag, 1998), 682.

34. Bentwich, *The Refugees from Germany*, 179.

35. Haffner, *Defying Hitler: A Memoir*, 231.

36. In England, Pretzel adopted the alias Sebastian Haffner, inspired by the two lights of German culture Sebastian Bach and Wolfgang Amadeus Mozart, the composer of the Haffner Serenade.

37. Rudolf and Ika Olden, *"In Tiefen Dunkel liegt Deutschland": Von Hitler vertrieben— Ein Jahr deutsche Emigration*, ed. Charmian Brinson and Marian Mallet (Berlin: Metropol, 1994), 65.

38. Letter Hermann Kesten to Ernst Toller, 23 March 1933, in Hermann Kesten, ed., *Deutsche Literatur im Exil: Briefe Europäischer Autoren 1933–1949* (Vienna, Munich, and Basel: Kurt Desch, 1964), 28.

39. Frankenthal, *Der dreifache Fluch: Jüdin, Intellektuelle, Sozialistin*, 208.

40. Olden, *"In Tiefen Dunkel liegt Deutschland,"* 64.

41. Lawrence Darton, *Friends Committee for Refugees and Aliens, 1933–1950* (London: Friends Committee for Refugees and Aliens, 1954), 16.

42. Ibid., 18.

43. Cabinet Committee on Aliens Restrictions, Report. PRO, CAB 27/549, 10686, 3.

44. "Proposals of Jewish Community as Regards Jewish Refugees from Germany," being an appendix to a memorandum entitled "The Present Position in Regard to the Admission of Jewish Refugees from Germany to This Country," by the home secretary for the Cabinet Committee on Aliens Restrictions. PRO, CAB 27/ 549, 10686, i.

45. Cabinet Committee on Aliens Restrictions, Report. PRO, CAB 27/549, 10686, 2ff.

46. See: Amy Zahl Gottlieb, *Men of Vision: Anglo-Jewry's Aid to Victims of the Nazi Regime, 1933–1945* (London: Weidenfeld and Nicolson, 1998), esp. 7–31; Louise London, *Whitehall and the Jews, 1933–1948: British Immigration Policy and the Holocaust* (Cambridge: Cambridge University Press, 2000), 16–57; A. J. Sherman, *Island Refuge: Britain and Refugees from the Third Reich, 1933–1939* (Berkeley: University of California Press, 1973,) 19–35.

47. Letter from Clara Wolfburn Sutro to the Lord Chamberlain, 31 July 1933. PRO, FO371/16740, 106726, 363.

48. Minute by Victor Perowne, dated 7 August 1933. PRO, FO371/16740, 106726, 361v.

49. Copy of letter from the Foreign Office to Mrs Sutro, August 1933. PRO, FO 371/16740, 106726, 376.

50. The library building in Hamburg survived the war and was bought in 1993 by the city of Hamburg and restored. A beautiful shell empty of books, it is an unintended but effective memorial to the losses Germany suffered in 1933 as the result of Nazi antisemitism.

51. "Admission of Jewish Refugees from Germany to United Kingdom or Dominions." PRO, FO 371/16740, 106726, 405; 422f.

52. Letter from the British Embassy to the Foreign Office, 24 January 1934. PRO, FO 371/17698, 106726, 190f.

PLACES: A HOMELAND IN PALESTINE

1. Theodor Herzl, *The Jewish State* (New York: Dover Publications, 1988), 69; 85; 92. See too: Alex Bein, *The Jewish Question: Biography of a World Problem*, trans. Harry Zohn (New York: Herzl Press, 1990), 284–312; 669–92; Jacques Kornberg, *Theodor Herzl: From Assimilation to Zionism* (Bloomington: Indiana University Press, 1993).

2. Herzl, *The Jewish State*, 95–6.

3. First Zionist Congress, *Zionisten-Congress in Basel (August 29, 30 und 31, 1897): Officielles Protocoll* (Vienna: Verlag des Vereines Erez Israel, 1898), 118.

4. For a description of the desperate situation of Romania's Jews, see Binjamin Segel, *Rümanien und seine Juden* (Berlin: Nibelungen Verlag, 1918).

5. Max Nordau, *Zionistische Schriften* (Berlin: Jüdischer Verlag, 1923), 109ff.

6. Mark Levene, *War, Jews, and the New Europe* (Oxford: Oxford University Press, 1992), 82ff.; 143.

7. Jewish Agency for Palestine, *Book of Documents* (New York: Jewish Agency for Palestine, 1947), 1.

8. *The Jewish Chronicle* (21 December 1917), 16.

9. Norman Bentwich, *Palestine of the Jews* (London: Kegan Paul, Trench, Trubner & Co., 1919), 125; 207.

10. Arthur James Balfour, Memorandum, 11 August 1919, as quoted in J. C. Hurewitz, ed., *The Middle East and North Africa in World Politics: A Documentary Record*, 2 vols. (New Haven: Yale University Press, 1979), vol. 2, 189.

11. On the way the Balfour Declaration burdened the League of Nations, see Elmer Bendiner, *A Time for Angels: The Tragicomic History of the League of Nations* (New York: Knopf, 1975), 322.

12. The League of Nations Non-Partisan Associations, *The Covenant of the League of Nations* (New York: League of Nations Non-Partisan Association, 1923), 15

13. Great Britain, Foreign Office, *The Constitutions of All Countries*, vol. 1: *The British Empire* (London: His Majesty's Stationery Office, 1938), 539ff.

14. See Vladimir Jabotinsky, *The War and the Jew* (New York: Dial Press, 1942), 190ff. Also Barukh Ben-Anat, "The Great Moment Found a Small Generation—the Nordau Plan 1919–1920," [Hebrew] in *Zionism*, vol. 19 (1995), 80–116.

15. Arthur Ruppin, "Mass Immigration and Finance," in Arthur Ruppin, *Three Decades of Palestine: Speeches and Papers on the Upbuilding of the Jewish National Home* (Jerusalem: Schocken, 1936), 108f.

16. Ibid.

17. David Ben Gurion, *From Class to Nation* (1933), quoted in Shlomo Avineri, *The Making of Modern Zionism: The Intellectual Origins of the Jewish State* (New York: Basic Books, 1981), 200.

18. See Ezra Mendelsohn, *Zionism in the Jewish Community of Poland During the Twenties* (Tel Aviv: Tel Aviv University, 1982).

19. Oscar I. Janowsky, *People at Bay: The Jewish Problem in East-Central Europe* (London: Victor Gollancz, 1938), 177ff.

20. Stephen M. Poppel, *Zionism in Germany, 1897–1933* (Philadelphia: Jewish Publication Society of America, 1977), 92f.

21. Cabinet Committee on Aliens Restrictions, Report, 7 April 1933, PRO, CAB 27/549.

22. Herbert A. Strauss, "Jewish Emigration from Germany: Nazi Policies and Jewish Responses (II)," in *Leo Baeck Institute Year Book*, vol. 26 (1981), 343ff.

23. As quoted in Abraham Margaliot, "The Problem of Rescue of German Jewry During the Years 1933–1939; the Reasons for the Delay in Their Emigration from the Third Reich," in Yisrael Gutman and Efraim Zuroff, eds., *Rescue Attempts During the Holocaust* (Jerusalem: Yad Vashem, 1977), 255.

24. Arthur Ruppin, "Settling German Jews in Palestine," in Ruppin, *Three Decades of Palestine*, 269ff. As the English translation of Ruppin's address is imprecise at points, we corrected the translation following the official German-language minutes of the conference: Arthur Ruppin, "Referat über die sesshaftmachung deutscher Juden in Palästina," in Zentralbureau der zionistischen Organisation, London, W.C. 1, *Stenographischer Protokoll der Verhandlungen des XVIII. Zionistenkongresses und der dritten Tagung des Council der Jewish Agency für Palästina, Prag, 21. August bis 4. September 1933* (Vienna: Fiba Verlag, 1933), 185; 188; 190.

25. Johann von Leers, *14 Jahre Judenpolitik: Die Geschichte eines Rassenkampfes*, 2 vols. (Berlin: NS.-Druck und Verlag, 1933), vol. 2, 126; for a general study on the Nazi view on Zionism and Palestine, see Francis R. Nicosia, *The Third Reich and the Palestine Question* (Austin: University of Texas Press, 1985).

26. On the ha'avara agreement, see Werner Feilchenfeld, Dolf Michaelis and Ludwig Pinner, *Haavara-Transfer nach Palästina und Einwanderung deutscher Juden, 1933–1939* (Tübingen: Mohr, 1972); Edwin Black, *The Transfer Agreement: The Dramatic Story of the Pact Between the Third Reich and Jewish Palestine* (New York: Macmillan, 1984).

27. Yfaat Weiss, "The Transfer Agreement and the Boycott Movement: A Jewish Dilemma on the Eve of the Holocaust," *Yad Vashem Studies*, vol. 26 (1998), 255–63.

28. Barnet Litvinoff and Gabriel Sheffer, eds., *The Letters and Papers of Chaim Weizmann, Series A*, vol. 16 (New Brunswick, NJ: Transaction Books, 1978), 78.

29. Werner Rosenstock, "Exodus 1933–1939: A Survey of Jewish Emigration from Germany," *Leo Baeck Institute Year Book*, vol. 1 (1956), 381f.

30. Black, *The Transfer Agreement*; see also Curt D. Wormann, "German Jews in Israel: Their Cultural Situation Since 1933," *Leo Baeck Institute Year Book*, vol. 15 (1970), 73–103; and Mordechai Eliav, "German Jews Share in the Building of the National Home in Palestine and the State of Israel," *Leo Baeck Institute Year Book*, vol. 30 (1985), 255–63.

31. Arthur Holzer and Rudolf Seiden, *Das Palästina Informationsbuch* (Vienna: Ludwig Nath, 1933), 82ff.

32. Ernst L. Freud, ed., *The Letters of Sigmund Freud & Arnold Zweig*, trans. W. D. Robson-Scott (London: Hogarth Press, 1970), 56; 108; 113; 122.

33. See for example: Erich Gottgetreu, "The German Jews in Palestine," *The Menorah Journal*, vol. 24, no. 1 (January–March, 1936), 63–4; the German-language literature on the adaptation of the German Jews in Palestine is immense. See among others: Shlomo Erzel, *Neue Wurzeln: 50 Jahre Immigration deutschsprachiger Juden in Israel* (Gerlingen: Bleicher Verlag, 1983), Anne Betten and Miryam Du-nour, eds., *Wir sind die Letzten. Fragt uns aus: Gespräche mit den Emigranten der dreissiger Jahre in Israel* (Gerlingen: Bleicher Verlag, 1995); Gabriele Koppel, *Heimisch Werden: Lebenswege deutscher Juden in Pälestina* (Hamburg: Europäischer Verlagsanstalt, 2000); Joachim Schlör, *Endlich im Gelobten Land?: Deutsche Juden unterwegs in eine neue Heimat* (Berlin: Aufbau-Verlag, 2003).

34. Marvin Rosenthal, *Henriette Szold, Life and Letters* (New York: Viking Press, 1942), 246; 245.

35. Ibid., 247f.; 252.

36. Anne Bradley, "New Home: German Jews Enter Zion," *The Menorah Journal*, vol. 22, no.1 (April–June 1934), 17–8.

37. Rosenthal, *Henriette Szold*, 252.

38. Recha Freier, *Let the Children Come: The Early History of Youth Aliyah* (London: Weidenfeld and Nicolson, 1961), 9. See also Nathan Höxter, *Jüdische Pionierarbeit: Nach Kindheit und früher Jugend in Berlin ein Leben im Kibbuz Geva und neue Brücken nach Deutschland, 1916–2000* (Constance: Hartung-Gorre Verlag, 2000), 31f. See too: Brian Amkraut, *Between Home and Homeland: Youth Aliyah from Nazi Germany* (Tuscaloosa: University of Alabama Press, 2006).

39. Freier, *Let the Children Come*, 10.

40. Ibid., 10.

41. Norman Bentwich, *Jewish Youth Comes Home* (London: Victor Gollancz, 1944), 36.

42. Freier, *Let the Children Come*, 12.

43. Bentwich, *Jewish Youth Comes Home*, 37.

44. Ibid.

45. Freier, *Let the Children Come*, 29.

46. Interview with Chaim Arlosoroff in *Jüdische Rundschau*, 23 May 1933, 214f.; quoted in Herbert A. Strauss, ed., *Jewish Immigrants of the Nazi Period in the USA*, 6 vols. (Munich: K. G. Saur, 1992), vol. 4/1,138f.

47. See Rudolf Melitz, ed., *Das ist unser Weg: Junge Juden schildern Umschichtung und Hachscharah* (Berlin: Joachim Goldstein Verlag, 1937).

48. Rosenthal, *Henriette Szold,* 263; see too: Bentwich, *Jewish Youth Comes Home*, 41.

49. Freier, *Let the Children Come*, 35; Arie Eflel (né Appel), "The First Youth Group," in Meir Gottesman and Alan Sillitoe, eds., *Out of the Fire* (London: Children and Youth Aliyah Committee, 1979), 23.

50. Eflel (né Appel), "The First Youth Group," 24.

51. Arie Appel, "One Year at Ein Harod," in Gottesman and Sillitoe, eds., *Out of the Fire*, 31–3.

52. Bentwich, *Jewish Youth Comes Home*, 42.

53. Alexandra Levin, ed., *Henrietta Szold and Youth Aliyah: Family Letters, 1934–1944* (New York: Herzl Press, 1986), 6.

54. Hannah Arendt, "Some Young People Are Going Home," in Hannah Arendt, *The Jewish Writings*, ed. Jerome Kohn and Ron H. Feldman (New York: Schocken Books, 2007), 34.

55. Ibid., 35f.

56. Ibid., 36.

57. Arthur Ruppin, "The Record of Twenty-five Years," in Ruppin, *Three Decades of Palestine*, 311.

58. Arthur Ruppin, "The Future," ibid., 319.

59. See Rashid Khalidi, *The Iron Cage: The Story of the Palestinian Struggle for Statehood* (Boston: Beacon Press, 2006), 31ff.

60. Great Britain. Palestine Royal Commission, *Report* (London: His Majesty's Stationery Office, 1937), 281.

61. Mark Tessler, *A History of the Israeli-Palestinian Conflict* (Bloomington and Indianapolis: Indiana University Press, 1994), 238ff.; Ann Mosely Lesch, "The Palestine Arab Nationalist Movement Under the Mandate," in William B. Quandt, Fuad Jabber, and Ann Moseley Lesch, *The Politics of Palestinian Nationalism* (Berkeley, Los Angeles, and London: University of California Press, 1973), 17.

62. Letter by John G. Erhardt to the Secretary of State, Washington, 16 May 1936, in John Mendelsohn, ed., *The Holocaust: Selected Documents in Eighteen Volumes*, 18 vols. (New York: Garland, 1982), vol. 5, 23f.

63. Arthur Prinz, "Thesen zur Wanderungsfrage," *Der Morgen*, vol. 12, no. 9 (1936), 390ff.

64. Great Britain, Palestine Royal Commission, *Report*, ix.

65. Ibid., 372ff.
66. Ibid., 389.
67. "Minutes of the Permanent Mandates Commission of the League of Nations for the Thirty-second Session at Geneva Devoted to Palestine," in Howard M. Sachar, *The Rise of Israel*, 39 vols. (New York and London: Garland, 1987), vol. 25, 318.
68. Germany, Auswärtiges Amt, *Documents on German Foreign Policy, 1918–1945, Series D*, 15 vols. (Washington, DC: Government Printing Office, 1949–83), vol. 5, 746. Also Nicosia, *The Third Reich and the Palestine Question*, 109ff.
69. *Documents on German Foreign Policy, 1918–1945, Series D*, vol. 5, 761.
70. Barnet Litvinoff, ed., *The Letters and Papers of Chaim Weizmann Series B*, vol. 2 (New Brunswick, NJ: Transaction Books, 1984), 286.
71. As quoted in Yossi Katz, *Partner to Partition: The Jewish Agency's Partition Plan in the Mandate Era* (London and Portland, OR: Frank Cass, 1998), 64; 19f.
72. Nahum Goldmann, *The Autobiography of Nahum Goldmann: Sixty Years of Jewish Life*, trans. Helen Sebba (New York: Holt, Rinehart and Winston, 1969), 180f.

PAPERS: PASSPORTS IN A CLOSED WORLD

1. Hannah Arendt, *The Origins of Totalitarianism* (New York: Schocken Books, 2004), 341.
2. Stefan Zweig, *The World of Yesterday: An Autobiography* (New York: Viking, 1943), 308f.
3. Werner Bertelsmann, *Das Passwesen: Eine völkerrechtliche Studie* (Strassburg: Heitz, 1914), 18f., as quoted in John Torpey, *The Invention of the Passport: Surveillance, Citizenship and the State* (Cambridge: Cambridge University Press, 2000), 111. Edwin Montefiore Borchard, *The Diplomatic Protection of Citizens Abroad or the Law of International Claims* (New York: Banks Law Publishing Co., 1915), 504.
4. Egidio Reale, "Le Problème des Passeports," in Hague Academy of International Law, *Recueil des Cours/Académie de Droit International*, vol. 50 (1934), 108. For a short summary in English of Reale's work, see Egidio Reale, "The Passport Question," *Foreign Affairs*, vol. 9 (1930–1), 506–9.
5. Borchard, *The Diplomatic Protection of Citizens Abroad or the Law of International Claims*, 493.
6. Valentin Groebner, *Who Are You? Identification, Deception, and Surveillance in Early Modern Europe*, trans. Mark Kyburz and John Peck (New York: Zone Books, 2007), 171.
7. Ibid., 175ff.
8. Torpey, *The Invention of the Passport*, 21f.

9. On the innate right to travel in early modern and enlightenment international law, see Franciscus de Vitoria, "On the Indians Lately Discovered," in James Brown Scott, *The Spanish Origins of International Law: Francisco de Vitoria and His Law of Nations* (Oxford: Clarendon Press, 1934), appendix A, xxxviff.; appendix C, lxxv; Hugo Grotius, *The Law of War and Peace*, trans. Louise R. Loomis (New York: Walter J. Black, 1949), 85; Emerich de Vattel, *The Law of Nations or Principles of the Law of Nature* (Dublin: Luke White, 1787), 262ff.

10. Reale, "Le Problème des Passeports," 99ff.

11. Ibid., 105ff.

12. Leo Lucassen, "A Many-Headed Monster: The Evolution of the Passport System in the Netherlands and Germany in the Long Nineteenth Century," in Jane Caplan and John Torpey, eds., *Documenting Individual Identity: The Development of State Practices in the Modern World* (Princeton and Oxford: Princeton University Press, 2001), 248.

13. Daniel C. Turack, *The Passport in International Law* (Lexington, MA, Toronto, and London: Lexington Books, 1972), 13.

14. John Torpey, "The Great War and the Birth of the Modern Passport System," in Caplan and Torpey, eds., *Documenting Individual Identity*, 256–70; Martin Lloyd, *The Passport: The History of Man's Most Traveled Document* (Stroud: Sutton, 2003), 90ff.

15. Ernst Isay, "De la Nationalité," in Hague Academie of International Law, *Recueil des Cours/Académie de Droit International*, vol. 5 (1924), 447f.

16. Reale, "Le Problème des Passeports," 112ff.

17. See inter alia: Jeremiah W. Jenks and W. Jett Lauck, *The Immigration Problem: A Study of American Immigration Conditions and Needs,* 6th edition (New York and London: Funk & Wagnalls, 1926), 455; Claudena M. Skran, *Refugees in Inter-War Europe: The Emergence of a Regime* (Oxford: Clarendon Press, 1995), 22f.

18. See John Hope Simpson, *The Refugee Problem: Report of a Survey* (London: Royal Institute of International Affairs, 1938), 99.

19. See inter alia: Sigismund Cargas, "Die Staatenlosen," *Bibliotheca Visseriana Dissertationem Ius Internationale Illustratum*, vol. 7 (1928), 1–130; Erwin Lowenfeld, "Status of Stateless Persons," *Transactions of the Grotius Society*, vol. 27 (1941), 59–112; Paul Weis, *Nationality and Statelessness in International Law* (London: Stevens & Sons, 1956), 53ff.

20. Lassa Oppenheim, *International Law*, 4th edition, ed. Arnold D. McNair, 2 vols. (New York: Longmans, Green, 1929), vol. 1, 521. It is for this reason that the Universal Declaration of Human Rights (1948) laid down that every human being has the right to a nationality and cannot be arbitrarily deprived of his or her nationality.

21. Richard Wilson Flournoy and Manley Ottmer Hudson, *A Collection of Nation-*

ality Laws of Various Countries as Contained in Constitutions, Statutes and Treaties (New York: Oxford University Press, 1929), 511.

22. Simpson, *The Refugee Problem*, 561.

23. Flournoy and Hudson, *A Collection of Nationality Laws of Various Countries as Contained in Constitutions, Statutes and Treaties*, 569.

24. Ibid., 571.

25. Simpson, *The Refugee Problem*, 558.

26. This figure can be found in Thomas Jürgens, *Diplomatischer Schutz und Staatenlose* (Berlin: Duncker & Humblot, 1987), 84; Jürgens calculated this high number on the basis of information given in Johannes Lepsius, *Deutschland und Armenien, 1914–1918: Sammlung diplomatischer Aktenstücke* (Potsdam: Tempelverlag, 1919), lxv.

27. John Fischer Williams, "Denationalization," *British Year Book of International Law*, vol. 8 (1927), 45ff.

28. See Vincent Chetail, "Fridtjof Nansen and the International Protection of Refugees: An Introduction," *Refugee Survey Quarterly*, vol. 22 (2003), 1–6; see too: Fridtjof Nansen, *The First Crossing of Greenland*, 2 vols. (London: Longmans, 1890), and idem, *Farthest North: Being a Record of a Voyage of Exploration of the Ship "Fram" 1893–96 and of a Fifteen Months' Sleigh Journey by Dr. Nansen and Lieut. Johansen with an Appendix by Otto Sverdrup, Captain of the Fram*, 2 vols. (Westminster: Archibald Constable & Co., 1897).

29. See the description of Baker by his colleague Thomas Frank Johnson. Thomas Frank Johnson, *International Tramps: From Chaos to Permanent World Peace* (London: Hutchinson, 1938), 163.

30. League of Nations, *Official Journal* (May 1922), annex 321, 385.

31. John Hope Simpson, *Refugees: Preliminary Report of a Survey* (London: Institute of International Affairs, 1938), 99f.

32. On the Nansen passport, see "Arrangement with Regard to the Issue of Certificates of Identity to Russian Refugees, Signed at Geneva, July 5, 1922," in League of Nations, *Treaty Series*, vol. 13 (1922), 238–42; Reale, "Le Problème des Passeports," 120ff.; Jürgens, *Diplomatischer Schutz und Staatenlose*, 87ff.; Otto Hieronymi, "The Nansen Passport: A Tool of Freedom of Movement and Protection," *Refugee Survey Quarterly*, vol. 22 (2003), 36–47.

33. Johnson, *International Tramps*, 261f.

34. On the importance of these quasi-consular services, see J. L. Rubinstein, "The Refugee Problem," *International Affairs (Royal Institute of International Affairs 1931–1939)*, vol. 15 (1936), 724f.

35. League of Nations, Organisation for Communications and Transit, *Passport Conference Held at Geneva, May 12th to 18th, 1926, Minutes of the Plenary Meetings of the Conference* (Geneva: League of Nations, 1926), 75.

36. Simpson, *The Refugee Problem*, 121. See also Ernest Kohn Bramstedt, *Dictator-*

ship and Political Police: The Technique of Control by Fear (London: Routledge, 2003), 51ff.

37. League of Nations, *Third General Conference on Communications and Transit, Geneva, August 23rd to September 2nd, 1927,* 3 vols. (Geneva: League of Nations, 1927), vol. 1, 25f.; vol. 3, 11ff.

38. Simpson, *The Refugee Problem,* 121f.

39. League of Nations, *Third General Conference on Communications and Transit,* vol. 3, 60.

40. Louise Holborn, *Refugees: A Problem of Our Times* (Metuchen, NJ: Scarecrow Press, 1975), 10.

41. Dorothy Thompson, *Refugees: Anarchy or Organization?* (New York: Random House, 1938), 28.

42. "Convention Relating to the International Status of Refugees, Signed at Geneva, October 28th, 1933," League of Nations, *Treaty Series,* vol. 159 (1933), 205.

43. Minute by M. H. Huxley, 3 May 1933. PRO, FO 371/16724.

44. Letter from Orme Sargent to Douglas Hacking, 20 May 1933. PRO, FO 371/16724.

45. Letter from Arthur Henderson to Sir John Simon, 13 May 1933. PRO, FO 371/16724, 43.

46. Letter from Maxwell Garnett to Sir John Simon, 23 May 1933. PRO, FO 371/16724, 84.

47. Letter from Walter Benjamin to Gershom Scholem, 20 March 1933, in Walter Benjamin, *The Correspondence of Walter Benjamin and Gershom Scholem,* ed. Gershom Scholem, trans. Gary Smith and André Lefevere (New York: Schocken, 1989), 34f.

48. Letter from Walter Benjamin to Gershom Scholem, 1 May 1933, ibid., 47.

49. Letter from Gershom Scholem to Walter Benjamin, 23 May 1933, ibid., 49.

50. Letter from Walter Benjamin to Gershom Scholem, 31 July 1933, ibid., 69.

51. See Hans Georg Lehmann, "Acht und Ächtung politischer Gegner im Dritten Reich: Die Ausbürgerung deutscher Emigranten 1933–1945," in Michael Hepp, ed., *Die Ausbürgerung deutscher Staatsangehöriger 1933–1945 nach dem im Reichsanzeiger veröffentlichten Listen,* 3 vols. (Munich: K. G. Saur, 1985), vol. 1, xiff.; also Martin Dean, "The Development and Implementation of Nazi Denaturalization and Confiscation Policy up to the Eleventh Decree to the Reich Citizenship Law, *Holocaust and Genocide Studies,* vol. 16 (2002), 217ff.

52. "Statement of James G. McDonald, High Commissioner for Refugees (Jewish and other) Coming from Germany, Made at the Second Session of the Governing Body at London, May 2, 1934." PRO, FO 371/17700, 151.

53. Minute by Victor Perowne, 6 September 1933. PRO, FO 371/16757, 342f.

54. Minute by Victor Perowne, 18 September 1933. PRO, FO 371/16757, 9.

55. Note from the French Embassy in London to British Foreign Office, 14 September 1933. PRO, FO 371/16757, 13.

56. Vicki Caron, *Uneasy Asylum: France and the Jewish Refugee Crisis, 1933–1942* (Stanford, CA: Stanford University Press, 1999), 13ff., 64ff.; Greg Burgess, "France and the German Refugee Crisis of 1933," *French History*, vol. 16 (2002), 211ff.

57. Norman Bentwich, *My 77 Years: An Account of My Life and Times, 1883–1960* (Philadelphia: Jewish Publication Society of America, 1961), 122ff.

58. See David Cohen, *Zwervend en Dolend: De Joodse Vluchtelingen in Nederland in de Jaren 1933–1940* (Haarlem: Bohn, 1955), 31f.

59. League of Nations, *Official Journal, Special Supplement 115: Records of the Fourteenth Ordinary Session of the Assembly, Plenary Meetings, Text of the Debates* (Geneva: 1933), 48.

60. League of Nations, *Official Journal, Special Supplement 117: Records of the Fourteenth Ordinary Session of the Assembly, Minutes of the Second Committee (Technical Organisations)* (Geneva: 1933), 22f.

61. Telegrams from William George Ormsby-Gore to the Foreign Office, 3 October, 7 October, and 9 October 1933. PRO, FO 371/16757, 70f.; 138f.; 174.

62. League of Nations, *Official Journal, Special Supplement 117*, 27.

63. Ibid., 47f.

64. For more on McDonald and his views, see: James G. McDonald, *German "Atrocities" and International Law* (Chicago: Germanistic Society, 1914); Claudene M. Skran, "Profiles of the First Two High Commissioners," *Journal of Refugee Studies*, vol. 1 (1988), 289f.

65. Norman Bentwich, *The Refugees from Germany: April 1935 to December 1936* (London: Allen and Unwin, 1936), 72ff.; John I. Knudson, *A History of the League of Nations* (Atlanta: Turner E. Smith & Co., 1938), 258.

66. Bentwich, *My 77 Years*, 131.

67. See inter alia: Reale, "Le Problème des Passeports," 158f.; Letter from Lord Cecil to Sir John Simon, 8 December 1933. PRO, FO 371/17698; Letter from the Under Secretary of State, Home Office, to Under Secretary of State, Foreign Office, 26 January 1934. PRO, FO 371/17689, 174; "Travel Documents for refugees from Germany Who Do Not Possess National Papers." PRO, FO 371/17689; S. A. Heald, "Report on the Meeting of the Permanent Committee of the Governing Body of the High Commission for Refugees (Jewish and Other) Coming from Germany," 30 January 1934. PRO, FO 371/176699, 243; also Bentwich, *The Refugees from Germany*, 92; Letter from Norman Bentwich to Under Secretary of State, Foreign Office, 6 February 1934. PRO, FO 371/17698, 225.

68. "Provisional Arrangement Concerning the Status of Refugees Coming from Germany. Signed at Geneva, July 4th, 1936," in League of Nations, *Treaty Series*, vol. 171 (1936–7), 77.

69. "Identity Certificate for Refugees Coming from Germany," ibid., 87.

70. Rudolf and Ika Olden. *In Tiefen Dunkel liegt Deutschland*, preface Lion Feuchtwanger, ed. Charmian Brinson and Marian Mallet (Berlin: Metropol, 1994), 123ff. This text was written in 1934, but published sixty years later.

71. James G. McDonald, "Letter of Resignation," in *The Christian Century*, vol. 53 (15 January 1936), 101.

PROBLEMS: MINORITY RIGHTS AND JEWS AS A MINORITY

1. The causal connection between minority politics and refugees was well recognized in the 1930s. See for example: John Hope Simson, *The Refugee Problem: Report of a Survey* (London: Royal Institute of International Affairs, 1938), 522ff.

2. See André Mandelstam, "La Protection des Minorités," in Hague Academy of International Law, *Recueil des Cours / Académie de Droit International*, vol. 1 (1923), 365–519; Lucy Philip Mair, *The Protection of Minorities: The Working and Scope of the Minorities Treaties Under the League of Nations* (London: Christophers, 1928); Carlile Aylmer Macartney, *National States and National Minorities* (London: Oxford University Press, 1934); Jennifer Jackson Preece, *National Minorities and the European Nation-States System* (Oxford: Clarendon Press, 1998).

3. See Georg Landauer, *Das geltende jüdische Minderheitenrecht mit besonderer Berücksichtegung Osteuropas* (Leipizg and Berlin: Teubner, 1924); Oscar J. Janowsky, *The Jews and Minority Rights, 1898–1919* (New York: Columbia University Press, 1933); Carole Fink, *Defending the Rights of Others: The Great Powers, the Jews, and International Minority Protection, 1878–1938* (Cambridge and New York: Cambridge University Press, 2004).

4. As quoted in Janowsky, *The Jews and Minority Rights*, 268.

5. For the complete text of the document, see Jacob Robinson a.o., *Were the Minorities Treaties a Failure?* (New York: Institute of Jewish Affairs, 1943), 324.

6. As quoted in Macartney, *National States and National Minorities*, 233.

7. Robinson, *Were the Minorities Treaties a Failure?*, 160.

8. Ibid., 161.

9. Each of these countries had significant minority populations. According to an article by Oscar I. Janowsky published in *Survey Graphic*, 8 percent of the population of Czechoslovakia was comprised of Germans, Jews, and Magyars; 28 percent of Romania's population were Magyars, Jews, Germans, Ukrainians, Bulgarians, Turks, and Russians; somewhere between 8 and 13 percent of the population of Greece were Turks, Bulgarian-Macedonians, Romanians, Albanians, and Jews; and more than 17 percent of the population of Yugoslavia were Germans, Bulgarian-Macedonians, Magyars, Albanians, Romanians, and Czechoslovaks. Oscar I. Janowsky, "Minorities: Pawns of Power," *Survey Graphic*, vol. 28, no. 2 (February 1939), 77.

10. In *The Origins of Totalitarianism*, Hannah Arendt has argued that these treaties were as heinous an idea as Wilson's call for nation states. The treaties both reflected and shaped a political structure that undermined the rights of minorities. Hannah Arendt, *The Origins of Totalitarianism* (New York: World Publishing, 1972), 275ff.

11. In Bulgaria, 16 percent of the population was comprised of Turks, Gypsies, and Romanians; more than 17 percent of the population of Hungary were Germans, Jews, and Slovaks. Janowsky, "Minorities: Pawns of Power," 77.

12. World Jewish Congress, *Unity in Dispersion: A History of the World Jewish Congress* (New York: World Jewish Congress, 1945), 31.

13. Robinson, *Were the Minorities Treaties a Failure?*, 248.

14. For an incisive portrait of the German Jew as an assimilationist, see Nahum Goldmann, *The Autobiography of Nahum Goldmann: Sixty Years of Jewish Life*, trans. Helen Sabba (New York: Holt, Rinehart and Winston, 1969), 59f.

15. Ibid., 125.

16. On the Centralverein, see Avraham Barkai, *"Wehr Dich": Der Centralverein deutscher Staatsbürger jüdischen Glaubens (C.V.) 1893–1938* (Munich: Beck, 2002).

17. *Protokoll der jüdischen Welt-Konferenz*, Geneva, 14–17 August 1932 (Berlin: Executiv-Komite für die Vorbereitung des jüdischen Welt-Kongresses, 1932), 64.

18. Letter of von Neurath to Frick, 21 April 1933, and letter of Frick to von Neurath, 22 May 1933, as quoted in Helmut Pieper, *Die Minderheitenfrage und das Deutsche Reich 1919–1933/34* (Frankfurt: Alfred Metzner Verlag, 1974), 296–7.

19. Max Hildebert Boehm, "Minderheiten, Judenfrage und das neue Deutschland," *Der Ring*, vol. 6 (1933), issue 17, 271.

20. Boehm's formulation was also endorsed by Ferdinand von Uexküll-Güldenband, a Baltic-German and the preeminent German scholar of minority issues and publisher of *Nation und Staat*, a prestigious journal about minority politics. See Ferdinand von Uexküll-Güldenband, "Deutschlands volkspolitische Programm," *Nation und Staat*, vol. 6 (1932–3), 539ff.

21. League of Nations, *Official Journal*, vol. 14, no. 7, part 1 (1933), 930; on the plebiscite and partition of Upper Silesia, see Sir Robert Donald, *The Polish Corridor and the Consequences* (London: Thornton Butterworth, 1929); J. Weinstein, *Upper Silesia: A Country of Contrasts* (Paris: Gebethner & Wolff, 1931); William Harbutt Dawson, *Germany Under the Treaty* (London: Allen & Unwin, 1933); Julius Stone, *Regional Guarantees of Minority Rights: A Study of Minorities Procedures in Upper Silesia* (New York: Macmillan, 1933); Georges Kaeckenbeeck, *The International Experiment of Upper Silesia: A Study in the Working of the Upper Silesia Settlement, 1922–1937* (London: Oxford University Press, 1942).

22. Max Beer, *The League on Trial: A Journey to Geneva* (Boston and New York: Houghton Mifflin, 1933), 360.

23. On the Bernheim case, see: Greg Burgess, *The Human Rights Dilemma in Anti-Nazi Protest: The Bernheim Petition, Minorities Protection, and the 1933 Session of the League of Nations,* CERC Working Paper Series, no. 2 (Melbourne: Contemporary Europe Research Centre, 2002); Philipp Graf, *Die Bernheim-Petition 1933* (Göttingen: Vandenhoeck & Ruprecht, 2008).

24. League of Nations, *Official Journal*, vol. 14, no. 7, part 1 (1933), 933.

25. Pieper, *Die Minderheitenfrage und das Deutsche Reich*, 299f.

26. League of Nations, *Official Journal*, vol. 14, no. 7, part 1 (1933), 833.

27. Ibid., 839.

28. See: Max Kohler, *The United States and German Jewish Persecutions: Precedents for Popular and Governmental Action* (Cincinnati: B'nai B'rith Executive Committee, 1934), 34f; J. W. Garner, "The Internationally Binding Force of Unilateral Oral Declarations," *American Journal of International Law*, vol. 27 (July 1933), 493–7.

29. League of Nations, *Official Journal*, vol. 14, no. 7, part 1 (1933), 840 ff.

30. Ibid., 843.

31. Alfred Wiener, "Zwischen Himmel und Erde," *Centralverein-Zeitung*, vol. 12, no. 22 (1 June 1933), 1.

32. League of Nations, *Official Journal*, vol. 14, no. 7, part 1 (1933), 934–5; see too 845f.

33. Pieper, *Die Minderheitenfrage und das Deutsche Reich*, 305.

34. International Federation of League of Nations Societies, *XVIIth Plenary Congress, Montreux, 3rd–7th June 1933: Proceedings and Resolutions* (Brussels and Geneva: General Secretariat, 1933), 36ff.; 118.

35. Ibid., 38.

36. *Protocole de la IIme Conférence Juive Mondiale, Genève, 5–8 Septembre 1933* (Genève: La Comité Exécutif du Congrès Juif Mondial, 1933), 57–8.

37. Ibid., 32f.

38. See Sabine Bamberger-Stemmann, *Der europäische Nationalitäten-kongress 1925 bis 1938: Nationale Minderheiten zwischen Lobbyistentum und Grossmachtinteressen* (Marburg: Verlag Herder-Institut, 2000).

39. Quoted ibid., 275.

40. Ibid., 278–9; see also Hannah Arendt, "Concerning Minorities," *Contemporary Jewish Record*, vol. 7 (1944), 359f.

41. "Minutes of the Conference of Ministers on September 12, 1933, at 4:30 p.m.," Germany, Auswärtiges Amt, *Documents on German Foreign Policy 1918–1945, Series C*, 7 vols. (Washington, DC: Government Printing Office, 1957–66), vol. 1, 796.

42. Joseph Goebbels, *Die Tagebücher von Joseph Goebbels*, ed. Elke Fröhlich, part 1:

Aufzeichnungen 1923–1941, 9 vols. (Munich: K. G. Saur, 1997–2006), vol. 2/III, 276f.

43. "Minutes of a Conference of Heads of Departments, Held at the Reich Chancellery, on Tuesday, September 26, 1933, at 4:15 p.m.," *Documents on German Foreign Policy 1918–1945, Series C*, vol. 1, 796.

44. "Dr Goebbels on National Socialist Germany and Her Contribution Toward World Peace," German League of Nations Union News Service. PRO, FO 371/16728.

45. Henri Bérenger, as quoted in Irene Harand, *Sein Kampf: Antwort an Hitler* (Vienna: Selbstverlag Irene Harand, 1935), 39.

46. Goebbels, *Die Tagebücher von Joseph Goebbels*, part 1, vol. 2/III, 281.

47. League of Nations, *Official Journal, Special Supplement 115: Records of the Fourteenth Ordinary Session of the Assembly, Plenary Meetings, Text of the Debates* (Geneva: 1933), 44; 48; 50f.; 60f.

48. League of Nations, *Official Journal, Special Supplement 120: Records of the Fourteenth Ordinary Session of the Assembly, Minutes of the Sixth Committee* (Political Questions) (Geneva: 1933), 23–4.

49. Ibid., 28; 34; 35; 39.

50. Ibid., 42.

51. Ibid., 49–50.

52. League of Nations, *Official Journal, Special Supplement 115*, 88.

53. A borderland territory, the Saar had belonged to both Germany and France. Most of the 828,000 inhabitants were German, but after World War I the French claimed the territory as compensation for the destruction of its mines and industries. A compromise struck in 1919 determined that the Saar would be an autonomous area under the sovereignty of the League of Nations for fifteen years, while France got its coalfield. See Sarah Wambaugh, *The Saar Plebiscite: With a Collection of Official Documents* (Cambridge: Harvard University Press, 1940).

54. Ibid., 150; also Schlomo Rülf, *Ströme im dürren Land: Erinnerungen* (Stuttgart: Deutsche Verlags-Anstalt, 1964), 94ff.

55. Document 25, *Dokumentation zur Geschichte der jüdischen Bevölkerung in Rheinland-Pfalz und im Saarland von 1800 bis 1945*, 9 vols. (Koblenz: Selbstverlag der Landesarchivverwaltung Rheinland-Pfalz, 1965–82), vol. 6, 329ff. See also Document 31, ibid., vol. 6, 358f.

56. Document 34, ibid., vol. 6, 370ff.

57. Document 38, ibid., vol. 6, 377f.

58. Goldmann, *Autobiography of Nahum Goldmann*, 155ff.

59. Document 47, *Dokumentation zur Geschichte der jüdischen Bevölkerung in Rheinland-Pfalz und im Saarland von 1800 bis 1945*, vol. 6, 387.

60. Hans-Walter Herrmann, "Das Schicksal der Juden im Saarland 1920 bis 1945," Document 31, ibid., vol. 6, 278. On 22 October 1940 all remaining

Jews in Saarland—except 14 who were either married to a non-Jew or in a hospital—were deported to the Gurs transit camp in Vichy France. Of these deportees, 134 died in Gurs; the rest began a journey that led, via other camps, to Auschwitz. Twelve survived.

61. Simpson, *The Refugee Problem: Report of a Survey*, 155ff.

1933–1938: THE SCREWS TIGHTEN

1. As we have seen, the ha'avara agreement suffered from significant inflation. Herbert A. Strauss, "Jewish Emigration from Germany: Nazi Policies and Jewish Responses (2)," *Leo Baeck Institute Year Book*, vol. 26 (1981), 351.

2. Werner Rosenstock, "Jewish Emigration from Germany," *Leo Baeck Institute Year Book*, vol. 1 (1956), 381.

3. Herbert A. Strauss, "Jewish Emigration from Germany: Nazi Policies and Jewish Responses (1)," *Leo Baeck Institute Year Book*, vol. 25 (1980), 343f.

4. Strauss, "Jewish Emigration from Germany: Nazi Policies and Jewish Responses (2)," 351.

5. As quoted in *The Yellow Spot—The Outlawing of Half a Million Human Beings: A Collection of Facts and Documents Relating to Three Years' Persecution of German Jews, Derived Chiefly from National Socialist Sources, Very Carefully Assembled by a Group of Investigators* (London: Victor Gollancz, 1936), 48f.

6. As quoted ibid., 175.

7. "The Central-Verein Balance Sheet, 1935," Lucy S. Dawidowicz, ed., *A Holocaust Reader* (New York: Behrman House, 1976), 164f.

8. Werner Rosenstock, "Jewish Emigration from Germany," *Leo Baeck Institute Year Book*, vol. 1 (1956), 381.

9. Ibid., 382.

10. Mark Wischnitzer, *To Dwell in Safety: The Story of Jewish Migration Since 1800* (Philadelphia: Jewish Publication Society of America, 1948), 187f. Little has been written about German Jews who fled to South Africa. Strassler Center doctoral candidate Lotte Stone is currently completing a much-needed dissertation, "Seeking Asylum: Jewish Refugees to South Africa, 1930–1948."

11. Arieh Tartakower and Kurt R. Grossmann, *The Jewish Refugee* (New York: Institute of Jewish Affairs, 1944), 314ff.

12. "Vermerk über die Besprechung am 29. September 1936," as printed in Brita Eckert, ed., *Die jüdische Emigration aus Deutschland 1933–1941: Die Geschichte einer Austreibung* (Frankfurt: Büchhandler-Vereinigung, 1985), 210.

13. On the political prehistory of the Anschluss, see Alfred D. Low, *The Anschluss Movement, 1931–1938, and the Great Powers* (Boulder, CO: East European Monographs/New York: Columbia University Press, 1985). On the events of

March 1938, see Gordon Brook-Shepherd, *Anschluss: The Rape of Austria* (London: Macmillan, 1963).

14. For a contemporary perspective, see Gerhard Schacher, *Central Europe and the Western World* (London: George Allen & Unwin, 1936), 142ff.

15. See Herbert Rosenkranz, "The Anschluss and the Tragedy of Austrian Jewry 1938–1945," in Josef Frankel, ed., *The Jews of Austria: Essays on Their Life, History, and Destruction* (London: Vallentine Mitchell, 1967), 479–546.

PEOPLE: OFFICIALS AND THEIR SOLUTIONS

1. On the events of March 1938, see Gordon Brook-Shepherd, *Anschluss: The Rape of Austria* (London: Macmillan, 1963) and Herbert Rosenkranz, "The Anschluss and the Tragedy of Austrian Jewry 1938–1945," in Josef Frankel, ed., *The Jews of Austria: Essays on Their Life, History, and Destruction* (London: Vallentine Mitchell, 1967), 479–546. For a contemporary account, see George Eric Rowe Gedye, *The Fallen Bastions* (London: Victor Gollancz, 1939).

2. Norman Bentwich, *My 77 Years: An Account of My Life and Times, 1883–1960* (Philadelphia: Jewish Publication Society of America, 1961), 145.

3. Dorothy Thompson, "Refugees: A World Problem," *Foreign Affairs*, vol. 16 (1938), 377.

4. Ibid., 382.

5. Ibid., 387.

6. Quoted in Henry L. Feingold, *The Politics of Rescue: The Roosevelt Administration and the Holocaust, 1933–1945* (New Brunswick, NJ: Rutgers University Press, 1970), 23.

7. Minute dated 25 March 1938 by Roger Makins. PRO, FO 371/22321.

8. "Austrian Refugees. Revised Record of Inter-Departmental Meeting," 28 March 1938. PRO, FO 371/22321.

9. For general discussions on the Evian conference and its aftermath, see inter alia: Shalom Adler-Rudel, "The Evian Conference on the Refugee Question," *Leo Baeck Institute Year Book*, vol. 13 (1968), 235–73; Feingold, *The Politics of Rescue*; Shlomo Z. Katz, "Public Opinion in Western Europe and the Evian Conference," *Yad Vashem Studies*, vol. 9 (1973), 105–32.

10. William Shirer, *Berlin Diary: The Journal of a Foreign Correspondent 1934–1941* (New York: Knopf, 1941), 119f.

11. Quoted in Adler-Rudel, "The Evian Conference on the Refugee Question," 249.

12. Quoted ibid.

13. On the massacres, see Ian Bell, *The Dominican Republic* (Boulder, CO: West-

view Press, 1981), 67f., and Albert C. Hicks, *Blood in the Streets: The Life and Rule of Trujillo* (New York: Creative Age Press, 1946), viff.; 98ff.

14. On the causal relationship between the massacres and Trujillo's offer and his financial expectations, see Hicks, *Blood in the Streets*, 166ff.; on Trujillo's attempt to "whiten" the Dominican population see Feingold, *The Politics of Rescue*, 112; 121.

15. Norman Bentwich, *Wanderer Between Two Worlds* (London: Kegan Paul, Trench, Trubner & Co., 1941), 281.

16. On the Inter-Governmental Committee, see Tommie Sjöberg, *The Powers and the Persecuted: The Refugee Problem and the Intergovernmental Committee on Refugees (IGCR), 1938–1947* (Lund: Lund University Press, 1991); Ralph Weingarten, *Die Hilfeleistung der westlichen Welt bei der Endlösung der deutschen Judenfrage: Das "Intergovernmental Committee on Political Refugees" (IGC) 1938–1939* (Bern, Frankfurt, and Las Vegas: Peter Lang, 1981).

17. Report by Myron C. Taylor to Sumner Welles on the Evian conference, 20 July, 1938, in John Mendelsohn, *The Holocaust: Selected Documents in Eighteen Volumes* (New York and London: Garland, 1982), vol. 5, 259ff.

18. Stenographic notes of the first meeting of the Inter-Governmental Committee to continue and develop the work of the Evian meeting, Foreign Office, London, 3 August 1938. PRO, FO 371/22573—106569.

19. Frank Shapiro, *Haven in Africa* (Jerusalem: Gefen, 2002), 5.

20. Magnus Brechtken, *"Madagascar für die Juden": Antisemitische Idee und politische Praxis 1885–1945* (Munich: Oldenbourg, Verlag 1997), 16; 34f.; 61.

21. Alfred Rosenberg, "Wohin mit den Juden?," *Völkischer Beobachter*, 8 July 1938.

22. Letter from Robert Benson & Co., London, to Reich Economics Minister Schacht, 24 August 1936, in Herbert Arthur Strauss, ed., *Jewish Immigrants of the Nazi Period in the U.S.A.*, 6 vols. (Munich, New York, London, and Paris: K. G. Saur, 1978–92), vol. 4: Norbert Kampe, ed., *Jewish Emigration from Germany: A Documentary History*, part 2, 323.

23. Mark Wischnitzer, "Jewish Emigration from Germany, 1933–1938," *Jewish Social Studies*, vol. 2 (1940), 43; also Mark Wischnitzer, *To Dwell in Safety* (Philadelphia: Jewish Publication Society of America, 1948), 191.

24. See Peter Berger, "The Gildemeester Organization for Assistance to Emigrants and the Expulsion of Jews from Vienna, 1938–1942," in Terry Gourvish, ed., *Business and Politics in Europe, 1900–1970: Essays in Honour of Alice Teichova* (Cambridge: Cambridge University Press, 2003), 215–45; Theodor Venus and Alexandra-Eileen Wenck, *Die Entziehung jüdischen Vermögens im Rahmen der Aktion Gildemeester: Eine empirische Studie über Organisation, Form und Wandel von "Arisierung" und jüdischer Auswanderung in Österreich 1938–1941* (Vienna and Munich: Oldenbourg Verlag, 2004).

25. Berger, "The Gildemeester Organization," 226–30.
26. The November pogrom commands an extensive literature. See among others: Lionel Kochan, *Pogrom: 10 November 1938* (London: Andre Deutsch, 1957); Rita Thalmann and Emmanuel Feinemann, *Crystal Night: 9–10 November 1938*, trans. Gilles Cremonesi (London: Thames & Hudson, 1974); Hans-Jürgen Dörscher, *"Reichskristallnacht": Die Novemberpogrome 1938* (Frankfurt and Berlin: Ullstein, 1988); Anthony Read and David Fisher, *Kristallnacht: Unleashing the Holocaust* (London: Michael Joseph, 1989).
27. Nuremberg Document 1816-PS, stenographic Record of a Conference with Göring, 12 November 1938, on the Jewish Question, International Military Tribunal, *Trial of the Major War Criminals Before the International Military Tribunal*, 41 vols. (Nuremberg: Secretariat of the International Military Tribunal, 1947–9), vol. 28, 532f.
28. Memorandum by Hjalmar Schacht, 16 January 1939, document 661 in Germany, Auswärtiges Amt, *Documents on German Foreign Policy, Series D*, 12 vols. (Washington, DC: Government Printing Office, 1949–62), vol. 5, 921–5.
29. Letter from Legationsrat Hinrichs to State Secretary von Weizsäcker, 7 January 1939, in Rolf Vogel, *Ein Stempel hat gefehlt: Dokumente zur Emigration deutscher Juden* (Munich and Zürich: Droemer Knaur, 1977), 225.
30. Memorandum by Hjalmar Schacht, 16 January 1939, *Documents on German Foreign Policy, Series D.*, vol. 5, 922.
31. The most likely author of the idea was John Wilfred Harvey, professor of philosophy at Leeds University, who proposed Birobidzhan in a letter to the editor of the *Times* of London. See "The Settlement of Refugees: Searching the Atlas," *Times*, 18 November 1938.
32. Letter from Gordon Vereker to Lord Halifax, 21 January 1939. PRO, FO 371/24097.
33. Ibid.
34. Note of Conversation Between Lord Winterton and the Russian Ambassador on 12 May 1939. PRO, FO 371/24097—106726.
35. Ibid.
36. On Wohlthat, see Vogel, *Ein Stempel hat gefehlt*, 82ff.
37. Helmuth Wohlthat, interview with Rolf Vogel, Düsseldorf, 1974, ibid., 244ff.
38. George Rublee's letter to Helmuth Wohlthat with Rublee's memorandum "The Emigration of Jews from Germany," 1 February 1939, in Strauss, *Jewish Immigrants of the Nazi Period in the U.S.A.*, vol. 4, part 2, 394–7.
39. In his speech to the Greater German Reichstag on 30 January 1939, Hitler made it clear that he did not approve of any Jewish assets leaving Germany. Jews had immigrated into Germany with "little more than infectious political and sanitary diseases," and they were to leave empty-handed. See Max

Domarus, *Hitler: Speeches and Proclamations, 1932–1945*, 4 vols. (Wauconda, IL: Bolchazy-Carducci, 1990–7), vol. 3, 1447.

40. Letter from German Ambassador Herbert von Dirksen to the German Foreign Office, 18 February 1939, in Germany, Auswärtiges Amt, *Documents on German Foreign Policy, Series D*, vol. 5, 937.

41. Minutes of a meeting of heads of German government departments concerned with Jewish emigration, 3 March 1939, in Strauss, *Jewish Immigrants of the Nazi Period in the U.S.A.*, vol. 4, part 2, 399f.

42. "Conversations Between Mr R.T. Pell and Dr Wohlthat." PRO, FO 371/24083.

43. Ibid., 14.

44. See: Feingold, *The Politics of Rescue*, 58–89; Naomi Shepherd, *A Refuge from Darkness: Wilfred Israel and the Rescue of the Jews* (New York: Pantheon Books, 1984), 156–63; A. Joshua Sherman, *Island Refuge: Britain and Refugees from the Third Reich, 1933–1939* (Berkeley and Los Angeles: University of California Press, 1973), 248.

45. Dorothy Thompson, "Financing by Ransom Money," *Let the Record Speak* (Boston: Houghton Mifflin, 1939), 273.

46. Dorothy Thompson, "Escape in a Frozen World," *Survey Graphic*, vol. 28 (1939), 168.

47. "Memorandum by Sir Herbert Emerson of a Meeting with Mr Wohlthat. 7 June 1939." PRO, FO 371/24084 –106569, 1–2; 7.

48. On Linton Wells, see his autobiography: Linton Wells, *Blood on the Moon* (Boston and New York: Houghton Mifflin, 1937).

49. Secret Memorandum by Sir Herbert Emerson, 7 November 1939. PRO, FO 371/24079, esp. 4–5. See too the Memorandum (strictly confidential) by Linton Wells, n.d., PRO, FO 371/24079—106569.

50. See letter from W. H. Ingrams to Sir Bernard Reilly, 15 April 1939, and letter from Sir Bernard Reilly to Sir John Shuckburgh, 25 April 1939. PRO, FO 371/24091.

51. "Summary of Information Received from Colonial Governments Regarding the Number of Refugees from Germany and Other European Countries." PRO, FO 371/24090.

52. Letter from Sir John Maybin to Malcolm MacDonald, 25 March 1939. PRO, FO 371/24091.

53. See Great Britain, Secretary of State for the Colonies, *Report of the British Guiana Refugee Commission to the Advisory Committee on Political Refugees Appointed by the President of the United States of America* (London: His Majesty's Stationery Office, 1939).

54. Joseph A. Rosen, "Problem of Large Scale Settlement of Refugees from Middle

European Countries in British Guiana," in *Report of the British Guiana Refugee*. PRO, FO 371/24089—106636, 2.

55. Cabinet Committee on the Refugee Problem, "Draft Conclusions of the Fourth Meeting of the Committee Held in the Home Secretary's Room, Home Office, S.W.1, on Tuesday, 9th May, 1939, at 11.30 a.m." PRO, FO 371/24090—106657, 2.

56. Dana G. Munro, ed., *Refugee Settlement in the Dominican Republic: A Survey Conducted Under the Auspices of the Brookings Institution* (Washington, DC: Brookings Institution, 1942). The publication of Archibald Grenfell Price's *White Settlers in the Tropics* (New York: American Geographic Society, 1939) undermined the idea that mass settlement of Jewish refugees in tropical areas provided a long-term solution to the refugee problem. Price maintained that white settlements in the tropics led to miscegenation and "negroidation" of white settlers, another form of the racism expressed by Maybin.

57. Marie Syrkin, "Rebirth in San Domingo?," *Jewish Frontier* (February 1941), 10f.

58. Ibid., 10.

59. Ibid.

60. Ibid., 11.

61. Heather Morgan, "Letter from Sosúa: Refugees and Kin Cling to an Island of Saved Souls," *The Forward* (13 December 2002). For a history of the Sosúa settlement, see Josef-David Ichen, *Sosúa: Una Colonia Hebrea en la República Dominicana* (Santiago: Universidad Católica Madre y Maestra, 1980) and Marion Kaplan, *Dominican Haven: The Jewish Refugee Settlement in Sosúa, 1940–1945* (New York: Museum of Jewish Heritage, 2008). For a description of Jewish life in Sosúa in the late 1940s, see Lore Segal, *Other People's Houses* (New York: Harcourt, Brace & World, 1964), 189ff.

PLACES: A LIFE ANYWHERE

1. Robert Rosner, oral history conducted by Debórah Dwork, Vienna, 3 July 1990, transcript, 14ff. N.B.: The English scientist who became Rosner's foster parent in Manchester was Dr Thomas Simm Littler, the founder of audiology in Britain.

2. Marianne Marco-Braun, oral history with Debórah Dwork, Wimbledon, 9 May 1987, 4.

3. Irene Butter-Hasenberg, oral history conducted by Debórah Dwork, Ann Arbor, 10 October 1986, transcript, 1.

4. Marianne Marco-Braun, transcript, 1ff.

5. Lore Gang-Saalheimer, oral history conducted by Debórah Dwork, Cardiff, 22 July 1985, transcript, 6f.

6. Mariánka May-Zadikow, oral history conducted by Debórah Dwork, New Paltz, 8–9 November 2000, transcript, 35f.

7. See George L. Mosse, *Germans and Jews: The Right, the Left, and the Search for a "Third Force" in Pre-Nazi Germany* (New York: Howard Fertig, 1970), 77ff. On the youth movements, see: Chaim Schatzker, "The Jewish Youth Movement in Germany in the Holocaust Period (I). Youth in Confrontation with a New Reality," *Leo Baeck Institute Year Book*, vol. 32 (London: Secker & Warburg, 1987), 157–82; Chaim Schatzker, "The Jewish Youth Movement in Germany in the Holocaust Period (II). The Relations Between the Youth Movement and Hechaluz," *Leo Baeck Institute Year Book*, vol. 33 (London: Secker & Warburg, 1988), 301–25.

8. Arthur Israelowitz, "Zum Weg des Haschomer Hazair," *Informationsblatt Hechalutz*, vol. 4, no. 37, 15, as quoted in Schatzker, "The Jewish Youth Movement in Germany in the Holocaust Period (II)," 305.

9. Georg Pape, "Die permanente Synthese," *Haboneh. Älterrenblatt der jüdischen Jugendgemeinschaft Habonim. Noar Chaluzi* (July 1933), 20, as quoted in Schatzker, "The Jewish Youth Movement in Germany in the Holocaust Period (II)," 307.

10. Otto Suschny, oral history conducted by Debórah Dwork, Vienna, 18 July 1991, transcript, 39ff.

11. Ibid., 43f.

12. Ibid., 48ff.

13. Marion Kaplan, *Between Dignity and Despair: Jewish Life in Nazi Germany* (New York and Oxford: Oxford University Press, 1998), 118.

14. "Länder-Teil Südamerika," *Jüdische Auswanderung: Korrespondenzblatt über Auswanderungs- und Siedlungswesen*, ed. Hilfsverein der Juden in Deutschland, September 1936 (Berlin: Schmoller und Gordon, 1936), 32.

15. Ibid., 35.

16. Ibid., 63.

17. Rudolf Stahl, "Vocational Retraining of Jews in Nazi Germany 1933–1938," *Jewish Social Studies*, vol. 1, no. 1 (January 1939), 182.

18. Ibid.

19. M. Mitzman, "A Visit to Germany, Austria and Poland in 1939," Eyewitness Accounts: Doc. #P II e, #178, Archive, Wiener Library: Institute of Contemporary History, London.

20. Robert Rosner, "Sommer 1938," ms., collection Debórah Dwork, 2.

21. Lore Gang-Saalheimer, transcript, 6.

22. Mariánka May-Zadikow, transcript, 36f.

23. "Länder-Teil Südamerika," *Jüdische Auswanderung*, September 1936, 34.

24. Stahl, "Vocational Retraining of Jews," 179.

25. Ibid., 183f.

26. H. B. J. Stegeman and J. P. Vorsteveld, *Het Joodse Werkdorp in de Wieringermeer 1934–1941* (Zutphen: De Walburg Pers, 1983); G. van Tijn, "Werkdorp Nieuwe Sluis," *Leo Baeck Institute Year Book*, vol. 14 (1969), 182–99.

27. Stegeman and Vorsteveld, *Het Joodse Werkdorp in de Wieringermeer*, 54.

28. Bob Moore, *Refugees from Nazi Germany in the Netherlands, 1933–1940* (Dordrecht and Boston: Martinus Nijhoff, 1986), 49.

29. Rudolf Melitz, ed., *Das ist unser Weg: Junge Juden schildern Umschichtung und Hachscharah* (Berlin: Joachim Goldstein Verlag, 1937), 64f.

30. Arieh Tartakower and Kurt R. Grossmann, *The Jewish Refugee* (New York: Institute of Jewish Affairs of the American Jewish Congress and World Jewish Congress, 1944), 381.

31. "Hausfrau und Auswanderung," *Jüdische Auswanderung*, September 1936, 11ff.

32. Kaplan, *Between Dignity and Despair*, 142f.

33. Robert Rosner, transcript, 28.

34. Robert Rosner, "Sommer 1938," 4.

35. Lore Gang-Saalheimer, transcript, 8.

36. Ibid., 8f.

37. Ibid., 10ff.

38. Robert Rosner, "Sommer 1938," 2. Damaged centers eventually reopened and students returned to retraining classes, but the mood had shifted to sheer desperation. In her dissertation, "The Nazification of Vienna and the Response of the Viennese Jews," Strassler Center doctoral student Ilana Offenberger scrutinizes Jews' resumption of daily life activities after the November pogrom.

39. Lore Gang-Saalheimer, transcript, 10.

40. Ibid., 13.

41. G. E. Miller, *Shanghai: Paradise of Adventurers* (New York: Orsay Publishing House, 1937), 38f.

42. Ibid., 254.

43. See Marcia Reynders, *Port of Last Resort: The Diaspora Communities of Shanghai* (Stanford, CA: Stanford University Press, 2001).

44. Miller, *Shanghai*, 64f. While visas were not required to enter Shanghai, the Chinese consul general in Vienna, Dr Ho Feng Shan, issued such visas to Jews, notwithstanding an explicit order not to do so by the Chinese ambassador in Berlin. In the wake of the November pogrom, these visas helped as many as a couple of thousand Jews obtain release from concentration camps, exit visas from Greater Germany, and transit visas to third countries. When war broke out in September 1939, most of these Shanghai visa holders had found refuge in these third countries; few of them actually went to Shanghai.

45. Moshe Ayalon, "'Gegenwaertige Situation': Report on the Living Conditions

of the Jews in Germany. A Document and Commentary," *Leo Baeck Institute Year Book*, vol. 43 (1998), 276.

46. Ibid., 273.

47. Avraham Altman and Irene Eber, "Flight to Shanghai, 1938–1940: The Larger Setting," *Yad Vashem Studies*, vol. 28 (2000), 60.

48. Minute by Frank Foley, January 1939. PRO, FO 371/24079.

49. See: Georg Armbruster, *Leben im Wartesaal: Exil in Shanghai 1938–1947* (Berlin: StiftungStadtmuseum, 1997); Georg Armbruster, Michael Kohlstruck, and Sonja Muhlberger, eds., *Exil Shanghai 1938–1947: Judisches Leben in der Emigration* (Teetz: Hentrich & Hentrich, 2000); Barbara Geldermann, " 'Jewish Refugees Should Be Welcomed and Assisted Here!': Shanghai: Exile and Return," *Leo Baeck Institute Year Book*, vol. 44 (1999), 227–43; David Kranzler, *Japanese, Nazis & Jews: The Jewish Refugee Community of Shanghai, 1938–1945* (New York: Yeshiva University Press, 1976); James R. Ross, *Escape to Shanghai: A Jewish Community in China* (New York: Free Press, 1994). Memoirs include Ernest G. Heppner, *Shanghai Refuge: A Memoir of the World War II Jewish Ghetto* (Lincoln and London: University of Nebraska Press, 1993); Evelyn Pike Rubin, *Ghetto Shanghai* (New York: Shengold, 1993); Sigmund Tobias, *Strange Haven: A Jewish Childhood in Wartime Shanghai* (Urbana and Chicago: University of Illinois Press, 1999).

PAPERS: VISA STAMPS OFFER HOPE

1. Ludwig Marcuse, *Mein Zwanzigste Jahrhundert: Auf dem Weg zu einer Autobiographie* (Munich: Paul List Verlag, 1960), 248ff.

2. Ibid., 249f.

3. Ibid., 250.

4. John Bassett Moore, *A Digest of International Law*, 8 vols. (Washington, DC: Government Printing Office, 1906), vol. 3, 994.

5. As quoted in Bat-Ami Zucker, *In Search of Refuge: Jews and US Consuls in Nazi Germany 1933–1941* (London and Portland, OR: Vallentine Mitchell, 2001), 50.

6. As quoted ibid., 79.

7. Jeremiah W. Jenks and W. Jett Lauck, *The Immigration Problem: A Study of American Immigration Conditions and Needs,* 6th edition (New York and London: Funk & Wagnalls, 1926), 472.

8. See Read Lewis and Marian Schibsby, "Status of the Refugee Under American Immigration Laws," *Annals of the American Academy of Political and Social Science*, vol. 203 (May 1939).

9. Martin Gumpert, *First Papers*, trans. Heinz and Ruth Norden (New York: Duell, Sloan and Pearce, 1941), 16; 19f.

10. Lewis and Schibsby, "Status of the Refugee Under American Immigration Laws," 79.

11. Letter from John G. Erhardt to the Secretary of State, 15 May 1936, in John Mendelsohn, ed., *The Holocaust: Selected Documents in Eighteen Volumes*, 18 vols. (New York and London: Garland, 1982), vol. 5, 36.

12. Zucker, *In Search of Refuge*, 149f.

13. Anton Kuh, "These Are the Refugees," *Jewish Frontier*, vol. 7 (December 1940), 8.

14. Anita Kassof, "Knocking at the Door: The German Jewish Refugees and U.S. Immigration Policy," in Anita Kassof, Avi Y. Decter, and Deborah R. Weiner, eds., *Lives Lost, Lives Found: Baltimore's German Jewish Refugees, 1933–1945* (Baltimore: Jewish Museum of Maryland, nd), 45–57. See too the text in the photographic images.

15. See Memorandum by C. B. McAlpine, 1 March 1938. PRO, HO 213/94.

16. Minutes of meeting of Sir Samuel Hoare and a deputation of the Board of Deputies, 1 April 1938. PRO, HO 213/42.

17. Ibid.

18. "Visas for Holders of German or Austrian Passports Entering the United Kingdom." PRO, HO 213/94, 1f.

19. Ibid., 2f.

20. For his emigration to Britain, see Paul Ferris, *Dr Freud: A Life* (London: Sinclair-Stevenson, 1997), 388ff.

21. As quoted ibid., 395.

22. Tina Walzer, "Vom Böhmerwald aus in die Welt: Einblicke in die Geschichte der Familie Fürth," *David: Jüdische Kulturzeitschrift*, vol. 67 (December 2005), 66ff.

23. Letter from Lothar Fürth to Martin Sherwood, 28 March 1938. PRO, HO 213/257.

24. Letter from the German Jewish Aid Committee to Martin Sherwood, 14 June 1938. PRO, HO 213/257.

25. Walzer, "Vom Böhmerwald aus in die Welt: Einblicke in die Geschichte der Familie Fürth," 69.

26. For a discussion of this issue, see the chapter "Problems: Life as a Refugee."

27. Tony Kushner, "An Alien Occupation—Jewish Refugees and Domestic Service in Britain, 1933–1948," in Werner E. Mosse, ed., *Second Chance: Two Centuries of German-speaking Jews in the United Kingdom* (Tübingen: J. C. B. Mohr [Paul Siebeck], 1991), 564; on the context, see: Frank Dawes, *Not in Front of the Servants: Domestic Service in England 1850–1939* (London: Wayland Publishers, 1973), 138ff.; Pamela Horn, *The Rise and Fall of the Victorian Servant* (New York: St. Martin's Press, 1975), 166ff.

28. Letter from Marjorie Watts to Sir Samuel Hoare, 22 October 1937. PRO, HO 213/322.

29. Ads from the *New Statesman and Nation* (24 November 1938), 1107; (15 October 1938), 589.

30. Letter from Maurice Jeffes, 21 October 1938. PRO, HO 213/99.

31. Letter from the British Passport Control Officer in Paris to Maurice Jeffes, 8 March 1939. HO 213/105.

32. Interview with Thea Scholl, March 1984, transcript, 136, Dokumentationsarchiv des österreichischen Widerstandes, as quoted in Wolfgang Muchitsch, ed., *Österreicher im Exil: Grossbritannien, 1938–1945: Eine Dokumentation* (Vienna: Österreichischer Bundesverlag, 1992), 24.

33. Letter from Maurice Jeffes to E. N. Cooper, 5 June 1939. PRO, HO 213/107.

34. Milena Roth, *Lifesaving Letters: A Child's Flight from the Holocaust* (Seattle: University of Washington Press, 2004), 51.

35. Ibid., 71; 80.

36. Ibid., 85.

37. Michael Smith, *Foley: The Spy Who Saved 10,000 Jews* (London: Hodder and Stoughton, 1999), 64–5.

38. Wim van Leer, *Time of My Life* (Jerusalem: Carta, 1984), 174.

39. Minutes of meeting of Coordinating Committee for Refugees, 1 May 1939. PRO, HO 213/268.

40. Central Office for Refugees, Domestic Bureau, *Domestic Service: Some Suggestions for Employers and Employees* (London: Bloomsbury House, 1938), 3–4; 7.

41. Great Britain, *Parliamentary Debates: House of Commons Official Report*, 5th series, vol. 341 (8 November—25 November 1938), 1437f.

42. Ibid., 1463f.

43. Ibid., 1472f.

44. See Amy Zahl Gottlieb, *Men of Vision: Anglo-Jewry's Aid to Victims of the Nazi Regime, 1933–1945* (London: Weidenfeld & Nicolson, 1998), 135–45.

45. Carl Ludwig, *Die Flüchtlingspolitik der Schweiz seit 1933 bis zur Gegenwart (1957)* (Bern: Verlag Herbert Lang & Cie, 1966), 57ff.

46. Patrick Kury, *Über Fremde reden: Der Überfremdungsdiskurs und Ausgrenzung in der Schweiz, 1900–1945* (Zurich: Chronos, 2003), 96ff., 132ff.

47. As quoted in Heinz Roschewski, *Rothmund und die Juden: Eine historische Fallstudie des Antisemitismus in der schweizerischen Flüchtlingspolitik 1933–1957* (Basel and Frankfurt: Schweizerischer Israelitischer Gemeindebund/Helbing & Lichtenhahn, 1997), 29f.

48. Shaul Ferro, "Switzerland and the Refugees Fleeing Nazism: Documents on the German Jews Turned Back at the Basel Border in 1938–1939," *Yad Vashem Studies*, vol. 27 (1999), 213.

49. Ibid., 214.

50. As quoted in Ludwig, *Die Flüchtlingspolitik der Schweiz*, 98f.

51. Nationale Kommission für die Veröffentlichung diplomatischer Dokumente der Schweiz: *Diplomatische Dokumente der Schweiz, 1848–1945,* 15 vols. (Bern: Benteli, 1984–94), vol. 12, 813; 833ff.

52. As quoted in Stefan Keller, *Grüningers Fall: Geschichten von Flucht und Hilfe* (Zurich: Rotpunktverlag, 1993), 49.

53. As quoted in Ludwig, *Die Flüchtlingspolitik der Schweiz*, 112; also Ferro, "Switzerland and the Refugees Fleeing Nazism," 217.

54. As quoted in Ludwig, *Die Flüchtlingspolitik der Schweiz*, 113f.

55. As quoted ibid., 115.

56. As quoted ibid., 116.

57. As quoted ibid., 119.

58. Ibid., 120.

59. Nationale Kommission für die Veröffentlichung diplomatischer Dokumente der Schweiz, *Diplomatische Dokumente der Schweiz*, vol. 12, 938.

60. German Reich, Interior Ministry, *Reichsgesetzblatt: Teil I* (1938), 1342.

61. Germany, Auswärtiges Amt, *Documents on German Foreign Policy, 1918–1945, Series D*, 15 vols. (Washington, DC: Government Printing Office, 1949–83), vol. 5, 898–900.

62. As quoted in Keller, *Grüningers Fall*, 200.

63. As quoted in Ferro, "Switzerland and the Refugees Fleeing Nazism," 231.

PROBLEMS: THE RUPTURE OF DEPARTURE

1. Gerda Freistadt-Geiringer, oral history conducted by Debórah Dwork, Vienna, 10, 12, and 15 July 1991, transcript, 13.

2. Ibid., 14–16.

3. Ibid., 16.

4. Ibid., 32.

5. Robert Rosner, oral history conducted by Debórah Dwork, Vienna, 3 July 1990, transcript, 33.

6. Geiringer, oral history, transcript, 38.

7. "Havoc in Munich: All Jews Given 48 Hours to Leave," *Times*, 11 November 1938.

8. "Munich Jews' Plight," *Times*, 15 November 1938.

9. "Vienna Jews' Fate," *Times*, 14 November 1938.

10. Yitzhak S. Herz, "*Kristallnacht* at the Dinslaken Orphanage," *Yad Vashem Studies*, vol. 11 (1976), 343; 353; 357.

11. Amy Zahl Gottlieb, *Men of Vision: Anglo-Jewry's Aid to Victims of the Nazi Regime, 1933–1945* (London: Weidenfeld and Nicolson, 1998), 103f.

12. Neville Chamberlain, *The Struggle for Peace* (Toronto: Thomas Allen, 1939), 315.

13. "Peace Saved by Action: Mr. Chamberlain on Munich," *Times*, 10 November 1938; also Chamberlain, *The Struggle for Peace*, 357ff.

14. As quoted in Louise London, *Whitehall and the Jews, 1933–1948: British Immigration Policy, Jewish Refugees and the Holocaust* (Cambridge: Cambridge University Press, 2000), 99.

15. "Plight of German Jewry: An Appeal to Other Communities," *Times*, 16 November 1938.

16. "German Jews' Future," *Times*, 16 November 1938.

17. "Jews to Be Turned Out of Homes: Wholesale Expulsion," *Times*, 18 November 1938.

18. "The Settlement of Refugees," *Times*, 18 November 1938.

19. Great Britain, *Parliamentary Debates: House of Commons Official Report*, 5th series, vol. 341 (8 November–25 November 1938), 1473f.

20. Ibid., 1474.

21. Great Britain, *Parliamentary Debates: House of Commons Official Report*, 5th series, vol. 342 (28 November–22 December 1938), 21.

22. Ibid., 1975–6.

23. As quoted in Corrie K. Berghuis, *Joodse Vluchtelingen in Nederland, 1938–1940: Documenten betreffende toelating, uitleiding en kampopname* (Kampen: J. H. Kok, 1990), 30.

24. File: Refugee Services. Children. Children in Europe. AFSC Archive. General Files, 1939: Refugee Services (Children to Country—Germany), 21 February 1939.

25. As quoted in Berghuis, *Joodse Vluchtelingen in Nederland, 1938–1940*, 41.

26. As quoted ibid., 89f.

27. Movement for the Care of Children from Germany, Ltd., *First Annual Report: November 1938-December 1939*, 4. CBF Archive, reel 153.

28. Claudia Curio, "'Unsichtbare' Kinder: Auswahl- und Eingliederungsstrategien der Hilfsorganizationen," in Wolfgang Benz, Claudia Curio, and Andrea Hammel, eds., *Die Kindertransporte 1938/39: Rettung und Integration* (Frankfurt: Fischer Taschenbuch Verlag, 2003), 62.

29. Movement for the Care of Children from Germany, Ltd., *First Annual Report: November 1938–December 1939*, 4–6. Central British Fund for Jewish Relief Archive, reel 153. See too: John Presland (Gladys Bendit), *A Great Adventure: The Story of the Refugee Children's Movement* (London: Bloomsbury House, 1944), 4–5.

30. Fred Dunston (né Fritz Deutsch), oral history conducted by Debórah Dwork, London, 2 January 1993, transcript, 4; 18.

31. Bertha Leverton and Shmuel Lowensohn, eds., *I Came Alone: The Stories of the Kindertransports* (Lewes, Sussex: Book Guild, 1990), 73; oral history of Fred Dunston, 21; 22; 27.

32. Leverton and Lowensohn, eds., *I Came Alone: The Stories of the Kindertransports*, 73; oral history of Fred Dunston, 21; 19.

33. Movement for the Care of Children from Germany, Ltd., *First Annual Report: November 1938–December 1939*, 4. Central British Fund for Jewish Relief Archive, reel 153.

34. Yvonne Kapp and Margaret Mynatt, *British Policy and the Refugees, 1933–1941* (London and Portland, OR: Frank Cass, 1997), 39.

35. London, *Whitehall and the Jews, 1933–1948*, 122.

36. Letter from Mrs McClelland, Hospitality Department, Movement for the Care of Children from Germany, to Mrs P. Shepherd, 19 May 1939. Correspondence reference number: H/BM/EC/74, authors' collection.

37. Letter from Mrs McClelland, Hospitality Department, Movement for the Care of Children from Germany, to Mrs P. Shepherd, 22 May 1939. Correspondence reference number: H/BM/EC/74, authors' collection.

38. Letter from Dr Herbert Neuwalder, Wien XVII. Dornbacherstr. 44, to Mrs P. Shepherd, 14 June 1939, authors' collection.

39. Susanne Harris-Neuwalder, oral history conducted by Debórah Dwork, New Haven, 20 September; 4 and 21 October; 17 November; 13 and 21 December 1993; 2 February and 9 March 1994, transcript, part 1, 54.

40. Ernest Stock, ed., *Jugend auf der Flucht: Die Tagebücher von Ernst und Julie Stock* (Berlin: Metropol, 2004), 56.

41. Ibid., 58.

42. Society of Friends, Germany Emergency Committee, Report from W. R. Hughes, 16 December 1938. PRO, FO 371/24074.

43. Statement by Norbert Wollheim, 1–2, Wiener Library Archive, London.

44. Hertha Nathorff, *Das Tagebuch der Hertha Nathorff: Berlin, New York, Auzeichnungen 1933 bis 1945*, ed. Wolfgang Benz (Munich: R. Oldenbourg, 1987), 60.

45. Ibid., 113.

46. Ibid., 134.

47. Ibid., 147.

48. Ibid., 148.

49. Ibid., 149f.

50. Ibid., 150.

51. *New York Times*, 11 December 1938.

52. "Report of the Children's Department of the Friends Centre, Vienna. November 1938–September 1939." AFSC Archive, General Files 1939, Refugee Services (Children to Country—Germany), 4. In her dissertation, "The Nazi-

fication of Vienna and the Response of the Viennese Jews," Strassler Center doctoral candidate Ilana Offenberger notes that the Viennese Kultusgemeinde encouraged mothers to send their children, and sought to reframe the social norm of maternal behavior.

53. Oral history of Susanne Harris-Neuwalder, 54–5.

54. Ibid., 56; 32–3.

55. "Women's Voluntary Services. Report on a visit to Dovercourt Refugee Camp, Jan. 12th, 1939," by Nancy de Selincourt, Evacuation Department, Women's Volunteer Services. PRO, MH 55/689, 1.

56. Note by C. F. Roundell, Chief General Inspector, and Miss Montagnon, Woman Inspector, on a Visit (19 December 1938) to the Jewish Refugee Camp in Dovercourt. PRO, MH 55/689.

57. Anna Essinger, *Bunce Court School, 1933–43.* CBF Archive, reel 154, 6.

58. Veronica Gillespie, "Working with the '*Kindertransports*,'" Sybil Oldfield, ed., *This Working-day World: Women's Lives and Culture(s) in Britain 1914–1945* (London: Taylor & Francis, 1994), 127f.

59. Oral history of Gerda Freistadt-Geiringer, 50.

60. Kitty Suschny-Pistol, oral history conducted by Debórah Dwork, Vienna, 19 July 1991, transcript, 8; 10–11.

61. Collective journal of the girls in the Southport Hostel. Manchester Jewish Museum. Anonymous entry.

62. Ibid., entries by Ilse Maurer and Gina Bauer.

63. Oral history of Kitty Suschny-Pistol, 16; 5.

1939–1942: TOWARD GENOCIDE

1. Quoted in Max Domarus, Hitler: *Speeches and Proclamations, 1932–1945,* 4 vols. (Wauconda, IL: Bolchazy-Carducci, 1990–7), vol. 3, 1447.

2. Ibid., 1448f.

3. Ibid., 1449.

4. See Helmut Krausnick, *Hitlers Einsatzgruppen: Die Truppen des Weltanschauungs-krieges 1938–1942* (Frankfurt: Fischer Taschenbuch Verlag, 1989), 26ff.; Hans Buchheim, "The SS—Instrument of Domination," in Helmut Krausnick, Hans Buchheim, Martin Broszat, and Hans-Adolf Jacobsen, *Anatomy of the SS State,* trans. Richard Barry, Marian Jackson, and Dorothy Long (New York: Walker and Co., 1968), 177ff.

5. See Debórah Dwork and Robert Jan van Pelt, *Auschwitz: 1270 to the Present* (New York and London: Norton, 1996), 127–59; Robert Lewis Koehl, *RKFDV: German Resettlement and Population Policy, 1939–1945. A History of the Reich Commission for the Strengthening of Germandom* (Cambridge: Harvard University Press, 1957).

6. "New Jewish State in Poland," *Times*, 24 October 1939.

7. As quoted in Poland: Ministry of Information, *The Black Book of Poland* (New York: Putnam, 1942), 239f.

8. "Draft Instructions to Passport Control Officers: Special Instructions Regarding the Grant of Visas for United Kingdom in the Event of an Outbreak of War." PRO, CAB 16/211, 175.

9. Note from the American Ambassador to Foreign Office, 30 September 1939. PRO, FO 371/24095, 167f.; Minute, Disposal of Palestine Immigration Certificates, 2 October 1939. PRO, FO 371/24095, 98f.

10. No minutes survive of the meeting, but the main points of the conversation were recapitulated in a letter from Moshe Shertok to Malcolm MacDonald, 27 October 1939. PRO, FO 371/24096, 96–100; see also the letter from Malcolm MacDonald to Moishe Shertok, 6 November 1939. PRO, FO 371/24096, 101ff.; and also Lewis Bernstein Namier, "Allocated but Undistributed Immigration Certificates in Greater Germany," unpublished ms. PRO, FO 371/24096, 250.

11. On the history of aliyah bet, see Dalia Ofer, *Escaping the Holocaust: Illegal Immigration to the Land of Israel, 1939–1944* (New York and Oxford: Oxford University Press, 1990).

12. David Ben Gurion, as quoted ibid., 18.

13. Berl Katznelson, as quoted ibid., 19.

14. Malcolm J. Proudfoot, *European Refugees, 1939–1952: A Study in Forced Population Movement* (London: Faber and Faber, 1957), 319.

15. From a note made by Martin Luther on 21 August 1942 about attempts to solve the Jewish Problem. As quoted in Kurt Pätzold, ed., *Verfolgung, Vetreibung, Vernichtung: Dokumente des faschistischen Antisemitismus* (Leipzig: Reclam, 1987), 350.

16. Raul Hilberg, *The Destruction of the European Jews*, rev. and definitive ed., 3 vols. (New York and London: Holmes and Meier, 1985), vol. 2, 397f.

17. Arieh Tartakower and Kurt R. Grossmann, *The Jewish Refugee* (New York: Institute of Jewish Affairs, 1944), 346.

18. Most Holocaust historians agree that in the second half of 1941 the Nazi plan to solve the Jewish Problem through forced emigration morphed into a policy to murder all of the Jews of Europe. Important contributions to our understanding of the emergence of the Holocaust in late 1941 include: Christopher R. Browning, *Fateful Months: Essays on the Emergence of the Final Solution*, rev. ed. (New York and London: Holmes & Meier, 1991); Christopher R. Browning with Jürgen Matthäus, *The Origins of the Final Solution: The Evolution of Nazi Jewish Policy, September 1939–March 1942* (Lincoln and Jerusalem: University of Nebraska Press and Yad Vashem, 2004); Henry Friedländer, *The Origins of Nazi Genocide: From Euthanasia to the Final Solution* (Chapel Hill and London: University of North Carolina Press, 1995).

19. Elke Fröhlich, ed., *Die Tagebücher von Joseph Goebbels: Teil II, Diktate 1941–1945*, 15 vols. (Munich: Saur, 1996), vol. 2., 498f.

PEOPLE: PASSEURS: GUIDES TO FREEDOM

1. For a general discussion of the history of Dutch Jews during the occupation, see Jacob Presser, *Ashes in the Wind* (Detroit: Wayne State University Press, 1988) [*Ondergang* (The Hague: Staatsuitgeverij, 1965)].
2. As quoted in Jenny Gans-Premsela, *Vluchtweg* (Baarn: Bosch & Keuning, 1990), 22.
3. Ibid., 24.
4. Ibid., 25.
5. Ibid., 32.
6. Neither Jenny nor Max Gans ever revealed Jean Louis's family name. Respecting their decision, we chose not pursue the matter.
7. As quoted in Unabhängige Expertenkommission Schweiz—Zweiter Weltkrieg, *Die Schweiz und die Flüchtlinge zur Zeit des Nationalsozialismus* (Zurich: Chronos Verlag, 2001), 118f.
8. As quoted in Carl Ludwig, *Die Flüchtlingspolitik der Schweiz seit 1933 bis zur Gegenwart (1957)* (Bern: Verlag Herbert Lang & Cie, 1966), 199.
9. As quoted ibid., 202.
10. As quoted in Unabhängige Expertenkommission, *Die Schweiz und die Flüchtlinge,* 158.
11. As quoted ibid., 148f.
12. As quoted ibid., 119.
13. As quoted ibid., 149.
14. As quoted ibid., 164.
15. As quoted ibid., 206.
16. As quoted ibid., 206f.
17. Stefan Mächler, "Ein Abgrund zwischen zwei Welten. Zwei Rückweisungen jüdischer Flüchtlinge im Jahre 1942," in Zeitschrift des Schweizerischen Bundesarchivs, *Die Schweiz und die Flüchtlinge 1933–1945* (Bern, Stuttgart and Vienna: Paul Haupt, 1996), 137–231.
18. Ibid., 151.
19. Ibid., 161.
20. Ibid., 170ff.; Claude Hauser, *Les Réfugiés aux Frontières Jurassiennes (1940–1945): Accueil et Refoulement—Internement* (St. Imier: Känel Walter, 1999), 47; Alfred A. Häsler, *The Lifeboat Is Full: Switzerland and the Refugees, 1933–1945,* trans. Charles Lam Markmann (New York: Funk & Wagnalls, 1969), 117.
21. Ludwig, *Die Flüchtlingspolitik der Schweiz,* 223.

22. As quoted in Unabhängige Expertenkommission, *Die Schweiz und die Flüchtlinge,* 159.

23. Ibid., 159.

24. As quoted, ibid., 154f.

25. Ibid., 155.

26. There is a fair amount of published literature on OSE and a wealth of archival documentation. See first inter alia: *American OSE Review*; Centre de Documentation Juive Contemporaine (CDJC), *L'Activité des Organisations Juives en France sous l'Occupation* (Paris: Centre de Documentation Juive Contemporaine, 1983; reissue of 1947 text); 117–79; Hillel J. Kieval, "Legality and Resistance in Vichy France: The Rescue of Jewish Children," *Proceedings of the American Philosophical Society*, vol. 124, no. 5 (October 1980), 339–66; Serge Klarsfeld, *The Children of Izieu* (New York: Abrams, Inc., 1985) [*Les Enfants d'Izieu: Une Tragedie Juive* (Paris: Publiée par Serge Klarsfeld, 1984)]; Anny Latour, *The Jewish Resistance in France* (New York: Holocaust Library, 1981) [*La Résistance Juive en France* (Paris: Stock, 1970)]; Lucien Lazare, *Rescue as Resistance,* trans. Jeffrey M. Green (New York: Columbia University Press, 1996) [*La Résistance Juive en France* (Paris: Stock, 1987)]; Ernst Papanek and Edward Linn, *Out of the Fire* (New York: William Morrow, 1975) especially 34–5; Vivette Samuel, *Rescuing the Children,* trans. Charles B. Paul (Madison: University of Wisconsin Press, 2002) [*Sauver les Enfants* (Paris: Editions Liana Levi, 1995)]; Zosa Szajkowski, *Analytical Franco-Jewish Gazetteer, 1939–1945* (New York: Frydman, 1966), 73–5 and passim. See also Jacques Adler, *The Jews of Paris and the Final Solution* (New York: Oxford University Press, 1987), 167; 226–7 [*Face à la Persécution: Les Organisations Juives à Paris de 1940 à 1944* (Paris: Calmann-Lévy, 1985)]; David Diamant, *Les Juifs dans la Résistance Française, 1940–44* (Paris: Le Pavillon, 1971), 56–9; Dorothy Macardle, *The Children of Europe* (London: Victor Gollancz, 1949), 184–8; Sabine Zeitoun, *Ces Enfants Qu'il Fallait Sauver* (Paris: Albin Michel, 1989), 145–70. The major archival collections are in the Centre de Documentation Juive Contemporaine (CDJC) and the OSE institution itself in Paris and in the YIVO in New York.

27. "Exposé sur le Circuit Garel," CDJC doc. CCXVII–12a, 1.

28. Ibid., 1–2.

29. For a discussion of these networks, see Debórah Dwork, *Children With A Star* (New Haven: Yale University Press, 1991), 59–64.

30. Georges Loinger, oral history conducted by Debórah Dwork, Paris, 26 June 1987, transcript, 6.

31. Ian Ousby, *Occupation: The Ordeal of France, 1940–1944* (New York: St. Martin's Press, 1998), 90–93; H. R. Kedward, *Occupied France: Collaboration and Resistance, 1940–1944* (Oxford: Blackwell, 1985), 28.

32. Oral history of Georges Loinger, 5–6; Georges Loinger, *Aux Frontières de l'Espoir* (Paris: Editions le Manuscrit, 2006), 100.
33. Oral history of Georges Loinger, 6; Loinger, *Aux Frontières de l'Espoir*, 95–6.
34. Oral history of Georges Loinger, 7; Loinger, *Aux Frontières de l'Espoir*, 96–7; 102.
35. Loinger, *Aux Frontières de l'Espoir,* 97–9; 103.
36. Oral history of Georges Loinger, 6–7; Loinger, *Aux Frontières de l'Espoir,* 108.
37. Elisabeth Hirsch, oral history conducted by Debórah Dwork, Paris, 25 June 1987, transcript, 9.
38. Ibid., 11.
39. Quoted in Vivette Samuel, *Rescuing the Children*, 107.
40. Ibid., 106–8; Anny Latour, *The Jewish Resistance in France*, 174–6; CDJC, *L'Activité des Organizations Juives en France*, 168–9.
41. CDJC doc. XXXIII-24.
42. "Rapport Concernant l'Organisation de Combat (OJC) et Son Activité Durant la Période de Occupation," August 1944, CDJC doc. CCXIV–118; "Rapport Provisoire du Movement de la Jeunesse Sioniste de France," CDJC doc. CCXIV-117.
43. "Rapport sur l'Activité du Mouvement des Éclaireurs Israelites de France de 1939 au Lendemain de la Libération," Lyon, 1 October 1944, CDJC doc. CCXVII-8, 19.
44. "American Joint Distribution Committee," CDJC doc. CCCLXVI–14, 5; oral history of Georges Loinger, 6.
45. "Au Sujet d'Informations Recueillies sur la Circulation et l'Emigration Clandestine de Juifs Etrangers," Vichy, 19 February 1943, CDJC doc. LXXII–34, 2; 4.
46. Isabel Silberg-Riff, oral history conducted by Debórah Dwork, London, 13 May 1987, transcript, 1; 8; 11; 14–8.

PLACES: CAUGHT IN INTERNMENT CAMPS

We thank Srassler Center doctoral candidate Jeffrey Koerber for all materials quoted here from the American Joint Distribution Committee (JDC) Archives and the Shoah Visual History Archive. Engaged in a groundbreaking study of the Jewish communities in Grodno and Vitebsk, he generously forwarded to us material he uncovered pursuant to his own work.

1. Ben-Cion Pinchuk, "Jewish Refugees in Soviet Poland, 1939–1941," *Jewish Social Studies*, vol. 40 (1978), 143.
2. Ibid.
3. Jerzy (Joram) Kagan, oral history conducted by Debórah Dwork, New Haven, 17 February; 7 March; and 8 April 1994, transcript, 20.

4. Cable from Rosen in Amsterdam to Joint in New York, quoting Beckelman and Giterman in Poland. 1 November 1939. C971 482 1/40 1 JDC Archives, Collection: 33/44; File: 874.

5. Chaim Kaplan, *Scroll of Agony: The Warsaw Diary of Chaim A. Kaplan*, ed. Abraham I. Katsh (Bloomington and Indianapolis: Indiana University Press, 1999), 70.

6. Cable from Rosen in Amsterdam to Joint in New York, quoting Beckelman and Giterman in Poland, 1 November 1939. C971 482 1/40 1 JDC Archives. Collection 33/44; File 874.

7. Ibid.

8. David Grodner (pseudonym), "In Soviet Poland and Lithuania," *Contemporary Jewish Record,* vol. 4 (1941), 137f.

9. Hans Schafranek, *Zwischen NKWD und Gestapo: Die Auslieferung deutscher und österreichischer Antifaschisten aus der Sowjetunion an Nazideutschland 1937–1941* (Frankfurt: ISP Verlag, 1990), 61f.

10. Bernard D. Weinryb, "Polish Jews Under Soviet Rule," in Peter Meyer a.o., *The Jews in the Soviet Satellites* (Syracuse: Syracuse University Press, 1953), 341.

11. For a general discussion of help offered by the JDC in Lithuania, see Yehuda Bauer, *American Jewry and the Holocaust: The American Joint Distribution Committee, 1939–1945* (Detroit: Wayne State University Press, 1981), 107ff.

12. Moses W. Beckelman, "Memorandum re Expulsions over the Lithuanian German Border," dated 8 November 1939. JDC Archives. Collection 33/44; File 874, 2–3.

13. Ibid., 3–4.

14. A new trade for young Jews emerged: clandestine letter carrier. Disguised as peasants, they brought messages back and forth over the border. See Dov Levin, *The Lesser of Two Evils: Eastern European Jewry Under Soviet Rule, 1939–1941*, trans. Naftali Greenwood (Philadelphia and Jerusalem: Jewish Publication Society, 1995), 186.

15. Oral history of Jerzy (Joram) Kagan, transcript, 24–5.

16. As quoted in Levin, *The Lesser of Two Evils*, 185.

17. Pinchuk, "Jewish Refugees in Soviet Poland, 1939–1941," 147.

18. Shoah Visual History Archive, testimony of Joseph Ceder.

19. Levin, *The Lesser of Two Evils*, 188f.

20. Pinchuk, "Jewish Refugees in Soviet Poland, 1939–1941," 149f.; Levin, *The Lesser of Two Evils*, 189ff.

21. Oral history of Jerzy (Joram) Kagan, transcript, 31.

22. Shoah Visual History Archive, testimony of Dora Huze.

23. As quoted in Levin, *The Lesser of Two Evils*, 195.

24. Pinchuk, "Jewish Refugees in Soviet Poland, 1939–1941," 153; Weinryb, "Polish Jews Under Soviet Rule," 345.

25. Levin, *The Lesser of Two Evils*, 194ff.

26. Joram Kagan, "Travelog: 1939–," unpublished manuscript, authors' collection, 97.

27. Oral history of Jerzy (Joram) Kagan, transcript, 36.

28. Kagan, "Travelog," 98.

29. Ibid., 102–3.

30. Oral history of Jerzy (Joram) Kagan, 39–40.

31. Ibid., 40–2.

32. Ibid., 44.

33. Julius Margolin, *Überleben ist alles: Aufzeichnungen aus sowjetischen Lagern* (Munich: J. Pfeiffer, 1965), 93f.

34. Shoah Visual History Archive, testimony of Dora Huze.

35. Ibid., testimony of Joseph Ceder.

36. Ibid., testimony of Dora Huze.

37. Oral history of Jerzy (Joram) Kagan), 36.

38. Weinryb, "Polish Jews Under Soviet Rule," 354f.

39. Hugh Thomas, *The Spanish Civil War*, revised edition (London: Penguin, 2003), 854ff.

40. Denis Peschanski, *La France des Camps: L'Internement, 1938–1946* (Paris: Gallimard, 2002), 42f.

41. Alfred Kantorowicz, *Nachtbücher: Aufzeichnungen im französischen Exil, 1935 bis 1939*, ed. Ursula Büttner and Angelika Voss (Hamburg: Christians, 1995), 218.

42. Christian Eggers, *Unerwünschte Ausländer: Juden aus Deutschland und Mitteleuropa in französischen Internierungslagern, 1940–1942* (Berlin: Metropol Verlag, 2000), 48ff.; 216ff.; Peschanski, *La France des Camps*, 72ff.

43. Quoted in Hanna Schramm, *Menschen in Gurs: Erinnerungen an ein französischen Internierungslager (1940–1941), mit einem dokumentarischen Beitrag zur französischen Emigrantenpolitik (1933–1944)* (Worms: Georg Heintz, 1977), 226.

44. Arthur Koestler, *Scum of the Earth* (New York: Macmillan, 1941), 36.

45. Ibid., 96f.

46. Eggers, *Unerwünschte Ausländer*, 54ff., 216ff.; Peschanski, *La France des Camps*, 152ff.

47. As quoted in Eggers, *Unerwünschte Ausländer*, 336.

48. Letter from Varian Fry, 19 September 1940, AFSC Archive. Emergency Rescue Committee (Varian Fry), 1940.

49. See Schramm, *Menschen in Gurs,* 371.

50. Paul Sauer, *Dokumente über die Verfolgung der jüdischen Bürger in Baden-Württemberg durch das nationalsozialistische Regime 1933–1945*, 2 vols. (Stuttgart: Kohlhammer, 1966), vol. 2, 231ff.; Erhard R. Wiehn, ed., *Oktoberdeportation 1940* (Konstanz: Hartung-Gorre Verlag, 1990).

51. Jochen von Lang, ed., *Eichmann Interrogated: Transcripts from the Archives of the*

Israeli Police, trans. Ralph Mannheim (New York: Farrar, Straus & Giroux, 1983), 70f.

52. "Reich Jews Sent to South France: 10,000 Reported Put into Camps," *New York Times*, 9 November 1940, 5.

53. Steve Fulton, "Gurs Camp Shocks Red Cross Officer," *New York Times*, 28 December 1940, 4.

54. "Reich Jews Sent to South France: 10,000 Reported Put into Camps," *New York Times*, 9 November 1940, 5.

55. Rapport d'Activité de la HICEM-France pour 1941, 1er Janvier 1941–1er Avril 1942, CDJC doc. CCXVII–15, 8.

56. Mark Wischnitzer, *To Dwell in Safety: The Story of Jewish Migration Since 1800* (Philadelphia: Jewish Publication Society of America, 1948), 157f.; 179f.

57. Rapport d'Activité de la HICEM-France pour 1941, 1er Janvier 1941–1er Avril 1942, CDJC doc. CCXVII–15, 11f.

58. Wischnitzer, *To Dwell in Safety*, 235ff.

59. Eggers, *Unerwünschte Ausländer*, 271ff.; 405ff.

60. Oral history of Vivette Samuel-Hermann, conducted by Debórah Dwork, Paris, 3 June 1987, 8.

61. Report, Camp Gurs, February 1941, AFSC Archive. Foreign Service (France-Relief: Internment Camps Gurs).

62. D. E. Wright, "Brief Report on Trip to Perpignan, January 21–25, 1941," AFSC Archive. Foreign Service (France-Relief: Internment Camps), 5f.; on Rivesaltes, see Eggers, *Unerwünschte Ausländer*, 92ff.; Anne Bottel, *Le Camp de Rivesaltes 1941–1942: Du Centre d'Hébergement au "Drancy de la Zone Libre"* (Perpignan: Presses Universitaires de Perpignan/Mare Nostrum, 2000); Joël Mettay, *L'Archipel du Mépris: Histoire du Camp de Rivesaltes de 1939 à Nos Jours* (Canet: Editions Trabucaire, 2001).

63. Joseph Weill, *Contribution à l'Histoire des Camps d'Internement dans l'Anti-France* (Paris: Editions du Centre, 1946), 32–3.

64. See United States Committee for the Care of European Children, Inc., "Plan for the Evacuation of Children from France in Relation to the Problem of Securing Admission of Such Children into the United States," AFSC Archive. Box: General Files, 1941, Committees and Organisations (Spanish Refugee Relief to War Resisters League); File: Committees and Organisations 1941, United States Committee for the Care of European Children, 3.

65. "Children's Immigration to the USA," Memorandum of OSE Montpellier to the AFSC, AFSC Archive. Foreign Service, France-Relief Children Transports, 1941.

66. Isaac Chomski, "Children in Exile," *Contemporary Jewish Record*, vol. 4 (1941), 522.

67. Ibid., 526.

68. Ibid., 526–528.
69. Letter from Margaret Frawley to Allen Bonnell, 18 July 1941, AFSC Archive. Foreign Service, France-Relief, Letters and Cables to Marseille, May–August 1941.
70. Ibid.
71. Letter from Marjorie McClelland to Margaret Frawley, 22 April 1942, AFSC Archive. Box: General Files 1942, Foreign Service, France; File: Relief and Refugees, Marseille, Letters and Cables, January–May 1942.
72. File Antoinette Steuer, AFSC Archive. Box: General Files 1942, Foreign Service Refugee Services; File: Refugee Services, June–August 1942, Children, U.S. Committee for the Care of European Children—AFSCA Cooperation.
73. File Henri and Miriam Mass, ibid.
74. "Refugees Reach Land of Freedom from the Prison That Is Europe," *New York Herald Tribune*, 26 June 1942.
75. Memorandum Donald A. Lowrie, 10 August 1942, AFSC Archive. Box: General Files 1942, Foreign Service, France; File: Relief and Refuges, General 1942, 1.
76. Memorandum Donald A. Lowrie, ibid., 2.
77. For the negotiations in Washington, D.C., see "Statement by Mr George L. Warren," 14 September 1942, AFSC Archive. Box: General Files 1942, Foreign Service, France. File: Relief and Refugees. Children's Transports 1942.
78. Burrit Hiatt, Activities log, AFSC Archive. Box: General Files 1942, Foreign Service, France; File: Relief of Refugees, Marseille, 5.
79. Lindsley H. Noble, Children's Emigration, 27 October 1942, AFSC Archive. Box: General Files 1942, Foreign Service; File: Refugee Jews, September–December 1942.
80. Donald A. Lowrie, "Conversation with Mr Bousquet, Secrétaire-Général de la Police. Vichy, October 16th," AFSC Archive. Box: General Files 1942, Foreign Service; File: Refugee Jews, September–December 1942.
81. Burrit Hiatt, Activities log, AFSC Archive. Box: General Files 1942, Foreign Service France; File: Relief of Refugees, Marseille, 112.
82. Agenda Board Meeting USCCEC, 24 November 1942, AFSC Archive. Box: General Files 1942, Foreign Service; File: Refugee Jews, September–December 1942, Children, U.S. Committee for CEC-AFSC Cooperation.
83. Koestler, *Scum of the Earth*, 107.

PAPERS: LOVED ONES BECOME LETTERS

1. Letter from Wilhelm Halberstam to the Hepner-Halberstam family, 11 May 1939, in Irmtrud Wojak and Lore Hepner, eds., *"Geliebte Kinder . . ." Briefe aus dem Amsterdamer Exil in die Neue Welt* (Essen: Klartext Verlag, 1995), 60.
2. Letter from Wilhelm Halberstam to the Hepner-Halberstam family, 10 May 1940, ibid., 117.

3. Letter from Wilhelm Halberstam to the Hepner-Halberstam family, 19 May 1940, ibid., 121.

4. Letter from Marjorie McClelland to Margaret Frawley, 9 May 1942. AFSC Archive. Box: General Files 1942, Foreign Service Refugee Services; File: Refugee Services, June–August 1942, Children, U.S. Committee for the Care of European Children–AFSCA Cooperation.

5. Letter from Robert Lang to Margaret Frawley, 8 June 1942. Ibid.

6. The German ocean liner *St. Louis* left Hamburg on 13 May 1939 carrying 937 passengers, mostly Jewish refugees with Cuban visas. Upon arrival in Havana, the Jewish passengers were not allowed to disembark. The *St. Louis* thus began a long journey in search of a safe harbor for its passengers that included a failed attempt to land in Miami and ended with the return to Europe on 19 June. The highly publicized failure of the passengers to find a haven overseas became a symbol of the Jews' agony: the search for "anywhere" had yielded only a "nowhere" in return. See inter alia: Georg Mautner Markhof, *Das St. Louis Drama: Hintergrund und Rätsel einer mysteriösen Aktion des Dritten Reiches* (Graz: Leopold Stocker Verlag, 2001); John Mendelsohn, ed., *The Holocaust, Jewish Emigration, the S.S. St Louis Affair, and Other Cases*, vol. 7 (New York and London: Garland Publishing, 1982); Gordon Thomas and Max Morgan Witts, *Voyage of the Damned* (New York: Stein and Day, 1974). See too: Stefanie Fischer's M.A. thesis, "The Fiasco of the SS *St. Louis*—History and Myth," held at the Rose Library, Strassler Center for Holocaust and Genocide Studies, Clark University.

7. Letter from Adele Halberstam-Mamroth to Käthe Hepner-Halberstam, 19 June 1939, in Wojak and Hepner, eds., *"Geliebte Kinder . . . ,"* 72.

8. Letter from Wilhelm Halberstam to Hepner-Halberstam family, 20 July 1939, ibid., 76f.

9. Letter from Martha Levi to Elisabeth Luz, 8 February 1941, authors' collection [letter #186/1].

10. Letter from Martha Levi to Elisabeth Luz, 29 April 1941, authors' collection [letter #186/3] .

11. Postcard from Elisabeth Luz to Martha Levi, 6 September 1942, authors' collection [letter #197].

12. For a reflection on the role of letters in the lives of refugees and their families see Oliver Doetzer, *"Aus Menschen werden Briefe": Die Korrespondenz einer jüdischen Familie zwischen Verfolgung und Emigration, 1933–1947* (Cologne, Weimar, and Vienna: Böhlau Verlag, 2002). See too publications of family correspondence; inter alia: John S. Conway, "The Last Letters of the Brandt-Meyer Family from Berlin," in *Yad Vashem Studies*, vol. 11 (1976), 91–130; Michael Philipp, "'Unsere Correktheit trägt traurige Früchte': Aus einer Familienkorrespondenz im Exil," in *Exil: Forschung, Erkenntnisse,*

Ergebnisse, vol. 8 (1988), issue 2, 11–29; Raya Czerner Schapiro and Helga Czerner Weinberg, *One Family's Letters from Prague* (Chicago: Academy Chicago Publishers, 1996). Friends too carried on correspondence. See for example: the letters between Lion Feuchtwanger and Bertold Brecht, which elucidate Feuchtwanger's help at every stage in Brecht's flight from Helsinki to America, via Moscow and Vladivostok. See Lion Feuchtwanger, Harold von Hofe, and Sigrid Washburn, *Briefwechsel mit Freunden*, 2 vols. (Berlin and Weimar: Aufbau-Verlag, 1991), esp. vol. 1, 45–55; also Bertold Brecht, *Letters*, trans. Ralph Manheim, ed. John Willett (London: Methuen, 1990), 322–34.

13. Hannah Arendt and Heinrich Blücher, *Within Four Walls: The Correspondence Between Hannah Arendt and Heinrich Blücher, 1936–1968,* ed. Lotte Kohler, trans. Peter Constantine (New York: Harcourt, 2000), 52.

14. Letter from Adele Halberstam-Mamroth to Käthe Hepner-Halberstam, in Wojak and Hepner, eds., *"Geliebte Kinder . . . ,"* 92.

15. Letter from Susi Guttmann to Elisabeth Luz, 11 February 1940, authors' collection [letter #782a]; letter from Eva Guttmann to Elisabeth Luz, 14 February 1940, authors' collection [letter #782b].

16. Card from Susi Guttmann to Elisabeth Luz, 13 June 1940, authors' collection [letter #781].

17. Card from Susi Guttmann to Elisabeth Luz, 19 July 1940, authors' collection [letter #780].

18. Letter from Ernst Matzdorff to Elisabeth Luz, 5 November 1941, authors' collection [letter #408].

19. Carl Zuckmayer, *Aufruf zum Leben: Porträts und Zeugnisse aus bewegten Zeiten* (Frankfurt: Fischer, 1976), 15.

20. Letter from Phyllis Shepherd to Herbert Neuwalder, n.d., Family Archive of Susanne Harris-Neuwalder; copy in possession of authors.

21. Letter from Herbert Neuwalder to Phyllis Shepherd, 4 December 1939, Family Archive of Susanne Harris-Neuwalder; copy in possession of authors.

22. Letter from Phyllis Shepherd to Herbert Neuwalder, 9 January 1940, Family Archive of Susanne Harris-Neuwalder; copy in possession of authors.

23. Letter from Herbert Neuwalder to Phyllis Shepherd, 25 January 1940, Family Archive of Susanne Harris-Neuwalder; copy in possession of authors.

24. Letter from Phyllis Shepherd to Herbert Neuwalder, 7 February 1940, Family Archive of Susanne Harris-Neuwalder; copy in possession of authors.

25. Letter from Robert and Adolf Hess to Elisabeth Luz, 19 April 1941, authors' collection [letter #795].

26. Letter from Heinz Pfützner to Elisabeth Luz, 30 May 1941, authors' collection [letter #833a].

27. The words are part of the first sentence of an untitled poem published in the collection *Zahme Xenien* (Gentle Ironies).

Sei du im Leben wie im Wissen
Durchaus der reinen Fahrt beflissen,
Wenn Sturm und Strömung stossen, zerrn,
Sie werden doch nicht deine Herrn,
Kompass und Pol-Stern, Zeitenmesser
Und Sonn und Mond verstehst du besser,
Vollendest so nach deiner Art
Mit stillen Freuden deine Fahrt.

In rough translation:

Always be assiduous
in life and in the pursuit of knowledge
and when storm and current push and pull
they will not get the better of you
because compass and polar star, clock
and sun and moon you understand better
Thus complete in your own manner
with quiet satisfaction your journey.

Johann Wolfgang von Goethe, "Zahne Xenien VI," in Johann Wolfgang von Goethe, *Sämtliche Werke nach Epochen seines Schaffen*, ed. Karl Richter, 21 vols. (Munich and Vienna: Carl Hanser Verlag, 1985–98), vol. 13, 1, 227.

28. Letter from J. Bingen to Elisabeth Luz, 28 September 1942, authors' collection [letter #907].

29. Letter from Ursel Matzdorff to Elisabeth Luz, 12 September 1942, authors' collection [letter #598].

30. Letter from Captain Schauber to Elisabeth Luz, 22 December 1942, authors' collection [letter #599].

31. Letter from Flore Loinger to Elisabeth Luz, 12 November 1942, authors' collection [letter #64].

32. Letter from Adele Halberstam-Mamroth to Käthe Hepner-Halberstam, 2 July 1940, in Wojak and Hepner, eds., *"Geliebte Kinder . . . ,"* 126.

33. Letter from Wilhelm Halberstam to the Hepner family, 13 April 1942, ibid., *"Geliebte Kinder . . . ,"* 208f.

34. Letter from Wilhelm Halberstam to the Hepner family, 5 May 1942, ibid., 212.

35. Letter from Adele Halberstam-Mamroth to Käthe Hepner-Halberstam, 20–21 July 1942, ibid., 223.

36. Letter from Norbert Roth to Elisabeth Luz, 2 January 1942, authors' collection [letter #265a].

37. Letter from Norbert Roth to Elisabeth Luz, 13 April 1942, authors' collection [letter #263].
38. Letter from Norbert Roth to Elisabeth Luz, 10 May 1942, authors' collection [letter #262].
39. Letter from Regina Roth-Kaczinsky to Norbert Roth, 1 November 1942, authors' collection [letter #266].
40. Letter from Walter Beyth to Elisabeth Luz, 17 February 1941, authors' collection [letter #456].
41. Letter from Fée Beyth to Elisabeth Luz, 25 February 1942, authors' collection [letter #249a].
42. Letter from Fée Beyth to Elisabeth Luz, 9 May 1942, authors' collection [letter #251].
43. Ibid.
44. International Committee of the Red Cross, *Report of the International Committee of the Red Cross on Its Activities during the Second World War (September 1, 1939–June 30, 1947)*, 3 vols. (Geneva: International Committee of the Red Cross, 1948), vol. 2, 63ff.; Ivor Halsted, *Post Haste: The story of the Post Office in Peace and War* (London: Lindsay Drummond, 1944), 108f. See also: Henri Coursier, *The International Red Cross*, trans. M. C. S. Phipps (Geneva: International Committee of the Red Cross, 1961), 34f., 42; Hans Haug, *Humanity for All: The International Red Cross and Red Crescent Movement* (Bern: Paul Haupt, 1993), 61; International Committee of the Red Cross, *Handbook of the International Red Cross and Red Crescent Movement*, 13th edition (Geneva: International Committee of the Red Cross, 1994), 145.
45. Red Cross Message from Adele Halberstam-Mamroth to Hepner family, 8 August 1943, in Wojak and Hepner, eds., *"Geliebte Kinder . . . ,"* 249.
46. Red Cross Message from Adele Halberstam-Mamroth to Hepner family, 5 October 1943, ibid., 252.
47. Red Cross Message from Adele Halberstam-Mamroth to Hepner family, 31 October 1943, ibid., 255.
48. Letter from Hanna-Ruth Klopstock to Elisabeth Luz, 30 April 1942, authors' collection [letter #251a].
49. Letter from Frieda Klopstock to Elisabeth Luz, 21 December 1942, authors' collection [letter #443].
50. Letter from Werner Klopstock to Elisabeth Luz and Hanna-Ruth Klopstock, n.d., authors' collection [letter #367].
51. Postcard from Elisabeth Luz to Werner Klopstock, 23 February 1943, authors' collection [letter #445].
52. See Julien Lajournade, *Le Courrier dans les Camps de Concentration: Système et Rôle Politique, 1933–1945* (Paris: Editions l'Image Document, 1989), especially 129ff. On letters from concentration camps, see also Frauke Dettmer, "'Ich bin gesund und es geht mir gut': Briefe aus Konzentrationslagern und Ghettos,"

in *Informationen zur Schleswig-Holsteinischen Zeitgeschichte*, no. 33–34 (1998), 213–18.

53. Postcard from Werner Klopstock to Elisabeth Luz and Hanna-Ruth Klopstock, 18 July 1943, authors' collection [letter #633].

54. International Military Tribunal, *Trial of the Major War Criminals*, 46 vols. (Nuremberg: Secretariat of the International Military Tribunal, 1947), vol. 5, 11.

PROBLEMS: LIFE AS A REFUGEE

1. For an excellent biography in English, see Donald Arthur Prater, *European of Yesterday: A Biography of Stefan Zweig* (Oxford: Clarendon Press, 1972).

2. Letter to Romain Rolland, 10 May 1933, in Stefan Zweig, *Briefe 1932–1942*, ed. Knut Beck and Jeffrey B. Berlin (Frankfurt: S. Fischer, 2005), 60. In a "Hymn on Exile" that Zweig included in his biography of Joseph Fouché (written in the late 1920s), Zweig valorized the émigré experience. Exile, Zweig argued, was a crucible in which people might develop their full potential. Experience taught him to think differently. When Zweig committed suicide in 1942, the Jewish refugee Theodor Wolff observed that he had recanted and disavowed his "Hymn on Exile"—and appropriately so. Stefan Zweig, *Joseph Fouché: The Portrait of a Politician*, trans. Eden and Cedar Paul (New York: Viking, 1930), 112ff.; Theodor Wolff, *"Die Juden": Ein Dokument aus dem Exil 1942/43*, ed. Bernd Sösemann (Königstein: Jüdischer Verlag Athenäum, 1984), 42ff.

3. Letter to Romain Rolland, 10 June 1933, in Zweig, *Briefe 1932–1942*, 62.

4. This search marked a watershed in his life. See: letter to Romain Rolland, 1 May 1938, ibid., 219f.; and Stefan Zweig, *The World of Yesterday* (London: Cassell & Co., 1943), 292f.

5. Irmgard Keun, "Stefan Zweig, der Emigrant," in Hanns Arens, ed., *Stefan Zweig im Zeugnis seiner Freunde* (Munich and Vienna: Langen Müller, 1968), 161.

6. Letter to Friderike Maria Zweig, postmarked 12 May 1937, in Zweig, *Briefe 1932–1942*, 190.

7. Zweig, *The World of Yesterday*, 310.

8. Klaus Mann, "Er war ein Verzweifelter . . . ," in Arens, ed., *Stefan Zweig im Zeugnis seiner Freunde*, 163.

9. Käthe Frankenthal, *Der dreifache Fluch: Jüdin, Intellektuelle, Sozialistin* (Frankfurt and New York: Campus Verlag, 1981), 216.

10. Letter to Friderike Zweig, 10 September 1941, in Stefan and Friderike Zweig, *Their Correspondence 1912–1942*, trans. Henry G. Alsberg with Erna MacArthur (New York: Hastings House, 1954), 330.

11. Letters to Friderike Zweig, 15 December 1941 and 22 February 1942, in Zweig, *Briefe 1932–1942*, 340; 344.

12. See Prater, *European of Yesterday*, 331ff.

13. Jules Romains, *Stefan Zweig: Great European* (New York: Viking, 1941), 29.

14. Konrad Kwiet, "The Ultimate Refuge: Suicide in the Jewish Community Under the Nazis," *Leo Baeck Institute Year Book*, vol. 29 (1984), esp. 146; 150; 156; John Hope Simpson, *The Refugee Problem: Report of a Survey* (London, New York, and Toronto: Oxford University Press, 1939), 126.

15. Hannah Arendt, "We Refugees," *The Menorah Journal*, vol. 31 (1943), 72f.

16. Jean Améry, "How Much Home Does a Person Need?," *At the Mind's Limits: Contemplations by a Survivor on Auschwitz and Its Realities*, trans. Sidney Rosenfeld and Stella Rosenfeld (Bloomington: Indiana University Press, 1980), 58.

17. "Meeting Between the Home Secretary and members of the Medical Profession," 4 July 1938; accompanying notes by Ernest Cooper to Sir Maxwell and to the file on 27 April 1938; note by Ernest Cooper of 27 July 1938. PRO, HO 213/257—106681, 1–3; 8–9; 31. Letter from Charles Hill, deputy secretary of the British Medical Association, to Cooper, 19 August 1938. PRO, HO 213/258—06738.

18. Hertha Nathorff, *Das Tagebuch der Hertha Nathorff: Berlin, New York, Aufzeichnungen 1933 bis 1945*, ed. Wolfgang Benz (Munich: R. Oldenbourg, 1987), 13.

19. Ibid., 186.

20. Ibid.,188.

21. Ibid., 189f.

22. Ibid., 191.

23. Martin Gumpert, *First Papers*, trans. Heinz and Ruth Norden (New York: Duell, Sloan and Pearce, 1941), 42f.

24. Ibid., 27f.

25. In the late 1930s and early 1940s many studies appeared in the United States on the way refugees were coping with the stresses and opportunities of their new lives. These studies include: Willi Schlamm, "The Cultural Dilemma of the Refugee," *Jewish Frontier*, vol. 6 (February 1939), 6–9; Gerhart Saenger, "The Psychology of the Refugee," *Contemporary Jewish Record*, vol. 3 (1940), 264–73; Gerhart Saenger, *Today's Refugees, Tomorrow's Citizens: A Story of Americanization* (New York and London: Harper & Brothers, 1941); Maurice R. Davie, *Refugees in America: Report of the Committee for the Study of Recent Immigration from Europe* (New York and London: Harpers, 1947); Donald Peterson Kent, *The Refugee Intellectual: The Americanization of Immigrants, 1933–1941* (New York: Columbia University Press, 1953); see also Yvonne Kapp and Margeret Mynatt, *British Policy and the Refugees, 1933–1941* (London and Portland, OR: Frank Cass, 1997), 62ff.; Alfred Döblin, "Eindrücke von New York," *Schriften zu Leben und Werk* (Olten and Freiburg: Walter-Verlag, 1986), 243–57; an unsurpassed portrait of the psychology of the refugee remains Kazys Claude Cirtautas, *The Refugee: A Psychological Study* (Boston: Meador Publishing Company, 1957).

26. See inter alia: Anthony Heilbut, *Exiled in Paradise: German Refugee Artists and*

Intellectuals in America from the 1930s to the Present (Berkeley: University of California Press, 1997).

27. Gumpert, *First Papers*, 30f.

28. Hilde Spiel, *Die hellen und die finsteren Zeiten: Erinnerungen 1911–1946* (Munich: List Verlag, 1989), 204f.

29. Meir Gottesman and Alan Sillitoe, eds., *Out of the Fire* (London: Children and Youth Aliyah Committee, 1979), 25.

30. Marie Syrkin, "Rebirth in San Domingo?," *Jewish Frontier* (February 1941), 13.

31. Ibid., 12.

32. Otto Suschny, oral history conducted by Debórah Dwork, Vienna, 18 July 1991, transcript, 58; 42; 59–60; 42.

33. Gerda Freistadt-Geiringer, oral history conducted by Debórah Dwork, Vienna, 10, 12, and 15 July 1991, transcript, 75–8.

34. Ibid., 79–80.

35. *Young Austria in Grossbritannien: Wiedersehenstreffen anlässlich des 50. Jahrestages der Besetzung Österreichs* (Vienna: Verein Wiedersehenstreffen 1938–1988, Young Austria, 1988), 7. See also Erich Fried, *Mitunter sogar Lachen: Zwischenfälle und Erinnerungen* (Berlin: Wagenbach, 1986), 103ff.

36. Oral history of Gerda Freistadt-Geiringer, 97–101.

37. Georg Eisler, oral history conducted by Debórah Dwork, Vienna, 2 July 1990, transcript, 5.

38. Oral history of Gerda Freistadt-Geiringer, 102.

39. Robert Rosner, oral history conducted by Debórah Dwork, Vienna, 3 July 1990, transcript, 39.

40. Ibid., 57.

41. Lena Jedwab Rozenberg, *Girl with Two Landscapes: The Wartime Diary of Lena Jedwab, 1941–1945* (New York and London: Holmes & Meier, 2002), 15f.

42. Ibid., 35.

43. Ibid., 48; 104; 107; 121.

44. Ibid., 129; 136ff.

45. Ibid., 142.

46. Ibid., 148; 155; 159.

1942–1946: HOLOCAUST

1. "Extermination of Polish Jewry: What Happened in the Warsaw Ghetto," *Polish Fortnightly Review*, no. 57 (1 December 1942), 3.

2. As quoted in Bernard Wasserstein, *Britain and the Jews of Europe 1939–1945* (Oxford: Clarendon Press, 1979), 173.

3. On the blockade, see W. N. Medlicott, *The Economic Blockade*, 2 vols. (London: His Majesty's Stationery Office, 1952–9).

4. Great Britain, *Parliamentary Debates: House of Commons*, 5th series (London: His Majesty's Stationery Office, 1943), vol. 386, 31.

5. On the Bermuda conference, see Arieh Tartakower and Kurt R. Grossmann, *The Jewish Refugee* (New York: Institute of Jewish Affairs, 1944), 420ff.; Henry L. Feingold, *The Politics of Rescue: The Roosevelt Administration and the Holocaust, 1938–1945* (New York: Holocaust Library, 1970), 167ff.; Bernard Wasserstein, *Britain and the Jews of Europe 1939–1945* (Oxford: Clarendon Press, 1979), 188ff.; Irving Abella and Harold Troper, *None Is Too Many: Canada and the Jews of Europe 1933–1948* (New York: Random House, 1983), 126ff.; David S. Wyman, *The Abandonment of the Jews* (New York: Pantheon, 1984), 104ff.; Monty Noam Penkower. *The Jews Were Expendable: Free World Diplomacy and the Holocaust* (Detroit: Wayne State University Press, 1988), 98ff.

6. Quoted in Feingold, *The Politics of Rescue*, 206.

7. "To 5,000,000 Jews in the Nazi Death-Trap Bermuda Was a 'Cruel Mockery,'" Ad in the *New York Times*, 4 May 1943, as printed in David S. Wyman, *America and the Holocaust*, 13 vols. (New York and London: Garland, 1990), vol. 3, document 27 (between 292 and 293).

8. As quoted in Paul A. Levine, "From Indifference to Activism: Swedish Diplomacy and the Holocaust, 1938–1945" (Ph.D. thesis, Uppsala University, 1996), 139.

9. Ibid., 229.

10. See inter alia: Tatiana Brustin-Berenstein, "The Historiographic Treatment of the Abortive Attempt to Deport the Danish Jews," *Yad Vashem Studies*, vol. 17 (1986), 181–218; Harold Flender, *Rescue in Denmark* (New York.: Holocaust Library, 1963); Raul Hilberg, *The Destruction of the European Jews,* 3 vols. (New York: Holmes & Meier, 1985), vol. 2, 558–68; Steven L. B. Jensen and Mette Bash-olm Jensen, *Denmark and the Holocaust* (Copenhagen: Danish Institute for International Studies, 2003); Hans Kirchhoff, "*SS-Gruppenführer* Werner Best and the Action Against the Danish Jews," *Yad Vashem Studies*, vol. 24 (1994), 195–222; Levine, *Indifference to Activism*, 229–45; "Sweden," *Review of the Foreign Press, Series B*, no. 205 (20 October 1943), 409f.; Hugo Valentin, "Rescue Activities in Scandinavia," *YIVO Annual of Jewish Social Science*, vol. 8 (1953), 224–51; Leni Yahil, *The Rescue of Danish Jewry: Test of a Democracy*, trans. Morris Gradel (Philadelphia: Jewish Publication Society of America, 1969).

11. Peter Weiss, "Vanishing Point," in *Exile*, trans. E. B. Garside, Alastair Hamilton, and Christopher Levenson (New York: Delacorte Press, 1968), 194f.

PEOPLE: SHERIT HAPLEITA: THE SURVIVING REMNANT

1. Quoted in United Nations Information Office, *War and Peace Aims: Extracts from Statements of United Nation Leaders*, issue 1 (30 January 1943), 27.

2. During the war the term "United Nations" referred to allies, the nations united

against the Axis forces. The present-day United Nations was established in August 1945, just a few months after the war.

3. Preamble to the Agreement for the United Nations Relief and Rehabilitation Administration, 9 November 1943, in George Woodbridge, ed., *UNRRA: The History of the United Nations Relief and Rehabilitation Administration,* 3 vols. (New York: Columbia University Press, 1950), vol. 3, 23.

4. Eugene M. Kulischer, *The Displacement of Population in Europe* (Montreal: International Labour Office, 1943), i.

5. Ibid., 166.

6. Tommie Sjöberg, *The Powers and the Persecuted: The Refugee Problem and the Intergovernmental Committee on Refugees (ICGR), 1938–1947* (Lund: Lund University Press, 1991), 126.

7. Sir Herbert Emerson, "Postwar Problems of Refugees," *Foreign Affairs,* vol. 21 (1942–3), 213.

8. Ben Halpern, "We and the European Jews," *Jewish Frontier,* vol. 10 (August 1943), 16.

9. Ibid., 16f.

10. United Nations Relief and Rehabilitation Administration, *First Session of the Council of the United Nations Relief and Rehabilitation Administration: Selected Documents* (Washington, DC: Government Printing Office, 1944), 159.

11. Letter A. Leon Kubowitzki and Arie Tartakower to Sir George Rendel, 24 November 1943, as quoted in Zorach Warhaftig, *Relief and Rehabilitation: Implications of the UNRRA Program for Jewish Needs* (New York: Institute of Jewish Affairs, 1944), 117.

12. Hannah Arendt, "Guests from No-Man's Land," in Hannah Arendt, *The Jewish Writings,* ed. Jerome Kohn and Ron H. Feldman (New York: Schocken, 2007), 212.

13. Zorach Warhaftig, *Refugee and Survivor* (Jerusalem: Yad Vashem, 1988), 102–11.

14. Warhaftig, *Relief and Rehabilitation,* 151.

15. UNRRA, *First Session of the Council,* 159.

16. Warhaftig, *Relief and Rehabilitation,* 114.

17. Ibid., 115.

18. UNRRA, *Journal,* vol. 3, no. 4 (10 August 1945), 38. The Soviets arrested many of their repatriated citizens (including POWs), and executed them as traitors or deported them to gulags for having conspired with the enemy.

19. Letter from Zalman Grinberg, Samuel Gringauz, and A. Bergmann to the World Jewish Congress, 31 May 1945, as quoted in Leo W. Schwarz, *The Redeemers: A Saga of the Years 1945–1952* (New York: Farrar, Straus and Young, 1953), 320f.

20. Ernst M. Lorge, "A Tragic Object-Lesson," *Jewish Frontier,* vol. 12 (August 1945), 11.

21. Ibid., 12; for the crucial role of the Jewish chaplains in the rescue of the Jewish survivors, see Alex Grobman, *Rekindling the Flame: American Jewish Chaplains and the Survivors of European Jewry, 1944–1948* (Detroit: Wayne State University Press, 1993).

22. Leonard Dinnerstein, *America and the Survivors of the Holocaust* (New York: Columbia University Press, 1982), 34ff.

23. On Sherit Hapleita, see: Yisrael Gutman and Avital Saf, eds., *She'erit Hapletah, 1944–1948: Rehabilitation and Political Struggle* (Jerusalem: Yad Vashem, 1990); Abraham J. Klausner, *A Letter to My Children: From the Edge of the Holocaust* (San Francisco: Holocaust Center of Northern California, 2002), 27; Ze'ev Mankowitz, "The Formation of She'erit Hapleita: November 1944–July 1945," *Yad Vashem Studies*, vol. 20 (1990), 337–70; Ze'ev Mankowitz, "The Affirmation of Life in She'erith Hapleitah," *Holocaust and Genocide Studies*, vol. 5 (1990), 13–21; Zeev W. Mankowitz, *Life Between Memory and Hope: the Survivors of the Holocaust in Occupied Germany* (Cambridge: Cambridge University Press, 2002). In his address to the Twentieth Zionist Congress (August 1937), Chaim Weitzmann had applied the concept of Sherit Hapleita to an estimated two million young European Jews who could be absorbed by the small Jewish state proposed by the Peel Commission. See Barnet Litvinoff, ed., *The Letters and Papers of Chaim Weizmann Series B*, vol. 2 (New Brunswick, NJ: Transaction Books, 1984), 286.

24. As quoted in Schwarz, *The Redeemers*, 320f.

25. Report of Earl G. Harrison, "Displaced Persons in Germany," *Department of State Bulletin*, vol. 13, no. 327 (30 September 1945), 456.

26. Ibid., 458.

27. Ibid., 462.

28. Ibid., 460.

29. Ibid., 461.

30. See for example: Hitler's speech to the Greater German Reichstag on 30 January 1939; see Max Domarus, *Hitler: Speeches and Proclamations, 1932–1945*, 4 vols. (Wauconda, IL: Bolchazy-Carducci, 1990–7), vol. 3, 1447ff.

31. Sebastian Haffner, *Germany: Jekyll and Hyde* (New York: Dutton, 1941), 233.

32. Letter from President Harry S. Truman to General Dwight D. Eisenhower, in Report of Earl G. Harrison, "Displaced Persons in Germany," 456.

33. Telegram from General Dwight D. Eisenhower to President Harry S. Truman, 14 September 1945, in Alfred D. Chandler, Jr., and Louis Galambos, eds., *The Papers of Dwight David Eisenhower*, 21 vols. (Baltimore and London: Johns Hopkins Press, 1970–2001), vol. 6, 353.

34. Letter from General Dwight D. Eisenhower to President Harry S. Truman, 18 September 1945, ibid., vol. 6, 358.

35. Schwarz, *The Redeemers*, 38ff.

36. Letter from General Dwight D. Eisenhower to Lieutenant General George

S. Patton, 29 September 1945, in Chandler and Galambos, eds., *The Papers of Dwight David Eisenhower*, vol. 6, 394.

37. George S. Patton, diary entry 1 October 1945, in Martin Blumenson, *The Patton Papers, 1940–1945*, 2 vols. (Boston: Houghton Mifflin, 1974), vol. 2, 787.

38. "Problems Confronting Displaced Persons Program in Germany," *Department of State Bulletin*, vol. 13, no. 327 (30 September 1945), 464.

39. Shlomo Katz, "The Jewish 'Displaced Persons,'" *Jewish Frontier*, vol. 13 (July 1946), 6.

40. Minutes, cabinet meeting, 4 October 1945, in Michael J. Cohen, *The Rise of Israel*, 39 vols. (New York and London: Garland, 1987), vol. 35, 60ff.

41. "Address of Bartley C. Crum, Member, Anglo-American Committee of Inquiry, 12 June 1946," Aaron S. Klieman and Adrian L. Klieman, eds., *American Zionism: A Documentary History*, 15 vols. (New York and London: Garland, 1990–1), vol. 11, part II, 214.

42. "Report of the Anglo-American Committee of Enquiry Regarding the Problems of European Jewry and Palestine, Lausanne, 20 April 1946," in Cohen, *The Rise of Israel*, vol. 35, 185ff.; 196f.

43. Chaim Weizmann, *The Letters and Papers of Chaim Weizmann*, ed. Barnet Litvinov (Oxford: Oxford University Press, 1968–84), vol. 22, series A, 118.

44. Richard Crossman, *Palestine Mission* (London: Hamish Hamilton, 1947), 175.

45. Richard Crossman, "Notes on Palestine Report of Anglo-American Committee, Lausanne, 22 April 1946," in Cohen, *The Rise of Israel*, vol. 35, 336ff.

46. "Report of the Anglo-American Committee," 152f.

47. Letter of Chaim Weizmann to Sir James Grigg, 21 June 1945, in Weizmann, *The Letters and Papers of Chaim Weizmann*, vol. 22, series A, 23f.

48. As quoted in Tom Segev, *The Seventh Million: The Israelis and the Holocaust*, trans. Haim Watzman (New York: Hill and Wang, 1993), 120.

49. Judah Nadich, *Eisenhower and the Jews* (New York: Twayne Publishers, 1953), 231f.

50. As quoted in Segev, *The Seventh Million*, 121.

51. Bernard D. Weinryb, "Poland," in Peter Meyer a.o., *The Jews in the Soviet Satellites* (Syracuse: Syracuse University Press, 1953), 244.

52. Ibid., 252ff.; For the problems of returning Jewish refugees in Poland, see Ewa Kozminska-Frejlak, "Polen als Heimat von Juden: Strategien des Heimischwerdens von Juden im Nachkriegspolen 1944–1949," in Fritz Bauer Institut, ed., *Überlebt und unterwegs: Jüdische Displaced Persons in Nachkriegsdeutschland* (Frankfurt and New York: Campus Verlag, 1997), 71–107.

53. Abraham J. Klausner, "The Central Committee," in *Sharit Ha-Platah: An Extensive List of Survivors of Nazi Tyranny Published So That the Lost May Be Found and the Dead May Be Brought Back to Life* (Munich: Central Committee of Liberated Jews in Bavaria, 1946), n.p.

54. "The Hearings in Washington: Excerpts of Testimony," *Jewish Frontier*, vol. 13 (February 1946), 31.

PLACES: WHERE NOW?

1. Jenny Gans-Premsela, *Vluchtweg* (Baarn: Bosch & Keunig, 1990), 153.

2. Abel Jacob Herzberg, *Kroniek der Jodenvervolging, 1940–1945* (Amsterdam: Meulenhoff, 1978), 7; Herzberg's 250-page chronicle of the persecution of the Dutch Jews was first published in 1950 as numbers 23 through 26 of a 36-issue periodical entitled *Onderdrukking en Verzet: Nederland in Oorlogstijd*.

3. "Der Hexensabbat der Verjudung in den Wiener Theatern," *Völkischer Beobachter*—Vienna edition (18 March 1938).

4. Ernst Lothar, *Das Wunder des Überlebens: Erinnerungen und Ergebnisse* (Hamburg and Vienna: Paul Zsolnay Verlag, 1960), 124.

5. Ibid., 211.

6. Ibid., 313.

7. Ibid., 290.

8. Ibid., 435. The republic of Austria had been reestablished in 1945, and with it Austrian nationality. Repatriating after 1945, refugees who had been stripped of their citizenship automatically regained an Austrian passport under the *Nichtigkeitsgesetz* (Nullity Law) of 1946. Thus the German denationalization decree of November 1941, which had rendered all Jewish refugees stateless, was annulled. Refugees like the Lothars, who had obtained foreign nationality, faced a substantial legal hurdle, however. Pre-war law applied: Austrians who accepted foreign nationality lost their Austrian citizenship. The postwar state refused to recognize the particular nature of the refugees' wartime circumstances. The law was amended for repatriates only in 1973, and it took another twenty years before another amendment facilitated the restoration of citizenship to Austrian refugees who had remained abroad after the war. See Dieter Kolonovits, Hannelore Burger, and Harald Wendelin, eds., *Staatsbürgerschaft und Vertreibung* (Munich: Oldenbourg, 2004). Also Harald Wendelin "'. . . denn heut kann man nirgendwo mehr ohne ein gestempeltes Papier existieren.' Die Restitution der Staatsbürgerschaft," in Verene Pawlowsky and Harald Wendelin, eds., *Die Republik und das NS-Erbe: Raub und Rückgabe, Österreich von 1938 bis Heute* (Vienna: Mandelbaum Verlag, 2005), 27–39.

9. Passports issued to Edith Sara Gruber and Armin Israel Gruber, 22 and 17 February 1939, respectively, and lease by R. Kikoin and Edith Gruber of Mr I. I. Sachkovich's premises (signed by all parties), Shanghai, China, 4 August 1939. Family Archive of Gabriel Gruber; copies in possession of the authors. Recollections of Gabriel Gruber, conversation with Debórah Dwork, 14 October 2007.

10. Georg Armbrüster, "Das Ende des Exils in Shanghai: Rück- und Weiterwan-

derung nach 1945," in Georg Armbrüster, Michael Kohlstruck, and Sonja Mühlberger, eds., *Exil Shanghai 1938–1947: Jüdisches Leben in der Emigration* (Teetz: Hentrich & Hentrich, 2000), 184.

11. [Wilhelm Meier], "Zwischen Schanghai und Berlin: Die Ankunft der 295 Rückkehrer," *Der Weg*, 29 August 1947, 3.

12. On the restoration of property in the immediate postwar period in Germany and Austria, see inter alia: Constantin Goschler, *Wiedergutmachung: Westdeutschland und die Verfolgten des Nationalsozialismus, 1945–1954* (Munich: R. Oldenbourg Verlag, 1992), 91–148; idem, *Schuld und Schulden: Die Politik der Wiedergutmachung für NS-Verfolgte seit 1945* (Göttingen: Wallstein Verlag, 2005), 61–124; Monroe Karasik, "Problems of Compensation and Restitution in Germany and Austria," *Law and Contemporary Problems*, vol. 16 (1951), 448–68; Nehemiah Robinson, *Restitution Legislation in Germany: A Survey of Enactments* (New York: Institute of Jewish Affairs, 1949); Walter Schwarz, *Rückerstattung nach den Gesetzen der Alliierten Mächte* (Munich: Beck, 1974); Ignaz Seidl-Hohenveldern, "Austria: Restitution Legislation," *American Journal of Comparative Law*, vol. 2 (1953), 383–9.

13. "Bundesgesetz vom 15. Mai 1946 über die Nichterklärung von Rechtsgeschäften und sonstigen Rechtshandlungen, die während der deutschen Besetzung Österreichs erfolgt sind," *Staatsgesetzblatt für die Republic Österreich* (30 July 1946), 141.

14. Letter from Siegmund Fischel, President, Communal Association of Central European Jews, Shanghai, 12 May 1947; immigration visas, 24 May 1947; smallpox vaccination papers. Family Archive of Gabriel Gruber; copies in possession of the authors.

15. See Armbrüster, "Das Ende des Exils in Shanghai," 187ff.

16. Peter Fabrizius, "Gerettet aus Shanghai," *Aufbau*, 25 February 1949, 17.

17. "4,000 Juden in der Falle von Shanghai," *Aufbau*, 6 May 1949, 7.

18. "'Operation Flying Dragon': Evakuierung der Shanghai-Flüchtlinge in Flugzeugen," *Aufbau*, 13 May 1949, 2.

19. These 108 refugees were among those evacuated by ship from Shanghai to San Francisco and, refused admission to the United States, sent on to Germany. The future of "the 108 from Shanghai" became a matter of public debate. See Armbrüster, "Das Ende des Exils in Shanghai," 194f.

20. Isidor F. Stone, *Underground to Palestine* (New York: Pantheon, 1978), 46f.

21. Lena Jedwab Rozenberg, *Girl with Two Landscapes: The Wartime Diary of Lena Jedwab, 1941–1945* (New York: Holmes & Meier, 2002), 159–60; 189–90.

22. Hilde Spiel, *Die hellen und die finsteren Zeiten: Erinnerungen 1911–1946* (Munich: List Verlag, 1989), 207.

23. Hilde Spiel, *Rückkehr nach Wien: Tagebuch 1946* (Munich: Nymphenburger Verlagsbuchhandlung, 1968), 17.

24. Ibid., 78f.

25. Note the complete absence of any discussion of the persecution of the Jews in post-Anschluss Austria in the official government publication *Rot-Weiss-Rot-Buch: Darstellungen, Dokumente und nachweise zur Vorgeschichte und Geschichte der Okkupation Österreichs, Erster Teil* (Vienna: Österreichischen Staatsdruckerei, 1946), 69ff.

26. Robert Knight, "'Neutrality,' Not Sympathy: Jews in Post-war Austria," in Robert S. Wistrich, ed., *Austrians and Jews in the Twentieth Century: From Franz Joseph to Waldheim* (New York: St. Martin's Press, 1992), 228.

27. Stefan Heym, *Nachruf* (Munich: Bertelsmann, 1988), 363.

28. Ibid.

29. Ludwig Marcuse, Letter to the von Hofe and Townsend families, 17 July 1949, in Harold von Hofe, ed., *Briefe von und zu Ludwig Marcuse* (Zurich: Diogenes, 1975), 80.

30. Ibid., 81f.

31. Ludwig Marcuse, *Mein zwanzigste Jahrhundert: Auf dem Weg zu einer Autobiographie* (Munich: Paul List Verlag, 1960), 370.

32. Diary entry, 27 April 1945, Thomas Mann, *Tagebücher 1944–1.4.1946*, ed. Inge Jens (Frankfurt: S. Fischer, 1986), 194f.

33. Thomas Mann, "Die deutschen KZ," in Thomas Mann, *Essays*, ed. Hermann Kurzke und Stephan Stachorski, 6 vols. (Frankfurt: Fischer, 1993–7), vol. 6, 11.

34. "Kommentar zu die deutschen KZ," ibid., 375ff.

35. Yvonne Wolf: *Frank Thiess und der Nationalsozialismus. Ein konservativer Revolutionär als Dissident* (Tübingen: Niemeyer, 2003).

36. Frank Thiess, "Die innere Emigration," *Münchener Zeitung* (18 August 1945), quoted in Johannes Franz Gottlieb Grosser, ed., *Die grosse Kontroverse: Ein Briefwechsel un Deutschland* (Hamburg: Nagel, 1963), 24.

37. Viktor Matejka, "And die österreichischen Künstler und Wissenschaftler in der U.S.A.," *Austro American Tribune*, vol. 4, no. 4 (November 1945), 7.

38. Robert Rie, "Offener Brief aus der Emigration," *Austro American Tribune*, vol. 5, no. 2 (September 1946), 17.

39. Ibid.

40. Paul E. Moeller, Memorandum, Office of Military Government for Bavaria, in Jost Hermand and Wigand Lange, *Wollt ihr Thomas Mann wiederhaben?: Deutschland und die Emigranten* (Hamburg: Europäische Verlagsanstalt/Rotbuch verlag, 1999), 62.

41. As quoted in Hermand and Lange, *Wollt ihr Thomas Mann wiederhaben?*, 118.

42. As quoted ibid., 161.

43. Arthur Koestler, *The Invisible Writing* (New York: Macmillan, 1954), 247f.

44. Ibid., 426f.

45. Martin Gumpert, *First Papers*, trans. Heinz and Ruth Norden (New York: Duell, Sloan and Pearce, 1941), 191f., 195.

46. Gerda Freistadt-Geiringer, oral history conducted by Debórah Dwork, Vienna, 10, 12, and 15 July 1991, transcript II, 8; 9; 37.

47. Robert Rosner, oral history conducted by Debórah Dwork, Vienna, 3 July 1990, transcript, 62.

48. Ernst M. Lorge, "A Tragic Object-Lesson," *Jewish Frontier*, vol. 12 (August 1945), 13.

49. Zeev M. Mankowitz, *Life Between Memory and Hope: The Survivors of the Holocaust in Occupied Germany* (Cambridge: Cambridge University Press, 2002), 124.

50. Bartley C. Crum, *Behind the Silken Curtain: A Personal Account of Anglo-American Diplomacy in Palestine and the Middle East* (Jerusalem and New London: Milah Press, 1996), 85.

51. As quoted ibid., 9.

52. Ibid., 107f.

53. Richard Crossman, *Palestine Mission: A Personal Record* (London: Hamish Hamilton, 1947), 87f.

54. Judah Nadich, *Eisenhower and the Jews* (New York: Twayne Publishers, 1953), 234.

55. Samuel Gringauz, "Jewish Destiny as the DP's See It: The Ideology of the Surviving Remnant," *Commentary*, vol. 4 (December 1947), 502.

56. Koppel L. Pinson, "Jewish Life in Liberated Germany: A Study of Jewish DP's," *Jewish Social Studies*, vol. 9 (1947), 116.

57. Jorge García Granados, *The Birth of Israel: The Drama as I Saw It* (New York: Knopf, 1948), 255.

58. Ibid., 256.

59. Ibid., 219.

60. Yehuda Bauer, *Flight and Rescue: Brichah* (New York: Random House, 1970).

61. See Idith Zertal, *From Catastrophe to Power: Holocaust Survivors and the Emergence of Israel* (Berkeley, Los Angeles, and London: University of California Press, 1998), 129ff.

62. Abraham S. Hyman, *The Undefeated* (Jerusalem: Gefen, 1993), 375.

63. See: Louise London, *Whitehall and the Jews: 1933–1948* (Cambridge: Cambridge University Press, 2000), 268–9, and Beth Cohen, *Case Closed: Holocaust Survivors in Postwar America* (New Brunswick, NJ: Rutgers University Press, 2007), 8–17.

64. Hyman, *The Undefeated*, 377.

65. Ibid., 378.

66. Nahum Goldmann, as quoted in Abraham Klausner, *Letter to My Children from the Edge of the Holocaust* (San Francisco: Holocaust Center of Northern California, 2002), 170.

67. Sara Grossman-Weil, oral history conducted by Debórah Dwork, Malverne, N.Y., 29–30 April 1987, transcript, 37–41.

PAPERS: LISTS OF THE LIVING

1. Postcard from Lotti Rosenfeld to Elisabeth Luz, 22 September 1943; letters from Lotti Rosenfeld to Elisabeth Luz, 27 September 1943 and 5 December 1943, authors' collection [letters 50g, 51a, 51b].
2. H. G. [Hans Günther] Adler, *Theresienstadt, 1941–1945: Das Antlitz einer Zwangsgemeinschaft*, 2nd edition (Tübingen: J. C. B. Mohr, 1960), 199f.
3. Letter from Lotti Rosenfeld to Elisabeth Luz, 8 February 1945, authors' collection [letter #51f1].
4. Letter from Lotti Rosenfeld to Elisabeth Luz, 13 February 1945, authors' collection [letter #51c2].
5. Letter from Verband schweizerischer jüdischer Flüchtlingshilfen to Elisabeth Luz, 28 February 1945, authors' collection [letter #71a].
6. Postcard from World Jewish Congress, Geneva, to Elisabeth Luz, 19 July 1945, authors' collection [letter #57].
7. Letter from William H. Forster [Heinz Pfützner] to Elisabeth Luz, 12 January 1945, authors' collection [letter #298b].
8. Letter from William Forster [Heinz Pfützner] to his mother, no date, authors' collection [letter #298a].
9. Letter from William H. Forster [Heinz Pfützner] to Elisabeth Luz, 7 April 1945, authors' collection [letter #301].
10. Letter from Lutz Scheucher to Elisabeth Luz, 3 August 1941, authors' collection [letter #788].
11. Letter from Lutz Scheucher to Elisabeth Luz, 7 July 1945, authors' collection [letter #282d].
12. Letter from Agnes Scheucher to Elisabeth Luz, 30 May 1945, authors' collection [letter #282g].
13. Cable from Agnes Scheucher née Fränkel to Elisabeth Luz, 22 May 1945, authors' collection [letter #34b].
14. Letter from Central Office OSE to Elisabeth Luz, 29 May 1945, authors' collection [letter #34a].
15. Letter from Central Office OSE to Elisabeth Luz, 1 June 1945, authors' collection [letter #36].
16. Letter from Agnes Scheucher to Elisabeth Luz, 30 May 1945, authors' collection [letter #282g].
17. Letter from Lutz Scheucher to Elisabeth Luz, 7 July 1945, authors' collection [letter #282d].
18. Letter from Lutz and Agnes Scheucher to Elisabeth Luz, 25 January 1946, authors' collection [letter #273].
19. Ibid.

20. Abraham J. Klausner, "The Central Committee," in *Sharit Ha-Platah: An Extensive List of Survivors of Nazi Tyranny Published So That the Lost May Be Found and the Dead May Be Brought Back to Life* (Munich: Central Committee of Liberated Jews in Bavaria, 1946), n.p.

21. Isidor F. Stone, *Underground to Palestine* (New York: Pantheon, 1978), 79f.

22. Abraham J. Klausner, *A Letter to My Children: From the Edge of the Holocaust* (San Francisco: Holocaust Center of Northern California, 2002), 13.

23. Judah Nadich, *Eisenhower and the Jews* (New York: Twayne Publishers, 1953), 74f.

24. Abraham S. Hyman, *The Undefeated* (Jerusalem: Gefen, 1993), 38.

25. Klausner, *A Letter to My Children*, 11.

26. Ibid., 13f.

27. Ibid., 26.

28. Hyman, *The Undefeated*, 38f.

29. Larry Lubetsky, *Berlin JDC Tracing Office, 1945–1947* (Berlin: American Joint Distribution Committee, 1948).

30. Hans Steinitz, "Aufbau, Neubau, Brückenbau," in Will Schaber, ed., *Aufbau Reconstruction: Dokumente einer Kultur im Exil* (New York and Cologne, Overlook Press and Kiepenheuer & Witsch, 1972), 13.

31. "Die Quoten-Einwanderung nach U.S.A.: Tatsachen aus der Praxis," *Aufbau*, 1 March 1939, 1.

32. I. Gillis and M. Raileanu, "Say It in English," *Aufbau*, 1 April 1939, 17.

33. "Es Suchen," *Aufbau*, 1 May 1939, 11.

34. "Erste Liste der aus Gurs Deportierten," *Aufbau*, 6 November 1942, 14.

35. "Achtung: Botschaften aus Europa—Adressen, die das Rote Kreuz sucht," *Aufbau*, 13 November 1942, 12.

36. "Erste wiener jüdische Totenliste," *Aufbau*, 29 January 1943, 18.

37. "Flüchtlinge in Russland suchen Verwandte in Amerika," *Aufbau*, 23 April 1943, 24.

38. Death announcement Bernhard Hausner, *Aufbau*, 26 February 1943, 18.

39. Death announcement Ludwig Allmeyer, *Aufbau*, 24 August 1945, 18.

40. Death announcement Ida Wittner née Pollak, *Aufbau*, 24 August 1945, 18.

41. Death announcement Benjamin Wolff, *Aufbau*, 24 August 1945, 19.

42. "Rückwanderer—Dritte Liste, Ziel: München," *Aufbau*, 24 August 1945, 21.

43. "Nach Wien Zurürchgekehrt," *Aufbau*, 24 August 1945, 26.

44. "Nach Belgien zurückhekehrt," *Aufbau*, 24 August 1945, 31; "Juden in Berlin," *Aufbau*, 24 August 1945, 29.

45. "Das erste Lebenszeichen," *Aufbau*, 24 August 1945, 26.

46. Ibid.

47. Ibid.

48. Advertisement in *Aufbau*, 24 August 1945, 26.

49. "Gesucht wird," advertisement, *Aufbau*, 24 August 1945, 27.

50. On the history of tracing, see: Caroline Moorehead, "A History of Tracing," in Michael Johnstone, *Reunited!: Loved Ones Traced by the British Red Cross* (Henley on Thames: Aidan Ellis, 1995), 4ff.; also Georges Dunand, *Ne Perdez Pas Leur Trace!* (Neuchâtel: Baconnière, 1950).

51. Stefan Zweig, "Das Herz Europas," *Begegnungen mit Menschen, Büchern, Städten* (Vienna: Herbert Reichner Verlag, 1937), 204.

52. Ibid., 214.

53. International Committee of the Red Cross, *Report of the International Committee of the Red Cross on Its Activities During the Second World War (September 1, 1939–June 30, 1947),* 3 vols. (Geneva: ICRC, 1948), vol. 2, 299f.

54. Ibid., 301f.

55. Ibid., 302.

56. The British Tracing Bureau and its successor organizations proved a key source. On the initiative of Allied forces headquarters as well as Jewish organizations, the British Red Cross Department of International Affairs was transformed into a search office. As the allies prepared to invade, Supreme Headquarters Allied Expeditionary Forces (SHAEF) reorganized this unit to serve as a Central Tracing Bureau, charged with investigating the whereabouts of prisoners, forced laborers, and refugees in central Europe. The bureau accompanied the front from London to Versailles to Frankfurt. War's end brought a shift in responsibilities, and SHAEF turned over the Central Tracing Bureau to UNRRA in October 1945. Responsible for coordinating the work of the tracing bureau in each of the four occupation zones of Germany and for sharing information with national and Red Cross tracing bureaus in some 46 countries outside Germany, the Central Tracing Bureau moved to Bad Arolsen in January 1946. UNRRA wound up its operations on 30 June 1947, and the International Refugee Organization took over the Central Tracing Bureau, renaming it the International Tracing Service. Hundreds of thousands of people still searched for family and friends. Managed by the International Committee of the Red Cross since 1954, it continues to function today. See Charles-Claude Biedermann, *More Than 10.5 Million . . . : 60 Years of History and Benefit of the Personal Documentary Material About the Former Civilian Persecutees of the National Socialist Regime Preserved in Bad Arolsen* (Bad Arolsen: International Tracing Service/Wildner Druck, 2003).

57. International Committee of the Red Cross, *Report of the International Committee of the Red Cross,* vol. 2, 83.

58. Ibid., 85.

59. Information from Ruth K. Westheimer with Ben Yagoda, *All in a Lifetime* (New York: Warner Books, 1987) and Alfred A. Häsler and Ruth K. Westheimer, *Die Geschichte der Karola Siegel* (Bern: Benteli Verlag, 1976).

60. Westheimer with Yagoda, *All in a Lifetime*, 51.
61. Ibid., 71.

PROBLEMS: ADJUSTMENT

1. Ruth K. Westheimer with Ben Yagoda, *All in a Lifetime* (New York: Warner Books, 1987), 69.
2. The government included two exceptions: those who were engaged in activities against the Jewish people and those likely to endanger the public health or the security of the state.
3. "Middle East," *American Jewish Year Book*, vol. 49 (1947–8), 473.
4. See Siegfried Landshut, *Jewish Communities in the Muslim Countries of the Middle East* (London: Jewish Chronicle, 1950); Joseph B. Schechtman, *On Wings of Eagles: The Plight, Exodus, and Homecoming of Oriental Jewry* (New York and London: Thomas Yoseloff, 1961); Reeva Spector Simon, Michael Menachem Laskier, and Sara Reguer, eds., *The Jews of the Middle East and North Africa in Modern Times* (New York: Columbia University Press, 2003).
5. Naim Kattan, *Farewell, Babylon: Coming of Age in Jewish Baghdad*, trans. Sheila Fischman (Vancouver: Raincoast Books, 2005), 59.
6. Lukasz Hirszowicz, *The Third Reich and the Arab East* (London: Routledge & Kegan Paul, 1966), 122ff.; Bernd Philipp Schröder, *Deutschland und der Mittlere Osten im Zweiten Weltkrieg* (Göttingen: Musterschmidt, 1975), 63ff.
7. Kattan, *Farewell, Babylon*, 21.
8. On the Anglo-Iraq war, see Compton Mackenzie, *Eastern Epic: 1 September 1939–March 1943, Defence* (London: Chatto & Windus, 1951), 82ff.
9. Nissim Rejwan, *The Last Jews of Baghdad: Remembering a Lost Homeland* (Austin: University of Texas Press, 2004), 132.
10. Kattan, *Farewell, Babylon*, 34.
11. With the birth of their first child, Mnashee, Aliza binti-Frayim (daughter of Frayim) and Salem ibn-Hiskil (son of Hiskil) acquired the names Aliza emmi Mnashee (mother of) and Salem abu-Mnashee (father of).
12. The story of Aliza emmi-Mnashee and Salem abu-Mnashee was related to Robert Jan van Pelt in a number of conversations and e-mail exchanges with Aliza's daughter Zmira Birnbaum, her son Menashe Arbel, and her grandson Omer Arbel, 6, 12, 13, and 19 November 2007.
13. See also Rejwan, *The Last Jews of Baghdad*, 189ff.
14. As quoted in Moshe Gat, *The Jewish Exodus from Iraq, 1948–1951* (London and Portland, OR: Frank Cass, 1997), 71.
15. Ibid., 70.
16. Ibid., 79ff., 101ff.

17. Kattan, *Farewell, Babylon*, 177.

18. Ibid., 186.

19. Accounts of the self-liquidation of the Iraqi-Jewish community also warrant an analysis in terms of the group psychology proposed in Elias Canetti, *Crowds and Power*, trans. Carol Stewart (London: Gollancz, 1962). The contagion would have been aided by unreliable information about life in Israel obtained through broadcasts and unrealistic expectations based on biblical notions of Israel as a Land of Milk and Honey; see Avraham Shama and Mark Iris, *Immigration Without Integration: Third World Jews in Israel* (Cambridge, MA: Schenkman, 1977), 39ff. Finally, there are many interpretations that see the wave of applications to emigrate wholly or partially as the result of Zionist conspiracies. For example: David Hirst, *The Gun and the Olive Branch: The Roots of Violence in the Middle East* (London: Faber and Faber, 1977), 155ff.; Marion Woolfson, *Prophets in Babylon: Jews in the Arab World* (London: Faber and Faber, 1980), 182ff.

20. Robert Rosner, oral history conducted by Debórah Dwork, Vienna, 3 July 1990, transcript, 61.

21. Otto Suschny, oral history conducted by Debórah Dwork, Vienna, 18 July 1991, transcript, 64–5.

22. Ibid., 71–2.

23. As quoted in Eli M. Rosenbaum with William Hoffer, *Betrayal: The Untold Story of the Kurt Waldheim Investigation and Cover-Up* (New York: St. Martin's Press, 1993), 338.

24. Gerda Freistadt-Geiringer, oral history conducted by Debórah Dwork, Vienna, 10, 12 and 15 July 1991, transcript I, 86–7.

25. Leo Katcher, *Post Mortem: The Jews and Germany—Now* (London: Hamish Hamilton, 1968), 91.

26. Ibid., 92.

27. Susanne Harris-Neuwalder, oral history conducted by Debórah Dwork, New Haven, CT, 20 September; 4 and 21 October; 17 November; 13 and 21 December 1993; and 2 February and 9 March 1994, transcript I, 65.

28. Letter from Mary A. Hobbins to Herbert Neuwalder, 29 April 1944, Family Archive of Susanne Harris-Neuwalder, copy in possession of authors.

29. Letter from Mary A. Hobbins to Herbert Neuwalder, 15 November 1944, Family Archive of Susanne Harris-Neuwalder, copy in possession of authors.

30. Letter from Susanne Neuwalder to Herbert Neuwalder, 16 January 1945, Family Archive of Susanne Harris-Neuwalder, copy in possession of authors.

31. Letter from Herbert Neuwalder to Mary A Hobbins, 4 December 1945, Family Archive of Susanne Harris-Neuwalder, copy in possession of authors.

32. Susanne Harris-Neuwalder, oral history, transcript I, 106.

33. Ibid., transcript II, 30.

34. Ibid., transcript I, 49–50.
35. Isabelle Silberg-Riff, oral history conducted by Debórah Dwork, London, 13 May 1987, transcript, 21–2.
36. Ibid., 22–3.
37. Ibid., 23–4.
38. Letter from Eva Guttmann to Elisabeth Luz, 10 September 1945, authors' collection [letter #616].
39. Letter from Susi Sachs-Guttmann to Elisabeth Luz, 13 April 1958, authors' collection [letter #611b].
40. Letter from Susi Sachs-Guttmann to Elisabeth Luz, 27 May 1958, authors' collection [letter #611c].
41. Letter from Susi Sachs-Guttmann to Elisabeth Luz, 26 January 1959, authors' collection [letter #611g].
42. Letter from Susi Sachs-Guttmann to Elisabeth Luz, 7 May 1960, authors' collection [letter #611f]
43. Letter from Hanna-Ruth Klopstock to Elisabeth Luz, 24 August 1954, authors' collection [letter #368b]
44. Letter from Hanna-Ruth Klopstock to Elisabeth Luz, 7 December 1954, authors' collection [letter #370]
45. C. L. Lang, "Second Start in France," in Association of Jewish Refugees in Great Britain, ed., *Dispersion and Resettlement: The Story of the Jews from Central Europe* (London: Association of Jewish Refugees in Great Britain, 1955), 22.
46. Werner Rosenstock, "Between the Continents," ibid., 58f.
47. Mariánka May-Zadikow, oral history conducted by Debórah Dwork, New Paltz, NY, 8–9 November 2000, transcript, 75–6.
48. Ibid., 98–8.
49. Ibid., 102–4.
50. Jean Améry, "How Much Home Does a Person Need?" in *At the Mind's Limits: Contemplations by a Survivor on Auschwitz and Its Realities*, trans. Sidney Rosenfeld and Stella Rosenfeld (Bloomington: Indiana University Press, 1980), 50.
51. Ibid., 57; 59.

ACKNOWLEDGMENTS

ONE OF THE GREAT PLEASURES OF FINISHING A BOOK IS THAT IT gives authors the opportunity to thank those who helped make the project a product.

Our first debt is to the women and men who recounted their personal histories and gave us their artifacts from the Holocaust years: letters, diaries, photographs, drawings, ration coupons, identity cards. We are grateful for their time, and for the care they devoted to the enterprise. We do not forget for an instant the searing nature of such recollection.

Individuals and families in every country where Debórah conducted oral histories took on this project with enthusiasm. They offered hospitality and help with the practical problems of everyday life away from home. Most important, these friends provided opportunities to meet those whose histories we sought to learn. Our acknowledgments are in alphabetical order by city.

We are indebted to Esther Fine, a lifelong resident of Cardiff, who welcomed Debórah into her home and her community; Sylvia and Henry Starkman who did the same in Detroit; Chantal and Isabelle Brotherton-Ratcliffe in London took Debórah in as their flatmate summer after summer; and to Carolyn and Richard Rampton, who offered warm hospitality to Debórah and Robert Jan when they returned to the

Public Record Office to scan those archives yet again (and again). The entire Tolya Barsky–Odette Bérujeau family was involved in Paris, and we thank them all—grandparents Tolya, Olga, and Odette of blessed memory, parents, and children—for their energy and cheer. Finally, we are sincerely grateful to the Katz-Badian family in Vienna.

Research materials emerge through unexpected doors. One fine day Debórah received a letter from Ulrich Luz, a renowned Swiss theologian. His deceased aunt had carried on an extensive correspondence with German-Jewish refugee children in France and their parents in Germany. Over half a century later the letters remained in his possession, and he did not quite know what to do with them. Might she be interested? Thus, a window opened onto the daily difficulties of Jews during the Nazi era. We thank Elisabeth Luz, of blessed memory, for her compassion and the activities it prompted. And we thank Ulrich Luz for his generosity to Debórah, a scholar known to him solely by reputation.

Robert Jan came to an unexpected encounter with this history through quite a different route. While working on this book, he married Miriam Greenbaum, and he found her father, Jakob Grünbaum, on a list of survivors compiled in the summer of 1945 by the indefatigable U.S. army chaplain Abraham Klausner. The list recorded Altötting as his place of residence, and it was in that Bavarian town that Jakob met and married Miriam's mother.

Our colleagues at Clark and Waterloo support us in myriad ways. At the Strassler Center, Margaret Hillard, Tatyana Macaulay, Mary Jane Rein, and Ghi Vaughn encouraged Debórah and sought to give her the time to write. We thank them for lightening her load and for cheering her through to the finish line. Debórah's colleagues as she wrote, Thomas Kühne, Bob Melson, Marion Pritchard, and Shelly Tenenbaum, snapped her synapses and brightened her day. She is grateful to dean of research Nancy Budwig, who championed her efforts to focus on scholarship, and to provost David Angel, a staunch advocate of research centers at Clark University. Robert Jan thanks Margaret Hillard at the Center for dealing with the financial bureaucracy of research reimbursement. And at the University of Waterloo, Adel Sedra and Rick Haldenby warmly endorsed his collaboration with Debórah as a valid research project in a Faculty of

Engineering and a School of Architecture and provided practical help in approving a sabbatical leave that allowed him to write full-time.

This book grew over a number of years and was supported along the way by many individuals and organizations. David Strassler, founding donor of the Strassler Center for Holocaust and Genocide Studies, was always there. Sidney and Rosalie Rose and Ralph and Shirley Rose endowed a chair Debórah came to occupy, and we thank Rosalie and Sidney for the research fund attached to the professorship, as we remember Ralph and Shirley with affection. Debórah is grateful to businessman and philanthropist Robert Weil for his support of this work in Sweden and for his sturdy friendship stretching over a decade. He does not quite understand why she does the work she does—but he supports her just the same. Al Tapper, by contrast, understands in a profound way but despairs of its utility. Yet he too remains unstinting in his generosity. We hope the anonymous donor who singled out Debórah for support when she was a professor at Yale reads these lines and accepts our thanks. Most recently, an unexpected and most welcome grant from the Shillman Foundation—thanks to Dr Bob Shillman and Dr Dianne Parrotte— enabled Robert Jan and Debórah to sit together month after month to complete the manuscript. We are utterly grateful.

The Wellcome Trust (London), the American Philosophical Society, American Council of Learned Societies, National Endowment for the Humanities, Guggenheim Foundation, Social Sciences and Humanities Research Council (Canada), and the Woodrow Wilson International Center for Scholars provided generous aid that defrayed the cost of travel, tape transcription, research assistance, and salary support.

It is a pleasure to thank photo archivists Judy Cohen and Caroline Waddell at the USHMM. Extraordinarily knowledgeable and helpful, they are legends in our field.

Flight from the Reich has been produced by people who extended themselves beyond all definitions of a "job." We thank copyeditor Pearl Hanig, jacket art director Eleen Cheung, designer Judy Abbate, and editorial assistant Erica Stern for their astute and sympathetic eyes, as well as their patience and good humor.

To our literary agent Anne Borchardt and our editors Ed Barber and Amy Cherry we offer thanks for instruction and advice. From them we learned many lessons we take with us into the future. Indeed, the Strassler Center's PhD students are the beneficiaries, secondhand.

Finally, we thank our parents, aunts, and uncles for nourishing our interest in the past with family stories. Surely they inspire our work: hiding in the Netherlands during the German occupation, Robert Jan's maternal uncle Sas Bunge gave benefit piano concerts in the private homes of courageous people to raise funds to support others in hiding. Robert Jan's father, Willem (Wim) van Pelt went into hiding also, not because he faced racial persecution but because, like many other high school graduates, he objected to the loyalty oath the Germans demanded as a precondition for university matriculation. Refusing to accept the alternative—forced labor in Germany—he went underground. Sheltered by his Latin teacher, he developed a passion for the language. Nearly seventy years later, he is still able to recite the whole of Cicero's indictment of Cataline. Debórah's family stories come from her mother's sister, her aunt Sara Grossman-Weil. Years later, she recorded her aunt's oral history, and a bit of it has been included in our text.

Family stories are passed to the next generation, and we both leave our tales to Debórah's daughters Hannah and Miriam, who grew up as we researched and wrote this book.

DD
RJvP
Wellfleet and New Haven
December 2008

ILLUSTRATION CREDITS

123 Courtesy USHMM and the Bildarchiv Preussischer Kulturbesitz.

125 Courtesy Bildarchiv Abraham Pisarek, Berlin.

130 Courtesy USHMM and the Central Zionist Archives.

134 Courtesy USHMM and the Bildarchiv Preussischer Kulturbesitz.

139 Courtesy Leo Baeck Institute, New York.

143 Courtesy USHMM and the Bildarchiv Preussischer Kulturbesitz.

153 Courtesy Bildarchiv Abraham Pisarek, Berlin.

165 Courtesy Spaarnestad Fotoarchief, Haarlem, the Netherlands.

171 Courtesy USHMM and Ilse Lichtenstein Meyer.

177 Courtesy USHMM and the Bibliothèque Historique de la Ville de Paris.

183 Courtesy USHMM and the Institute of Contemporary History and Wiener Library, London.

186 Courtesy USHMM and Michel Reynders.

203 Courtesy USHMM and Charles Martin Roman.

211 Courtesy Beth Hatefutsoth, Tel Aviv, Israel.

215 Courtesy USHMM and Norbert Bikales.

224 Courtesy USHMM and the National Archives and Records Administration, College Park, Maryland.

229 Courtesy USHMM and Hynda Szczukowski Halpren.

233 Courtesy USHMM and Hanna Meyer-Moses.

238 Courtesy USHMM and the American Joint Distribution Committee, New York.

241 Courtesy USHMM and the American Joint Distribution Committee, New York.

247 Authors' collection.

248 Courtesy USHMM and the American Joint Distribution Committee, New York.

253 Authors' collection.

273 Authors' collection.

284 Courtesy USHMM and the National Archives and Records Administration, College Park, Maryland.

299 Courtesy Michael Bohnen.

304 Courtesy USHMM and Saul Sorrin.

307 Courtesy Michael Bohnen.

311 Courtesy USHMM and Sara Huberfeld.

313 Courtesy USHMM and Samuel (Rakowski) Ron.

321 Courtesy USHMM and the National Archives and Records Administration, College Park, Maryland.

323 Courtesy USHMM and Shlomo Liwer.

333 Courtesy USHMM and Abraham Atsmon.

336   Courtesy USHMM and Alice Zev.
341   Courtesy USHMM and YIVO Institute.
349   Courtesy USHMM and the Jacob Rader Marcus Center of the American
      Jewish Archives, Cincinnati, Ohio.
356   Courtesy USHMM and Willy Fogel.
365   Authors' collection.
377   Authors' collection.

INDEX

Page numbers in *italics* refer to illustrations.